Shakespeare on Film

Inside Film

SHAKESPEARE on FILM

Judith Buchanan

PEARSON
Longman

Harlow, England • London • New York • Boston • San Francisco • Toronto
Sydney • Tokyo • Singapore • Hong Kong • Seoul • Taipei • New Delhi
Cape Town • Madrid • Mexico City • Amsterdam • Munich • Paris • Milan

Pearson Education Limited
Edinburgh Gate
Harlow
Essex CM20 2JE
England

and Associated Companies throughout the world

Visit us on the World Wide Web at:
www.pearsoned.co.uk

First published 2005

British Library Cataloguing-in-Publication Data
A catalogue record for this book is available from the British Library

Library of Congress Cataloging-in-Publication Data
Buchanan, Judith.
    Shakespeare on film / Judith Buchanan.
       p. cm. — (Inside film)
    Filmography: p.
    Includes bibliographical references (p.) and index.
    ISBN 0-582-43716-4
    1. Shakespeare, William, 1564–1616—Film and video adaptations. 2. English
drama—Film and video adaptations. 3. Film adaptations. I. Title. II. Series.

    PR3093.B77 2004
    791.43'6—dc22

                                                          200405749

10 9 8 7 6 5 4 3 2 1
09 08 07 06 05

Typeset in 10/13 pt Giovanni by 35
Printed and bound in Malaysia (CTP-VVP)

The publisher's policy is to use paper manufactured from sustainable forests.

CONTENTS

Island of Lost Souls (Erle C. Kenton, 1932), *Iguana* (Monte Hellman, 1988), *Forbidden Planet* (Fred McLeod Wilcox, 1956), *Men of Respect* (William Reilly, 1991), *O* (Tim Blake Nelson, 2000)

PART II: Moment and Context: How History Works on Story   **119**

5.   Historically Juxtaposed Beans (I): *A Midsummer Night's Dream* on Film   **121**
     A Midsummer Night's Dream (Vitagraph, 1909), *A Midsummer Night's Dream* (Paulo Azzuri, 1913), *A Midsummer Night's Dream* (Reinhardt/Dieterle, 1935), *A Midsummer Night's Dream* (Celestino Coronado, 1984), *A Midsummer Night's Dream* (Adrian Noble, 1995), *A Midsummer Night's Dream* (Michael Hoffman, 1999)

6.   Historically Juxtaposed Beans (II): *The Tempest* on Film   **150**
     Forbidden Planet (Fred McLeod Wilcox, 1956), *Magic Island* (Michael Powell, 1969), *The Tempest* (Derek Jarman, 1979), *Tempest* (Paul Mazursky, 1982), *Prospero's Books* (Peter Greenaway, 1991)

7.   Boxing with Ghosts: The Shakespeare Films of Kenneth Branagh   **184**
     Henry V (1989 & Olivier, 1944), *Much Ado About Nothing* (1993), *Hamlet* (1996), *Love's Labour's Lost* (2000)

8.   Leaves of Brass and Gads of Steel: Cinema as Subject in Shakespeare Films, 1991-2000   **220**
     The King is Alive (Kristian Levring, 2000), *Prospero's Books* (Peter Greenaway, 1991), *William Shakespeare's Romeo+Juliet* (Baz Luhrmann, 1996), *Hamlet* (Michael Almereyda, 2000), *Titus* (Julie Taymor, 2000)

     Filmography   **261**
     Bibliography   **264**
     Index   **283**

LIST OF ILLUSTRATIONS

AUTHOR'S ACKNOWLEDGEMENTS

I have accrued many pleasurable debts in writing this *Inside Film* reader. For helping me refine the questions that could be asked of Shakespeare and of the cinema both separately and in combination, I am grateful to Ian Christie, Tony Nuttall, John Pitcher, Dennis Kay, Barbara Everett, Ann Pasternak-Slater, the late Don McKenzie, and Sarah Street. They have provided a heady cocktail of influences, scholarship and catching enthusiasms from which I am still being fed. I also thank The Fulbright Commission and the University of Rochester, New York who funded me to pursue research in the excellent film archives of George Eastman House and the Library of Congress, and Worcester College, Oxford for post-doctoral research fellowships that nurtured my thinking not only in relation to my research, but much more besides.

In the last two years I have learned much from conversations with colleagues and students in the Department of English and Related Literature at the University of York – in particular with Mike Cordner, Director of Writing and Performance, himself an extraordinary walking archive of Shakespeare performance. Jonathan Statham and Corrie Burton nobly acted as guinea-pig undergraduate readers of the final chapter and I have greatly appreciated their incisive comments about how the material might work best for the book's intended reader. Gareth Davies gave me a discriminating reading of the Introduction and Chapters 4 and 6 and I have made considerable use of his comments on each of these. I would also like to thank Carol Chillington Rutter for her warmth and wit in response to the manuscript, Pat Palmer for her searchingly editorial eye in relation to Chapter 3, Zinnie Harris and Di Buchanan for their comments in response to the Introduction and Julie Taymor for her generously attentive reading of the section on *Titus* and for taking the time to discuss her extraordinary film with me on a couple of occasions. Steve Pethick, with whom discussing the flicks has long been an illuminating pleasure, has made helpful interjections into my reading and thinking about transmediating Shakespeare over the years, and Andrea Richter Hume's company and generous hospitality have always made research trips to the United States an unqualified delight. I thank them all warmly.

For expert assistance with viewing and reading archival materials, I am grateful to Karen Everson at George Eastman House, Rosemary Hanes at The

Library of Congress Motion Picture Reading Room, Betsy Walsh at the Folger Shakespeare Library, the staff in the study room at the Theatre Museum Covent Garden, Bryony Dixon and Janet Moat at the British Film Institute and Signior Cocchi at the Cineteca in Bologna. Mariengela Tempera of the University of Ferrara has kindly helped with access to some films, and Luke McKernan, Russell Jackson, Ian Christie, Tony Davies, Ken Rothwell, Colin Buchanan, Gabriella Misuriello, José Ramón Díaz-Fernández, Don Boyd and Sue Gillingham have all generously answered questions at various times that have helped in my research. Tim Parker at Pearson has steered the manuscript through the later stages of publication with great patience and Ellen Little of the Little Film Company has been a tremendous fixer when we became stumped by questions of industry rights. Thank you both.

An earlier version of the section on *Forbidden Planet* in Chapter 3 here appeared as Chapter 11, '*Forbidden Planet* and the Retrospective Attribution of Intentions' in D. Cartmell, I. Hunter, H. Kaye and I. Whelehan (eds), *Retrovisions: Reinventing the Past in Film and Fiction* (London and Chicago: Pluto, 2001), pp.148–62. A fuller tracing of the Hieronymite influence in both *Prospero's Books* and *The Tempest* (discussed in Chapter 8 here) first appeared as 'Cantankerous Scholars and the Production of a Canonical Text: The Appropriation of Hieronymite Space in *Prospero's Books*', in Christel Stalpaert (ed.), *Peter Greenaway's 'Prospero's Books': Critical Essays* (Ghent: Academia Press, 2000), pp.43–85.

The delivery of the manuscript has been a little impeded by a delivery of another kind. As a result, the speed of completion of the book has not quite lived up to expectations. I am, therefore, particularly grateful to Alex Ballinger, the original series editor, whose attentiveness, suggestions, consideration and timely boots I have greatly appreciated. The final, and not unrelated, thank you goes to young Douglas, whose contribution in slowing down my work rate has been more than matched by the extent to which his arrival has enriched my life.

Late extra: sufficient time has elapsed since the original submission of the manuscript for a baby girl, Freddie, now to have arrived to join the fray. So, though not around when this book was being written, Frederike Hope, we salute you warmly too.

A NOTE ON EDITIONS

For reasons of long-standing personal familiarity, unless otherwise noted, all quotations from Shakespeare are taken from the Arden II editions.

PUBLISHER'S ACKNOWLEDGEMENTS

We are grateful to the following for permission to reproduce copyright material:

Stills from 'Titus' (2000) © 2000 Twentieth Century Fox. All rights reserved. Reprinted by permission of Twentieth Century Fox; Still from 'Ran' (1985) reprinted by permission of Studio Canal Image; Film poster image and still from 'Henry V' (1989) reprinted by permission of Britannia Films Ltd.; Still from 'The Tempest' (1979) reprinted by permission of Don Boyd; Still from 'A Midsummer Night's Dream' (1935) © Turner Entertainment Co. A Warner Bros. Entertainment Company. All Rights Reserved. Reprinted by permission of Warner Bros. Entertainment Inc.; Still from 'Men of Respect' (1990) © 1990 Grandview Avenue Pictures, Inc., Central City Film Co. and Columbia TriStar Home Entertainment, Inc. All Rights Reserved. Courtesy of Columbia Pictures; Stills from 'William Shakespeare's a Midsummer Night's Dream' (1999) © 1999 Twentieth Century Fox. All rights reserved. Reprinted by permission of Twentieth Century Fox; Still from 'William Shakespeare's Romeo and Juliet' (1996) © 1996 Twentieth Century Fox. All rights reserved. Reprinted by permission of Twentieth Century Fox; Still from 'Hamlet' (2000) used under license from Miramax Film Corp. All Rights Reserved; Still from 'Forbidden Planet' (1956) © Turner Entertainment Co. A Warner Bros. Entertainment Company. All Rights Reserved. Reprinted by permission of Warner Bros Entertainment Inc.;_Cartoon from *Punch*, 18 October 1899, © Punch Ltd. Reprinted by permission of Punch Ltd.; Poster by Candido de Faria edited by Pathé frères circa 1908–1910. Copyright collection Pathé/DR. Reprinted by permission of Patrimoine Pathé; Saint Jerome in his Study by Antonello da Messina, © National Gallery, London. Reprinted by permission of National Gallery; Crucified Christ from *Prospero's Books* by Peter Greenaway, published by Chatto & Windus. Reprinted by permission of The Random House Group Ltd. (Greenaway, P. 1992)

All photos kindly supplied by the British Film Institute, The Ronald Grant Archive and Photofest, New York.

In some instances we have been unable to trace the owners of copyright material, and we would appreciate any information that would enable us to do so.

for Kostja

INTRODUCTION

One day in 1990, on the set for the shooting of Franco Zeffirelli's *Hamlet*, a member of the production team gave Mel Gibson a white billowy shirt. This version of the standard Hamlet garb had a history, having been worn by Laurence Olivier in his 1948 film of *Hamlet*. As a gift, it was presumably intended to give Gibson a sense of the rich heritage in which he was now working. Since the first screen Hamlet had appeared as early as 1900, when the famous French classical actress Sarah Bernhardt was shot on film performing the duel scene opposite Pierre Magnier as Laertes, by 1990 a lengthy performance tradition of screen Hamlets had accrued for Gibson to inherit. The wearing of a shirt (literally too small for him, symbolically a little on the large side perhaps) from a particularly prestigious moment in that history offered a tangible representation of the continuity and accumulated dependences of a cinematic performance legacy.

Six years later, on the set for the shooting of Kenneth Branagh's film of *Hamlet*, Derek Jacobi (who played Claudius) gave Branagh (who played Hamlet) an old, much thumbed copy of the play. This gift too was more significant than might at first appear. The particular *Hamlet* edition given to Branagh was a volume which had once belonged to Johnston Forbes-Robertson, the acclaimed Shakespearean actor from the turn of the century. In each generation since Forbes-Robertson, this volume had been entrusted into the care of an actor whose Hamlet performance had achieved some distinction. Since *Hamlet* is considered the supreme actor's play, the bestowing of the Forbes-Robertson edition inevitably became a sign of privileged election among actors. Through the latter half of the twentieth century, for example, it passed from Laurence Olivier to Michael Redgrave to Derek Jacobi in recognition of their stage Hamlets.[1]

The symbolic weight gathered by the Forbes-Robertson copy of *Hamlet* in its passage through the century is of a more extensive character than that which attaches to Olivier's shirt (pleasing though such a gift evidently was for Gibson).[2] For, in addition to conferring a certain consecrated status upon Branagh himself, Jacobi's gift also served as a symbol of the coming of age for filmed Shakespeare more generally. Before Branagh, it had always been in response to a *stage* performance of the role that the honour of being the guardian of Forbes-Robertson's edition had been conferred.[3] *The* Hamlet of a generation was, by implication, necessarily a theatrical one. Branagh had himself achieved a profile for his stage Hamlet in Adrian Noble's 1992 production at the Barbican, but it was not for this that he received the prize. Jacobi's notable intervention in the tradition of appointing an actor as privileged custodian of the book was not so much, therefore, in his choice of candidate to receive it, as in the moment in which he chose to bestow it. For it was as Branagh remade his performance for *film* that Jacobi handed over the book. For the first time, it was upon a screen Hamlet that the honour was bestowed.

Shakespeare on film as a subject worthy of study has a history almost as long as Shakespeare films themselves do. In 1911, for example, as part of a local publicity campaign to bring in the crowds and so maximise revenue for a film of *Henry VIII*, an enterprising picture-house manager in Ipswich advertised 'two guinea prizes to the boy and girl who writes [*sic*] the best 200 words essay on the subject of *King Henry VIII* as presented in the pictures'.[4] The manager's motivation for organising the essay competition had a sound basis in finance, as no doubt did the motivation of any boy or girl who took up the essay-writing challenge. And it is perhaps appropriate that educational and economic ambition should have joined forces early in the launch of Shakespeare on film as a discipline; it was, after all, just such a cocktail that had given birth to Shakespeare films themselves in the early years of the new medium.

The attempt to describe and evaluate a Shakespeare play 'as presented in the pictures' has animated a plentiful supply of critics since 1911. Although largely sidelined by serious criticism before the 1970s, Shakespeare on film has now long been sanctioned as part of the legitimate performance history of a Shakespeare play. As a subject, it has carved out a space for itself both within Shakespeare performance studies as part of the history of the ongoing life of a play, and within film studies as part of the debate about adaptation and the encounter between differing cultural registers. Jacobi's decision to designate Branagh's *film* Hamlet the performance of his generation adds a symbolic layer of legitimacy to the medium as a vehicle for Shakespearean production. Future recipients of Forbes-Robertson's edition of *Hamlet* will be free to select a performance from stage or screen in a way that is genuinely medium-blind. Establishment prejudices about theatrical legitimacy as opposed to cinematic triviality have been symbolically laid to rest.

*

Whether on stage or screen, all performances that begin life as a script are acts of recreation. Even when the formal properties of the words remain the same across productions, their meanings may be transformed. Translating a scripted line into a specific performance involves a set of intricate negotiations between the words and the actor, the actor and the production, the production and its audience, the audience and its wider contexts. Performance words, as Feste reminds us, are 'but a chev'ril glove to a good wit' (*Twelfth Night* III.i.12), capable of being turned inside out in a trice. The mutability of a text's meanings in performance therefore alerts us to the provisional character of that originating text. It is inherently a document of possibilities that can ambush us anew in performance as its multiple points of collaborative interaction come together in ways not before experienced. This book makes it its project to map some of the adjustments and transformations of the meanings of Shakespeare's words, and the adjustments and transformations of the contexts in which they are sited, across cinematic productions.

But the brief is necessarily wider than this, extending to productions that appropriate extra-linguistic material (plots, themes, characters) from Shakespeare's plays while rejecting the language itself. If the meanings of a single line may prove pliably subject to multiple interventions across productions, the meanings of a plot when divorced from the linguistic particularities of its original composition are yet more so. The films considered here include versions of Shakespearean plots recouched in different idiom, different registers, different languages, or even different communicative systems (such as a language of gesture rather than of words). The chapter on 'American Shakespearean offshoots' also considers some films whose points of correspondence with a Shakespeare plot may not necessarily depend upon a conscious strategy on the part of the producers. The films discussed in the pages that follow therefore testify to a wide variety of processes of interpretation, modification, reconception, translation and even accidental collision with Shakespeare plays.

The Shakespeare plays from which the films derive are dynamic, performance-inflected and in many cases surviving in variant textual forms. The source material for the films is therefore far from being a stable given. Since the nature of the engagements between a film and its source may not only be interpretively transcriptive, but also oblique, unpredictable, playful, tangential, parodic and even accidental, what constitutes a 'Shakespeare film' is therefore by no means a self-evident category. It is part of the project of the book to explore ways of demarcating the territory.

*

It has long been a critical project to discern or create definitional categories in relation to adaptation. John Dryden's late 1690s discussion of the available approaches to translating Ovid into English usefully offers a pattern in this respect. In his *Preface to Ovid's Epistles*, Dryden defined a set of possible relationships between a poetic translation and its source:

> *All translation, I suppose, may be reduced to these three heads.*
> *First, that of metaphrase, or turning an author word by word, and line by line,*
> *from one language into another. . . . The second way is that of paraphrase, or*
> *translation with latitude, where the author is kept in view by the translator, so*
> *as never to be lost, but his words are not so strictly followed as his sense; and*
> *that too is admitted to be amplified, but not altered. . . . The third way is that*
> *of imitation, where the translator (if now he has not lost that name) assumes*
> *the liberty, not only to vary from the words and sense, but to forsake them both*
> *as he sees occasion . . .* [5]

This tripartite division into 'metaphrase', 'paraphrase' and 'imitation' has been echoed in many later theories of translation and adaptation. The three broad categories of Shakespeare films identified by Jack Jorgens in *Shakespeare on Film* in 1977, for example, work along broadly similar lines. Jorgens classified Shakespeare films according to their relative distances from their source, which he saw as the language and conventions of the theatre: the 'theatrical' mode which in essence produces minimally directed film recordings of stage productions making few concessions to the capabilities and tendencies of the recording medium; the 'realist' mode in which, while the text is adhered to as closely as possible, detailed attention is paid to establishing setting and visual detail in ways that graphically realise the implications of the text beyond anything stageable in the theatre; the 'filmic' mode in which most liberties are taken with the original text in order to fuse the spirit of the original material with the essential fabric of the new medium.[6]

Grigori Kozintsev, the Russian film-maker, clearly approving and extending a style of adaptation that accords with Dryden's last 'imitative', and Jorgen's last 'filmic', categorisation, described how absolute a reconception of the dramatic material needs to be for the process of medium translation to be effective: 'The aural has to be made visual. The poetic texture itself has to be transformed into a visual poetry, into the dynamic organisation of film imagery.'[7] Dudley Andrew has described this same process of transmediation in the language of semiotics, as 'the systematic replacement of verbal signifiers by cinematic signifiers'.[8] Discussing the 'replacement' of one communicative scheme by a supposed equivalent in this way presumes essential significance to be detachable from the text. If one believes this significance can be relocated in, or re-evoked by, other sign clusters, it must necessarily have an identity that can transcend any one expression. The implication both of Kozintsev's theoretical writings and of his own film-making is that he believed

4

such a separation of the significance of a source from the specificity of its language is indeed possible.

After detailing his similarly tripartite categorising scheme for Shakespeare films in 1968, Donald Skoller concluded, somewhat simply, that 'the most effective films are those which take greatest liberties with original play-script material'.[9] The extremity of Skoller's position is, in many ways, a reaction against the earlier position adopted by a small core of Shakespeareans who had, more conservatively, regretted cinema's populist appropriation of hallowed dramatic material. Laurence Kitchin, for example, in an article for *Shakespeare Survey* in 1965 concluded that: 'In its . . . capacity . . . [as a] trend-setter, the screen is potentially a menace. It has given Shakespeare its biggest audience. Up to a point it can lead that audience, but it is a mass audience which demands concessions.'[10]

In examining what is 'conceded' in adapting Shakespeare for the cinema, and what gained, it has often been the subject of study to consider how the conflicting, even perhaps antithetical, demands of the medium (film) and material (Shakespeare) have jostled against, and accommodated themselves to, each other. Theatrically 'metaphrased' versions, that is films which take little account of the demands or strengths of the medium but attempt a near transparent recording of a stage production, do not engage with these processes of adjustment and accommodation and so need make few of those 'concessions' whose prospect appalled Kitchin. In this refusal, however, they can become a curiously permanent monument to an art form whose essence more usually depends for much of its power upon its very *im*permanence. In their attempt to preserve the life of a theatre performance whose ephemeral moment is, or should more properly be allowed to be past, they can appear as exercises in celluloid taxidermy – valuable primarily as records of the thing now lost. In discussing the value of Shakespeare performance criticism, as opposed to purely textual criticism, Douglas Lanier has issued a caveat about the selection of performance texts for study purposes. A filmed version of a live theatrical production cannot, he writes:

> . . . *capture the horizon of anxiety that live actor and audience share, the possibility that lines might be forgotten or mangled, props fall apart or become misplaced, cues missed, the anxiety that mundane material contingency may mar the performance. It thereby robs a live performance of some of its power.*[11]

Seen through the other end of the glass, of course, Lanier's 'horizon of anxiety' in the theatre is also a 'horizon of excitement'. That which has the anxiety-inducing potential to be marred by material contingency in one performance has the toe-tingling possibility of being *made* by crackling atmospheric magic in another. This, in part, is what theatre is. The process of deracinating

5

theatrical material from such a live performance context and resituating it in the cinema inevitably transforms that dramatic material. Since any medium of presentation is not merely a neutral vehicle for the transparent transmission of an artistic message, the processes of transmediation inevitably alter what that message is and how it will be received. Typically, film recordings of live productions have a deadening effect upon the performance since Lanier's 'horizon of anxiety that live actor and audience share' has been lost. Since they are also literally uncinematic – that is, not made for cinematic exhibition – they lie outside the scope of the present study.

Made-for-television productions constitute a trickier discrimination since this body of work is not such a clearly distinct unit as it once was. Most films, irrespective of provenance, are for study purposes now viewed on DVD or video on the small screen. This democratising of viewing conditions at the point of attentive study can obfuscate a series of differences that exist at the point of production and first exhibition. These might, for example, include differences in shooting format (between gauges of film, or between material shot on film and that shot digitally), or, for example, between the contexts of reception for which films were initially destined. Eliding both the viewing format and reception contexts post-release increasingly challenges some of the old distinctions between made-for-television films and those made for theatrical exhibition. Despite the processes of post-release homogenisation, however, typically it *is* still possible to differentiate between the spectatorship targeted and viewing experience offered by the domestic screen as opposed to the movie theatre *at their moment of first release*. As first conceived, made-for-television films still play to a differently perceived market in a different reception context – domesticated, isolated and with myriad competing claims on the attention – and as a result tend to operate under different aesthetic and commercial imperatives. The prevailing conditions of presentation of cinema and television have led to an accepted characterisation of their dominant modes of viewing as 'the gaze' and 'the glance' respectively. These distinctions have understandably had an effect on the nature of the productions designed to meet these differing viewing styles.

The challenge of adapting Shakespeare for the television might be defined as finding a means of penetrating to the imaginative, intellectual and emotional heart of an audience which is viewing on a reduced scale, in a contained format, often in bite-sized chunks to accommodate commercial breaks and, importantly, in a domestic context laden with possible distractions. The core of the challenge in adapting Shakespeare for the cinema, by contrast, lies not principally in how to reach the heart of an audience, since the scale and intensity of cinematic presentation can, potentially at least, absorb the spectator into the flux of the narrative. Rather the challenge for the cinema lies centrally in how most intelligently to treat the suggestive depths of poetically laden language which it inherits from its source, without disrupting the balance of the movie as a whole. That is to say that a Shakespeare movie needs to have a peculiar degree of poise in order to absorb a considerable weight of concentrated Shakespearean dialogue without in the process slipping into visual paralysis or stentorian obsession. Julie Taymor, whose playful and disturbing mixed-period *Titus* (2000) starring Anthony Hopkins is discussed in Chapter 8, expresses the challenge in more punchily concrete terms: 'You can't have a battery of dialogue, dialogue, dialogue in a movie.'[12] Staple to the repertoire of television drama has traditionally been the word-based set-up known as 'talking heads'. As a result, a battery of dialogue – when required – tends to be more deftly managed in televisual than in cinematic production since words have always been more integral to television's communications.

The implications of viewing a Shakespeare film on a small screen in private space as opposed to on a big screen in communal space forms part of the discussion that follows. The viewing spaces in prospect are relevant to a discussion of cinematic Shakespeares in part because they become part of the implicit discussion of the films themselves, aware as they increasingly are of the dominant spaces of consumption that await them in their life post-theatrical release. The striking conjunction of a television screen and a ruined (movie) theatre in Baz Luhrmann's *William Shakespeare's Romeo+Juliet* (1996), for example, provides its own implicit commentary on the presentation spaces currently able to make the most pervasive claim on Shakespeare performances. The variant character of viewing spaces, public and domestic, televisual and cinematic, as specifically explored within recent Shakespeare films, comes under the spotlight in Chapter 8.

*

Roger Manvell, whose pioneering study of Shakespeare films appeared in 1971, partly made it his project to identify what is inherently 'Shakespearean', and what inherently 'cinematic'.[13] His analyses of individual films implicitly or explicitly considered how these two potentially antithetical forms – the one, so the argument runs, imaginatively evoking the image through the suggestive power of the word, the other apt to erode the power of the word by its impressive privileging of the image – have been creatively modified to accommodate each other to greatest effect. Cinematic form and Shakespearean dramatic character were, therefore, implicitly posited as competing absolutes as the premise for considering the interestingly hybrid nature of their union.

The medium of transmission *is*, of course, a potent influence upon the dramatic material presented and needs always to be borne in mind in reading any text that has been transmediated. Film's principal formal characteristics are well known: its play of light and shade on a screen unfolds in two dimensions; the actor is physically absent from its exhibition space; the composition of the frame (and therefore the irresistible direction of spectatorial attention) is predetermined; proximity to or distance from a character or object is not dependent upon spectator placement but on camera position or focal length; space and time are edited – seemingly fluid but actually disjoint; the filmic world on offer is prescribed, controllable and mediated. These characteristics necessarily make their own interventionist commentary on any narrative told in moving pictures. As such they reward analysis. However, the range of ways in which these base-line medium characteristics have been employed in cinematic interpretive treatments of Shakespearean material does not tend to add up to a stable category of specifically 'cinematic' attributes that might be considered universally true. There is too much exciting variation between, for example, the epic sweep of Laurence Olivier's *Henry V* (1944) and the intimacy of Kenneth Branagh's *Henry V* (1989), or between the excessive explosion of digital technology on display in *Prospero's Books* (Peter Greenaway, 1991) and the deliberate technological self-denial of *The King is Alive* (Kristian Levring, 2000), or between the gritty-edged fragmented close-ups of Peter Brook's *King Lear* (1969) and the saccharinely filtered imagery of Michael Hoffmann's *A Midsummer Night's Dream* (1999), or between the studied realism of costume and setting in Franco Zeffirelli's *Hamlet* (1990) and the spare minimalism of Derek Jarman's *The Tempest* (1979) to be able to extract many general principles from this body of material as to what might constitute the 'cinematic'.

To cling to a notion of the 'cinematic' as a particular body of medium characteristics (which in practice is nearly always distilled to mean the epic photographic sweep and some deft effects of montage) is to adhere to what Noël Carroll has designated the 'specificity thesis': 'The specificity thesis seems to urge that a medium pursue only what it does best . . . appear[ing] to envision each art form on the model of a highly specialized tool with a range of determinate functions.'[14] Carroll's objection to this is that a medium may effectively be inhibited from doing something well simply because, in terms relative to other media, there may be something that it does better. If adhered to, the pursuit of medium purity implied by the specificity thesis would create, at best, an unhelpful bias in how critics value each art form and, at worst, an unnecessary fettering of innovative practice. To commend those films which observe a particular set of medium-specific characteristics, for example, and to dismiss as 'uncinematic' those which stray from the prescribed uses is almost always to crudify an understanding of filmic potential and diversity. (Eschewing an essentialist definition of the cinematic should not, however, be confused with sidelining questions of technique and style in reading a film. It simply resists prejudging how those things *should* be employed.)

The 'cinematic' is not the only unhelpfully over-defined constituent element detectable in some theories of Shakespearean transmediation: notional categories of 'the Shakespearean' and 'the theatrical' are both as subject to variation, revision and contradiction in their own right. The institutional encounters that take place in a Shakespeare film cannot be considered those between absolutes. None of the key players in the encounter – Shakespeare, the cinema, the theatre – exists in ideal forms that transcend particular expressions; rather each is constantly being defined and redefined by usage.

Formalist studies of Shakespeare films as a body of work responsive to, and determined by, a series of medium-specific imperatives tended, in any case, to cede in the 1980s. And by the 1990s, examinations of the films as cultural products emerging from, and illustrative of, a series of economic, industrial and cultural predispositions and priorities had firmly taken precedence. There is, of course, a vital contiguity between any cultural expression (in this case a film) and the world from which it emerges. However, because a film, unlike a play, can survive long enough to slough off the particularities of its production context, it can give the impression of floating through history relatively unencumbered by questions of history and culture. It is one of the tasks of the critic, therefore, to puncture this illusion of ahistoricity and attempt, in as much as this is possible, to particularise a film's engagements with its production context. This is not to deny a film's capacity to be subsequently transformed in reception: a film, like any cultural expression that endures, needs to be allowed to reinvent itself across time as it engages successively with renewed contexts. It is, however, to assert that whatever happens to it subsequently, it remains the product of specific origins which, when offered as a critical backdrop, can help to bring the film into sharper interpretive relief. And just as a knowledge of the production context can illuminate a reading of the film, equally a sensitive reading of the film can help to illuminate aspects of the cultural context that gave birth to it. To say as much is simply to assert that the relationship between a published text and its cultural contexts is necessarily symbiotic.

In the pages that follow, a hybridising of these critical traditions – the formalist and the cultural-historical – will be represented. The book falls into two parts and although both approaches are represented in both parts, the relative balance tips in the direction of formalist considerations in Part I, and of contextual considerations in Part II. The project is therefore, in varying degrees of balance, both to consider the filmic mechanisms of the particular spectatorial pleasures on offer *and* to weigh the broader contexts from which the films emerge, and into which they have been received. It is neither possible nor desirable to keep these areas of enquiry entirely separate since what counts as a 'text' can never be wholly isolated from the network of supporting structures that gives it form.

True of all texts, this is so in particularly obvious ways of mainstream movie releases. Each movie release is typically accompanied by a bombardment of anecdote, location report, publicity stills, teaser trailers, celebrity appearances, interviews and production information strategically put into the public domain. Some of this will seep irresistibly into our reading of the film, compromising any hypothetical notion of textual autonomy. The sheer prevalence of such extra-textual information gives it a power of penetration that binds it in to what we might call the 'textual penumbra' of a film: that body of information that, although not literally part of what is seen on screen, attaches to the film so closely as to become inextricably associated with it. At its most intrusive, a film's potential inclusions in its 'penumbra', or textual identity in the broadest sense, might include, for example, what the director is on record as saying the film 'is about'. At its most innocuous, it might, more simply, include an awareness of an actor's previous roles, or a knowledge of the shooting locations used. We know, for example, that Anthony Hopkins had already played a gleeful butcher (Hannibal Lecter) on film before playing Titus in Julie Taymor's 2000 film. We cannot, therefore, read Hopkins' screen presence in this film in isolation from some of his earlier work: it will necessarily inflect our readings at the very least of all butchery-related humour in the film. Equally, the well publicised fact of the Croatian setting of the amphitheatre in the same film – unnervingly close to the scene of real world atrocities to rival even those in Shakespeare's play – cannot but effect our reading of the film's topical engagements with acts of institutionalised violence beyond the movie theatre. Knowing of the politically charged location for the shoot makes the analogy the more pressingly immediate. The pervasiveness of such extraneous information about a film, and its capacity to insinuate itself fully into the fabric of the film we view, complicates any simple putative divide between what constitutes the 'textual' and what the 'extra-textual' in the case of such an industrially driven, mass-market art form. The text itself is constantly gathering accretions – some diversionary, some interpretively pertinent – by means of the plethora of shared information in circulation about it.

Shakespeare films are too diverse in their interpretive and cultural operations to cohere obligingly into an identifiable body of work about which homogenising claims may legitimately be made, or which, therefore, may be submitted with equal rewards to a 'one-size-fits-all' critical approach. In acknowledgement of this, a range of analytical strategies is employed. In addition to finding points of inextricable relation between the text and its various contexts, for example, another central project is to read the films as illuminating interpretive tools in relation to the Shakespeare plays. To consider a film as in part a work of literary criticism *put into practice* is by no means to excuse it the requirement to work as an entertaining film in its own right. It is, however, to acknowledge that the networks of relationship it establishes with its advertised source will be an influential interpretive referent for many spectators. Inviting the two texts – source and adaptation – to comment on each other also has the potential benefit of being interpretively enriching for both. In practice, therefore, films are discussed in whichever critical framework seems calculated to yield the most interesting reading in each case. As an approach, the embracing of varying critical traditions has none of the virtues of theoretic purity. Nevertheless, it is hoped that it may have the more prosaic advantage of being flexibly responsive to the films in their multiple identities.

The book offers a series of studies of films that range from 1899 (in Chapter 1) to the early 2000s (in Chapter 8). Cumulatively, these studies tell an emerging story of the cinema's collaborative engagements with the work of one iconic dramatist. The book's progress between the temporal end-markers of Chapters 1 and 8 is, therefore, sequential in its drift, if divertable in its detail. In the four chapters that make up Part I, 'Degrees of Remove: Translating the Language, Translating the Story', some of the contested definitional boundaries of the putative category 'Shakespeare on film' are implicitly interrogated. In the first two, films from the era pre-1927 (when the first commercial sound film was released) are considered. Although these films are conventionally known as 'silent' Shakespeare films, the label is, of course, misleading: for all their lack of spoken dialogue, they were always accompanied by music, and sometimes additionally by other vocal comment-ary, at the point of exhibition. Nevertheless, the removal of spoken language from Shakespeare is, undeniably, a significant act of 'silencing' and strikes many as the explicit denial of the beauties of the dramatic material, or even the wilful creation of an oxymoron. It is this charge that silent Shakespeare films typically have to counter on a first exposure. However, it is important to resist an anachronistically patronising smirk at their expense. In their own moment of first exhibition – used as it was to various other forms of pantomimic, wordless Shakespeare performance, and with no sense that such a thing as the *talkies* might one day become the norm – they will have seemed less of an oxymoron than they do now in ours.

In practice, these films are sometimes, to borrow Alonso's phrase from *The Tempest*, 'an excellent dumb discourse' (III.iii.39), a system of communication whose eloquence and whose wordlessness are intimately related. At others they can seem principally anxious to signal the absence of that which might make them meaningful in ways that would accord more easily with tra-ditional understandings of (worded) Shakespearean performance. To ignore the first can lead critics to dismiss the body of silent Shakespeare films simply as a risible curiosity. To ignore the second, however, can lead to a view of the films clouded by sentiment. In the two chapters on the silent era, I therefore attempt to see the films as illuminating the theatrical and cinematic conventions of their moment and as touching, innovative and exciting films in their own right. However, I also try to keep the readings alive to the ways in which some films broadcast their frustration at not being a worded performance, advertising as they do a pained sense of verbal absence and defining themselves most resolutely in terms of what they are not. In the films' progressive movement across the era from offering conciliatory compensation for that which is not there (words) to a fulsome celebration of that which is (spectacle, plot, performance), silent Shakespeare films may even be seen as growing *into* Alonso's appreciative sense of the potentially 'excellent' character of dumbshow. A changing relationship to the conventions of the theatre is therefore charted across the period, as are the emerging tonal distinctions between the British, American and continental European releases.

In Chapter 3, a case study on Japanese director Akira Kurosawa's exquisite Shakespeare-inspired films *Throne of Blood* (1957) and *Ran* (1985) brings foreign-language films from the sound era under the spotlight. Kurosawa's painterly eye, purposeful engagements with his collaborators about the use of musical underscoring and interest in finding points of intersection between European and Japanese myths form the basis of the discussion about his work. The chapter analyses both how Kurosawa encourages Shakespearean narratives to intersect with Japanese narratives, and how a selective slice of Japanese exoticism has been marketed under a Shakespearean label with a sensitive but strategic eye to Western funding and Western audiences.

The films discussed in Chapter 4 effectively do to Shakespearean material what the picture on a beach towel on sale in the Metropolitan Opera gift shop in 1991 did to Verdi's *Aida*. I am indebted to John Glavin for his nimble report of the beach towel's decoration:

> The top of the towel proclaims: 'The Original Ending of Verdi's Aida.' The middle displays a pyramid, some palm trees, and two figures in Egyptian dress, one male, the other female, peeking, suspicious and surprised, through an opening in the structure. And at the bottom: 'Who would have thought there was a back door to this place?'[15]

Unlike their operatic counterparts, this cartoon Radames and Aida are not condemned to death by being buried alive but are here impishly released from their scripted fate into the possiblity of other adventures. It is the unentombing of Shakespearean material and Shakespearean characters into other adventures and new contexts that is, in effect, the subject of Chapter 4. The delighted discovery of a 'back door' out of the (Shakespearean) monument is explored through the horror films *Island of Lost Souls* (1932) and *Iguana* (1988), the American sci-fi fantasy *Forbidden Planet* (1956), the noir-esque *Men of Respect* (1991) and the teen flick *O* (2001). The first three of these share narrative and thematic ground with *The Tempest*, the fourth is a closely worked updating of the plot and language of *Macbeth* to a contemporary world of New York mafia syndicates and the last, *O*, reworks *Othello* as a story about a black basketball hero in an all-white American high school. In post-production, *O* was found to chime so neatly with a contemporary news story that it nearly did not make it to the screen for fear of being too closely identified with that real-world event. *O*'s points of intersection with a contemporary news story prompt me to revisit, by way of comparison, the Othello/OJ Simpson parallels to which Oliver Parker's *Othello* contributed in 1995. It is no surprise that the films chosen for Chapter 4 should all be American. It is by now almost a truism that British cinema's deference to British literary sources has tended to translate into less radically reconceived filmic interpretations. By contrast, since its earliest days, American cinema has felt the liberty to make free with Shakespearean narratives in pursuit of its own less riven agendas. The films considered in this chapter, therefore, represent a sample of the many less than entirely deferential American engagements with Shakespearean source material that mischievously seek a back route out of the pyramid.

As the range of material in Part I demonstrates, there is a plurality of possible types of film which either advertise a relationship to Shakespeare, or which can be usefully brought into a comparative frame with Shakespeare in a way that is illuminating. By considering silent Shakespeare films, foreign-language Shakespeare films and narrative borrowings from Shakespearean material, it is the project of Part I to explore some of the more complex and intriguing sets of engagements between Shakespeare and his cinematic relations. Definitional debates about 'Shakespeare films' as opposed to 'films with a Shakespearean resonance' or 'films on a Shakespearean subject' are of less concern here than what of interpretive use or interest might emerge from thinking about the films as enjoying some derivative relationship to Shakespeare. If a useful interpretive purpose may be served by placing a particular film alongside a Shakespeare play, that seems sufficient justification for doing so. As the work of both Dryden and Jorgens can perhaps testify, beyond a very few givens, the precise degrees of remove of an adaptation from its source are notoriously difficult to quantify with any useful exactitude.

In Part II, 'Moment and Context: How History Works on Story', the balance of attention shifts to concentrate more on the films as products of a particular cultural historical moment. In Chapters 5 and 6, two Shakespeare plays – *A Midsummer Night's Dream* and *The Tempest* – are tracked across a century of cinematic adaptation. Considering how the dramatic material has been moulded, shaped and reinvented across time to suit the altered contexts of production and reception inevitably makes of each drama a sensitive indicator of cultural change. Michael Almereyda reports that before he made his 2000 film of *Hamlet* (discussed in Chapter 8), he 'went to every film library and museum in New York, where I watched every Hamlet on record, plays recorded on video, even silent films'.[16] This manifest desire to understand the cumulative legacy of *Hamlet* performances that preceded his own directly informs Almereyda's production. The film is shot through with an awareness that it is working in, and itself now contributing to, a long tradition of interpretive readings of a classic play. It is just such a desire to trace a cumulative interpretive legacy that animates Chapters 5 and 6, making possible a consideration of what George Steiner has referred to as the 'processes of canonization and of discard' at work in the interpretive evolution of a single story across time.[17] According to the workings of these processes, some elements of a classic tale become enshrined as central to an understanding of the work while others necessarily fall into neglect, in line with the interpretive priorities of an age. It is the project of these two chapters to plot these shifts in interpretive emphasis in relation to *A Midsummer Night's Dream* and *The Tempest* in turn, and to ask in what ways the resulting adjustments of concentration may be culturally eloquent about the moments which have produced them.

In Chapter 7, the films of Kenneth Branagh are considered. It is almost *de rigeur* in considering Branagh's work to use Laurence Olivier as a comparative foil, and I do not break with tradition in this respect. The chapter therefore includes some lengthy asides about the Olivier mantle that Branagh has in some respects adopted and in others defined himself against. What I hope to bring fresh to this discussion is a consideration of some of Olivier's defining screen roles in British films of the 1940s that helped to determine what his screen presence meant to audiences. His performance as Nelson, an English military hero pitted against a European foe, in Alexander Korda's *Lady Hamilton* (1941), for example, serves as a useful analogue to, and anticipation of, his heroic portrayal of Henry V in the celebrated 1944 Two Cities film. Also discussed is the Ministry of Information's strategic decision to protect Olivier's valuable patriotic image by refusing to release him from other war duties to star in Powell and Pressburger's controversial *The Life and Death of Colonel Blimp* (1943). The chapter's weight of concentration, however, is on the remarkable and remarkably varied collection of Branagh's Shakespeare films produced to date, and on the engaging presence of Branagh himself in the midst of each of them. Not only have Branagh's Shakespeare films themselves taken on a considerable public profile, but his influence on at least a decade of Shakespeare film-making has been profound. Had I been assigning a single chapter to an anglophone director in a book such as this one before the 1990s, it would almost certainly have been Olivier, Orson Welles or Franco Zeffirelli who presented themselves as the obvious stand-alone candidates in this respect. Writing as I am in the early 2000s – and notwithstanding the box-office and critical failure of *Love's Labour's Lost* – the territory is Branagh's.

Branagh's success with *Henry V* (1989) and *Much Ado About Nothing* (1993) encouraged other film-makers to test the 'cinematability' of Shakespeare themselves. By 1996, therefore, when Branagh's *Hamlet* was released, the renaissance of Shakespeare film production was well into its stride. 1996, for example, saw the release not only of Branagh's *Hamlet* but also of Luhrmann's stylishly paced box-office hit *William Shakespeare's Romeo+Juliet*. Luhrmann's film worked with a text even more heavily edited than is the norm with Shakespeare films (which tend to use no more than 40 per cent of the text). Strikingly, for a film with such a celebrated word-based heritage, the main theatrical trailer for Luhrmann's *Romeo+Juliet* included no dialogue at all. Branagh's *Hamlet*, by contrast, famously used an uncut text – and, as famously, received an Academy Award nomination in 1997 for 'best adapted screenplay' (which raised a quizzical smile or two about what 'adapted' might mean in this context). These two 1996 films therefore neatly offer polar extremes of possible approaches to the Shakespeare text(s) they take as their sources. Branagh/Hamlet's mildly contemptuous glance askance at Polonius's undiscriminating comments made about the length of the 'Fall of Priam' speech encapsulates the central premise of Branagh's film. For Polonius (Richard Briers), the first player's speech is 'too long': for Branagh/Hamlet, its mesmeric length holds a cumulative power and must be protected in its entirety. In Luhrmann's film, almost no speech survives uncut: *Romeo+Juliet* works to the priorities of pace, passion and hip appeal and the text tends to be used in fairly snappy chunks in the service of these ends. The glance askance with which Branagh's Hamlet responds to the suggestion that a scripted speech might be 'too long' is, therefore, the sort of sideways glance that Branagh's textually expansive film as a whole may even be taken as implicitly making to Luhrmann's textually far thriftier one. If Branagh had opened up a potential market for Shakespeare films, however, it was Luhrmann's production, in all its textual thriftiness, that proved to have both the teen-sensitive sensibility and the cinematic savviness to exploit it.

Romeo+Juliet is considered in detail in Chapter 8, alongside *Prospero's Books* (Peter Greenaway, 1991), *The King is Alive* (Kristian Levring, 2000), *Hamlet* (Michael Almereyda, 2000) and *Titus* (Julie Taymor, 2000). Even in their points of resistance to Branagh, these films have all benefited from the enhanced interest in Shakespearean cinema among both audiences and backers that Branagh's work has elicited. In personalised and idiosyncratic ways, each of these films also proves to be of its moment in trailing an interest in its own narrative, technological and artistic purposes. The burning of books as part of the cinematic spectacle in *Prospero's Books*; the self-conscious siting of part of *Romeo+Juliet*'s action in the shell of a crumbling theatre; Michael

Almereyda's Hamlet intent upon documenting his own story in film; the strip down, no frills production of a Shakespeare play in *The King is Alive*; the ghostly galleries of a Roman coliseum in *Titus*, all prompt reflection upon the operations of the cinema as a medium that cannot help but compete with, and to some extent displace, both the text and the theatre as a cultural force. To be self-referentially alive to the characteristics of the medium within which one is working is, of course, itself a thoroughly Shakespearean project and in this final chapter I consider what purpose a medium-specific reflexivity might serve explicitly in relation to these films.

The sadness in a study of this modest length on a subject of this magnitude is inevitably about the films that cannot be included. The omissions here are of necessity many. It is hoped that the inclusions – some of which (Branagh, Olivier, Kurosawa, Luhrmann, *Forbidden Planet*) are well known, others (including much of the silent material, Michael Powell's proposed *Tempest* and some of the offshoots) as yet very little known – will provide some compensation for that which did not make the final cut. The selected further reading suggestions at the end of each chapter are intended to enable readers profitably to pursue a subject further. If this book can serve as a lively route into an entertaining, complex and endlessly evolving subject, while offering some navigational aids to the scholarly body of work beyond itself, it will have served its purpose.

NOTES

1. Kenneth Branagh gave an account of the history of the Forbes-Robertson edition in an interview for *Woman's Hour*, BBC Radio 4, February 1997. I heard the interview myself but, because the *Woman's Hour* archive records were not consistently computerised before 1998, I have not since been able to verify the exact date of broadcast.
2. Gibson reports his own excitement about trying on the shirt in the HBO film he narrates, entitled *Classic Mel Gibson: The Making of Hamlet* (1991). Copy viewed in the video library of the University of Rochester, New York. Deborah Cartmell also discusses Olivier's shirt in 'Franco Zeffirelli and Shakespeare', Chapter 12 in *The Cambridge Companion to Shakespeare on Film*, edited by Russell Jackson (Cambridge: Cambridge University Press, 2000), p.216.
3. Forbes-Robertson, Olivier and Jacobi had all themselves played Hamlet on screen but it was not their screen performances that were recognised in this way.
4. Quoted in Robert Hamilton Ball, *Shakespeare on Silent Film* (New York: Theatre Arts Books, 1968) p.80.
5. John Dryden, *Works*, edited by W. Scott (London, 1808), vol. XII, pp.11–12.
6. Jack Jorgens, *Shakespeare on Film* (Bloomington: Indiana University Press, 1977), pp.7–12.
7. Grigori Kozintsev, *Shakespeare, Time and Conscience* (London: D. Dobson, 1967), p.191.

8. Dudley Andrew, *Concepts in Film Theory* (Oxford: Oxford University Press, 1984), p.101.
9. Donald S. Skoller, 'Problems of Transformation in the Adaptation of Shakespeare's Tragedies from Play-Script to Cinema' (Unpublished PhD Dissertation: New York University, 1968), p.578.
10. Laurence Kitchin, 'Shakespeare on the Screen', *Shakespeare Survey* 18 (Cambridge, 1965), pp.70–4. This quotation, p.74.
11. Douglas Lanier, 'Drowning the Book', in James C. Bulman (ed.), *Shakespeare, Theory and Performance* (London: Routledge, 1996), pp.187–209. This quotation, p.204.
12. Taymor, November 1999, quoted in Miranda Johnson-Haddad, 'A Time for *Titus*: An Interview with Julie Taymor', *Shakespeare Bulletin* 18, 4 (Fall 2000), p.35.
13. Roger Manvell, *Shakespeare and the Film* (London: Dent, 1971). See particularly the discussion of Shakespeare's poetry and the cinema as 'oil and water' (p.15).
14. Noël Carroll, *Philosophical Problems of Classical Film Theory* (Princeton, NJ: Princeton University Press, 1988), pp.85–6.
15. John Glavin, *After Dickens* (Cambridge: Cambridge University Press, 1999), p.13.
16. Quoted in Miramax's Production Notes to *Hamlet*, p.13. Copy held on microfiche at the British Film Institute.
17. George Steiner, *Antigones: The Antigone Myth in Western Literature, Art and Thought* (Oxford: Oxford University Press, 1984), p.110.

PART I

'Degrees of Remove':

Translating the Language, Translating the Story

One of the purposes of the book is to explore a multiplicity of possible engagements between a notion of a source and a cinematic counterpart. In considering silent Shakespeare films, foreign-language Shakespeare films and narrative offshoots from Shakespearean material, the four chapters of Part I explore some of the more tangential of these possible engagements. All of the films considered in these four chapters have performed a double act of divorce from the inherited dramatic material, turning away both from the live playing space of the stage and from the specificity of Shakespeare's language. The new presentational and linguistic spaces – silent, gestural, non-anglophone, radically updated – in which they find themselves vary enormously. For all their points of divergence, however, they all manage to prompt renewed reflection on the Shakespearean material which has inspired them while simultaneously asserting their own autonomy as distinct cultural products with agendas of their own to pursue.

CHAPTER ONE

'An Excellent Dumb Discourse':

British and American Shakespeare Films, 1899-1916

> *I cannot too much muse*
> *Such shapes, such gesture, and such sound, expressing –*
> *Although they want the use of tongue – a kind*
> *Of excellent dumb discourse.*

> (Alonso, *The Tempest* III.iii.36–39)

Until fairly recently, silent Shakespeare films have not had a good press. 'There was little point in tackling Shakespeare seriously until the movies could speak', wrote Laurence Kitchen in 1966. The Shakespeare films that were made in the pre-sound period were, he continued, 'half piously theatrical and half frivolous'.[1] More damning yet was Jack Jorgens' summary account of the phenomenon: 'First came scores of silent Shakespeare films, one- and two-reelers struggling to render great poetic drama in dumb-show. Mercifully, most of them are lost . . .'[2] To anyone with an interest in the history of Shakespeare film, or in the preservation of early cinematic material more generally, Jack Jorgens' swift dismissal of this body of silent films makes difficult reading. If a mercy *is* to be identified in this history, it is not, as Jorgens would have it, that most silent Shakespeare films are lost, but rather that not all of them are. As is the case for so many films from the silent era, large quantities have gone missing, or been destroyed, or disintegrated beyond the point of possible restoration. Equally, however, many silent Shakespeare films have survived. That this is so is partly testimony to the staggering numbers that were made. The tally is impossible to log definitively since what might count as a Shakespeare film can vary so dramatically in the freewheeling experiments of the pre-sound era. Nevertheless, by any count, it clearly exceeds three hundred.

In this chapter I discuss some of the many Shakespeare films that emerged from Britain and the United States in the early pre-sound era (up to and, for present purposes, including the First World War). In the next chapter I discuss some which emerged from Continental Europe in both the early pre-sound period and on into the 1920s.

BRITISH SILENT SHAKESPEARE FILMS

The story of Shakespeare film begins in 1899 with the British Mutoscope and Biograph Company's filming of Herbert Beerbohm Tree's performance of scenes from his London stage production of *King John*. One film fragment survives from the production. It depicts King John, played by Tree, shot square-on from a static camera against a theatrical back-drop, writhing in pain, earnestly mouthing inaudible words, gripping his chair, frantically wiping his hand to rid himself of Prince Henry's solicitous attentions, clutching at his chest, stretching out his arms in despair and eventually dying with histrionic ceremony. Probably accompanied by two or three other filmed scenes from the same stage production, it was exhibited through the autumn and winter of 1899 as part of the varied Biograph programme at London's Palace Theatre. This Biograph programme ran concurrently with the early part of the run of Tree's stage production of *King John* at the more respectable Her Majesty's Theatre. The exhibiting of the filmed scenes from *King John* at the Palace Theatre, whose fragmentary character prevented them from making autonomous sense, therefore served partly as a brief advertisement for the more substantial live production that could be enjoyed by buying a separate ticket for a different show at another venue.

The 1899 date for the *King John* film – just four years after the Lumières brothers' pioneer screening in Paris – is striking. Shakespeare was recognised as a plunderable source of filmable material almost as soon as the new medium recognised itself as such. One of the attractions of Shakespeare to the emerging industry was his unquestioned place on the cultural (and moral) highground of British, American and European life. Film-makers were conscious of the need to shake off the disreputable reputation that clung to the medium partly by association with the titillating tastes of the optical toys that had preceded it. Key to the commercial success of many of these technological forerunners to the cinematograph (including mutoscopes, what-the-butler-saw machines and zoopraxiscopes) was their saucy subject matter. Moreover, titles such as *The Artist's Model*, *Yvette Retiring to Bed*, *A Parisian Lady's Bath*, *The Undressing of a Model*, *Should Ladies Wear Bloomers?*, *Mixed Bathing Allowed* and *Why Marie Blew Out the Light* continued to contribute to the commercial success of the cinematograph in its early days too. With this salacious (or 'giddy' as it was then known) heritage visibly in tow, and under significant pressure from the voice of respectability and public decency, the industry

King John signing the Long Lease of Her Majesty's Theatre.

The popularity of Tree's stage production of *King John* can be gauged from a satirical engraving that appeared in *Punch*. The engraving depicts Tree as King John signing not the Magna Carta but the 'Long Lease of Her Majesty's Theatre'
(18 October, 1899), p.189.

Source: *Punch*, 18 October 1899. (c) Punch Ltd.

felt the need to place some moral distance between itself and its inherited legacy.

By September 1899, when the film of *King John* was made, bitter personal experience had made the British Mutoscope and Biograph Company keenly aware of this need for a respectabilising sheen both for the industry in general and for their company in particular. Opposition to a BMBC film entitled *Studio Troubles* (also known as *Wicked Willie*) had been building since January of that year: by the summer the company had a significant public relations battle on their hands. The one-reeler over which the controversy raged featured a naked model being tickled by a young boy (Willie) in an artist's studio until caught and evicted by his mother and the artist. During its short life, this particular animated picture gained quite a public profile. It was denounced in newspapers, in the pulpit, in town meetings, and eventually, as the row reached its peak, it even received a mention in Parliament from Samuel Smith, the Liberal MP for Flintshire, North Wales. In his subsequent letter to *The Times*, Smith claimed it was 'hardly possible to exaggerate the corruption of the young' from these 'vicious and demoralizing pictures' which, he continued, would bring about 'a rapid decay of English morals to the level of Paris, with the same deadly results on the life of the nation'.[3] For the 'studio' at the centre of the row, the beleaguered BMBC, *Studio Troubles* proved to have been remarkably aptly named.

It would be wrong to suggest that *King John* might have been made as a direct result of the bad publicity generated by *Studio Troubles*. The BMBC were churning out far too many other films each month to be able to draw too close a causal link between any two. Nevertheless, the opprobrium heaped upon the company's executives by the summer of 1899 must, once the suggestion was raised, have made them then reach the more eagerly and gratefully for the culturally respectable and morally edifying sanctuary of a Shakespeare production as one of their next projects. As distractions from bad publicity went, this was undoubtedly a good one. It was certainly hoped that the mere fact of a Shakespeare film would, as Smedley, the company's chairman put it, help to 'remove the stigma, which, justly or unjustly, at present is apt to be cast on moving pictures'.[4] Having been himself thoroughly immersed in exactly this stigma through the mixed reception of *Studio Troubles*, Smedley must have particularly enjoyed having the chance to come off the defensive and claim the moral high ground freshly armed, as he was, with the company's pioneering film of Shakespeare's *King John*.

The crusade to 'remove the stigma' was not, of course, quickly won (and in many respects is still being waged) but Shakespeare continued to be cited in the campaign to gain some incontrovertible kudos for an industry that undoubtedly still had a set of rather saucy associations to shed. In order to become a useful tool in this respect, Shakespeare films were presented not simply, therefore, as quality drama, but also as a morally edifying influence on humanity. Or rather, they seemed to gain their moral validity directly *from* their artistic validity, the two value schemes becoming increasingly elided.

Tree was not the only pioneer in bringing Shakespeare before the cameras, but his name appears several times subsequently in the history of British and American Shakespeare films. Following the *King John* film, his next Shakespearean skirmish with the cinema was, in its overall conception, more innovative. It too had its clear roots in a stage production – his 1904/05 production of *The Tempest* at His Majesty's Theatre in London. The opening shipwreck scene of this production was particularly commended by theatre reviewers for its startling and dramatic effects. Its sensational impact depended upon such extravagances as the snapping of the ship's mainmast and the

It was not only the British film industry that used Shakespeare to boost its own artistic and moral legitimacy. An advertising poster from 1910 shows how the French studio Pathé sought to to validate its own cinematic products by aligning itself with a host of literary figures, including Dante, Goethe, Hugo and 'Schakespeare' (*sic*). A parade of literary and operatic characters emerges symbolically from the cameo inset images of the 'meilleurs auteurs'.

Source: Poster by Candido de Faria edited by Pathé frères circa 1908–1910. Lithographie 120 × 160 cm. Copyright: Collection Pathé/DR. Reprinted by permission of Patrimoine Pathé.

appearance of little fires in different parts of the ship. It was this dramatic *tour de force* of the opening storm scene and shipwreck from the stage production that was caught on film by Charles Urban a few months into the theatrical run. The blue-tinted two-minute film that resulted seems to have been intended to facilitate the company's plans to tour the provinces – providing the drama and spectacle of the storm and shipwreck in a format that was both re-viewable and relatively portable. A projected first scene dispensed with the need to transport cumbersome props around the country, while the second scene onwards could still be presented, more conventionally, as live action. The multi-media event that must have resulted was both an inventive and pragmatically-minded fusion of the available presentational forms.

Although also exhibited as a subject in its own right (through the Charles Urban Trading Company) as part of the varied programme of one-reelers in moving picture houses, the film of Tree's storm scene was clearly *primarily* conceived as an effect subservient to, and enhancing, the original theatrical production. In 1905 Shakespeare on film was, as yet, chiefly a novelty to promote Shakespeare on stage, and its difference from theatrical Shakespeare, far from being a point of pride, was even a cause of some concern in relation to potential adverse audience reaction. The *Optical Lantern and Cinematic Journal*, for example, felt the need to reassure potential exhibitors that the audience would 'not be made *painfully conscious* that they are looking at animated pictures' (my emphasis).[5] Rather the full theatricality of the effects and the 'original mechanical contrivances' were, the advertisement assured its reader, marvellously maintained in the film. It was not even, therefore, as a passable rendering of a *real* storm that the film storm scene seems to have been appreciated, but rather as a successful rendering of the *theatrical* storm to which previous audiences had been privy. It was, that is, as an act of recording not of creation that it was principally valued.

Even as late as 1908 in England, Gaumont's *Romeo and Juliet* was being applauded in terms that revealed a similar set of priorities: 'The production of *Romeo and Juliet* is so finely accurate in its leading details, and the scenery, costumes and acting so realistic that we sit and forget for the time that we are looking at the kinematograph art, but fancy ourselves seated in a theatre.'[6] Such comments define simulating theatre as the goal of cinema. They testify to an attitude as yet a long way from Tree's own enthusiasm for the special capabilities of film in rendering Shakespeare, as expressed in 1916 after spending one day in the Triangle Fine Arts studio on the filming of *Macbeth* in California:

> It is quite wonderful . . . how many things can be done in pictures for the Shakespeare tales that cannot be done on the stage. With all due reverence to the master dramatist, it is possible to illuminate and accentuate many details so as to produce a marvellously truth-telling commentary on the text and at the same time heighten the dramatic values. . . . The pictorial possibilities . . . grow, as one studies it in the light of this strange, new art, into something very beautiful and wonderful – not precisely a play in the Shakespearean sense, perhaps, but a dramatic narrative of great power.[7]

The anxiety that audiences might be made *painfully* conscious that they were watching animated pictures has been replaced by an awareness that they may be *delightfully* conscious that they were doing so. In other words, by 1916 Shakespearean film was no longer being considered a dilution or distortion of the real thing, but a real thing in its own right, whose difference from theatre could be a virtue rather than a flaw.

A production which finds itself torn between wanting to assert its allegiance to theatrical forms and conventions on the one hand and to vaunt its independence from them on the other was Percy Stow's 1908 film of *The Tempest* that emerged from the Clarendon Film Company. Unlike many of the early Shakespeare films, in particular the British ones, the Clarendon *Tempest* did not have its genesis in a stage production. Rather it was conceived as an autonomous piece of cinema. Nevertheless, it alternates between contradictory impulses in relation to theatre. On the one hand, it enjoys its capacity to present real locations and effects of superimposition beyond the scope of the stage. On the other, it pursues its parallel desire to authenticate itself as a Shakespeare performance by simulating stage sets, and so acknowledging some sort of theatrical allegiance. Thus an ambiguity of styles is sustained, the production courting a realism and a representational allusiveness by turns. And from the contrasting styles of presentation Prospero's island emerges as an oddly self-contradictory territory.

In order to clarify the telling of the drama as a tale, Stow reordered the events of the play so that the story unfolds chronologically. Much of that which in the play is reported narrative about the drama's pre-history – such as the arrival on the island, or Caliban's lustful, but unsuccessful, advances on Miranda – becomes in the film part of the sequential unfolding of the action. Thus, whereas the processes and effects of *remembering* the past are one of the driving impetuses of the play, the film removes the disrupting function of memory from the drama by ironing out the play's eloquent a-chronologies. In constructing a single linear narrative from the play, the drama thereby loses the force generated by the intermittent eruption of powerful and disturbing recollections from the past into the flux of present-time action. What it gains, of course, is greater narrative clarity.

The 1908 *Tempest* is intertitled with explanatory captions which often pre-empt the action, and sometimes disambiguate the motivations for action which in the play are less clear. For example, the film's anticipatory intertitle 'To humble Prince Ferdinand, Prospero sets him to log-shifting' leaves no room for doubt about why Prospero gives him this task: a definitive reason is offered from outside the internal subjectivities of the play. The play leaves more room for speculation than this. Might the log-shifting be designed to align Ferdinand with Caliban? Might Prospero be setting himself up as a conventional fairytale father-in-law testing the strength of the potential son-in-law? Does he want Ferdinand to engage with the fabric of the island before returning to Milan? Does he feel displaced by Ferdinand and so simply want to punish him – under the guise of testing his resolve – for being the pretender to his daughter's affections? The apparent objectivity of the film's pre-emptive pronouncement about motivation ('To humble Prince Ferdinand . . .') effectively renders such speculations redundant.

Nevertheless, the film can by no means be dismissed as simply an over-explained, simplified retelling of a Shakespeare 'tale'. It specifically exploits, for example, some capabilities of its medium to illustrate and enliven the narrative and, in so doing, draws attention to some of the arguments about the transmediation of dramatic material more generally. In Ariel's first encounter with Ferdinand, it is evident that the airy spirit is visible and invisible to Ferdinand by turns. Ferdinand, glad in the belief that he has found a companion, chases Ariel across a field, and yet every time he reaches out as if to embrace the dancing spirit, he finds himself clutching ludicrously at air. On each occasion Ariel has magically disappeared, only to reappear tantalisingly in another part of the field for the whole game to start again. Stow ensures at this stage that the audience is able to appreciate Ferdinand's bemusement by partially aligning the spectator's perspective with that of Ferdinand, Ariel being alternately present and not present on the screen exactly as he clearly is and is not for Ferdinand.[8] In the next shot, however, in which Miranda first sees Ferdinand, Stow re-employs film's ability to subjectivise perceptions in a sympathetic joke at Ferdinand's expense. Ferdinand is once again shown running across the field and clutching at air. This time, however, he is shown from *Miranda's* perspective for whom Ariel is consistently invisible. Whereas, therefore, the spectator has been made aware from the previous shot of how things seem to Ferdinand and of what he is attempting to grasp by the repeated, though futile, clutching gestures, the spectator is now made aware of how idiotic Ferdinand must seem to Miranda since, with Ariel invisible, his lunging actions now seem utterly inexplicable. Her willing collapse into his arms at the first opportunity therefore seems the more magical and mysterious (and entertaining) bearing in mind how extravagantly foolish he had seemed at first sight.

Film can toy with perspectives and show differing points of view on the same scene in ways beyond the scope of theatre which, in the main, is limited to offering a single third-person perspective on any given scene. Whereas on the stage, for example, a directorial choice needs to be made about whether Ariel (or, say, Banquo's ghost) is present or absent to the audience, on film he can clearly be both present and absent depending on which character's perspective is privileged by the subjective identification of the camera at any given moment. This same capability of film, identified and exploited by Stow in order to show how characters might see each other, has, naturally, continued to inform Shakespeare films into the sound era. For example, in both Polanski's *Macbeth* (1971) and William Reilly's *Men of Respect* (1991), the ghost of Banquo is present not only to Macbeth but also to the spectator, thus to some extent validating Macbeth's horror and invalidating Lady Macbeth's scepticism. In Trevor Nunn's *Macbeth* (1978), the ghost of Banquo is not visible to the spectator at all – although it is powerfully evoked both by camera placement and Ian McKellen's performance as Macbeth. By contrast, in Orson Welles' *Macbeth* (1948), the ghost is sometimes present and sometimes not present according to the play of perspectives in the film's construction, thus apparently validating the differing responses of both Macbeth and Lady Macbeth.

Prospero's island is a territory made and unmade according to the subjective impressions of individual perceivers – being, for example, green to one and tawny to another, lush to one and meagrely resourced to another. By showing the same scene a second time as an entertainingly different event since now seen through the eyes of a different perceiver, the film's implication that no event on the island has a definitive character, only a variety of ways of being understood by different perceivers, therefore comments intelligently on the nature of the Shakespeare play.

In 1911 Tree's name surfaces again in relation to the early history of British Shakespeare films. In that year his stage production of *Henry VIII* from His Majesty's Theatre was made into a film. William Barker of Barker Motion Photography released the film in a limited edition print in March 1911. The film was an immediate commercial and critical success and was declared the 'film of the year' by the *Kinematograph and Lantern Weekly*.[9] In line with the peculiar deal struck with the exhibitors ahead of time, however, the prints were only released for a pre-determined six-week period. This appears to have been the most strategic of marketing ploys, designed to generate an intense burst of enthusiasm to see the film, and so to maximise box-office takings in the given six-week exhibition period. And having generated the desired enthusiasm (and revenue), the film prints *were*, as arranged, all recalled. Then on 13 April 1911, an extraordinary ceremony was held at Ealing, to which the press and other visitors were invited. The recalled prints were counted, unwound into a loose pile, and set alight.[10] The conflagration this generated was doubtless impressive. There is, as a film such as Peter Greenaway's *Prospero's Books* (1991) was later to demonstrate, something transfixing, and inherently photographic, about watching highly flammable material burning. Certainly Barker was sufficiently struck by the cinematic and/or symbolic potential of the moment to take the odd step of arranging for the burning of the films itself to be shot on film. Thus a film of almost cannibalistic character was made; a film of the burning of real films. It is perhaps the most perversely performative moment in the history of Shakespeare films. This filmic record of the destruction of the *Henry VIII* films has not, alas, survived as a lasting memento of the public burning (and as a text which seems inadvertently to have played neatly to a postmodernist agenda). It has either itself since been lost, or perhaps, as so often happened with films from the era stored in unsuitable conditions, it may well have spontaneously combusted at some point, so joining its Shakespearean predecessors from the Barker stable as a pile of celluloid ash.

Thankfully, Barker's ceremonial print burning was not the sort of marketing gimmick that could be successfully repeated. Prints of other British Shakespeare films from the pre-war years were spared such spectacular treatment. In the same year that Barker's *Henry VIII* was going up in smoke, Frank Benson's *Richard III* was, for example, released by the Co-operative Cinematograph Company. It was not the only one of Benson's many Shakespeare Stratford productions to have been shot on film, but it does seem to be the only one that has survived.[11] Since 1886 the Benson Company had regularly included *Richard III* in their annual programme for the Stratford-upon-Avon summer festival and it was, from Benson himself to the most humble spearbearer, the regular Benson Company who appear in the film. The film's cast therefore has a substantial theatrical pedigree behind it. The film is shot in long takes – one per scene – from a static camera placed in mid-stalls at the Shakespeare Memorial Theatre in Stratford. As such it has attracted a certain amount of critical flak for its refusal to make more imaginative use of the camera, of more camera-appropriate acting styles and/or of the possibilities of film editing. The film 'reads' far more as an attempt to enshrine in lasting form a telescoped version of a celebrated theatrical moment from a celebrated theatrical actor in a prestigious venue than as an engagement with the possibilities of the medium to animate and comment upon a dramatic narrative.

It is unproductive, however, to condemn the film for not achieving something that so clearly lay outside its brief. The film makes little pretence to be anything other than a compressed recording of an acclaimed theatrical moment. Even filming *in situ* was still a fairly unusual decision. In 1899 Tree, for example, had transported his actors complete with theatrical backdrops and properties to the British Mutoscope and Biograph Company's Embankment studio for the filming of *King John*. Even by 1911, it was still a far more technically complicated task to light a theatrical venue sufficiently to produce a satisfactory film image than it was to relocate the theatrical event to a film studio lit for the purpose. There is, therefore, something deliberately self-authenticating about the Benson *Richard III* as a captured piece of theatre happening in its own legitimate performance space. The film is illuminating about Benson's emphatically, sometimes frantically, gestural acting style, about the uses of sets, costumes, extras, properties and blocking on Stratford's

Memorial Theatre stage in 1910/11 and, of course, about Benson's hyper-physical and sometimes callously humorous interpretation of Richard (nicely in evidence, for example, when he wipes clean his blood-stained knife with grisly and almost cartooned exaggeration). As a piece of cinema, it is less than scintillating, but as a complex record both of theatrical priorities and, interestingly, of what in its moment must have been considered potentially marketable as cinema – for some sections of the market at least – it remains of significant interest.

Within two years of the release of *Richard III*, however, multi-reel productions of feature-length were in production, and in the vanguard of these was the Gaumont–Hepworth *Hamlet*. Even prior to its release, it was the subject of an intense and enthusiastic publicity campaign. In June 1913, for example, the *Bioscope* referred to the project as 'without doubt one of the most interesting events that has ever taken place in the cinematograph industry'. No expense, it was claimed, had been spared in the filming (reported to have cost an impressive £10,000) or in the hiring of Sir Johnston Forbes-Robertson 'on the eve of his retirement' to immortalise on screen his well-weathered but still popular Hamlet. The *Bioscope* was confident about the film's prospects, particularly when bearing in mind the Hepworth Company's 'achievements in the past with this class of work'.[12]

A litany of indisputably 'quality' elements came together in this film which made it possible for producers, distributors and even reviewers to eulogise with almost nationalistic fervour. In July 1913, the *Bioscope* surpassed even its own enthusiasm of the previous month:

> *The filming of 'Hamlet,' the greatest English play, with Sir Johnston Forbes-Robertson, the greatest living exponent of the most famous part in the whole world's drama, in the title rôle, has been perhaps the most notable event up to the present in the history of British cinematography, and it was only natural that Mr. Cecil Hepworth, the greatest British producer of cinematograph plays, should have been approached by Messrs. Gaumont, the originators of the enterprise, as the man capable before all others of carrying through successfully this most difficult of undertaking. There can be no man in this country today who has a deeper knowledge of cinematography, nor a greater capacity for applying his knowledge to artistic ends than Mr. Hepworth, and, although one has not yet had an opportunity of inspecting the result of his latest and most ambitious production, one has the utmost confidence in its success.[13]*

The film oozed prestige almost from every frame. From its source material (Shakespeare) to its cast list (Forbes-Robertson, his wife Gertrude Elliott and the rest of their Drury Lane company); from its production team (Hay Plumb and Cecil Hepworth) to its locations (which included a complete

With his aquiline nose, fine bone structure and measured dignity, Sir Johnston Forbes-Robertson was an impressive presence in both his stage and screen Hamlets.

Source: Hamlet (1913)

reconstruction of Elsinore Castle at Lulworth Cove, the gardens of Harts-bourne Manor, home of Lady Robertson's sister, a private garden at Halliford-on-Thames and a private lake at Walton-on-Thames): in every respect, the film's faultless, even aristocratic, pedigree made itself felt. It was not a quality to be ignored by reviewers either at the time or subsequently: 'Haste, as we know, had no place in the aristocratic ideal and there is no haste here.'[14] Even the film's lack of pace, therefore, which elsewhere might have been considered a fault, is here turned to critical advantage as a further assertion of the film's impressively aristocratic credentials.

There are undoubtedly some pleasing moments in the film – in particular the repeated cross-cut between Ophelia's poetically distracted walk through the woods and along the river bank with her dress reflected in the water on the one hand and the evolving conspiracy between Claudius and Laertes on the other. The insistent cross-cutting nicely relates and contrasts male and female responses to the death of Polonius: the men plot death for another while Ophelia heads for the brook in search of her own. Moreover, the appearance of the intertitles 'There with fantastic garlands did she come' and subsequently 'There is a willow grows aslant a brook / That shows his hoar leaves in the glassy stream' as apparently simple location indicators for Ophelia's river-side walk adds an exquisite pathos to the scene. The lines are taken (out of sequence) from Gertrude's elegy for Ophelia's death (IV.vii.165ff.). The title cards thus poignantly acknowledge, and gently advertise, the inevitable destination of Ophelia's walk. It is difficult for those who recognise the appropriation and displacement of the words not to feel that even as they watch her tripping along the river bank collecting her flowers, they are simultaneously hearing the prophetically whispered news of her impending death. The sequence is beautiful in its elegiac qualities.

During the filming of this prestigious English *Hamlet*, Forbes-Robertson is reported to have stomped through a wood shouting at the poor cameraman, 'Lines, damn you, give me lines!'[15] The absence of words from the production was a source of constant frustration to him. Like Tree in his death scene in *King John* and Benson in his filmed *Richard III*, this Hamlet is clearly visible throughout the film earnestly mouthing entirely inaudible speeches. This does more than signal to an audience the mere fact that a conversation is taking place, since the speeches can stretch to considerable length. That is, it exceeded the standard practice in relation to many films from the silent era. It is as if English Shakespearean actors were anxious to signal their unerring allegiance to the value of the spoken word, even (perhaps especially) in a medium partly characterised by its absence. The determination of such actors visually to signal their reverence for Shakespeare's language in this way self-subvertingly seems to advertise the very thing these films are not – a vehicle for spoken poetry.

The intertitles in the Gaumont–Hepworth film are unusually long, and stay unusually close to the Shakespeare text rather than, as was more often the case in American silent Shakespeare films for example, restricting themselves predominantly to interpolated plot summaries. Neither their length nor their fidelity to Shakespeare is, however, sufficient to compensate the spectator for the feeling that there is meaning being conspicuously transmitted at the moment of production that is unrecoverable at the moment of reception. Forbes-Robertson's sustained mouthing of the words, and the production's respectful dwelling on him for the duration of some of his prolonged speeches, make this an inevitable spectatorial response.

The performance we see in the film is grave, unhurried and physically contained. It is, by design, very far from being showy. And not only is the pace of the acting stately, but the pace of the film as a whole attempts to keep step with that of the central performance. With a very few exceptions, the basic cinematic building blocks of the film are scene-length takes. That this is so virtually dissolves any potential distinction between a notion of scenes and shots. As if fractionally embarrassed about changing shot at all, the film even has a marked tendency to disguise its shot changes coyly under cover of an intertitle, thus minimising the advertisement of a fundamentally untheatrical narrational device.[16] Hepworth may have claimed that the detail of the stage production had been changed 'tremendously . . . for presentation under the novel conditions of the cinematograph'.[17] Nevertheless, such a prestigious Shakespearean *event* could not help but be riven about the extent to which it wished to celebrate its difference from theatre.

The inaudible mouthing of lines at length was slightly less in evidence in American silent film productions, which tended to prefer to move the action on faster than such moments of sustained recitation would allow. As will be discussed at the beginning of Chapter 7, the difference between English and American priorities in filming Shakespeare in the period was made painfully and obviously apparent in 1916 when Tree proudly imported an undeflectable devotion to the Shakespearean text to the Triangle–Reliance Californian film set for the making of *Macbeth*. His energetic adherence to the text in the making of this film seems particularly ironic when the savage nature of the cuts he made to Shakespeare's texts for his own stage productions is considered. In California, he was met by consternation at his stubbornly uncinematic wordiness and then by a resolute commitment to preserve the pace of the movie even in defiance of the visiting English star's desire to recite entire speeches.

In America, the 1916 celebrations of the tercentenary of Shakespeare's death inspired a clutch of serious-minded Shakespeare films: the Triangle-Reliance *Macbeth*, two separate *Romeo and Juliets* (from Fox and Metro), and the Thanhouser *King Lear*.[18] In Britain, by contrast, it seems to have been taken as the excuse for some cinematic fun – partly at the expense of American Shakespeare films. Thus in the same year that Tree was in California making his American *Macbeth*, the playwright James Barrie wrote and co-directed a British all-star film entitled *The Real Thing At Last*, which, as Robert Hamilton Ball explains, was 'a delightful spoof' on *Macbeth*.[19] Barrie based the film's narrative upon an entertaining juxtaposition of two hypothetical productions of *Macbeth*, one an underplayed British version, the other a brasher American one. The film traded upon comically stereotyped contrasts. In the British production, properties were small, the acting style contained and the plot recognisably Shakespearean; in the American one, properties and sets were enormous, the action exaggeratedly melodramatic and the potential for both goriness and sexuality enhanced. The British version ended with typically coy understatement: 'The elegant home of the Macbeths is no longer a happy one', while the American version blithely opted for closure of another kind: 'The Macbeths repent and all ends happily.'

Unfortunately, no print of *The Real Thing At Last* has survived. Most of what can be known about it must therefore be gleaned from contemporary trade journals and from the recorded anecdotal accounts of those involved in its production. In its sympathetic burlesque on the imperatives of the American as opposed to the British film market, it was no doubt inflected by the American Vitagraph 1908 *Macbeth* (whose goriness had specifically attracted the attention of the censors). The moment of its release makes it possible that it also had the Triangle-Reliance forthcoming film production of *Macbeth* in its satirical sights. The fictional productions of *Macbeth* lampooned in Barrie's films may therefore have had some basis in fact. By 1916, Shakespearean cinema was already establishing its own networks of conscious and purpose-ful cross-reference.

At the London première of *The Real Thing At Last*, on 7 March 1916, the entire cast appeared in person on stage before the screening began. Rather than then returning to their seats in the auditorium, they exited instead through doors on the stage, only to make their next, transformed appearance, as it were, in the film itself. *The Real Thing At Last*, therefore, highlights two significant developments in the relations of the cinema to Shakespearean productions. First, it seems to make parodic reference to at least one other contemporary film (Vitagraph's *Macbeth*, and possibly the Triangle-Reliance also), suggesting that Shakespearean cinema already considered itself estab-lished enough to wish to interrogate and satirise its own processes. Secondly, it draws attention, by the careful choreography at its première, to its clear distinction from theatre by first advertising what the physical presence of a live cast of actors looks like, and then conspicuously replacing that with their projected, ghostly substitutes. Even in Britain, therefore, cinema was no longer apologising for its difference from theatre but was now beginning to vaunt its distinction. Moreover, it was doing so with confidence in relation to a film that presented Shakespearean material – material that is, from the heart of respectable theatrical culture.

AMERICAN SILENT SHAKESPEARE FILMS

An entry in the American Mutoscope and Biograph Company's production log for 15 July 1905 announces that G.W. (Billy) Blitzer had shot the 'Duel Scene from Macbeth'.[20] This tartan-clad, studio-staged fight in which Macbeth kills Young Siward before himself being slain by Macduff enjoyed two years of life in its Shakespearean guise. Then, in 1907, its original title was removed and the scene was renamed simply 'A Scottish Combat' in order to be incorporated into AMBC's patriotically contrived sequence entitled 'Fights of Nations'. The sequence included little cameos of fights involving not only the Scottish but also the Spanish, the Mexicans, 'our Hebrew friends', the Irish and 'sunny Africa', each engaged upon a form of combat considered characteristic in some way. The culmination of the sequence of geographically ranging fights was a scene entitled 'America' in which Uncle Sam presided over a 'Congress of the Powers' thus ensuring peace for the whole world. What had begun life as a scene from Shakespeare had therefore been absorbed into a cinematic celebration of American greatness. It may have been the first, but was certainly not the last time that a Shakespeare film would be pressed into patriotic service. Famously, and on a very different scale, Olivier's *Henry V* (1944) was made explicitly to a patriotic agenda. As will be discussed in Chapter 7, a series of strategic editorial selections allowed that film to become a wonderfully stirring hymn to (English) national character at a needful wartime moment. However, in the case of the Olivier film, Shakespeare's conspicuous presence in the fabric of the film was an integral part of the patriotic celebration. Anonymising the origins of the Scottish broadsword fight by subsuming it into a broader hymn to (American) nationhood was by contrast a turning away from Shakespeare, simply and pragmatically driven by the need to maximise returns on each film made, even if necessary by re-releasing it under a different name.

Also in 1907, but across the Atlantic in France, the experimental film-maker Georges Méliès engaged yet more directly with Shakespeare on the question of nationhood. Rather than subsuming Shakespearean material into a celebration of individual patriotism, Méliès advertised Shakespeare as himself the means of dissolving national divides. His innovative film *Shakespeare writing Julius Caesar* concluded with the magical appearance of a bust of Shakespeare 'around which all the nations wave flags and garlands'.[21] The trick photography in the magical appearance of the bust bears the Méliès authorial stamp. As a sentimental vision of universal, and universalising Shakespeare, however, it nicely counterpoints the specifically *American* flag-waver into which the 'Duel Scene from Macbeth' was simultaneously being absorbed.

A single fight scene, with or without its Shakespearean label, was, however, small fry compared to the prodigious number of more substantial silent Shakespeare films that were subsequently to emerge from the United States. In the years leading up to the First World War, there were two principal American studios which regularly included Shakespearean subjects among their output of prestige films: the Vitagraph Company, who were one of the major international operators, and the far smaller, independent Thanhouser Corporation. Unlike in 1905, when a single scene still tended to be the standard repertoire of moving pictures, by 1908 whole Shakespearean plots made up of multiple scenes were being compressed into a one-reel (and, within a couple of years, a two-reel) format.

1908 was Vitagraph's most prolific year for Shakespearean productions. The year's tally included: *Antony and Cleopatra*, *A Comedy of Errors*, *Julius Caesar*, *Macbeth*, *The Merchant of Venice*, *Othello*, *Richard III* and *Romeo and Juliet*. In 1909 they produced *King Lear* and *A Midsummer Night's Dream*; in 1910 *Twelfth Night* and in 1912 *As You Like It*. In addition to these fairly straight, if largely languageless, plot romps through Shakespeare's plays, Vitagraph also put out a small collection of other Shakespearean spin-offs and spoofs, including *A Midwinter Night's Dream* (1906), *Cardinal Wolsey* (1912), *Indian Romeo and Juliet* (1912) and *Freddy Versus Hamlet* (1916). Of these, the *Indian Romeo and Juliet* is particularly noteworthy in finding a transplanted context in which the action of *Romeo and Juliet* could be played out. A Native American landscape becomes the back-drop for the story which focuses on the forbidden romance, secret marriage and tragic ending of a Mohican Princess and young Huron brave. Much later Stephen Sondheim and Leonard Berstein's *West Side Story* (the 1961 movie which was directed by Robert Wise and Jerome Robbins) was to transplant the play's action to the streets of gangland New York, and Baz Luhrmann's 1996 *William Shakespeare's Romeo+Juliet* to Verona Beach, a fictional reinvention of Mexico City. Vitagraph's 1912 *Indian Romeo and Juliet* demonstrates that both of these later movies were working in a tradition of resiting and updating with a considerable history. The Mohicans and the Hurons, the Jets and the Sharks, the white beach bums and the Hispanic youths – each finds a context and idiom in which to capture and refresh the story of the feuding of the Montagues and the Capulets.

Although a little slower out of the blocks in this respect than Vitagraph, Thanhouser added the following titles to the overall American output: *A Winter's Tale* (1910), *Romeo and Juliet* (1911), *The Tempest* (1911), *The Merchant of Venice* (1912), *Cymbeline* (1913), *Two Little Dromios* (1914) and

King Lear (1916). Thanhouser also waded into the controversial debate about the authorship of Shakespeare's plays with a film entitled *Master Shakespeare, Strolling Player*, released in 1916.

Vitagraph and Thanhouser were working on quite different commercial scales. Vitagraph was part of the powerful consortium of film producers called the Motion Picture Patents Company and had its own distribution networks in both America and Europe. Thanhouser, by contrast, was a small independent struggling to secure and maintain a market in the uncompromising commercial environment of the early cinema period. Despite their differences in operating scale, however, both companies were similarly anxious to promote their own company label whenever possible. As was common practice for the period, they both displayed their own company logo prominently and regularly throughout their films. The Thanhouser Corporation placed the entwined letters 'TCo' on the title cards of their early films, Vitagraph the V-shaped company eagle on theirs. But Vitagraph also went one step further. In a rather insistent piece of product placement, the Vitagraph 'V', or its representative eagle (whose raised wings formed a 'V'), was also brazenly included as part of the set in some of their films. In the Vitagraph *Romeo and Juliet*, for example, there is a circled 'V' prominently displayed in centre frame on the canopy above Juliet's bed. The Vitagraph eagle perched upon a circled 'V' is also fixed in centre frame above the church door arch at Friar Lawrence's cell and above Juliet's sepulchre.[22] At the end of the Vitagraph *Julius Caesar* the Roman eagles that appear above the SPQR banners are in fact Vitagraph eagles – an eloquent elision between a film company and an imperial power which was perhaps intended as a cheeky covert assertion of Vitagraph's own imperial aspirations. Moreover, the same eagle was, of course, also the symbol of America itself, thus simultaneously associating Vitagraph with two different imperial powers. And in a scene between Kent and his man-servant in the Vitagraph *King Lear* there is a curious moment when both actors are simultaneously out of shot (Kent exits out of frame right, man-servant out of frame left), leaving the set temporarily empty. The disconcerting effect of the static, empty set, however, quickly yields to an awareness that the set is not, after all, *entirely* empty: a free-standing model of the Vitagraph eagle, with no pretence of narrative or thematic relevance to the scene, has been left incongruously holding the fort. The eagle's moment in the sun is occasioned by the unusual blocking of the scene and was, presumably, part of the choreography as corporate promotional strategies temporarily won out over narrative imperatives.

Neither Vitagraph's flagged Americanism nor its ongoing engagements with the culturally respectable material of Shakespeare placed it above censure in the United States. In 1908 the three goriest scenes of its *Macbeth* (the stabbing of Duncan, the brandishing of the bloody dagger and the fight between Macbeth and Macduff) had to be cut for the film's Chicago exhibition.

Lieutenant Joel A. Smith, the Chicago police censor, was reported as saying, 'I am not taking issue with Shakespeare. As a writer he was far from reproach. . . . But . . . when it gets on the canvas it's worse than the bloodiest melodrama ever.'[23] The incident directly called into question the many contemporary claims made about the 'improving' influence that Shakespearean film subjects could have both on the motion picture industry and, yet more ambitiously, on society at large. Shakespeare, it transpired, could not consistently be relied upon to 'remove the stigma' from the industry as Smedley had hoped he might, and could even, on occasions, be found contributing to it. Meanwhile, Vitagraph's Shakespearean output continued unabashed, although after the run-in with the Chicago censor, perhaps with a little less gore.

For a studio such as Vitagraph with a significant output of prestige subjects, regularly revisiting similar story pools had several advantages. These included the pragmatic possibility of reusing stock properties. The rather loosely strung lyre, for example, played with ironically exaggerated sentimentality by a bearded servant at the reunion of Cordelia and Lear in *King Lear* (1909), had made its first appearance, in less ironised vein, when played by Brutus's slave boy in *Julius Caesar* the year before. In each case an identical shield is propped up at the lyre-player's feet. In *Julius Caesar*, once the boy has played his seren-ade and taken his exit, the ghost of Caesar then appears to Brutus in his tent and the nicely unrealistic organisation of screen space for this spectral appear-ance is worthy of note. The ghost appears as a superimposed presence in the centre of the frame behind Brutus. As we watch, however, the ghost's presence is transformed from a translucent shadow to a far more substantial presence, plausibly sharing the same literal space with Brutus. Yet even as the ghost's substantiality seems to be the more asserted, there is a contrary impulse at work in the scene to sustain an ambiguity about the status of its presence. For in his desire to make contact with Caesar's spectral image, Brutus does not turn to face it at its point of visibility to us, but instead reaches forward away from the image and almost towards the camera, addressing Caesar's ghost as he does so. By ambiguating the placement of the ghost in this way, the screen thus advertises its potential to play with spatial organisation in an alogical and allusive way more typically the province of the theatre. And in the process, the ambivalence of the ghost's location in the frame (behind or in front of Brutus?) also destabilises a sense of the ghost's solidity within the narrative by alerting us to the subjectivity of its dimensions and co-ordinates.

Out of the comedically unpromising raw material of the capitol scene in *Julius Caesar*, the Vitagraph film creates one of the funniest moments to be found in any silent Shakespeare film. Caesar is seated in left of frame, rows of senators in banked benches on the right while the conspirators mill around on the floor in between. Having callously ignored the repeated suits of the conspirators to enfranchise Publius Cimber, Caesar is stabbed first from behind by Cassius and then, as he rises wounded and descends to the floor of the capitol, subsequently from all sides by the other conspirators. He staggers from side to side with measured symmetry and dies a rather stylised (and pragmatically ungory) death in centre frame. All the senators unconnected with the conspiracy show their horrified consternation by rising from their benches, waving their arms in the air and then fleeing the chamber to spread the word abroad. All, that is, except one. For there is one elderly senator who sleeps on his bench throughout. As the suits are presented to Caesar, the senator sleeps. As Caesar is stabbed, he sleeps. As the conspirators rouse themselves to proclaim the liberation of Rome in the streets, he sleeps still. As Antony breaks through the crowd and is then left alone with the body to assert his allegiance to the dead emperor, the senator snoozes happily on the benches now deserted by his colleagues. In fact, were it not for an occasional sleepy twitch from the senator to remind us of his incongruous presence at the edges of the frame, his sleeping performance would be almost missable. Vitagraph were clearly aware of the contrapuntal fun that could be had by juxtaposing dramatically contrasting tones of action within a single frame. When the cataclysmic, earth-shattering, history-making piece of action is taking place in centre frame, therefore, its gravitas is gently ironised by the figure of the nodding senator at the peripheries of the frame.

It was a daring decision to add a comic touch to this famously big scene, just as it was to detract from the emotional intensity of the Lear–Cordelia reunion by adding the eye-catching distraction of the self-consciously soppy lyre-player. However, Vitagraph's desire to poke gentle fun at the silently frantic and/or narratively significant gesticulations in centre frame was one that was also on occasion felt by Thanhouser. In fact the Thanhouser *Winter's Tale* of 1910/11 includes near its close an even more obvious joke about a possible set of relations between the action at the centre and that of the peripheries of the frame than that to be found in the Vitagraph *Julius Caesar*. Present throughout the Sicilia scenes in the Thanhouser *Winter's Tale* is a slightly curious figure – a court jester/fool who seems to have been parachuted in from beyond the orbit of this play's action. If this fool has any Shakespearean provenance at all, it is surely in *King Lear*. He even looks remarkably similar in costume and in chubbiness of face to the fool in the Vitagraph *Lear* from the previous year. Curiously, his importation into *A Winter's Tale* seems to have been uncommented upon in review – and the film was much reviewed (though principally by cineastes not Shakespeareans who might have been more alive to such non-Shakespearean interventions). In the reunion scenes at the end of Thanhouser's *A Winter's Tale*, the fool sits in the bottom left corner of the frame, at the edge of the action, blatantly ironising all the touching scenes of reconciliation taking place at its centre. Thus when Perdita appears in Leontes' court and her story is recounted by the old shepherd, the fool alternates between leaning forward with excessively intense interest to hear the tale, and turning straight to camera, arms thrown in the air in mock-consternation, with a deliberately hammed 'did-you-ever-hear-the-like?' expression on his face. When it transpires that Perdita is the daughter whom Leontes had banished to her death years earlier, the fool cradles and rocks his jester's stick as if a baby, again looking straight to camera, head now on one side, with an exaggeratedly hammed 'ah-how-sweet' expression. As a succession of events of escalating narrative and emotional significance unfold before him and us, he takes delight in his position at the margins of the action, and the frame, to comment satirically upon them in turn. The excessive nature of his interest, of his concern, of his sentimentality, of his joy at reunion, combined with his position outside the immediate sphere of the story – both narratively and spatially – gives him the perfect platform from which to become an ironic commentator on the action. His project is uncompromising pastiche and this cannot help but effect the way in which we read the scene as a whole. No potentially touching effect is left unpunctured by the fool's ironising intervention, no moment of potential anxiety is left undisturbed by his own heightened mock-anxiety that serves as a lightning conductor and so partial diffuser of our own. The metanarrative he provides suggests a hint of embarrassment on the part of the company who felt the need to poke fun at the gesturally emphatic and emotionally charged nature of the climactic scenes, before, perhaps, an audience had the chance to do so. The film's internal satirising of its own narrative and performative processes cleverly left little room for subsequent would-be satirists or critics: it had stolen a march on them by its own entertaining processes of self-interrogation. While exploring the potential of the frame edges tonally to adjust the action taking place at its centre, there is also a suggestion that both Vitagraph in its Roman capitol scene and in the Lear–Cordelia encounter, and Thanhouser in their reunion scene at the end of *Winter's Tale*, lacked the confidence to allow such portentously charged moments, deprived as they were of words, to play entirely sincerely. Each company seemed to think that the big scenes as played on silent film needed rescuing from ridicule by the addition of a satirical inflection of their own.

Since many of the performance priorities of the late nineteenth and early twentieth century stage did not in any case privilege language over spectacle, the slight nervousness on the part of these American film companies about the credibility of some scenes without the aid of language may have been misplaced. The most famous stage production of *The Winter's Tale* from the second half of the nineteenth century, for example, starred Johnston Forbes-Robertson as Leontes and Mary Anderson in the parts of Hermione and Perdita and toured both England and American in the late 1880s. The text for this production, as for so many other Shakespearean stage productions of the period, was butchered pretty savagely, and in the preface to the acting edition, its priorities were made fairly clear.

> *No audience of these days would desire to have the 'Winter's Tale' produced in its entirety. . . . A literal adhesion to the text as it has been handed down to us would in any case savour of superstition . . . [T]he First Folio that Heminge and Condell pitch-forked into type so abounds with obvious blunders . . . that any scrupulous reproduction of this mutilated text would be mere pedantry.*[24]

Given the nineteenth-century stage's desire to avoid the 'mere pedantry' of fidelity to the text, there was, perhaps, less of a dramatic corner to be negotiated in producing entirely wordless productions at the beginning of the twentieth century than there might seem to be from our perspective. Silent Shakespeare films can even be seen as the natural inheritors of the priorities of the popular theatre of the nineteenth century that had so frequently and so insistently weighed the value of spectacle, narrative and star performance over the precise character of the text. Where the theatre had deprivileged the significance of the text, silent films dispensed with it almost entirely, thus providing an exaggerated resting place for the aspirations its more respectable sister medium had already exhibited.

In general the Thanhouser output of Shakespearean films tended to be a slightly slower and stagier product than the Vitagraph films. Following the release of *A Winter's Tale, The Moving Picture World* commended the owner and producer of Thanhouser, Edwin Thanhouser, specifically for having evidently sprung

> *from English stock. He holds the old conservative English characteristics of 'going slow, but sure.' He looks before his leaps, hence the quality of his productions. . . . Undoubtedly Mr. Thanhouser's long knowledge of stagecraft stood him in good stead in posing this picture. It was one long evidence of attention to detail and technique that has made the Thanhouser stock productions so popular among the trade.*[25]

The association of the slowness of a production with an English heritage was one that was, of course, to be felt yet more keenly in relation to the Gaumont–Hepworth *Hamlet*. By 1910, however, it was clearly already considered a national English characteristic, even specifically in relation to film style. The speed with which such national reputations are established and confirmed, and the incapacity of national industries subsequently to adjust or shed those reputations, is still, of course, influencing the way in which the British film industry is viewed on the world market today.

Edwin Thanhouser was still new to the film industry in 1910, having previously worked in the theatre. His aptitude for the new art, and his presumptuous daring in producing a Shakespeare film in his first year in the industry, won him commendation from the trade. A knowledge of stagecraft is certainly evident in his films. *A Winter's Tale*, his earliest Shakespeare production, demonstrates particularly obviously a theatrical style of blocking and of camera work. Some reviewers could not help but think that in relation to Shakespearean material, a clear advertisement of a theatrical pedigree (in style if not in actual production history) was preferable to an uncompromising rejection of the codes of the theatre in favour of those of the new medium. In context, such comments could be taken as a coded commendation of Thanhouser's approach as distinct specifically from the more energetic, more mobile and typically more cinematically adventurous productions that had emerged from the Vitagraph Company. In response to the Thanhouser *A Winter's Tale*, *The Nikolodeon* wrote:

> . . . there is no reason why tales from Shakespeare illumined and apostrophized as has been done in The Winter's Tale *should not be given a better reception by the public than some of the cheap, gaudy modern productions now commanding so much attention in the moving picture field. I hope to see others of this type in the market in the near future.*[26]

The Nikolodeon was not to be disappointed: Thanhouser went on to produce a clutch more Shakespearean films in the next seven years, not to mention a handful of other status-conscious literary adaptations, including *The Old Curiosity Shop* (1911), *Little Dorrit* (1913), *Silas Marner* (1916) and two versions of *The Vicar of Wakefield* (1910 and 1917). Its *Romeo and Juliet* included a considered balance between beautiful outdoor locations and more cramped and limiting indoor studio sets, but its action was, in general, static and a bit dull. The one-reel Thanhouser *Tempest* (1911), now lost, was particularly commended for its exquisite storm effects ('easily better than any ever seen in a stage production of this play'),[27] but in a later interview with Robert Hamilton Ball, Edwin Thanhouser himself could remember almost nothing about it.[28] Prints of the Thanhouser *Cymbeline* (1913) and *King Lear* (1916), however, have survived and these films merit attention.

Despite a lively performance from the film star Florence LaBadie as Imogen at the centre of the film,[29] the Thanhouser *Cymbeline* is wordy – alternating between plot-summarising intertitles and little nuggets of direct quotation to assert its credentials as a production closely allied to the text. It also includes a striking number of screened letters in an attempt to clarify and explain the action. Notwithstanding the weight of wordiness by which the production is dogged – and perhaps even partly because of this wordiness – *Cymbeline* helped to confirm the reputation of Thanhouser as a producer of prestige pictures. Moreover, Florence LaBadie's whimsically charming presence on screen was likely to be a draw irrespective of any flaws in the production surrounding her. (It is also perhaps worth noting that no one before or since has yet taken on the challenge of producing a *Cymbeline* for the big screen.) A reviewer for the *Moving Picture World* even made the considerable claim that the emergence of such pictures should 'strengthen our hope in the future of kinematography'.[30] The implication was, once again, that with such subjects on the screen the medium might yet attain to the status of an art.

The most pleasing sequence in the film comes near the end, in the battle between the Romans and the Britons. A series of shots in which Imogen (as a page) and the Roman general anxiously watch the progress of the battle from the entrance to their striped battle tent are cross-cut with location shots of the battle itself, shot entirely as if from their point of view. By cutting the scene in this way, no single shot of the battle needed to be elaborately choreographed, particularly lengthy or, therefore, unusually expensive. Nevertheless, the battle sequences seem dramatic, lent force partly by the intensity of the reaction shots by which they are framed. As a mechanism for depicting a battle, it was, in its own moment, evidently considered effective: these battle scenes, reported one contemporary reviewer, 'hold the interest well'.[31] In 1989 Kenneth Branagh was to use a similarly economical and effective narrative device for filming the Agincourt scenes in *Henry V* (discussed in Chapter 7). Long before this, however, Thanhouser had themselves reused the shot/reaction shot sequence from the battle in *Cymbeline* to intensify the effect of the battle scene in *King Lear* (1916).

King Lear was longer, more ambitious, more imaginative and more effective than any previous Shakespearean Thanhouser production, with a greater variety of shot lengths and technical effects. It also knocked spots off the Vitagraph *King Lear* (1909) both in terms of its cinematography and its performances. Lear was played with some power and subtlety by Frederick Warde, who had considerable experience acting Shakespeare on the stage, and had already starred in James Keane's celebrated and entertaining American film of *Richard III* (whose 1912 release had come hard on the heels of Frank Benson's far stagier British one). Frederick Warde also made a name for himself by giving lectures and recitations as live accompaniment to screenings of his films in those venues prestigious enough to be able to afford his services. *King Lear* was directed by Frederick Warde's son Ernest Warde, who cast himself to play alongside his father as a touching Fool. The other memorable performance is given by Hector Dion as Edmund, whose intimate moments of straight-to-camera address in close-up are prophetically evocative of the knowingly conspiratorial looks to the camera that were later to become part of the standard repertoire of a host of screen Iagos.

Late in the Thanhouser *Lear*, the progress of the battle between the forces of Cordelia's France and Goneril and Regan's Britain is measured and charted by the reaction of the three watching women. The battle scenes are difficult to decipher on their own. However, the cross-cuts between Cordelia's sweet and eager observation on the one hand, and on the other the voracious and vicious interest with which Goneril and Regan follow the fight make it clear at every point the respective fortunes of the opposing sides. The idea of narrating a battle by registering female reactions to it was lifted wholesale from *Cymbeline*, in which the progress of the battle between the Romans and the Britons was mapped through Imogen's reactions to it. Here, however, a layer of interest has been added by now counterposing the faces of two opposing observing parties as the narrative mechanism. Thus in *King Lear*, the contrasted reactions of the Lear sisters provide an antiphonal commentary on the progress of this battle.

A series of cross-cut shots that comment upon each other was part of the narrative design of the Thanhouser *King Lear* more generally. When Kent meets Oswald outside the walls of Regan's castle, the film cuts between shots of their bruising encounter and shots of Regan and her husband inside the castle going about their business. The relationship between the two spaces is made plain when those inside the castle hear the cries of Oswald and run to respond. Eventually the two fields of action fuse when the castle gates open and those inside rush out to discover the cause of the disturbance. Having been schooled to recognise the relationship between different shot sequences from such simple juxtapositions, the spectator is subsequently invited to infer a relationship of a less neutral, more value-laden character in a later series of shots. Here the cross-cutting not only furthers the narrative but also offers a wry commentary on it. As an iris closes on the Fool hugging Lear out in the windy wild storm, the scene cuts swiftly to a group, including Goneril, Regan, Cornwall, Gloster (*sic*) and Edmund, sitting snugly indoors by a roaring fire while Edmund chats animatedly to both sisters. The iris then reopens on the hapless souls caught in the storm, showing Lear railing to Heaven. The juxtaposition of the warmth on the one hand and the weather on the other is savage, clearly designed to emphasise the extent of the cruelty in robbing Lear of those most symbolically emotive of possessions – hearth and home.

Having the Fool represented by the son of the actor playing Lear effects the way in which the Lear/Fool relationship may be read. Knowing of their off-screen relationship invests their on-screen intimacy and paternal/filial mutual responsibility with an additional charge. Furthermore, knowing that the actor playing the Fool was also the film's director additionally creates an interestingly composite presence in the film – an elision which Ernest Warde seems to have used with some self-consciousness. Throughout Cordelia's banishment, for example, the scene intermittently cuts to a close-up of the Fool cowering and watching, timid and yet disapproving. His look presages disaster. By giving himself a series of bemused, concerned and troubled reaction shots in this way, Ernest Warde casts himself as a sort of surrogate for us and for our concern at the way in which the action is tending. Warde's Fool does not approach the parodic heights of his predecessor Fool from the Thanhouser stable, who had made such an entertainingly unShakespearean appearance in *A Winter's Tale* six years earlier. Nevertheless, a slight connection with that Fool is felt by any spectators who know both films since this Fool is wearing the same jester's hat and carrying the same jester's stick topped by a mini-Punch on its end. The re-emergence of these stock properties from the company's store cannot but serve as a visual reminder of the function of the earlier Fool. Unusually, Thanhouser seem to have offered the parody of a fool in anticipation of a straighter version. One of the effects of the obliquely referenced visual association is to evoke the parodic functions of the Fool's role while allowing Ernest Warde to offer a more reigned in, and altogether more serious version of Shakespearean professional folly. Whereas the Fool in *A Winter's Tale* had been the entertained, and entertaining, internal spectator, Warde's use of his own image in this film is as the troubled, and slightly troubling, internal spectator of the drama. This not only draws attention to the Fool's conventional role as distanced observer of and commentator upon this play's action but also partly advertises Warde's own extra-diegetic role as the eye through which the action is literally being seen. In this way, the conflated presence of director/Fool in this film provides a mediated vision of the drama that prompts reflection both on the processes of the play *and* of the medium into which it has been translated.

The year 1916, the tercentenary of Shakespeare's death, saw a small flurry of Shakespearean filmmaking, including the Thanhouser *King Lear*, the Triangle-Reliance *Macbeth* and the British parody *The Real Thing at Last*. By then, Shakespeare films were not only multi-reeled but had also begun to reflect upon their own interpretive legacy and performance practices. As is evident from, for example, the straight-to-camera address, the cross-cut sequences, the play of subjectivised perceptions and the use of star personae to promote less accessible material, they had also already established a set of conventions in their use of the camera, of editing and of stardom, upon which contemporary Shakespeare films are still trading.

FURTHER READING

Robert Hamilton Ball, *Shakespeare on Silent Film* (New York: Theater Arts Books, 1968).

John Collick, *Shakespeare, Cinema, Society* (Manchester: Manchester University Press, 1989), pp.12–57.

Luke McKernan, 'A Scene – *King John* – Now Playing at Her Majesty's Theatre', in Linda Fitzsimmons and Sarah Street (eds), *Moving Performance: British Stage and Screen, 1890s–1920s* (Trowbridge: Flicks Books, 2000), pp.56–68.

Kenneth S. Rothwell, *Shakespeare on Screen* (Cambridge: Cambridge University Press, 1999), pp.1–27.

Emma Smith, ' "Sir J. and Lady Forbes-Robertson left for America on Saturday": Marketing the 1913 *Hamlet* for Stage and Screen', in Linda Fitzsimmons and Sarah Street (eds), *Moving Performance: British Stage and Screen, 1890s–1920s* (Trowbridge: Flicks Books, 2000), pp.44–55.

William Uricchio and Roberta E. Pearson, *Reframing Culture: The Case of the Vitagraph Quality Films* (Princeton, NJ: Princeton University Press, 1993), pp.41–110.

NOTES

1. Laurence Kitchen, *Drama in the Sixties: Form and Interpretation* (London: Faber and Faber, 1966), p.142.

2. Jack Jorgens, *Shakespeare on Film* (Bloomington: Indiana University Press, 1977), p.1.

3. 'Demoralizing Moving Pictures', *The Times*, 3 August 1899, p.12, col. 5. Quoted in Richard Brown and Barry Anthony, *A Victorian Film Enterprise: The History of the British Biograph and Mutoscope Company, 1897–1915* (Trowbridge: Flicks Books, 1999), p.108.

4. W.T. Smedley, ' "King John" in the Mutoscope. A Glimpse at Mr. Tree for a Penny', *The Westminster Gazette*, 21 September 1899, p.4. See Brown and Anthony (1999), p.63; Luke McKernan, 'Beerbohm Tree's *King John* Rediscovered', *Shakespeare Bulletin* 11, 1 (Winter 1993), pp.35–6; and McKernan, 'Further News on Beerbohm Tree's *King John*', *Shakespeare Bulletin* 11, 2 (Spring 1993), pp.49–50.

5. *Optical Lantern and Cinematic Journal*, March 1905. Quoted in Robert Hamilton Ball, *Shakespeare on Silent Film* (New York: Theater Arts Books, 1968), p.30.

6. *Kinematograph and Lantern Weekly*, 18 June 1908. Quoted in Ball (1968), p.76.

7. Sir Herbert Beerbohm Tree, interviewed on 4 January 1916; interview published as 'Sir Herbert Tree Pleased' in *Pictures and the Picturegoer* 9, 105 (19 February 1916), pp.483–4.

8. I follow Shakespeare in using the male pronoun for Ariel. In the Stow production, however, as in so many of those on the Victorian and Edwardian stage, Ariel is played by a young girl. The girl's identity, like that of the rest of the cast, is not known.

9. *Kinematograph and Lantern Weekly*, 16 February 1911. Quoted in Ball (1968), p.80.

10. Ibid., p.82.

11. The Co-operative Cinematograph's Company certainly made four, and possibly as many as six, Benson Shakespeare productions from his Stratford repertoire. In addition to the surviving *Richard III*, the titles about which we can be sure are *Julius Caesar*, *Macbeth* and *The Taming of the Shrew*. For the surviving evidence about these three, and for further details about the making of *Richard III*, see Russell Jackson, 'Staging and Storytelling, Theatre and Film: *Richard III* at Stratford, 1910', *New Theatre Quarterly* 62 (May 2000), pp.107–21.

12. *The Bioscope* 19, 348 (12 June 1913), p.773.

13. 'The Filming of "Hamlet": Interview with Mr. Cecil Hepworth', *The Bioscope* 20, 354 (24 July 1913), p.275.

14. 'Silent Film of 1913 Brings Back a Great Hamlet', *The Illustrated London News*, 14 May 1960. Review on file at the Theatre Museum, Covent Garden.

15. Paul Dehn, 'The Filming of Shakespeare', in John Garrett (ed.), *Talking of Shakespeare* (New York: Hodder and Stoughton, 1954), p.50.

16. The dramatic exception to this is, of course, the cross-cut sequence of Ophelia's drowning and Claudius's plotting. The neatly and eloquently edited nature of this sequence is, however, not characteristic of the film as a whole.

17. See *Bioscope*, 24 July 1913, p.275. Other films released at the time included noticeably faster editing. These long takes might even, therefore, have taxed the attention span of a 1913 spectatorship.

18. For an excellent discussion of America's tercentenary Shakespeare films, and especially the Triangle–Reliance *Macbeth*, see Roberta E. Pearson and William Uricchio, ' "Shrieking From Below the Gratings": Sir Herbert Beerbohm-Tree's *Macbeth* and His Critics', in A.J. Hoenselaars (ed.), *Reclamations of Shakespeare* (Amsterdam and Atlanta: Rodopi, 1994), pp.249–71.

19. Ball (1968), p.225. See also J.A. Hammerton, *Barrie: The Story of a Genius* (New York: Sampson Low, Marston & Co., 1929), p.286.

20. The AMBC's production log is available to consult in the Motion Picture Division Reading Room at the Library of Congress. The film itself is included on the recent AFI DVD release of the Keane/Warde *Richard III* (1912).

21. From the scenario given in *Complete Catalogue of Genuine and Original 'Star' Films (Moving Pictures) Manufactured by Geo. Méliès of Paris*, compiled in 1908. Quoted in Ball (1968), pp.35–6.

22. I am grateful to Janet Costa for first introducing me to this film.

23. *Moving Picture World* 2, 24 (13 June 1908), p.511.

24. Preface to Mary Anderson's acting edition of *The Winter's Tale* (1887). Quoted in Dennis Bartholomeusz, *The Winter's Tale in Performance in England and America 1611–1976* (Cambridge: Cambridge University Press,1982), p.117.

25. *The Moving Picture News*, 21 May 1910. Quoted in Q. David Bowers, *CD Rom of History of the Thanhouser Film Company* (1995).

26. *The Nickelodeon*, 1 June 1910. Quoted in Bowers (1995).

27. Thanhouser advertisement in *Moving Picture World* 10, 8 (25 November 1911), p.598.

28. See Ball (1968), p.317.

29. It was Florence LaBadie's friendship with Mary Pickford that had first introduced her to the world of moving pictures and, more specifically, to D.W. Griffith who signed her up in 1909 to work for the Biograph Company. She stayed with Biograph until 1911 when she joined Thanhouser as their principal lady. In her time at Thanhouser, she acquired a star following.

30. *The Moving Picture World*, 5 April 1913. Quoted in Ball (1968), p.153.

31. Ibid. Quoted in Ball (1968), p.152.

CHAPTER TWO

'Wresting an Alphabet':

Continental European Shakespeare Films, 1907-22

Thou shalt not sigh, nor hold thy stumps to heaven,
Nor wink, nor nod, nor kneel, nor make a sign,
But I of these will wrest an alphabet . . .

(Titus to Lavinia, *Titus Andronicus* III.ii.42–44)

At the turn of the twentieth century there was a European view that a cripplingly respectful approach to Shakespeare was hampering the English stage. In 1899, for example, the French publication *Le Théâtre* had this to say on the subject:

Although the English admire, almost worship, Shakespeare, although they read and reread him and learn his works by heart, although they make him, along with the Bible, into their ideal literary model, for some extraordinary reason they have long neglected him in performance . . .[1]

The charge of a tentative and over-respectful treatment of literary sources in British performance practice could not, in truth, stick in relation to Victorian stage Shakespeares (*not* typically characterised by a paralysing respect for the text). Nevertheless, the allegation of a fettered national mindset about Shakespearean performance has proved both durable and ranging. It is in relation to the British film industry's supposed timidity in the face of a prestigious literary heritage that it has bitten with particular force – and perhaps with some justification. Examining the imaginative range of ways in which European cinemas treated Shakespeare in the pre-sound era can certainly make some British makers of Shakespeare films appear stiff in their respectful strivings to render the character of the verbal text in a series of visual equivalents.

The impression that an inherited and unshakeable reverence for Shakespeare has made the British poor custodians of his work in performance has enjoyed some sustained currency in continental Europe. A paralysing sense of the sanctity of the text and an inherited set of stultifying cultural prejudices have, runs the argument, debarred the British from being the true heirs of the raw energies of early Shakespearean performance practice. The implied corollary of this is clear: the contrasting freedom that can characterise the engagements of non-anglophone communities with Shakespeare has invigorated and emboldened their interpretations. Responses to foreign-language Shakespearean performances are instructive in this regard. In 1926, for example, an Italian critic reported that the celebrated Italian actor Ruggero Ruggeri's Hamlet had been received in London as 'a rendition of Hamlet such as that Burbage must have given', and this despite the fact that Ruggeri's performance was given exclusively in Italian.[2] Needless to say, to be aligned with Burbage (the original player of Hamlet) was a big statement about the perceived truth and authenticity of the performance. There is perhaps something pleasingly paradoxical about attributing a Burbagian (and by implication Shakespearean) authority to individuals and communities linguistically removed from the original.

In an era in which language could not be the driving force of a film production, film-makers from non-anglophone communities felt justifiably confident in taking on Shakespeare. Moreover, in the years before 1927 (when the first commercial sound film was released), the market offered a level playing field to all language communities in ways it has not been able to do since. One of the reasons that Shakespeare films from continental European countries were able to compete on more even terms was because the international distribution of films in different language prints was a simpler process in the pre-sound era than it was subsequently to become in the sound era. In this period, film prints would typically be exported without their titles cards. Upon arrival in the country of exhibition, a new set of translated title cards in the appropriate language would be shot and spliced in, in accordance with the instructions about content and placement sent by the production company or distributor.[3] Since import duties were paid per foot of film, calculating the total footage without the intertitles in this way could represent a considerable saving. Where producers' instructions lacked precision, or if the distribution agent in the country of import was slapdash, there was always the possibility that intertitles could be cut back in in slightly different places. Where this happened, a film not only in a different language but one also differently punctuated by its moments of action-suspending dialogue was generated. Despite the slight discrepancies in prints that occasionally resulted – and that are still in some cases detectable where prints in more than one language survive – the ease with which silent Shakespeare films could receive a multi-lingual distribution encouraged continental French, German, Danish and Italian film-makers to invest their energies in adapting Shakespearean material.

This chapter offers a selective illustration of the body of silent Shakespeare films to emerge from continental Europe. It considers a range of little known Italian Shakespeare films of the early pre-sound period and then moves to a more concentrated focus on two better known German Shakespeare films of the later pre-sound period. In acknowledgement of the ongoing legacy of silent Shakespeare films, however, it begins with a brief reference to a more recent American release.

*

Michael Almereyda's film *Hamlet* (2000) recasts Hamlet (Ethan Hawkes) as an amateur film-maker. This Hamlet invites reflection upon the material of his life by recording, reshaping and then cinematically exhibiting it. In place of Shakespeare's play-within-the-play, a select audience in this film is invited into a private movie theatre to view Hamlet's latest, provocative piece of home video-art. The reflexivity of this movie's interest not just in the story told but also in the mechanisms of its telling seems throroughly of its postmodernist moment. However, such introspection is far from being new to Shakespearean film-making. Ninety years before Ethan Hawkes' moody adolescent American Hamlet became an amateur film-maker, an Italian cinematic version of Hamlet's ghostly father had already beaten him to it by explicitly demonstrating *his* interest in the processes of cinematic exhibition and reception.

The Rome-based film company Società Italiana Cines put out two versions of their frenetically-paced one-reel *Hamlet* (*Amleto*) – one in 1908 and the next in 1910. One of the most interesting scenes in the film is the ghost's narration of how he met his death. Rather than slowing down the action with long intertitles of explanation (a tendency more common in English films), *this* ghost has a more efficient means of communicating the story to his son. Having led Hamlet (Amleto Novelli) across a field to a rocky cavern, he is discovered standing in depth of field frame left with his left arm dramatically raised, impresario-like, to highlight the space in depth of field frame right.[4] In the designated space, and with all the drama and magic of cinema itself, the scene featuring his own self sleeping in the orchard and then falling poisoned from his garden bench is being played out in projected moving images on the back wall of the cave. Hamlet, his back to us, is himself thus briefly turned into a film spectator, transfixed by the brief but inflammatory screening to which he has been made privy by his cinematically savvy father. Once the action of the film-within-the-film has run its course and the internal screen goes dark, the ghost too, as an equally spectral presence, disappears. Hamlet turns to face the camera, clearly incensed at the import of the film shown to him by his impresario-cum-projectionist father, and rushes off, apparently to act upon the news he has received.

Both this silent Italian *Hamlet* and Michael Almereyda's more recent *Hamlet* form part of the single ongoing interpretive story of film *Hamlets*. The Italian film's cinematic self-consciousness appears trail-blazingly early in that history. Its oblique anticipation of one of the interests of the Almereyda film illustrates a principle about the history of Shakespeare films more generally: namely that some of the things most celebrated as interpretively innovative in recent Shakespeare films are far from new.[5] Shakespeare films from the silent era reward a sustained critical airing not only as fascinating films in their own right, but also for the light they can shed upon current Shakespearean cinema. The standard repertoire of Shakespearean cinematic grammar (and indeed that of cinematic grammar more generally) has its roots in the experiments made with narrative mechanism and interpretive trends during the silent era. And yet so self-effacing, or perhaps simply so relatively neglected, has this history been that the provenance of resurgent cinematic ideas, or even the fact that those ideas may have already had earlier outings, is rarely acknowledged. And it is not only in the case of a distant kinship between the Almereyda *Hamlet* and the Cines film from 1908 that tracking a recent film's interpretive heritage happens to reveal precedents in a non-anglophone tradition. It was *frequently* in European cinemas of the pre-sound era that the daring and influential experiments with both cinematic form and interpretive ideas were being tried. It is, therefore, no surprise that the relevance of these films to more recent cinemas is often felt at least as keenly than that of their counterparts from British and American studios.

PRE-1917 ITALIAN SILENT FILMS

It was for their lavish sets, dramatic location shooting, huge crowds of extras and resulting big spectacles that the Italian film industry was most known on the world market in the early pre-sound period. Big cinematic spectacles such as *Cabiria* (1914) and *Il Leone di Venezia* (1914) seized the attention of distributors and exhibitors across continents. In fact, until the American film-maker D.W. Griffith decided specifically to try to emulate the Italian spectacular style with his big-budget films *Judith of Bethulia* (1914), *Birth of a Nation* (1915) and *Intolerance* (1916), the exoticism and visual appeal of the Italian film product was difficult to rival. Though none of the many (now much neglected) silent Italian films on Shakespearean themes in this period attempted to compete with *Cabiria* for sheer scale or impact, many do clearly emerge from a culture steeped in the need to give detailed attention to the visual composition of the frame. The look of these Italian films is often, therefore, as important as the narrative drive.

The Italian studio Film d'Arte Italiana was founded in Rome by Charles Pathé in 1909 as the Italian equivalent to Film d'Art in France. It shared Film d'Art's aim to nurture a literary and theatrical cinema as a prestigious alternative to the more populist films emerging from other studios. FAI's first Shakespeare production was a one-reel *Othello* (*Otello*, 1909) shot in Venice. The location of the shoot became one of its key selling points on the international market. Here was a drama shot in the very city in which it was partly set. 'Many have seen *Othello* but never in such a setting', boasted the distributor's advertisement to mark the American release of the film:

> *The stage has been noted for wonders of scenic fidelity but to enact this marvelous tragedy along the very waters and in the very gardens and palaces as the immortal Shakespeare pictures them with his versatile pen is to add an interest which could not be obtained in any other way.*[6]

With an eye on international distribution, the company was keen to capitalise on the possibility of authentic Italian settings for their subsequent Shakespearean films too. A cast and crew were consequently dispatched to Venice and Verona in turn for the shooting of *The Merchant of Venice* (*Il Mercante di Venezia*, 1910) and *Romeo and Juliet* (*Romeo e Giulietta*, 1911) respectively, each of which starred the gently beguiling Francesca Bertini. If Britain could claim an authenticity in its access to Shakespearean language and a theatrical tradition that technically had its roots in the theatre of Shakespeare's day, Italy was difficult to rival for locations that were both extremely photogenic *and* literally stipulated by Shakespeare's texts.

FAI films tended to court the look and feel of the theatre by shooting from entirely static camera placements and in fairly long takes, as if gazing admiringly at their own sets and actors. Prints were then enhanced by colour stencilling. This involved cutting out the precise areas to be coloured on duplicate black and white prints, one for each colour to be used. Each cut stencil was then attached in turn to the projection print and run across a colour dye pad. Effects of stencilling, in combination with some blocks of colour tinting (an historical 'sepia' in one scene, a more detached, night-time blue in the next, a more urgent red in the next) that decisively altered the dramatic mood across scenes, creating a strangely heightened sense of unreal colour.

The company's *Romeo e Giulietta* (1911) was more carefully choreographed than its predecessors, shot on attractive waterways, little bridges, courtyards and stone staircases and dominated by a Catholic iconography of a sort that was to surface prominently again in Baz Luhrmann's much later *Romeo+Juliet*

(1996). The film was also more sensibly paced than its FAI Shakespearean predecessors since it had the luxury of unfolding not over one reel but now over two. The story was simplified in the interests of narrative clarity so that Tybalt (Tebaldo), for example, becomes an approximation of Tybalt and Paris combined, being both wounded (though not killed) by Romeo (Gustavo Serena) *and* the paternally sanctioned suitor for Juliet (Bertini).

The benefits of the longer length and simplified plot are obvious, leaving more space and time for memorable effect. A scene near the end of the film must serve as synecdochic illustration of the greater degree of care taken with the whole. Romeo appears cloaked in the close foreground at the end of Juliet's long funeral procession. Romeo turns away from the procession to face the camera lest he be discovered by the Capulet mourners, and as he does so the procession is shown winding its way into depth of field into the chapel behind him. Finally, reluctant to allow Juliet's body to pass out of his sphere entirely, Romeo adds himself surreptitiously to the end of the procession and thus is himself admitted to the chapel. This study in perspective is more than a mere technical flourish of focusing acumen (though it is partly that) and more than a mere demonstration of the resources that have been invested in a moment of controlled spectacle (though it is also partly that): the sight of the disappearing body flanked by a steady stream of Capulet mourners and religious attendants is also psychologically expressive of Romeo's despair at Juliet's seeming unattainability and enforced removal from him. The coherence of the organisation, visual impact and psychological import of this scene is characteristic of a film that demands and holds the attention in ways beyond the scope of its predecessor films from the same stable.

Although FAI were keen to trade upon the Shakespearean associations of Italian cities, the *best* (and most commercially astute) use of narratively apposite Italian scenery was made by another studio altogether – Ambrosio. The Ambrosio four-reel *Othello* (*Otello*) of 1914, whose early sequences were shot along the waterways of Venice, is an exquisite film. It was given a wide distribution, including in Britain and the United States, where it received the standard marketing 'puff' that traded upon Italian scenic beauty and a sense of Old World authenticity. One whole-page illustrated advertisement in an American trade journal proclaimed:

The Super Film – By All Odds the Most Pretentious, Beautiful and Accurately-Screened Version of Shakespearean Stories! MADE AT VENICE, ITALY! That's a Tremendous Advertising Feature in itself! VENICE, rendezvous of the modern tourist – a very fountain-head of Romance and Adventure! The waterways of Historic Venice with its tales ten centuries old, of Passionate Loves and Fierce Vendettas – the indolent, dreamy sweep of these Gondola-ridden highways are scenes of the quaintest stories in any language! . . .

In Othello, we offer a real masterpiece. It is the first of Shakespeare's stories filmed in its proper environment, as the Master would have wished.[7]

Whether or not filming Italian stories in Italy might have been what 'the Master would have wished', it certainly in this case made for a beautiful film. The gondolas, the canals, the sumptuous clothes, the villas, the scenes of Desdemona's attentive listening to Othello's stories from outside a decorative window, the coy close-up of a hand dropping a rose from an upstairs window into Othello's gondola below, the silhouette of Iago leaning pensively against an arch watching the water traffic, the balanced symmetry of Desdemona's and Othello's early trysts on a coastal wall in Cyprus, all contribute to a rich array of visually pleasing moments. *The Cinema News and Property Gazette* proudly reported that the film was well received in Wales, giving as the reason for its popularity that '[t]he masses have a keener taste for classic drama than some of their destructors [*sic*] would have us believe'.[8] However, the French publication *Ciné-Journal* reported that 'the local censors in Villefranche-sur-Rhône have refused to allow the exhibition of *Othello* on the screen, because Desdeomona is killed . . .'.[9] That the death of Desdemona managed to offend the squeamish censors of Villefranche-sur-Rhône is particularly surprising given the manner in which the death is shot. In most films of *Othello* since, the killing of Desdmona has been the excuse for some desperate grappling, often of a quasi-sexual character, and usually involving a tense close-up at some stage. In the Ambrosio film, however, it is treated with a striking degree of discipline. The camera follows the central action of the scene as Othello throws Desdemona on to the bed prior to killing her. Then, however, at the very moment when we would expect it to move in to view the sensational action from close quarters, it announces its lack of prurient interest in the details of that encounter by panning away right. The murder therefore takes place teasingly out of shot, frame left. Meanwhile the camera reveals instead, with obvious metaphorical significance, a lit candle illuminating a painting of the virgin Mary. As we watch, the candle is magically extinguished, releasing a little trail of smoke that winds upwards past the painting. The inference to be drawn is clear: in Othello's own phrase, the light has been 'put out'. In leaving Desdemona's off-screen fate principally at the level of suggestion, however, the film resists the temptation to exploit the potential spectacular force of the moment. The fact that the camera *could* show so much (and in grisly close-up if it chose to) makes its decision to show almost nothing the more striking and the more welcome. No modern film production of *Othello* has been as self-denying.

The power to narrate a story visually in this way, free from an over-dependence on wordy intertitles, was a characteristic feature of the best Italian Shakespeare films. It is gloriously in evidence in the 1917 film of

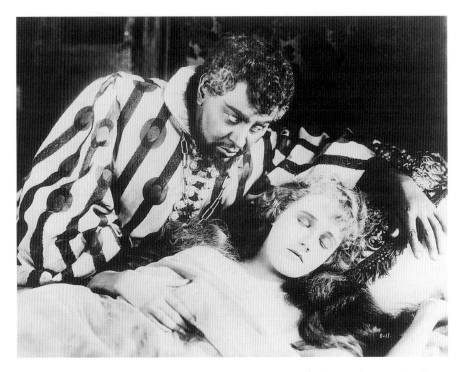

Unlike the self-denial of the Ambrosio *Otello* (1914) in relation to the murder of Desdemona, Buchowetski's 1922 German production, starring Emil Jannings and Ica von Lenkeffy, was to milk the potential sensationalism of the moment.
Source: Othello (Buchowetski, 1922).

Hamlet (*Amleto*), directed by Eleuterio Rodolfi and starring Ruggero Ruggeri (whose stage Hamlet in London, it will be recalled, was later to be hailed as Burbagian). Although Ruggeri, like Forbes-Robertson before him, can sometimes be seen speaking to his fellow actors on screen, for large swathes of the film he has trained himself *out* of speaking the lines and *into* trying to communicate their sense as precisely as possible through non-verbal means. His strategic, and striking, use of compensatory facial expression and gesture, and reflections on his own use of gesture, are illustrated with particular force in the sequence in the film that begins with the nunnery scene and runs into the scene of the instruction of the players.

In the nunnery scene, Ophelia (Polish actress Elena Makowska)[10] is 'loosed' to Hamlet by the adults in her world, with her little casket of treasures that she is under commission to return to him. He rejects her proffered gifts. She looks to Heaven. With a marked gestural extravagance, he relents in depth of field and advances as if to embrace her tenderly from behind, only to stop himself mid-advance, change his mind suddenly and instead brutally reassume his antic disposition, illustrated in part by a grotesquely extreme close-up on his maniacal laugh. The maniacal laugh is exclusive to the Italian film: the choreography of the preceding action, however, is closely imitative of the 1913 Gaumont–Hepworth *Hamlet* starring Sir Johnston Forbes-Robertson (discussed in Chapter 1) which serves as a pattern for emulation in several respects.

The scene in the Ruggeri *Hamlet*, however, then cuts suddenly to Hamlet's instruction of the first player not to saw the air with his hands. Most other silent *Hamlet* films coyly cut this exchange[11] and it is not difficult to guess why. In this medium, the scene could so quickly boomerang upon its makers and expose the cartoon aspects not just of the first player's histrionic style, but more worryingly, of the gestural excesses of a silent Hamlet himself. Ruggeri, however, is happy to move seamlessly from his own gestural extravagance in the nunnery scene into a set of imperious instructions to the first player to moderate *his* gestural style. He even has the *sang-froid* to illustrate the point by imitating the player's gesticulations in order to expose its degree of excess. The film's intertitle (in the surviving French language print) at this point reads: 'Do not saw the air with your emphatic gestures. Be measured, moderate.' ('Ne fendez pas l'air de vos gestes emphatiques. Soyez sobres, modérés.') Since we have just seen Hamlet as himself an air-sawer *par excellence* in the nunnery scene, his subsequent attempts to reign in the melodramatic expressiveness of the first player cannot help but specifically draw attention to the performance codes of the piece and the role of excess in it. That is, the entertaining contradiction between Hamlet's articulated *theory* of acting and his own very recently demonstrated *practice* invites us to consider how emotion and ideas *are* communicated, and best communicated, in the film as a whole. Other little indications of self-aware humour in the film suggest that he and Rodolfi might perhaps even be consciously trading upon the comedy of the juxtaposition of this scene with the gesturally extravagant encounter with Ophelia – itself, of course, very far from 'measured' or 'moderate'.

It was not entirely uncharacteristic of Ruggeri (whose acting style was not typically marked by restraint) that he was willing to let the words go and embrace a visually expressive style of acting with such humour and enthusiasm. By contrast, Sir Johnston Forbes-Robertson seems to have considered it a matter both of professional principle and of personal taste to distance himself clearly from a high gestural style in his 1913 screen *Hamlet*. Forbes-Robertson's conspicuous and repeated allusion to the primacy of the communicative form definitively absent from this performance – the spoken word – creates an uneasy tension at the heart of his film. His principled resistance to some of the particular dynamic imperatives of the film medium undoubtedly preserves an aura of distinction in his own performance. However, this is achieved in many respects at the expense of the film as a whole, whose stately pace mostly mirrors that of the central performance. Ruggeri's approach to creating a Hamlet for the screen was more attentive to the particular opportunities that the medium afforded, and as a result the film as a whole is more energetically compelling as a viewing experience. It is a film which also employs a greater degree of thoughtfulness about how shooting and editing style could themselves act as interpretive agents in relation to the drama. This film, unlike its English counterpart, is less an act of preservation than of creation. As a result, its interpretive thinking is quite plainly often discernible *in* the specifics of its technical construction.

Near the beginning of the film, for example, an urgently distracted Hamlet kneels on the battlements, atmospherically under-lit by the flickering flames from a fire. From his position in right of frame he reaches out with his right hand across the dark space of the frame in a desperate attempt to make contact with his father's ghost. The scene then cross-cuts between Hamlet's marginalised, reaching figure and the superimposed ghost, shown in another part of the battlements, shot from a respectfully low angle and, like the object of the gaze he is, in the centre of his own frame. The sense of Hamlet's desperation to occupy the same space as his ghostly father but inability to transcend the space of the battlements (and the associated space of the frame) ever quite to reach him is therefore in part communicated by the edited style of the sequence. Indeed, so firmly established is the spatial separation between father and son that even when a master shot subsequently shows them in frame together at opposite ends of the battlements, the space between them remains, as it were, contractually impenetrable. Mise-en-scène and editing have by this point established a clear, fixed spatial relationship between them, which even appearing in the same shot together cannot now unfix or disturb. A truth about emotional relationship is therefore eloquently suggested by the style of the shooting and the sequence of the editing: these are characters who exist in entirely separate worlds.

Ruggeri's Hamlet's desperate reaching out from within the isolation of his own frame testifies not only to the character's action but also, implicitly, to his mindset. Later in the film, he reaches out resolutely with his right arm into frame left again, this time to make contact with the Yorick he remembers once incarnating the skull he now holds at arm's reach. The reaching gesture and the frame's spatial organisation at this point obliquely recall his earlier attempt to get in touch with his ghostly father. This visual echo in turn creates a suggestive association between the two quintessentially unattainable objects – father and Yorick – to which Hamlet's gaze, reach and memory tend in each case. The association is made to *take* all the more by the fact that Yorick's skull is temporarily animated by having the face of the living Yorick super-imposed upon it. (And it is perhaps worth noting that this was eighty years before Kenneth Branagh's 1996 film of *Hamlet* was similarly to use Yorick's skull as a trigger to conjuring the face of the living man.) By actually giving the skull the lips, the eyes of flashing merriment and the grin upon whose disturbing absence Hamlet usually comments, the Ruggeri film plucks Yorick from the realm of the purely skeletal and invites him temporarily instead into the realm of the spectral, a realm already partly occupied in the drama by the ghost. The resulting suggestion of an association between the two dead figures points up a truth about this Hamlet's obsessions. At the beginning of the film he encounters a risen ghost and near its end a reincarnated skull temporarily made to re-engage with the world it had left. The graveyard scene ends by Hamlet urgently picking flowers and strewing them over Ophelia's grave – activities that had, prior to her death, been clearly associated with Ophelia herself. It is as if Hamlet were symbolically trying to restore her to his world by himself *being* her, taking over her role as the urgent gatherer and distributor of flowers. This thematic book-ending to the film is expressive about the vision of Hamlet offered in it. There is a limit to how many spectres can be summoned from the grave, but not to how much Hamlet can refuse to be reconciled to a future when there is still a past, and a cast of past characters from it, with which to try to reconnect. Ruggeri's Hamlet is a character who constantly tries to find the means to reconnect with a lost world, and the film's stylistics – even its moments of trick photography – contribute coherently to that reading. The film medium is more, therefore, than a self-effacing vehicle for the delivery of predetermined meanings. Rather the operations of the medium are here crucially and consciously part of the mechanism for *generating* meaning.

Robert Hamilton Ball's judgement of Ruggeri's performance was that it was 'perhaps too Italianate'.[12] By alluding to the cultural otherness of the performance as he saw it, Ball implicitly reasserted the right of anglophone communities to feel their interpretive proprietorship over the Shakespearean performance legacy – a right, as we have seen, that was not undisputed. Ball's judgement that the performance was 'perhaps too Italianate' may almost certainly be taken as a reference to a degree of unembarrassed expressiveness that may not have played well in either Britain or the United States. In Britain – as suggested by, for example, the Forbes-Robertson *Hamlet* – there was a taste (if not a universal one) for playing down performance codes of too exaggerated a character. In the United States – as suggested by, for example, the Vitagraph *Julius Caesar* or the Thanhouser *Winter's Tale* (discussed in the previous chapter) – there was a taste for referencing such codes in order then to ironise them by some undermining buffoonery in the peripheries of the frame. As, for example, Buchowetski's German *Othello* suggests, it was principally in continental Europe that those codes could still be, and were, embraced without irony into the 1920s. Even in continental Europe, however, this was by no means always the case.

POST-WAR GERMAN SILENT FILMS

Hamlet (Gade/Schall, 1920)

In Svend Gade and Heinz Schall's adaptation of *Hamlet* starring Asta Nielsen, for example, there was an interesting tempering and distillation of the expressive performance codes. Nielsen's fame as a screen actress was in part justly derived from her huge, expressive eyes. As Hamlet, she deftly maximises the dramatic impact both of her eyes and of her languid bodily grace to produce a hauntingly memorable performance finely poised between pathos and comedy.

The film's central premise combines the speculations of a maverick American nineteenth-century researcher named Edward P. Vining with elements from a Saxo-Grammaticus twelfth-century Nordic saga. As a version of *Hamlet*, it borders on the racy: the 'prince', in this telling of the tale, is in truth a girl who at birth is publicly declared a boy in an attempt to safeguard the succession of the vulnerable Danish throne. Having grown up with this duplicity, she is obliged to sustain the pretence of maleness until her death when her 'tragic secret' is finally discovered. To attach its reading to some claim to scholarship, the film acknowledges its debt to Vining in an opening intertitle. Vining's 1881 publication *The Mystery of Hamlet* outlines a maverick but by no means carelessly worked theory that Hamlet's mental processes and the indecision that results from them are essentially feminine in character. Vining posited that the character's behaviour and characteristics of mind are therefore consistent with, and best explained by, 'his' being female. Needless to say, once the opening premise had been granted, other interpretive possiblities lined up obligingly to lend credibility to the thesis. Understanding Hamlet as a woman disguised as a man could, for example, shed new light upon the harsh brush-off Hamlet gives to Ophelia and add an interesting new dimension to the peculiar warmth of Hamlet's affection for Horatio. In fact, *Hamlet* as a whole could be rendered far more intelligible by being read in these radically regendered terms.

The theory also neatly intersected with, and perhaps drew upon, a long-standing theatrical fashion for the role to be played by women. The play's performance history suggests that the role lent itself to female actorly appropriation far more readily than did most other major tragic parts. Hamlet's thoughtfulness, sensitivity, capriciousness, vulnerability and indecision all rendered him ripe for feminising: the list of actresses who took up the challenge is extensive.[13] Mrs Siddons played the prince in the late eighteenth century. Mrs Glover impressed Edmund Kean for her mastery of the role at the Lyceum in 1821. In 1851 in the United States Charlotte Cushman seems to have traded upon her own extra-theatrical flamboyant lesbianism in her rendering of the role. Alice Marriott played a rather sturdy Dane at the Marylebone Theatre in 1861, and later at Sadlers Wells, to warm reviews. Julia Seaman played Hamlet in 1865. The redoubtable Millicent Bandmann-Palmer played the part in tours of the provinces in the 1890s. In the same period, Clare Howard played at London's Pavilion Theatre while Sophie Miles played at the Britannia, Hoxton in 1899. That year Janette Steer, an avant-garde American actress, played Hamlet in Birmingham. Ellen Terry did not herself play Hamlet but she did commend Julia Jennings on *her* performance in August 1900 at the Portable Theatre in Droitwich. Sarah Bernhardt visited England in 1899 with her celebrated Hamlet. Bernhardt was praised for her fencing and it was this she immortalised on film in Clement Maurice's five minute recording of the duel scene with synchronised sound (shown at the Paris Expo of 1900). The popularity of the role for classical actresses in the nineteenth century can perhaps be gauged by the otherwise inconsequential piece of theatrical trivia that in Henry Irving's revival of *Macbeth* at the Lyceum in 1888, all three of his witches – Marriott, Desborough and Seaman – had already themselves played Hamlet.

The Gade/Schall *Hamlet* used Vining as the springboard, and academic validation, for taking a well-established performance tradition one step further, moving Hamlet from being a part suitable to be *played by* a woman, to being a part that *was* a woman's. It was a step that had been partly prepared for by the prevalence of female actresses inhabiting the role. As an example of character regendering it was broadly comparable to that in evidence in Vitagraph's 1909 film of *A Midsummer Night's Dream* (discussed in Chapter 5) in which Oberon was morphed into a fairy spirit called Penelope. In the Vitagraph *Dream*, however, Penelope is publicly acknowledged as female, whereas in the Gade/Schall film, a layer of complicating subterfuge is added by keeping Hamlet's womanhood secret from her on-screen (though not her off-screen) audience.

The Hamlet we meet in Shakespeare could scarcely be considered a simple character. The processes of gender suppression with which the character is additionally burdened in the Gade/Schall film, however, invest an already notoriously intricate figure with yet further layers of interesting complexity. Nielsen's visually striking, intellectually thoughtful and emotionally complex Hamlet makes bravely tortured efforts to deny her womanhood to the world while acknowledging it keenly in her own private self as she has to own that she is jealous of Horatio's affection for Ophelia.

There is arguably something appealingly subversive in any era about the performance of an assumed masculinity. In 1920, however, that appeal takes on a particular force by chiming so neatly with emerging ideas of what was in any case considered desirable in a woman. With their curve-minimising straight dresses, short hair and taste for skinny boyish figures, flappers of the

Asta Nielsen's Hamlet wears a figure-denying short, straight tunic and wears her hair short. To some extent, therefore, she is simply exaggerating a tendency in female fashion of her 1920s moment.

Source: Hamlet (Gade, 1920)

period turned androgyny into a sexual aesthetic. Nielsen's Hamlet has short straight hair, wears a short straight tunic and adopts self-consciously manly poses to delude her on-screen (and to delight her off-screen) public. In the extra-cinematic world of 1920, however, this collection of character traits no longer represented the complete renunciation of socially acceptable womanhood that it is ostensibly offered as meaning within the story. At the moment of the film's release across Europe and the United States, fashionable manifestations of womanhood were themselves sufficiently on the move to complicate the gender landscape and perhaps even to give a broader application to some of this Hamlet's private agonies about the ambivalence of her gender constructions.

In order to avoid any lack of narrative clarity, there is a tendency in many silent Shakespeare films to resolve interpretive ambiguities and to render plain aspects of the drama that might otherwise have needed nuanced explanation. Plots are rendered understandable and motivation transparent lest the muteness of the medium be construed as having inhibited the clear communication of the drama. This tendency, discernible in many silent Shakespeare films, is felt with particular acuteness in the Gade/Schall *Hamlet*.

Partly under the influence of Vining, and partly responding to the imperatives of its own medium, the film goes to extravagant lengths to provide a coherent explanation for anything that might in the play have raised questions or opened up interpretive possibilities. Reconfiguring Hamlet as a girl masquerading as a boy, in love with Horatio (Heinz Stieda), jealous of Ophelia (Lilli Jacobson) and suppressing her femininity in order to protect the royal line of succession makes almost unprecedentedly orderly sense of Hamlet's angst-ridden relationship to his world, of the strength of his affection for Horatio and of his distinctly odd treatment of Ophelia. Moreover, the guilt of this Claudius (played by Eduard von Winterstein as a crude, lascivious boor) need not depend on anything so flimsy as the tale of a ghost, or a suspiciously hasty exit from a play. Material evidence to establish his culpability is found in the shape of his dagger. Additionally, any question about Gertrude's relationship to events is here disambiguated since this Gertrude (Mathilde Brandt) is clearly complicit in the crimes of her second husband. Young Fortinbras's interest in Hamlet is explained by the fact that Hamlet and he became friends during their school days together in Wittenberg (depicted in the film as part of the pre-history of the play). Claudius sends Hamlet not to England but to Norway in the hope that he might be there despatched. The warmth of Hamlet's subsequent reception in Norway is partly the result of the conventionally switched missives, and partly of Hamlet's long-standing personal connection with young Fortinbras. The implication is that Fortinbras's decision to march on Denmark is made in conjunction with Hamlet: the corrupt Danish regime needs overthrowing and the young Norwegian King is enlisted to help his friend of old in the endeavour. The film therefore subjects an impressive number of the play's interpretive cruxes to definitive explanation.

Disambiguating motivation, and finding a reason for the unreconciled mysteries in the play, ties up everything with peculiar neatness and makes the resulting drama psychologically coherent. For that very reason, however, it is discernibly adrift from its Shakespearean source, which is on balance less amenable to such thorough-going explanations. To counterbalance these departures from Shakespeare, the film occasionally asserts a superficial attachment to its Shakespearean source through the use of a direct quotation. The film's usual strategy in relation to its intertitles is to use plot-summarising descriptions and snippets of non-Shakespearean dialogue. Against such a background, the occasional, and overt, advertisement of a Shakespearean phrase such as 'to sleep perchance to dream' ('schlafen um zu träumen') is the more striking. Although on one level the inclusion of such a line anchors the production in a relation to the Shakespearean source, the specific use of the line here necessarily qualifies the nature of that relationship. The film does not quote 'to sleep perchance to dream' to punctuate Hamlet's consideration about the appeal or otherwise of death. Rather the line is divorced from its poetic and semantic context in the 'To be or not to be' soliloquy and used instead as the textual accompaniment to an image of Hamlet simply lying down to sleep. The apparent linguistic anchoring in some notion of a source therefore testifies only to a *superficial* connection and to a *desire* to be thus anchored. The misattributed quotation serves most of all as a demonstration of the distance between the Shakespearean text and this production. For a 'version' of *Hamlet* that includes snake-pits, arson attacks, a Hamlet who is secretly female and a Horatio who is in love with Hamlet though he does not know it, as this one does, a line from Shakespeare severed from its context and its prior meanings merely highlights how vibrantly and interestingly *un*Shakespearean most of the production is.

Othello (Buchowetski, 1922)

A less radical Shakespearean adaptation emerged from Germany two years later in the six-reel *Othello* (1922) directed by the Russian Dmitri Buchowetski, starring Emil Jannings as a blacked-up Othello and Werner Krauss as Iago. *Othello* was not Buchowetski's first literary adaptation for the screen, nor his first collaboration with Jannings and Krauss. Both had, for example, appeared in *The Brothers Karamazov* (1918) under Buchowetski's co-direction with Carl Frölich, and the year before *Othello* was made, Jannings had taken the title role as the doomed Danton to Krauss's dictatorially evil Robespierre in Buchowetski's own adaptation of Georg Büchner's famous German play *Danton*. As a piece of film-making, however, *Othello* was even more ambitious than *The Brothers Karamazov* or *Danton*. It included a series of enormous crowd scenes, a grand set of courtyards, arches, staircases and balconies, and (unlike the earlier silent Shakespeare films but like the Nielsen *Hamlet*) a plot rendered more complex than that to be found in the play. We do not quite get the piling-on of action that Shakespeare found in his source, the Cinthio novella. But whereas we are spared the sensational Cinthian heights of a clubbing to death with a sand-filled stocking or the pulling down of a ceiling to disguise the deed, there are many other bits and pieces of business added of a slightly tamer character. These include considerably more playful dwelling upon Iago's gulling of Roderigo (Ferdinand von Alten), more complex choreography on Iago's part to suggest the guilt of Desdemona (Ika von Lenceffy) in relation to Cassio (Theodor Loos), and the neat stabbing to death of Iago by Othello once his fatal error is made clear to him.

In addition to these extra pieces of domestic business, there is also a greater contextualising of the domestic drama within a larger social and political framework. Othello is sent to Cyprus not merely on the say-so of the Senate, but partly because the Venetian populace on the streets calls for him to be sent in their cause. Similarly, near the end of the film there is an uprising of people on the streets of Cyprus to lament his arrest. Moreover, the Turk in this version of the drama does not seem to have been as thoroughly routed at the arrival on Cyprus as he is in Shakespeare's rendering of events. Throughout the film there are, therefore, reports that he is pressing to attack, and these reports become more urgent as the climax approaches, reinforcing the claustrophobic pressure of their life on Cyprus and adding a political and military dimension to the mounting crescendo. The introduction of reports of the advancing Turk in effect *Hamletises* the usually far more domestically focused *Othello*, mimicking the rhythms of the advance of Fortinbras as events of a more familial character are played out at Elsinore. Although the Turk does not actually arrive to look upon the tragic loading of the bed at the end of the film, the repeated announcements of his increasing proximity do contribute to the rising pressure upon Othello, forcing events towards the crisis.

The climax, when it comes, is played out in a high key. Othello is glimpsed at a considerable distance through an archway in depth of field, left of frame. Simultaneously visible in shot is Desdemona's sleeping form (Ica von Lenkeffy) on the bed in near field, right of frame. Othello's advancing figure approaches and passes through the arch into the bedroom with a painfully unhurried deliberateness. In the context of Jannings' exaggerated performance throughout, the discipline of this walk is the more noticeable. The inevitable moment of the forthcoming murder is then further delayed by a series of dialogue cards (about whether Desdemona has prayed tonight, about the handkerchief, about Cassio). These interrupt a sequence of close-ups of Othello's anger and Desdemona's fear by turns. Characteristically, the film does not fight shy of sustaining its close-ups for an almost uncomfortable length of time. The effect of this here is both to generate a sense of embarrassing intrusion into the grotesque intimacy of these particular exchanges and to hold the poise of the pre-climactic moment for a daringly long period of time. When the moment finally comes, it is desperate and violent. Even the noise it generates is evoked by a repeated cut to Emilia's running figure, who has clearly been alerted to some danger by hearing cries. Unlike in the Italian Ambrosio *Othello*, there is no coy panning away or searching for a suggestive metaphor here: the scene only cuts to Emilia in order to add an implied realistic dimension – sound – to the horrific sensory specifics of the murder. In its final image, Othello grips Desdemona's throat with both hands forcing her head to dangle backwards over the edge of the bed, now seen upside down and centre frame. The sensationalised pathos of the image sets the seal on Iago's triumph over Othello.

Werner Krauss's screen persona was already well established as a darkly sinister force before he took the role of Iago. Parts such as 'the evil cripple' luring men to their deaths in *The Dance of Death* (*Totentanz* written by Fritz

Lang, directed by Otto Rippert, 1919) and, most famously, the mysterious Dr Caligari in *The Cabinet of Dr Caligari* (*Das Kabinett des Dr Caligari* directed by Robert Weine, 1920) had already left an indelible mark on his screen presence even before he played Jannings' powerful *bête noir* as an uncompromisingly vicious Robespierre in Buchowetski's 1921 film *Danton*. His casting as Iago, therefore – and even his casting recapitulating his role as Jannings' tormenter – ran with the grain of his screen career to date and was able to trade upon the accumulated associations of the previous arch-manipulators he had played.

It was a role that Krauss clearly relished. As he half limps, half hops swiftly across courtyards in the vigorous pursuit of his vicious schemes, clad in sleek black, with greased down hair, a small moustache, one piratical earring and heavy eye make-up, his Iago frequently flirts with becoming a cartoon of pure melodramatic villainy. What makes Krauss winning within the role – even entertainingly so – is that he creates a Iago who finds his own villainy irresistibly delicious. The understatedly stylish nonchalance of his pocketing of a stream of coins from Roderigo as part of his ongoing extortion racket, for example, makes it difficult for a spectator not to agree with him. Certainly it is easier to take pleasure in the self-conscious villainy of the Iago in this film than it is to feel pity for the Othello. Even in his calm moments, it would, for example, be a stretch to consider Jannings' Othello noble, and in his fits of passion he becomes a crude caricature of the wild and stary.

The scene of Othello's most significant fit is worth considering. As he lies down, a cameo of Desdemona in Cassio's arms is projected on to the curtain behind his bed as the implied visualisation of his own tormented thought life. This graphic conjuring of Desdemona's imagined adultery is a device that many filmed *Othellos* have employed since. Translating a series of verbal accusations into a publicly accessible visual image of her infidelity – as for example Oliver Parker's 1995 film does, or Andrew Davies' made-for-television updated *Othello* (London Weekend Television, 2001) – has an effect on the spectator's sense of Desdemona. In the play, an adulterous version of Desdemona is powerfully conjured by the extensive slander of her. So much is this the case that in response to the stage play we, like Othello, sometimes need to see her actual presence on stage in order to be reminded that there is another version of Desdemona, an innocent one, who is more real than her graphically discussed adulterous other self. If, however, we have *seen* an image of her infidelity as well as hearing about it, as we do in these films, the slander inevitably assumes a degree of quasi-photographic truth that is harder entirely to dismiss. Even at the level of our understanding of how filmic realities work, Desdemona's innocence *is* subtly compromised when she is shown in an imaginary scene with Cassio. From our point of view, both Desdemonas – the innocent one and her fictional adulterous counterpart – are now cinematic 'fictional truths' on a broadly equal representational footing. As a more recent film such as *The Usual Suspects* (Bryan Singer, 1995) forcibly demonstrates, there is a level at which if a cinema audience is *shown* an event happening, that event thereby assumes its own seductive truth. And even when we know, as we do, for example, that when we *see* Desdemona's infidelity, what we are witnessing is not *true*, this knowledge is not in itself sufficient to dismiss from our mind its claim of having in some sense happened. What we see with our own eyes is, after all, insidiously persuasive. The scene projected on to the curtain behind Jannings' Othello's bed cannot but help, therefore, subtly tarnish Desdemona – even though, as if in an attempt to temper exactly this effect, the scene cuts away to show the other Desdemona, the innocent one, kneeling at her *prie-dieu* throughout her husband's sullying dream of her.

In response to his horrific fantasy, Othello's level of writhing torment reaches such a pitch that he falls from the bed. Iago finds his general on the floor and tenderly cradles his head in his arms, dabbing his brow soothingly with the controversial handkerchief in a first attempt to bring it to his general's notice. As he then removes it from Othello's brow, he looks with interested surprise at what comes off on it before then refolding it and reapplying it as a palliative compress. The understated gesture clearly has the potential to be read as a moment whose significance extends beyond the internal story of the film. We might, that is, be expected to take the particularity of his look at, and subsequent refolding of, the handkerchief as simply signalling his disgust at having to come into contact with his general's feverish sweat. In the context of Jannings' blacked-up performance, however, Krauss's expression of interest in what comes off on the handkerchief cannot help but also register the fact that in their *performance* of this scene at least, it was very probably boot polish.

Two years before the Jannings/Krauss *Othello* was made, the British cartoonist Anson Dyer had made a skittish animated film of *Othello* with Cecil Hepworth. This short nugget of a film contributes an apposite joke to the performance history of blacked-up actors taking the role of Othello. A cartoonist's hand transforms a bare line-drawn figure sitting in front of a dressing table into a music-hall black minstrel complete with banjo slung across his back. Mid-task, however, the cartoonist's hand places the burnt cork he has been using on the dressing table in front of his half-coloured creation and withdraws from the frame. Left to his own devices the newly animated, but as yet only half-coloured, Othello picks up the piece of burnt cork and completes the task of blacking-up himself. The accompanying intertitles to this opening sequence make the joke yet more self-conscious. The opening intertitle, 'OTHELLO THE MOOR WAS BLACK', is immediately followed by a second, which puns on the literal and symbolic significances of 'black' to emphasise the constructed nature both of Othello's colour and of his degenerative reputation, 'BUT HE WAS NOT AS BLACK AS HE WAS PAINTED!' The fact that Dyer's Othello is made so obviously responsible for applying his own colour, and therefore for constructing his own racial self-projections, reflects back keenly upon the performance practices which the film parodies. The actor of Shakespeare's Othello has indeed rarely been as 'black as he was painted', since he has almost always been a white man painted black. Both his reputation and his colour have been blackened by deliberate decision. In the final shot of the Anson Dyer film, Othello's girlfriend (known familiarly as Mona) becomes comically and exaggeratedly smeared with black as his artificially applied colour rubs off on her. (Famously, Maggie Smith's Desdemona was to be similarly smeared when kissed by Olivier's highly polished Othello.) The Dyer cartoon ridicules by extravagant parody the practice of casting a white man as Othello who needs to turn himself into a comically grotesque side-show in order to play the part.

A blacked-up Emil Jannings appeared on screen in the pan-European release of Buchowetski's *Othello* only two years after the release of the Anson Dyer cartoon. When he then seemed to shed some of his colour on to the handkerchief in Iago's possession, Dyer's grotesque seaside minstrel must still have been a fresh, and relevant, memory for some sections of the audience. The cartoon had had an impish topicality: the Jannings/Krauss film, released so soon after, played beautifully to its points of parody. Both in the par-ticularity of Jannings' performance as an uncontrollably wild, wide-eyed and passionate Moor and in the film's meta-cinematic allusion to his status as a blacked-up performer, the film unwittingly points to a time when questions of racial representation would supplant almost all else in discussion about the play in performance.

*

Foreign language communities dealt confidently and interestingly with Shake-spearean source material in the pre-sound era. In this period there was, in effect, a level playing field for anglophone and non-anglophone film-makers alike since language was not, and could not be, the driving force of the interpretation. Once the talkies arrived, however, for a time the balance of power in relation to Shakespearean film-making seems to have shifted decisively in favour of anglophone communities. Others temporarily took a respectful step back, ceding the field to native English speakers. And when they did summon up the courage to re-enter the fray, it was no longer the Western Europeans who scooped the greatest honours for creative invention in relation to this pool of source material. By the 1950s and 1960s there were powerful players further afield whose cinematic imagination had been seized by the possibility of appropriating and adapting Shakespearean source material as a malleable vehicle through which to offer reflection upon their own culture. It is one of the most remarkable of these, the Japanese film-maker Akira Kurosawa, who forms the subject of the next chapter.

FURTHER READING

Robert Hamilton Ball, *Shakespeare on Silent Film* (New York: Theater Arts Books, 1968).

Jill Edmonds, 'Princess Hamlet', Chapter 3 in Viv Gardner and Susan Rutherford (eds), *The New Woman and Her Sisters: Feminism and Theatre 1850–1914* (Ann Arbor: University of Michigan Press, 1992), pp.59–76.

Kenneth S. Rothwell, *A History of Shakespeare on Screen: A Century of Film and Television* (Cambridge: Cambridge University Press, 1999).

Ann Thompson, 'Asta Nielsen and the Mystery of *Hamlet*', Chapter 14 in Lynda E. Boose and Richard Burt (eds), *Shakespeare the Movie: Popularizing the Plays on Film, TV and Video* (London: Routledge, 1997), pp.215–24.

NOTES

1. 'Par un phénomène curieux, les Anglais, qui ont pour Shakespeare une admiration, une vénération presque religieuse, qui le lisent et le relisent, et qui l'apprennent par coeur, qui en ont fait, avec la Bible, leur modèle littéraire, l'ont pendant très longtemps négligé a la scène . . .' 'Le Théâtre à Londres: *King John* de Shakespeare au Her Majesty's Theatre', *Le Théâtre* (20 September 1899), p.19.

2. 'A Londra, un giudice favorevole ha scritto che il Burbage . . . doveva averla intesa e rappresentata così.' Renato Simoni, 'Amleto di Ruggeri', in *Corriere della Sera*, 10 June 1926. Quoted in Anna Cavallone Anzi, *Shakespeare Nei Teatri Milanesi Del Novocento (1904–1978)* (Bari: Adriatica Editrice, 1980), p.51.

3. See Paolo Cherchi Usai, *Burning Passions: An Introduction to the Study of Silent Cinema* (London: BFI, 1994), p.57.

4. For a description of the entire action of the film, see the *Kinematograph and Lantern Weekly*, 14 May 1908, p.19.

5. Almereyda knew the 1910 version of this Cines film, and had even intended to use a clip from it in his own film until he discovered the cost of the rights. See Michael Almereyda, *William Shakespeare's Hamlet: A Screenplay Adaptation* (London: Faber, 2000), p.131.

6. *Moving Picture World*, 19 March 1910. Quoted in Robert Hamilton Ball, *Shakespeare on Silent Film* (New York: Theater Arts Books, 1968), p.104.

7. *Moving Picture World* 21, 1 (4 July 1914), p.21.

8. *The Cinema News and Property Gazette*, 13 April 1916. Quoted in Ball (1968), p.213.

9. *Ciné-Journal*, 8 August 1918. Quoted in Ball (1968), p.213.

10. Elena Makowska had been working in Italy since 1910 and seemed to draw plaudits for her screen performances in an impressively varied range of roles, from knock-about comedies to graceful romances, from classical drama to sentimental melodrama.

11. The exception is the 1910 French Lux production. Even Forbes-Robertson, who includes the extensive spoken duet of the Priam/Hecuba speech with his first player, cuts the instructions about suiting the word to the action, the action to the word.
12. Ball (1968), p.262.
13. The succession of female Hamlets is helpfully documented by Jill Edmonds in 'Princess Hamlet', Chapter 3 in Viv Gardner and Susan Rutherford (eds), *The New Woman and Her Sisters: Feminism and Theatre 1850–1914* (Ann Arbor: University of Michigan Press, 1992), pp.59–76.

CHAPTER THREE

Cross-cultural Narrative Rhymes:

The Shakespeare Films of Akira Kurosawa

In preparation for his 1969 film of *King Lear*, Peter Brook commissioned Ted Hughes to translate a cut version of the text into his own distinctive poetic idiom. Despite, as the film's producer Lord Michael Birkett put it, 'some remarkable work by Ted Hughes',[1] the resulting *Lear* was never given a public airing. Nevertheless, since Brook spent time working with Hughes' text of *Lear* before subsequently reverting to Shakespeare's own language, from his point of view, the 'translation' had already proved its worth. The play had been defamiliarised by being recast in language that could neither roll automatically off the tongue through years of intimate acquaintance nor provoke too much learned reverence. Having been jostled out of its usual linguistic cadences in this way, the play's 'essential nature, the themes behind it'[2] could be found striking and touching and painful in ways that then reinvigorated Brook's engagements with it.

As a process, Brook's purposeful flirtation with Hughes' text mimics that which non-anglophone communities habitually encounter when they approach a Shakespeare play. Since Shakespeare's plays are available to many language communities in competing texts – and well resourced productions will sometimes even commission their own translation – non-anglophone interpreters experience both the luxury, and the deprivation, of coming fresh and without prejudice to the specific language of a play. A translation is inevitably defined in part by the nature and extent of its deviations from its original. In comparison with that more stable given, a text in translation will, therefore, always seem relatively susceptible to adjustment and variation since it begins life itself as just that, an adjusted variant. As a result, interpreters working from a translation are less likely to feel clouded by the presence of something sacrosanct in ways that might hamper creativity. Creativity in this sense can, of course, mean a whole range of extravagant or distracting departures from the driving impulses of the play as received. At its best, however, it may also mean a freedom from the paralysing respect that can potentially dog productions in the original language.

Defamiliarising the language of a production is not in itself, of course, sufficient to inject fresh insight into a performance interpretation. Not only can the poetic losses incurred be severe in some cases, but there are also non-anglophone productions aplenty, just as there are updated productions in English aplenty, to give the lie to such a claim in practice. In the case of the work of Japanese film director Akira Kurosawa, however, the translation of the language is only the most obvious of the acts of adjustment and appropriation performed upon the inherited dramatic materal. Having uprooted the plays both linguistically and culturally, Kurosawa has been able to reracinate them in a new soil and climate with an organic sensitivity that obscures the signs of grafting and makes the material appear indigenous to that context. It is Kurosawa's acts of deracination and transplantation of Shakespearean material to a Japanese history and landscape that will be the subject of this chapter.

*

Kurosawa has twice used a Shakespeare play as his direct source for a film: *Kumonosu-jô* (*Throne of Blood*, 1957) is an adaptation of *Macbeth*, and *Ran* (*Chaos*, 1985) of *King Lear*. In addition to these two adaptations, in 1960 he also made a film entitled *Warui Yatsu Hodo Yoku Nemuru* (*The Bad Sleep Well*) which plucks elements from the story of *Hamlet* and weaves them into a broader narrative about corporate corruption in contemporary Tokyo. The scale of the inherited narrative is adjusted from issues of monarchy to those of big business, but then, in the closing moments of the film, it breaks these parameters. Mori, the film's counterpart to Claudius (who, in this version, gets away with his crimes), is seen conducting a telephone conversation with someone evidently far more powerful than himself. The identity of his interlocutor is not disclosed, but it is clearly someone capable of pulling even Mori's strings. The implication is that someone high in government has all along been secretly orchestrating the corruption. Later, Kurosawa made it known that he wished he had been braver in implicating the government explicitly in accusations of corruption: the political climate at that time had not, however, lent itself to anything so brazen.

Kurosawa's vision of a crisply corporate and wretchedly corrupt business world as a possible dramatic locale for the internecine struggles of *Hamlet* has found a resonance with later film-makers. Aki Kaurismäki's 1987 Finnish film *Hamlet liikemaailmassa* (*Hamlet Goes Business*) displaces the action to a rubber duck-producing Helsinki company, and Michael Almereyda's *Hamlet* (2000) transplants the drama to contemporary big business New York (with a nod in the direction of its Finnish predecessor in the rubber duck that features among Ophelia's treasures). Despite Kurosawa's trend-setting invitation of *Hamlet* to 'go business', however, *Throne of Blood* and *Ran* are adaptations far closer to Shakespeare in both sweep and detail than *The Bad Sleep Well*. It is these that will centrally absorb our attention here.

THRONE OF BLOOD (1957)

In *Throne of Blood* Kurosawa transposes the story of *Macbeth* to the samurai world of sixteenth-century feudal Japan. In the 'Japanesing' of the narrative, King Duncan is transmuted into Lord Tsuzuki (Sasaki Takamaru), Macbeth and Banquo into the samurai warriors Washizu (Toshirô Mifune) and Miki (Minoru Chiaki) respectively, and Lady Macbeth into Lady Asaji (Isuzi Yamada). The three witches are condensed into a single forest spirit (Chieko Naniwa) and the principal action transferred to Cobweb Castle and its neighbouring wood, the bafflingly labyrinthine Cobweb Forest.

The resulting film is almost universally admired by cineastes and Shakespeareans alike, having drawn praise from, among others, Peter Hall ('perhaps the most successful Shakespeare film ever made'),[3] Peter Brook ('[o]ne of the films we admire most'),[4] J. Blumenthal ('a masterpiece in its own right'),[5] Roger Manvell ('one of the finest, and most exact in spirit, of the screen adaptation from Shakespeare')[6] and Grigori Kozintsev ('the finest of Shakespearean movies').[7] Kurosawa first thought of making a film of *Macbeth* in the late 1940s, but delayed when he heard that Orson Welles was already embarked on such a project at that time. And even when, eight years later, he finally went into pre-production on *Throne of Blood*, it was then being strongly rumoured that Olivier had a film of *Macbeth* in development. The Olivier film never saw the light of day, but to have coincided first with Welles and then with Olivier in the planning stages must have focused the nature of the challenge for Kurosawa. In choosing to adapt a Shakespeare play for the cinema, he was occupying territory that, since the coming of commercial sound to the cinema, had been principally the province of the anglophone world, and typically of the key players in it.

Although new to the Japanese screen, in 1957 Shakespeare was far from new to Japan: for nearly a hundred years Japan had been accruing a rich history of nuanced and daring Shakespearean performances of its own. Following the 1868 Meiji Restoration, the country's cultural attention was at liberty to range further afield. Shakespeare was among those to catch Japan's cultural attention as a source of artistic stimulation that might be rendered compatible with Japanese predispositions and priorities and even to offer material with which it could refashion and represent its sense of itself.

Japanese theatre became adept at hybridising the adopted product, integrating Shakespearean dramas with performance styles drawn from its own traditional theatre arts (most prominently Noh and Kabuki). Thus expression was given to the imported dramatic material in culturally appropriate forms, a trend to which in due course Kurosawa would himself contribute influentially.

It was not only in relation to Shakespearean material, however, that Kurosawa was to perform such acts of cultural realignment. In the same year in which he made *Throne of Blood* (1957), for example, he also made *Donzoko* (*The Lower Depths*). For this adaptation of Gorky's play he transferred the action from Imperial Russia to Japan's Edo period in the final days of the Tokugawa shogunate, thus making the inherited story intersect with a slice of Japanese history. The search for a moment of Japanese history as an approximate cultural rhyme for a non-Japanese source drama was character-istic of Kurosawa's working method in relation to adaptation more generally.

In *Throne of Blood*, he found points of correspondence between the legendary history of medieval Scotland and that of sixteenth-century feudal Japan. In a spirit of rampant nationalism, Shakespeare had been banned, along with other non-Japanese authors, during the Second World War. But then, in the late 1940s backlash that followed defeat, non-Japanese authors enjoyed a resurgence of popular interest whereas all glorifications of Japanese militarism, or of the country's feudal past, were themselves temporarily banned.[8] Kurosawa's combination of Shakespeare with a Japanese feudal past in 1957 therefore sought some balance between the swings of censoriousness that had marked the previous twenty years.

At the opening of *Throne of Blood*, the camera sweeps slowly over a misty black and white landscape from which the looming wooden shape of Cobweb Castle seems to emerge as if organically summoned by our gaze. It is the same misty landscape into which the action, and the castle with it, slips back invisibly at the film's close, leaving only a marker stone to show where it had once been. Thus the enduring weight of the landscape that both predates and survives the castle throws into relief the relative transience and vanity of human construction upon it. These opening and closing shots of a desolate landscape (shot high on Mount Fuji) are accompanied by a long, low, intoned chant which alludes to the territory's human story of ambition and murder. The detached judgement of this choric voice and the black and white quality of the landscape place a sheen of removed history over what is reported to have passed there. The framing of the narrative by coolly uninvolved retrospective comment at its opening and close generates a sense of inevitability about the drama that plays out within its bounds. Moreover, nothing occurs between these end-markers to destabilise the sense of inevit-ability. Washizu, the samurai reincarnation of Macbeth, *is* caught within a prescribed fate already written into the history books and narrated in ballads.

The relationship of Shakespeare's Macbeth to his own destiny is complicated by consoling layers of self-delusion. Do, for example, the witches 'solicit' him to act (as he maintains at I.iii.130), or merely state what will occur? Is he ruled by forces beyond himself, or spurred by those within himself? The ambiguity sustained in the Shakespeare play is resolved in Kurosawa's film. Washizu's fate, as the forest spirit makes clear and the ensuing action confirms, is not his to determine.

The disengagement evident in the choric voice is also a feature of the film's shooting style. Kurosawa's famous 1954 film *Shichinin no samurai* (*Seven Samurai*) had used close-ups as one of its principal narrational devices. Both the samurai and the farmers in that film had been in part defined by the camera's intimate attention to their faces. In *Throne of Blood*, by contrast, the close-up is used extremely sparingly. Kurosawa reports that his crew were understandably baffled by his rejection of the standard cinematic grammar: 'I tried to do everything using full shots. Japanese almost never make films this way and I remember I confused my staff thoroughly with my instructions. They were so used to moving up for moments of emotion and I kept telling them to move back.'[9] The detachment that this distanced camera placement implies is strikingly felt in the scenes between Washizu (Macbeth) and Lady Asaji (Lady Macbeth) when they discuss murdering the Great Lord. Throughout these scenes, a close-up seems constantly to be hovering in the wings as the obvious possible next shot. This possibility is, however, consistently eschewed in favour of a sustained distance. Resisting what would have been the more intuitive, and more intimate, camera placement helps to minimise any personalised feeling *with* in the film. The film's action – even its violent action – is choreographed almost like ballet. It is the overall shapes that characters make, and the formal choreography of their arrangements in relation to each other and to their setting that claim the attention. For the balletic force of the whole to be appreciated, the frame needs to be generously inclusive in its treatment of the subject. Minimising the close-up in favour of the medium and long shot therefore helped to determine both the film's dominant aesthetic and its approach to character.

With his designer Yoshiro Muraki and art consultant Kohei Esaki (himself a scroll painter) Kurosawa examined early traditional Japanese scrolls depicting battle scenes (an art form known in Japanese as *mushaé*) as the inspiration for the look of the film. The aim was to evoke the effect of ink painting. As a result, castle interiors are coolly minimalist in style, with little beyond the lateral lines of the louvred partitions to distract from the fates of those contained within the castle walls. Ceilings on these interiors are low and exteriors, though shot in big landscapes, are regularly obscured by fog. This is, therefore, a world in which the horizon rarely stretches out invitingly. Rather it is constantly closing in on those caught within its sphere. The mesmeric sequence near the beginning of the film, in which we see the mounted figures of Washizu/Macbeth and Miki/Banquo repeatedly emerging from and disappearing back into the mist, is eloquent in this respect. These returning samurai are desperate to find a route to the castle, but there are other forces at work robbing them of direction and clarity and thwarting their progress at every turn. The teasing impediment posed by the fog is suggestively illustrative of the landscape's broader imperviousness to human endeavour. In the face of other determining forces in this world, characters' attempts to assert some power over their own lives are repeatedly shown to be doomed.

The voice of those other forces at work in human affairs is vested in the forest spirit. The spirit, an enigmatically sexless crone, is initially discovered crouching inside a fragile hut of sticks deep in Cobweb Forest. Within this flimsy parody of a castle, she teases out a fateful thread from a spinning wheel. Her presence as a spinning arbiter of destinies puns on the Japanese word *Ito* which is both the name of the Japanese goddess of Fate, and the word for thread. As she sits calmly working the thread, she also illustrates the relationship between literal and metaphorical yarn-spinning (more tangentially related in Japanese metaphor than in English but still with points of connection)[10] by simultaneously telling Washizu and Miki the stories of their own futures. Moreover, as many critics have observed, the shape and workings of the double-spooled apparatus over which she presides are also subliminally evocative of a film projector.[11] Washizu and Miki thus seem in this encounter with the forest spirit to be *verbally* confronted by the content of their own stories and *visually* by the medium in which it is told. Threatened by this level of knowledge and apparent extra-diegetic control, Washizu and Miki burst in on the spirit's hut to challenge her pronouncements. As an unsparing prophecy about the solidity of the film's other wooden construction, Cobweb Castle, the little hut collapses with unseemly haste. The spirit has vanished along with her multiply suggestive spools, leaving behind only the piles of skulls and skeletons that have accumulated in the forest over the years as a salutary symbol of human mortality. The battle from which Washizu and Miki have just come is evidently only one in a line to have taken place in the territory.

In interview with Tadao Sato,[12] Kurosawa explained that, to help the actress Chieko Naniwa (the forest spirit) prepare for her role, he had shown her the mask of *Yamanba*, the frightening female mountain-dwelling demon from the Noh play *Kurozuka*. Noh theatre depends upon a highly schematised view of character and upon each actor's sense of proprietorial kinship with the mask and the tradition that accompanies his or her part. In being offered the mask of *Yamanba*, Chieko Naniwa was thus being asked to find a connection between her role as a distilled variant of Shakespeare's witches on the one hand and an ancient character with which Japanese audiences were already familiar on the other. In similar vein, Kurosawa selected a Noh mask for each of his principal actors according to what he thought would most capture the spirit of their character in terms drawn from the Noh drama. Each was then asked to allow the chosen mask to infuse their thinking about the role. Toshirô Mifune (Washizu/Macbeth) was shown *Heida*, the mask of the warrior; Minoru Chiaki (Miki/Banquo) was shown *Chûjô*, the mask of a nobleman, and Isuzi Yamada (Lady Asaji/Lady Macbeth) was shown *Shakumi*, the mask of the 'beauty no longer young . . . a woman about to go mad'.[13] This evocation of known types from the Noh rooted the production squarely in a Japanese tradition and offered Japanese audiences an existing narrative and performance framework within which to make sense of these characters.

And the Noh influences in *Throne of Blood* extend beyond the basic conception of character, for both acting style and blocking are also inflected by Noh traditions. Noh acting involves a level of heightened and ritualised stylisation that Western audiences would almost certainly find precious or embarrassing were it to appear in a Western production. In a Japanese production, however, performed by actors versed in the conventions of the form, it has a curious power to move, even as it minimises the nuances of naturalistic expression upon which we would more typically rely for the communication of emotion. The film's homage to the conventions of Noh is felt in most concentrated form in the person of Lady Asaji (Lady Macbeth). Asaji's make-up is deliberately evocative of her Noh mask (*Shakumi*) and her dead-pan delivery of her lines, her disciplined stillness, her refusal to look at her interlocutor, her extraordinary self-containment and the rhythmic swish of her kimono across the floor boards all emerge clearly from a Noh world. As Donald Richie points out, she 'moves, heel to toe, as does the Noh actor; the shape of [her] face is used to suggest the Noh mask; her scenes with her husband have a very Noh-like composition, and her handwashing is pure Noh drama.'[14] As she sits on the ground manoeuvring Washizu into doing what she wants without looking at him, she certainly appears abstracted in style ('like a ceremonial doll' wrote Kozintsev)[15] – and in each of these respects she is curiously reminiscent of the film's other presiding female, the forest spirit.

An association between the forest spirit and Asaji is commonly felt.[16] In her first scenes, Lady Asaji's posture, movement and styles of utterance unconsciously mimic those of the forest spirit. Even when she leaves the room to fetch the drink with which she will drug the guards, she seems to disappear into the darkness of the doorway as if she, like the forest spirit before her, had simply vanished. Washizu's accusation that she has been possessed by the spirit may be in jest, but the iconography of the film adds weight to the jest. Each female character expresses her quiet control – of forest and castle respectively – through the filter of the stylised rituals of Noh. There are moments in the film when other characters also align themselves temporarily with this theatrical tradition – for example in the scene of the murder of Lord Tsuzuki/Duncan when Washizu stamps exaggeratedly to signal his fear in accordance with the Noh's performance grammar. Nevertheless it is consistently the forest spirit and Lady Asaji whose adherence to the stylistic codes of Noh makes clear their allegiances to it and, in the process, confirms their kinship with each other.

One of the effects of the implied connection between these two female presences is to help question the boundaries between the two competing domains in Washizu's world – the forest and castle. Cobweb Forest and Cobweb Castle are initially shown to be constructed along very different (literal) lines: the forest is defined by the impressive verticals of its tall trees, the castle by the insistent horizontals of its exterior construction and louvred character of its interior decoration.[17] The conflicting axes of these visuals seem to indicate a fundamental opposition, forest and castle working to different ruling principles and, for much of the film, pulling Washizu between them like opposed adamantine draws. As the film progresses, however, this impression of binary opposition requires modification. For all their superficial differences, forest and castle are increasingly shown to be susceptible to similar tendencies, to be agents of torment in similar ways and even to collaborate in closing in on Washizu.

The forest parodies the castle and its hut of sticks imitates the far grander neighbouring construction in bathetic spirit. Even the hut's demonstated fragility wryly anticipates the inability of the castle to protect its occupants in the face of opposition. However, the forest not only mimics the castle from a remove, but also literally encroaches upon it in stages. When trees from the forest are cut down to furnish the invading army with their offensive camouflage, a flock of birds is displaced. Deprived of their forest habitat, the birds fly straight to a new home in the castle, disrupting a council meeting and provoking a discussion about whether their arrival might be an omen of some description. The intrusion of the forest into the life of the castle then finds its most blatant (and most Shakespearean) expression in the cut boughs' celebrated march from one to the other. The forest's march is viewed by Washizu (and us) from a vantage point in the castle which makes the illusion of an advancing forest eerily persuasive.

The escalating invasion of the forest culminates in the sequence which is also the climax of the film – the scene in the castle in which Washizu is killed in a spectacularly excessive and prolonged deluge of arrows fired by his own men. Those familiar with the Shakespeare play might have expected this Japanese Macbeth to die in a one-on-one fight in the midst of a battle and then to have his head cut off as a trophy. Those familiar with samurai narratives might have expected him to die by the sword. The film's dispensing with both sets of expectations – Shakespearean and samurai – is both flamboyant and purposeful. Arrows form dense thickets and impromptu barricades as they stick in the woodwork around Washizu and, eventually, in the man himself. In a distilled and sensationalised replaying of his earlier disorientating experience in the labyrinthine forest, Washizu repeatedly doubles back and forward, trying to clear a path through the thick maze of arrows that accumulates around him. Such is their hyperbolic proliferation that the arrows cannot help but become a point of interest in themselves. Unlike a samurai sword, for example (by which Washizu might have been expected to meet his death), arrows are made from organic matter: the shaft is wooden, the fletchings feather. As such, not only does their amassed form recreate for Washizu the experience of floundering repeatedly to and fro in the forest, but in their own substance they also symbolically combine the elements from the forest already to have intruded separately upon the castle – wood (as camouflage for the marching army) and feathers (in the flock of displaced birds).[18] When Washizu eventually falls, he does so literally in the space of the castle. Metaphorically, however, the forest makes its presence felt. Having re-enacted the sense of trapped disorientation that the forest had engendered, *and* being covered in wounds administered by the fabric of the forest, Washizu's extravagantly punctured body is graphic testimony to the forest's final claiming of its own.

The movement of Birnam Wood to Dunsinane, as scoffed at in prospect, and then witnessed, by Macbeth in Act V Scene 5 of the Shakespeare play, has served as the trigger for a more pervasive encroachment of forest upon castle, and finally upon its lord, in Kurosawa's adaptation. The forest in *Throne of Blood*, like the spider's web from which it gets its name, traps those who intrude upon it, and, in Washizu's case at least, sticks to him in one form or another until he dies, bearing the marks of its influence on his body. The apparent dichotomy that the film offers between the realm of the forest and that of the castle is thus revealed as a misleading tease. Both realms are subject to the same forces of destiny. There can be no escape from the implications of one in the apparent safety of the other.

The film's early scenes had proceeded with an unhurried languor. By contrast, as the final crisis approaches, the film takes on a crazed energy. Scenes become shorter and the editing typically swifter, hurtling the action towards the catastrophe. Once Washizu dies, however, all trace of urgency drains quickly from the film. As the camera shows the castle dissolving back into the mist and the intoned choric song once again draws its considered moral, the immediacy of events cedes to a stilled sense of the historically remote. The chorus transmutes the drama into a cautionary tale about murder and ambition whose lessons are apparently as solid and incontrovertible as the castle's memorialising monolith.

RAN (1985)

Nearly thirty years after making *Throne of Blood*, and twenty five after making *The Bad Sleep Well*, Kurosawa was once again drawn to Shakespeare for *Ran*, an adaptation of *King Lear*. *Throne of Blood* had concluded as it began, with a vatic judgement reassuring the audience that the bad always receive their just deserts. It is no surprise that there is no moral explicitly drawn at the end of *Ran*. The title literally means 'Chaos', and the world to which we are admitted in the film testifies constantly to the moral appropriateness of the title. The world of Shakespeare's *King Lear* lacks consolation. That of *Ran* is every bit as unsparing of its audience in its denial of potential sources of comfort.

At the same time, however, there is an irony in the film's title, since for all its moral chaos, a more aesthetically beautiful or ordered film could scarcely be imagined. Its vividly schematic use of costume and colour,[19] its appreciation of landscape and its painterly eye for the drama inherent in pitting the individual against the crowd make for scenes of an almost aching beauty. As with many melancholic or bleak works of art, the pain generated by the sheer misery of the tale is bounded for the spectator, and perhaps even a little mitigated, by the exquisite form of its telling.

In keeping with his established approach to adaptation, Kurosawa looked for, and found, a Japanese story with sufficient points of connection to his source drama to make it possible to create a cross-cultural fusion of the two. On this occasion it was the sixteenth-century warlord Môri Motonari (1497–1571) who furnished Kurosawa with the Japanese half of his Anglo-Japanese narrative tryst. Môri Motonari's story has some resonances with Shakespeare's Lear. In 1546, twenty-five years before his own death, Motonari handed over control of the Mori clan to the eldest of his three sons, Takamoto. The following year, control of the Kikkawa clan passed to his second son, Motoharu. Having officially ceded the reins of power, Motonari nevertheless remained personally active in pursuing a series of territorial battles with neighbouring clans. Despite many differences in their respective stories, Motonari's three children, premature announcement of his retirement and subsequent reluctance to live the life of a retiree provided fruitful material for appropriation as Kurosawa approached the *King Lear* narrative.

From the encounter between Môri Motonari on the one hand and Lear on the other, Kurosawa created the central character of *Ran*, Lord Hidetora Ichimonji (Tatsuya Nakadai). The major shift that had to be managed in order to bring the *Lear* story more closely into line with that of Môri Motonari was to convert Lear's daughters into sons. Both the narrative and metaphorical life of the Shakespeare play is bound up in the femaleness of Lear's offspring. It is, for example, specifically to his daughters that Lear looks for compensation for the absence of mothers and of maternal influence more generally in the play, and their femaleness is far from incidental to his sense of betrayal.[20] Replacing daughters with sons in the surface structure of the story necessarily involves the loss of some of the poetic power that derives from the strongly gendered pull of need and repulsion in the relationships of Lear with his daughters. In *Ran*, Kurosawa exchanges Goneril, Regan and Cordelia for the three sons Tarô, Jirô and Saburô. A compelling and influential female binary is, however, reintroduced to the psychological landscape of the film in the dramatically divergent attitudes and actions of the two daughters-in-law, the pious and innocent Sué (Yoshiko Miyazaki) and the excitingly vicious Kaede (Mieko Harada).

In many narrative details Hidetora mimics Lear, ceding rule over his dominions, exiling his youngest child for insolence and then suffering the consequences of these decisions as his eldest two children incrementally disempower him. Hidetora's past, however, is murkier than Lear's, and will not, moreover, lie buried. His brutal raids on neighbouring clans in his years as Great Lord of the Ichimonji clan have resulted in victim survivors whose continued suffering stands as a discomforting testimony to his past cruelty. The influence of his past crimes is felt intermittently throughout the film in the varying attitudes of those whom he had wronged, and even in the shape of the landscape, scarred as it is by the ruins of the castles he has sacked.

Although not part of the present-time narrative of the film, the eye-gouging from *Lear* is retained as part of the film's back-story. Here, however, the guilt for this has shifted. When Gloucester is blinded in *Lear* he stands not only as an ally of, but also, to some extent, as a surrogate for Lear himself, the extent of whose own vision and blindness the play subjects to scrutiny. In *Ran*, however, far from being identified with the victim of the eye-gouging, Hidetora is now its perpetrator. It transpires he had gouged out the eyes of a young boy, Tsurumaru (Yakeshi Kato), during a raid on an opposing clan years earlier, and then married the boy's sister, Sué, to his own second son, Jirô (Jinpachi Nezu). The blinded Tsurumaru, ashamed of his disfigurement, has subsequently grown up as a hermit in a wilderness dwelling. It is with this alternative to Poor Tom that Hidetora has a salutary encounter during the storm. The boy's quiet stoicism about his blighted life serves as a more potent accusation of Hidetora's past guilt than any railing might have done. His only pleasure is to play the flute given to him by his sister, and when he plays every note of the other-worldly strain seems to act like a physical torture upon his erstwhile torturer. Hidetora staggers and falls backwards, horrified at the evidence of his own grotesque past that now seems to confront him in piercingly melodic form. It is this encounter that finally pushes Hidetora to a point of deranged and pitiable abstraction from his environment.

It is to the pathos-laden figure of the blind Tsurumaru that the film returns for its final sequence. In a series of shots of increasing focal length, he is seen on a high promontory amidst the ruins of Azusa castle where he grew up. He has been left to wait there for the return of his sister Sué that they might flee to safety together. To keep him company while he waits, she has given him a picture of the god Amitabha. As we watch, a gust of wind catches the picture and blows it out of his hands. Bereft, he taps around with his stick, perilously close to the edge. We are in possession of a piece of information that Tsurumaru lacks: the sister for whom he waits has been ambushed while trying to retrieve his flute and is now lying headless in a gully. The pathos of the scene is rendered the more acute by this terrible discrepancy in knowledge. The film ends without having shown the resolution of Tsurumaru's fate. His figure is left suspended in time, tapping his way towards a precipice he cannot see, waiting for a sister who will not come, poignantly accompanied on the soundtrack by the sound of the flute that might have offered him some solace if only it were accessible to him. For all its restraint, the effect of the scene is acutely and painfully eloquent.

It is a feature not just of this final sequence but of the film as a whole that its eloquence should depend upon a language separate from the spoken word. 'I have so much to say, Saburô,' announces Hidetora near the end of the film (a line not included in the original screenplay), but this desire to say things is quickly and cruelly thwarted by the sudden death of the son he wishes to say them to. Hidetora is destroyed: 'You cannot die: I have tales to tell.' That the

'You cannot die: I have tales to tell.' Hidetora (Tatsuya Nakadai) kneels over the dead body of his youngest son, Saburô (Daisuke Ryu) in *Ran* (1985).

Source: *Ran* (1985). Reprinted by permission of Studio Canal Image.

promised tales must remain untold is characteristic of a film which makes a habit of minimising or even eliminating speech whenever a moment may instead be communicated by a piece of visual drama. Saburô's death not only reminds us of the random cruelty of things (as Cordelia's death does in *Lear*), but also protects one of the film's stylistics, inhibiting the threatened eruption of language on to its communicative landscape.

The film's most dramatic, and most justly famous, renunciation of language is the grand battle scene in which the combined forces of Tarô and Jirô attack the fort which houses Hidetora and what remains of his retinue. It is the scene that ends with the self-imposed exile of Hidetora on to the plain. Not only is dialogue absent from almost the entire sequence, but so too for much of it is any other motivated sound – sound, that is, that emerges naturalistically from the scene depicted. The screenplay announces: 'The music superimposed on these pictures is, like the Buddha's heart, measured in beats of profound anguish, the chanting of a melody full of sorrow that begins like sobbing and rises gradually as it is repeated, like karmic cycles, then finally sounds like the wailing of countless Buddhas.'[21] In the finished film, it is Toru Takemitsu's grand, slow Mahleresque orchestral score with its haunting solo line for the cor anglais that renders the anticipated 'beats of profound anguish' and displaces the sound of gunshot, clashing swords, horse whinnies and human cries.[22] Here, as elsewhere, Kurosawa aestheticises the presentation of violence. Objectively, the battle is gruesome: soldiers lose limbs and heap ravaged bodies into piles in the mist while inside the castle tower Hidetora's concubines enact their mutually assisted suicides (*seppuku*). The brutality, however, is seen through layers of stylisation, the most obvious of which is the removal of any realistic sound. This dislocation, even contradiction, between sight and sound invests the scene with the quality of a balletic nightmare. The extra-cinematic laws of cause and effect seem not to apply here: metal can strike metal without generating a clang; a man can sustain a series of wounds without emitting an audible cry; a fire can burn fiercely without making a crackle; horses can stampede silently across a hillside. As the usual bond between action and consequence seems to have been severed, something in our appreciation of the scene is correspondingly numbed.

But then, just as we have become accustomed to a level of insulated removal from the immediacy of what we see, sound breaks in suddenly and crudely, returning us with a jolt to the import of the action as a battle rather than a ballet. Tarô is shot in the back as he rides across the castle forecourt. The shot rings out, banishing the sombre musical weight of the soundtrack and releasing the action from the sound-proof frame in which it had been locked. Beginning with the shot on Tarô, sight and sound resynchronise to mimic the collaborative rather than competitive nature of these things in the world we inhabit. Wailing voices are finally allowed to articulate their own horror, and this re-engagement with the laws of cause and effect invites us back into the scene with renewed force.

The scene ends with the dishevelled figure of the literally and emotionally scorched Hidetora descending from the castle's burning tower. The visual drama of the sequence spectacularly showcases Kurosawa's painterly interest in form, pattern and colour. Hidetora emerges unarmed and steps gingerly but unbowed down the steps on to the castle forecourt where the forces of Tarô and Jirô are massed. The bristling spears and brightly colour-coded banners of the two armies, seen in long shot, quiver and part before his fragile figure, almost as if frightened by his alarming vulnerability. To have survived the onslaught on the tower gives him a sort of force, frail though he is. In the face of this unnerving combination of fragility and dignity, the quivering, straining body of men holds itself back, protecting a channel through which he may pass. The screenplay anticipates the effect thus: 'From the donjon entrance comes Hidetora trailing smoke, which wraps around him. His white hair is bristling, and he is staggering as if treading on air, staring vacantly into space. . . . Samurai and foot soldiers slide away to open up his path but cannot avert their eyes from him.'[23] He staggers slowly through their midst in dramatic isolation and out of the castle into the howling wilderness beyond. His determination to commit suicide in the tower had been thwarted by his inability to find a dagger or sword that might serve. As his tiny figure becomes subsumed within the forbidding landscape beyond the castle, his flimsy clothes clinging to his bare legs in the wind, it seems likely that the environment will now do what a sword could not.

The bristling, quivering mass of soldiers parting like a sea to let Hidetora through is almost a signature scene for Kurosawa. The group life of a crowd and the visual patterns that can be created when they behave as a single organism has a place in many of his films. In *Seven Samurai*, for example, a crowd of peasant farmers expresses its unease, dissent, excitement and approval by the slightest of individual movements, whose effect is amplified by rippling through their ranks. When at a village meeting euphemistic reference is made to 'the cost' these farmers had to pay for holding a little of their crop back from the marauding bandits, it is the women who twitch. The moment is fleeting and each woman makes only the tiniest of movements. Nevertheless made in synchronisation with the others, the effect is telling. We are never told explicitly what 'the cost' demanded by the bandits was, but the women's collective twitching is more efficiently and powerfully communicative in this regard than any explanatory line of dialogue could have been. In *Throne of Blood*, when Washizu addresses his massed army near the end of the film, the men shuffle uncomfortably, causing their banners to flutter. Once again it is the tiniest of individual movements that generates the drama of the collective effect – expressive on this occasion of a collective scepticism in the face of their leader's hollowly triumphalist talk. The crowd scenes in *The Bad Sleep Well* testify once again to the trademark Kurosawa effect. In the opening wedding scene, for example, crowds of pressmen and paparazzi rush around from one place to another, seeking out the story and the photograph that will sell their newspapers. The movements made by their massed presence are suggestive of that of a single, unwieldy, segmented creature rather than of a collection of individuals. And as always in a Kurosawa film, it is against the background of this undulating, anonymised mass that a few individual fates then emerge in sharp definition.

*

Kurosawa was much admired in the West: he twice received an Academy Award for Best Foreign Picture,[24] was nominated for the Best Director Academy Award for *Ran*, and in 1990 was honoured by the Academy with a Lifetime Achievement Award. In Japan, by contrast, his reputation waned considerably in the latter part of his career. In an interview with Donald Richie earlier in his career, Kurosawa declared himself 'very Japanese' and interested above all in the compression, symbolism and subtlety of Japanese art forms.[25] His inclusion of specifically Japanese elements (such as components of Noh) in his films, however, was increasingly read in Japan as the strategic imprinting of an exoticised stamp of *token* Japaneseness upon his films, with an eye to an international market. When Japanese films fared better than expected at international film festivals, the explanations reached for in Japan to explain the success were revealing about how the Western reception of Japanese films was viewed. Anderson and Richie cite the analogy proposed by one Japanese critic: 'In the same way, foreigners – forever souvenir-hunting – always pick Japanese style paintings on silk (*nihonga*) rather than our oils on canvas (*yoga*).'[26] That is to say, it was that which could be economically labelled as incontrovertibly Japanese that was thought to appeal to the international market. The product branding for a Japanese film had to be clear in courting an exoticism, but this sheen of well-advertised Japaneseness should not, of course, penetrate deep enough to alienate a Western market. Kurosawa's films became viewed by some sections of the Japanese film industry as the equivalent of the kimonos the Japanese garment industry made specifically for export. As Anderson and Richie explain: 'Before the war, and to some extent even now, the kimono industry made two kinds of garments, those intended for domestic use and those destined for export. The latter, distinguished by their bright colours, were alive with embroidered dragons and stalking tigers.'[27] The suggestion is clear: products designed for a non-Japanese market exaggerated, even perhaps cartooned, aspects of Japanese expression in order to render them readily appreciable to an untrained eye, and appealingly exotic to non-Japanese consumers.

As Kurosawa's films began to be seen as strategically heightening selective elements of Japaneseness for a Western reception, funding from within Japan became correspondingly harder to secure. Conversely, foreign money needed some reassurance about the Japanese character of the films before being willing to commit. Kurosawa thus found himself in one cultural community looking to another not only for an audience of a sufficient size to justify the expenditure but also for primary economic support: the process of securing funding for his later films was, therefore, neither easy nor quick.

In pre-production for *Ran*, as for all of his films from *Kagemusha* (1980) onwards, Kurosawa planned the precise look of the photography by himself story-boarding with a lavish attention to detail. Drawing upon his own earlier artistic training, he envisaged some frames as full-blown paintings. Creating these story-board drawings and paintings proved to be one of the ways of using the time profitably in the quiet periods between projects, and the resulting works were themselves then also helpful support material in pitching to potential investors. *Ran* cost over $10 million to produce (the most expensive Japanese film of its time), which allowed, among other things, for an enormous array of extras, a collection of expensive sets and some flamboyant battle scenes,[28] and it was eventually French money that was found to bankroll this. In 1994, Kurosawa's collection of story-boards and film-related artwork were sought for an exhibition in their own right. Given his popularity among a generation of film-makers in the United States, it is perhaps unsurprising that this exhibition should have been mounted not in Japan but Manhattan, at the Ise Foundation Gallery on Broadway.[29] As Kurosawa reports in his introduction to the *Ran* screenplay, before cinema supplanted painting as his chosen primary mode of creative expression, it had been one of his youthful ambitions to mount an exhibition of his art in the West.[30] There was a pleasing sense of circular completeness about his career that this ambition should have been finally fulfilled shortly before his death in 1998 and, moreover, in a way that was not in competition but directly in collaboration with his dominant career as a film-maker.

When Kurosawa died, in September 1998, he drew eulogies from many of the most prominent film-makers working in the West, including George Lucas, Steven Spielberg, Martin Scorsese and Brian de Palma, each of whom wished to record his debt of gratitude to Kurosawa's extraordinary, and extraordinarily influential, cinematic style. When he brought that style to bear upon Shakespearean narratives, the results were intelligently engaged with many of the driving impetuses of the source plays and yet still decidedly, even perhaps strategically, Japanese. He moulded the Shakespearean material to intersect purposefully with a translated cultural context, viewing the narratives through the filter of a specific Japanese history, milieu and set of performance codes. In his treatments, both *Macbeth* and *King Lear* proved to be extremely culturally malleable – just as they already had done when Shakespeare himself inherited them from Holinshed and the traditional tale of *Leir* respectively.

Shakespeare's *King Lear* was almost certainly first performed in 1605, just two years after James VI of Scotland had acceded to the throne as James I of England. As played in 1605, therefore, the king who struts on to the theatrical stage and promptly divides his kingdom might well have been received as a comparison by opposition with that other king who had recently strutted on to a stage – the English political stage. The play suggests that for a king to divide his kingdom is an act of political folly. The implicit corollary of this is that for a king to unite his kingdoms (as James had symbolically done by becoming king of both Scotland and England) is, by contrast, an act of political acumen. As such, the folly of Lear might be read as a canny, if obliquely inverted, tribute to the wisdom of James. Even as first played, therefore, *King Lear* was laced with matters of strategic interest to its intended reception community. And *Macbeth's* dramatic engagements with witchcraft, rebellion and Scottish monarchy were, if anything, yet more topically charged.

Kurosawa's approach to adaptation in *Throne of Blood* and *Ran* is thus to some extent in line with the original operations of these plays. He, like Shakespeare before him, strips the dramatic narrative to its bones and then, combining the remote with the familiar, finds a framework in which it can play best to its intended audience. And one of the effects of the narrative palimpsests that result is to prompt revivified reflection on the Shakespeare plays that were part of their inspiration. Writing about Japanese interpretations of Shakespeare in general, the Japanese academic Anzai Tetsuo suggests that 'The very peripherality of our position might give us a vantage point from which we might command a better view'.[31] Steven Spielberg's claim that Kurosawa was 'the pictorial Shakespeare of our time',[32] and, more importantly, the intelligence and sensitivity of the films themselves, might even make us question the validity of the hierarchy implicit in a continuing geography of 'centre' and 'peripheries' in this context.

FURTHER READING

Joseph L. Anderson and Donald Richie, *The Japanese Film: Art and Industry* (Rutland, Vermont and Tokyo: Charles E. Tuttle Company, 1959).

J. Blumenthal, 'Macbeth into *Throne of Blood*', *Sight and Sound* 34, 4 (Autumn 1965), pp.190–5.

Anthony Davies, 'Peter Brook's *King Lear* and Akira Kurosawa's *Throne of Blood*', Chapter 8 in A. Davies, *Filming Shakespeare's Plays* (Cambridge: Cambridge University Press, 1988), pp.143–66.

Robert Hapgood, 'Kurosawa's Shakespeare Films: *Throne of Blood, The Bad Sleep Well,* and *Ran*', in Anthony Davies and Stanley Wells (eds), *Shakespeare and the Moving Image: The Plays on Film and Television* (Cambridge: Cambridge University Press, 1994), pp.234–49.

Keiko McDonald, 'The Noh Convention in *The Throne of Blood* and *Ran*', in Kevin K.W. Chang (ed.), *Kurosawa: Perceptions on Life, An Anthology of Essays* (Honolulu: Honolulu Academy of Arts, 1991), pp.24–32.

Roger Manvell, 'Akira Kurosawa's *The Castle of the Spider's Web* (1957)', Chapter 9 in R. Manvell, *Shakespeare and the Film* (London: J.M. Dent and Sons, 1971), pp.101–13.

Minami Ryuta, Ian Carruthers and John Gillies (eds), *Performing Shakespeare in Japan* (Cambridge: Cambridge University Press, 2001).

Stephen Prince, *The Warrior's Camera* (Princeton, NJ: Princeton University Press, 1999).

NOTES

1. See Michael Birkett's account of the Brook *Lear*, written for Roger Manvell and reproduced in Roger Manvell, *Shakespeare and the Film* (London: J.M. Dent and Sons, 1971), pp.136–43. This quotation, p.137.
2. Ibid.
3. *The Sunday Times*, 26 January 1969. Quoted in Manvell (1971), p.107.
4. Michael Birkett about his and Brook's shared taste. Quoted in Manvell (1971), p.136.
5. J. Blumenthal, 'Macbeth into *Throne of Blood*', *Sight and Sound* 34, 4 (Autumn 1965), pp.190–5. This quotation p.190.
6. Manvell (1971), p.xvi.
7. Grigori Kozintsev, *Shakespeare: Time and Conscience*, trans. by Joyce Vining (New York: Hill and Wang, 1966), p.29.
8. See John Collick, *Shakespeare, Cinema and Society* (Manchester: Manchester University Press, 1989), pp.161, 163.
9. Quoted in Donald Richie, *The Films of Akira Kurosawa* (Berkeley and Los Angeles: University of California Press, 1965), p.121.
10. The Japanese noun *arasuji* can, for example, apparently mean both a plot (as in a play) and a sinewy fibrous thread. I am grateful to Kao Richter and Harald Suppanschitsch for their advice about Japanese metaphor.
11. See, for example, Jack Jorgens, *Shakespeare on Film* (Bloomington: Indiana University Press, 1997), p.156; Peter S. Donaldson, *Shakespeare Films/Shakespearean Directors* (Boston: Unwin Hyman, 1990), p.76; Neil Forsyth, 'Shakespeare the Illusionist: Filming the Supernatural', Chapter 16 in Russell Jackson (ed.), *The Cambridge Companion to Shakespeare on Film* (Cambridge: Cambridge University Press, 2000), pp.274–94, especially p.288.
12. Quoted in Manvell (1971), pp.102–5.
13. See Manvell (1971), p.103. See also Keiko McDonald, 'The Noh Convention in *The Throne of Blood* and *Ran*', in Kevin K.W. Chang (ed.), *Kurosawa: Perceptions on Life, An Anthology of Essays* (Honolulu: Honolulu Academy of Arts, 1991), pp.24–32.

14. Richie (1965), p.117.

15. Kozintsev (1966), p.30.

16. See Richie (1965), p.118; John Gerlach, 'Shakespeare, Kurosawa, and *Macbeth*: A Response to J. Blumenthal', *Literature/Film Quarterly* 1, 4 (1973), pp.352–9, especially p.355; Anthony Davies, 'Peter Brook's *King Lear* and Akira Kurosawa's *Throne of Blood*', Chapter 8 in A. Davies, *Filming Shakespeare's Plays* (Cambridge: Cambridge University Press, 1988), p.165.

17. For an illuminating discussion of the counterposing of horizontal and vertical lines in the film, see Davies (1988), pp.167–72.

18. To these are added the arrow-heads made of bone, another substance to which our attention has already been drawn in the forest.

19. *Ran* won the Academy Award for costume design in 1985.

20. See Coppélia Kahn, 'The Absent Mother in *King Lear*', in Margaret W. Ferguson, Maureen Quilligan, Nancy J. Vickers (eds), *Rewriting the Renaissance* (Chicago: University of Chicago Press, 1986), pp.33–49.

21. Akira Kurosawa, *Ran: The Original Screenplay and Storyboards* (Boston and London: Shambhala, 1986), scene 67, p.46.

22. Takemitsu's remarkable score for *Ran* earned him the Los Angeles Film Critics' Award for 1987.

23. Kurosawa (1986), scenes 108, 110, p.52.

24. Kurosawa won the Oscar for Best Foreign Film in 1951 for *Rashomon* and in 1975 for *Dersu Uzala*.

25. Richie (1965), p.117.

26. Joseph L. Anderson and Donald Richie, *The Japanese Film: Art and Industry* (Tokyo: Charles E. Tuttle Company, 1959), p.233.

27. Anderson and Richie (1959), p.37.

28. See David Kehr, 'Samurai *Lear*', *American Film* 10, 10 (September 1985), p.24.

29. See Stephen Prince, *The Warrior's Camera: The Cinema of Akira Kurosawa*, revised and expanded edition (Princeton, NJ: Princeton University Press, 1991), p.341.

30. Kurosawa, 'Drawing and Directing', translated by Margaret Benton, in Kurosawa (1986), p.5.

31. Anzai Tetsuo, 'What Do We Mean by "Japanese" Shakespeare?', Chapter 1 in Minami Ryuta, Ian Carruthers, John Gillies (eds), *Performing Shakespeare in Japan* (Cambridge: Cambridge University Press, 2001), p.19.

32. Elizabeth Snead, 'Cinema Loses Its Shakespeare,' *USA Today*, 8 September 1998, p.2D. Quoted in Prince (1991), p.341.

CHAPTER FOUR

Roguish Interventions:

American Shakespearean Offshoots

When Hector Berlioz visited London in 1846, he expressed his consternation that, as he saw it, some considered themselves sufficiently superior to Shakespeare to 'correct[ ] and augment[ ]' his plays. Such 'rogues', he wrote in a letter to Joseph-Louis Duc, 'should have their bottoms publicly spanked'.[1] The tradition of adapting Shakespeare's plays has a long history, and it has often proved contentious. From the Restoration onwards, Shakespeare plays have been adapted for the legitimate stage, and also been re-spun into many other forms of cultural expression including operas, operettas, ballets, dumb-shows, burlesques, novels, cartoons, comic skits, musical suites, symphonies and advertisements. It is, needless to say, the particular endeavours of those 'rogues' who have stolen part or all of Shakespeare's plots while adapting his language for the cinema that will be the subject of this chapter.

It has long been the charge thrown at British cinema that it has been tentative and over-respectful in its approach to adaptation. Hollywood, by contrast, has long been willing to subject literary texts, as Brian McFarlane expresses it, to a 'robust exploitation'. As a result it has frequently been capable of producing something 'more dangerous and flamboyant and vigorous'.[2] The comparison drawn between a tentative British approach and a vigorous American approach to adaptation is, by now, a little clichéd. Like many clichés, however, it also has an element of truth about it. It is no accident, therefore, that all the films chosen for this chapter should be American.

The films centrally discussed in this chapter are *Island of Lost Souls* (1932), *Iguana* (1988), *Forbidden Planet* (1956), *Men of Respect* (1991) and *O* (2001). The first three have narrative correspondences with *The Tempest*, a play discussed at greater length in Chapter 6. Readers with an interest in how a single dramatic narrative has fared across time and a variety of treatments in the cinema may wish to read these two chapters as part of a connected narrative.

The three *Tempest*-evocative films considered in this chapter, however, have a more ambivalent relationship to Shakespeare than do those adaptations discussed in Chapter 6. As will be discussed, their points of narrative and thematic correspondence might *arguably* derive from the play, although these correspondences might equally be coincidental. A discerned similarity between texts need not, of course, be fully intentional for it to have an impact on the ways in which the film subsequently can make most sense for an audience. It is quite possible innocently to reproduce some narrative or situational elements, or collections of character types present in an earlier text without being completely aware of the points of duplication. Whether a sense of significant correspondence with a Shakespeare play is identified in the film's reception is, as history has shown and this chapter will explore, of greater interpretive significance than whether the film-makers were fully in control of those points of correspondence at the moment of production. The section on *Forbidden Planet* explicitly examines this question of intentionality versus coincidence in the narrative chiming of one text with another. A briefer introductory section on *Iguana* and *Island of Lost Souls* is offered principally as comparative illustration for the case of *Forbidden Planet* in this respect. No film in the history of *Tempest* adaptations, and perhaps of Shakespeare film adaptations generally, has generated such widespread critical misapprehensions as *Forbidden Planet*. It is, therefore, a film whose reception history merits examination.

In the second half of the chapter I consider two adaptations of Shakespearean source plays that clearly advertise the deliberateness of their points of reference to the original. The first is *Men of Respect* (William Reilly, 1991), a mobster update of *Macbeth* set in contemporary New York. The second is *O* (Tim Blake Nelson, 2001), a domesticated and 'teenified' modernisation of *Othello* set in an all-white American high school.

For all five films, the range of ways in which they are distinguished from their Shakespearean analogues becomes part of their identity. Having consciously or otherwise referenced a Shakespeare play, they are then defined not only in alliance, but as significantly in contradistinction to it. Their status as not *The Tempest*, not *Macbeth* and not *Othello* both helps to clarify what is specific to each as a new work *and* prompts renewed reflection on the particular character of the plays which has either eluded the grasp of the adaptor or been forsworn in the pursuit of other goals.

*

. . . the story in The Tempest *is a thing of naught, for any story will provide a remote island, a shipwreck, and a co-incidence.*[3]

ISLAND OF LOST SOULS (ERLE C. KENTON, 1932)

Although Paramount was not principally known for horror, its 1932 horror film *Island of Lost Souls* is creepy in effective ways. It was adapted from H.G. Wells' short novel *The Island of Dr. Moreau* (1896). Both Wells' novel and the Paramount film find representation for several of *The Tempest*'s principal narrative elements.

The novel relates the story of an elite and hubristic scientist, Dr Moreau. Wells himself referred to his depiction of Moreau as the savage indictment of an interventionist god, the novel as a whole adding up to 'an exercise in youthful blasphemy'.[4] The novel's pool of linked narrative and thematic reference – from *Robinson Crusoe* to *Gulliver's Travels*, from the book of Genesis to *Frankenstein* – is extensive. Unsurprisingly, amidst such a cluster of narrative allegiances, the correspondences between the essential situation of Wells' tale and that of *The Tempest* are easy to discern.

Moreau, like Prospero, is banished from his home to a remote island where he proclaims himself the absolute authority. His banishment, like Prospero's, results from having closeted himself away in the pursuit of hermetic knowledge. Moreau, like Prospero in relation at least to Caliban, then governs his island exile by means of a reign of terror, while tutoring his brutish creatures in language skills and in 'civilised' codes of behaviour. Moreau, like Prospero, works on the assumption that the savages he has at his command are *tabula rasa* and therefore amenable to being inscribed with any moral character he chooses. About one, Moreau says: 'I taught him the rudiments of English, gave him ideas of counting, even made the thing read the alphabet. . . . He began with a clean sheet, mentally.'[5] Moreau, like Prospero, has high hopes of what might be possible by way of the suppression of instinct and the elevation of reason: 'This time I will burn out all the animal, this time I will make a rational creature of my own.'[6] Moreau, like Prospero, however, is ultimately disappointed in his own capacity to divert nature from its instinctive drives. Although the single anarchic Caliban figure in *The Tempest* has proliferated into a *range* of primitive figures in the Wells novel, the essential identity of the untutorable 'slave' is recognisable across works as alike in tendencies, influences and dramatic function. Moreau, like Prospero, subsequently plays host to a shipwrecked man, who is able to observe how Moreau is deified by the island's brutish inhabitants as, among other things, the controller of 'the lightning-flash' and 'the deep salt sea'.[7]

The film *Island of Lost Souls* (starring Charles Laughton as a darkly imperious and yet impeccably civil Moreau) takes the material of the Wells narrative and moves it yet closer to the dramatic interests of *The Tempest*.[8] Most significant of the film's several adjustments of the narrative in the direction of the Shakespeare play is its reduction of the female presence on the island.

Whereas in the novel 'the females were less numerous than the males', in the film there is only one woman, Lota, the most perfect of Moreau's creations.[9] The presence on a remote island of a lone woman who has never seen a civilised man except her elderly male 'creator' confirms the *Tempest* resonance to this island community. Because of her sexual vulnerability Lota needs, and receives, the special protection of Moreau himself, whose care for her is both as tender and as calculating as Prospero's is for Miranda. Moreau decides to expose her to the shipwrecked visitor (Parker in the film), with the deliberate intention of observing her naïve responses to the first young man she has ever seen. His degree of clinical forethought in engineering this meeting is reminiscent of Prospero's approach to the strategically choreographed encounter between Miranda and Ferdinand. Prospero says to Miranda:

> *The fringed curtains of thine eye advance,*
> *And say what thou seest yond . . .*
> *. . . This gallant which thou seest*
> *Was in the wreck, and but he's something stained*
> *With grief – that's beauty's canker – thou mightst call him*
> *A goodly person.*   (I.ii.409–10, 414–17)

In the film, Moreau prepares Lota for the social task ahead even more explicitly:

> *Lota, I've taught you many things. All that you know I have taught you. I'm going to let you learn something for yourself. A man has come from the sea. I will take you to him. I'm going to leave you alone with him. You may talk with him about anything you please. About the world he comes from.*

What is more, Moreau does not try to veil his purposes, even when Parker is present. Having introduced Parker to Lota, he adds, without subtlety, 'She is the only woman on the entire island. Well, I'll leave you two young people together: I've got work to do,' before disappearing from sight in order to watch them, Prospero-fashion, himself unobserved. Moreau's quasi-scientific interest in exploiting the island's socially and sexually controlled environment to observe how well courtship and mating instincts function when deprived of any instruction or patterns for emulation makes of his island even more blatant a sexual laboratory than Prospero's.

The distillation of the novel's *several* female innocents down to the film's *single* female *naïve* in Lota indicates a pull towards a simplifying of the material in the interests of dramatic and emotional clarity. And from the paring away of some of the novel's more elaborate margins, the more focused narrative of the film emerges looking more Shakespearean in its dramatic interests. In this and other respects, the film intensifies the novel's broad correspondences with the Shakespeare play. This happens as an accidental by-product of streamlining the narrative, apparently with no deliberate *intention* to mimic or even evoke the substance of *The Tempest*.

The presence of a primary literary source with a significant profile in Wells' novel has shielded the film from the need for any more distant narrative sources to be identified. As a result, its considerable points of coincidence with Shakespeare's narrative – a shipwreck, an uncharted island, an exiled magus, a primitive savage, an aspiration to imprint civilisation upon the barbarous and a carefully choreographed encounter between an unsocialised virgin and a shipwrecked man – have scarcely prompted comment. In some cases, stories of such a fundamental and primal character are able to be in circulation without exhaustive labels of derivation and narrative indebtedness being attached to them.

IGUANA (MONTE HELLMAN, 1988)

Like *Island of Lost Souls*, cult director Monte Hellman's *Iguana* sits at a slight remove from *The Tempest* while offering some interesting narrative parallels to it. It is a cinematic study of one man's revenge upon a world which has wronged him. The central character (Everett McGill) exorcises the memory of the abuse he has suffered by establishing his own Mediterranean island kingdom in which, as he says, he obeys no laws but his own. On this island he is then seen living out his own twisted power fantasies. Those who have the misfortune to be washed up on his shores are enslaved, their tormentor enjoying the power imbalance between his situation and theirs: 'I hold the power of life and death over you.' The relish with which he exercises his despotic control is in some measure reminiscent in exaggerated form of Prospero, who also manifestly enjoys the power he is able to wield, saying:

> . . . *these mine enemies are all knit up*
> *In their distractions: they now are in my power.*   (III.iii.89–90)

and later:

> *At this hour*
> *Lies at my mercy all mine enemies.*   (IV.i.262–263)

Hellman's central character quite deliberately turns his island kingdom into a living hell for those held captive there, designing horrific emotional torments not so much '[t]o lay upon the damn'd' (*The Tempest* I.ii.290) as to secure the future damnation of the sufferers. At one stage in the film, he boards the ship upon which his enemies of old are travelling, battening down the crew's hatches and, Ariel-fashion, setting light to the ship. He also ensures, once again evoking resonances of *The Tempest*, that the principal target of his vengeance is tormented with the knowledge that his sons have been drowned. Unlike Ariel's achievement, however, this is no mere *illusion* of destruction. There are no 'calm seas' and 'auspicious gales' (V.i.314) in prospect here. Hellman's anti-hero is a partial version of Prospero, but unlike Prospero he is never persuaded of the moral, or even strategic, benefits of virtue over vengeance. Prospero manages to combine the vengeful satisfaction of watching his enemies suffer with the moral luxury of subsequently undoing all his 'apparent' cruelties through the exercise of magic. Hellman's protagonist shares Prospero's satisfaction at the suffering of his enemies but has no interest in subsequently redescribing torment as the mere illusion of torment. The torments enacted on this island are irreversible.

Although *The Tempest* ends in forgiveness and reconciliation, until the last act it has seemed to be pursuing a muted, considered revenge plot leading to a revenge climax. At the beginning of Act V, Prospero's 'project' seems to have a direction, and it does not sound like a pleasant one. He describes his project as 'gather[ing] to a head' (V.i.1), his choice of metaphor implying that the gathered head must at some stage blow to release the accumulated pressure. In a boil or volcano – each of which 'gather[s] to a head' – the accumulated tension on the surface of the skin or land needs at some stage to be relieved by a moment of releasing eruption. Prospero makes it clear that the 'drift of [his] purpose' would have extended *at least* 'a frown further' had his wrongdoers *not* been, or not been described by Ariel as being, 'penitent' (V.i.28–30). Since there is no evidence that two of the prime culprits (Antonio and Sebastian) *are* penitent, however, it is possible to see the final resolution as, more than anything else, a structural necessity to enable the drama to remain, if under strain, within the generic exigencies of tragicomic form. Although the gathered 'head' is not allowed the anticipated satisfaction of erupting, it does nevertheless continue to seep messily throughout the denouement, as a reminder of the potential for a more dramatic, cathartic ending that was eschewed. The irritants to a neat resolution include Antonio's dogged refusal to be grateful for the forgiveness he receives and Prospero's own double-edged forgiveness of him:

> For you, most wicked sir, whom to call brother,
> Would even infect my mouth, I do forgive
> Thy rankest fault, – all of them; and require
> My dukedom of thee, which perforce, I know,
> Thou must restore. (V.i.130–134)

This forgiveness, which still seems at least as bitterly judgemental as it is merciful, and Antonio's stubbornly eloquent silence in response to it, testify to the pressure under which the 'happy' ending labours.

Both *Iguana*'s correspondences with and departures from *The Tempest* prompt reflection on the course of action upon which Shakespeare's central character seems set for most of the play, and on the intensity of the violent potential inherent, although finally dissipated, in the play. In the exclusivity of its concentration on the strategic control of one man over the lives of others beyond the reach of civilising or moderating influences, however, it necessarily ignores other key elements that contribute to the more mixed drama of *The Tempest*. It has, for example, no daughter, no innocence in need of awakening, no miracle-performing magic and, most importantly, no final forgiveness or redemption from physical or emotional thraldom. It is a grim, and grimly partial, allusion to *The Tempest*, offering not Gonzalo's Utopian fantasy, or even Antonio's sense of a land ripe for exploitation, but rather only Ariel-as-Harpy's 'most desolate isle' (III.iii.80), making good on his threat of '[l]ing'ring perdition' (III.iii.77) to those washed up there. As such, *Iguana* is a salutary speculation on the direction in which *The Tempest* might have tended if Prospero's purpose had extended the threatened 'frown further'.

FORBIDDEN PLANET (FRED MCLEOD WILCOX, 1956)

Unlike both *Island of Lost Souls* and *Iguana*, whose correspondences with *The Tempest* have raised little interest, the popular American science fiction film *Forbidden Planet* (1956) is widely acknowledged as a creative reworking of the Shakespeare play. The parallels between the two texts are easy to discern.

At a fundamental level, *Forbidden Planet* shares with *The Tempest* (and *Island of Lost Souls* and *Iguana*) an understanding of the intensity and concentration of action possible in a removed and inaccessible location where one reclusive man conducts innovative experiments in the personal exercise of secret power. In both play and film that reclusive central character – Prospero/Dr Morbius (Walter Pidgeon) – prizes his own quest for private knowledge above his engagements with the rest of humanity. His present isolation is therefore partly the natural outworking of his own prejudices (whatever mischance may *ostensibly* have determined his separation from others). Each has a beautiful daughter whose naïve innocence he jealously guards[10] – Miranda/Altaira (Anne Francis) – and a strange and multi-competent spirit to enact his power fantasies – Ariel/Robby the Robot. Each is troubled by a more primitive presence – Caliban/invisible monster – whom he claims is entirely untamable by civilised values. In both play and film a group of visitors – shipwrecked Neapolitan courtiers/the crew of an intergalactic spacecraft – arrives in the isolated territory. Among both groups is a young and handsome pretender to the daughter's affections – Ferdinand/Commander Adams (Leslie Nielsen). Each magus-father interprets the younger man as a direct rival to himself and treats him harshly before finally surrendering his exclusive claim on his daughter and resigning himself to the transfer of her allegiance to the younger man. As each drama reaches its resolution, the magus-father finally accepts a degree of responsibility for the primitive character he has previously disowned. Prospero looks at Caliban and says, 'this thing of darkness I / Acknowledge mine' (V.i.275–276). Morbius admits in his final moments that the destructive monster is in fact the horrible embodiment of his worst subconscious impulses. It is, as Commander Adams' colleague reveals in a marvellously diagnostic dying breath, a monster from the id.[11]

The narrative parallels between *The Tempest* and *Forbidden Planet*, in particular the magus's relationship to the untameable creature in his world and the rendering of a mythic tale with an overlaid contemporary political resonance, are treated in more detail in Chapter 6. My concern here is not to expand on these, but to query what they may legitimately be taken to signify about the nature of the relationship between the two texts.

Bob Carlton's popular stage musical, derivatively entitled *Return to the Forbidden Planet*, first performed in 1990 and advertised as 'Shakespeare's Forgotten Rock'n'Roll Masterpiece', both trades upon and, in doing so, confirms the Shakespearean association of the 1956 film. It leaves no room for ambiguity about the deliberateness of its references to Shakespeare, so consolidating the impression, if only accidentally, that this too is what its inspiration, *Forbidden Planet*, had done. In the case of *Forbidden Planet*, however, there are grounds for questioning this.

Forbidden Planet makes no mention of *The Tempest* in its title or credit sequences and was not advertised with any claim of a Shakespeare associ-ation during its early exhibition runs or in its press releases. As a landmark production for MGM, and a costly one, it was much reviewed in the year of its release. *Films in Review, Monthly Film Bulletin, Variety, Motion Picture Herald, Film Daily, Hollywood Reporter, The New York Times, Kinematograph Weekly* and *Today's Cinema* were, for example, among those publications that reviewed the film between its preview (22 February 1956) and late June of the same year. None of these contemporary reviews mentions a Shakespearean resonance to the film.

Those reviewers who considered what might have inspired the film pro-duced speculative descriptions such as this from *The New York Times*: 'Weird science fiction based primarily on fact, on present experimentation and on fertile imagination.'[12] Those who considered the film's possible literary or dramatic precedents were still not struck by any Shakespearean affinities, tending to arrive at more recent or populist models instead: 'a King Kong of space'; 'Walter Pidgeon play[s] the Jekyll-and-Hyde scholar'.[13] Even when in May 1956 Bosley Crowther, with unconscious irony, drew attention to the appropriateness of the Globe movie theatre as the film's New York venue, he clearly only intended that 'appropriateness' to refer to the planetary associations of the theatre's name for the showing of a space fantasy rather than to anything about Shakespearean playhouses.[14] Even this accident of location that might, with hindsight, have been expected to sensitise an audience to any latent Shakespearean narrative patterning in the film still triggered no spark of recognition among critics or reviewers. The film was received as an innovative and impressive work of cinema in terms of its ambitious special effects, its awe-inspiring sets, its groundbreaking use of robotics and its original soundtrack. Any suggestion of a Shakespeare association, however, seems to have been entirely absent from contemporary readings.

The earliest published comment connecting *Forbidden Planet* to *The Tempest* that I have been able to trace was made by Kingsley Amis in 1961. In *New Maps of Hell* he suggested that there had been 'a work oddly omitted' from previous considerations of the sources for science fiction in general and *Forbidden Planet* in particular. While *The Tempest*, he claimed, could only be considered 'a very dilute and indirect influence on science fiction', it was nevertheless 'a distant anticipation'. [15] Once given its first, slightly tentative airing, the idea that *Forbidden Planet* was partially indebted to *The Tempest* then percolated gradually through the critical community so that later critics were not even aware that it had, or needed to have had, an author and moment of first saying.

By the early 1970s *The Tempest* was being regularly discussed alongside *Forbidden Planet* with the unthinking confidence of a well-rehearsed, uncontested argument. By then, the weight of critical writing even implied that the association had *from the first* been an integral part of the film's conception and reception. This critical trend, retrospectively investing the film with intentions it did not communicate at the time, has persisted. And from 1970 onwards the critical line has been as consistently attentive to the Shakespearean association as it had been negligent of it in the film's early years. In 1976 and 1977 respectively, it was suggested that audiences in 1956 had been 'shocked to discover that this film bore an eerie resemblance to Shakespeare's *The Tempest*'[16] and had found in it 'an intelligent blending of the wild creature storyline and a retelling of Shakespeare's play, *The Tempest*'.[17] By 1982 Philip Strick was even making fine distinctions between the type of Shakespearean attention that he claimed the film *had* received upon first release and that which it *should* have received: 'While critics [at the time] made passing allusions to *The Tempest*, it was overlooked that Shakespeare's play had already dealt with disenchantment.'[18] The evidence available suggests that audiences overlooked considerably more that was arguably Shakespearean in the film than the single theme of disenchantment. Shakespeare, that is, was not partially but entirely absent from their frame of reference.

Once established, however, this revisionist critical tendency – remembering, for example, 'passing allusions to *The Tempest*' where there had been none – has passed so authoritatively into the popular mythology surrounding the film that it seems to have escaped sceptical interrogation. The actual first audiences for *Forbidden Planet*, who did not, it would seem, identify anything Shakespearean in the film worthy of comment, have been written out of the story. Since 1970 they have been conveniently reconfigured as an extra-historical *ideal* audience who would have recognised every possible latent allusion in the text and who were therefore at once struck, as has been claimed, by the film's 'eerie resemblance' to *The Tempest*. Such an ideal spectatorship is, however, an interpretive construct of a later period, revealing much about modern tendencies to project contemporary patterns of critical reception back on to earlier contexts. About the film's actual reception at the time of its release, however, it is actively misleading.

The possibility that the Shakespeare parallels in *Forbidden Planet* were deliberately evoked, simply not publicly acknowledged, cannot, of course, be wholly discounted. Indeed, in 1975, nineteen years after the film's release, Irving Block, who had co-written the story upon which the screenplay was based, emerged from the shadows to tell *Cinéfantastique* that it had been he who had 'suggested they use Shakespeare's *The Tempest* as a premise on which to build the science fiction story'.[19] This may well have been the case. It was certainly a claim that was beyond dispute as made in 1975 since no other key players in the production (co-writer Allen Adler, screenwriter Cyril Hume, director Fred McLeod Wilcox, producer Nicholas Nayfack) was by then still alive to query the account. Even being true in relation to the original story, however, need not make it automatically true also for the film. Indeed, the movie narrative was sufficiently adjusted from the original story to leave space for a subsequent novel – *Forbidden Planet* by W.J. Stuart (Bantam, 1956) – to be commissioned as a movie tie-in. This narrated the story as told in the movie rather than that which had originally inspired the movie: they were not, that is, the same tale. In addition, as part of the post-release frenzy to sustain the interest and enthusiasm for the film, Will F. Jenkins was commissioned to write a summarised version of the film's narrative for the April 1956 edition of *Screen Stories*.[20] Neither of these post-release versions of the story made any allusion to Shakespeare, nor even drew the possible narrative parallels to the fore. On the contrary, the story seems, if anything, *less* discernibly Shakespearean in these published narrative accounts than it does in the film.

Until 1975 nobody associated with the production seems to have publicised a Shakespearean connection, or even to have mentioned it casually to a reporter. It may be that the narrative correspondences with *The Tempest* were generally understood as the film was in production but that nobody thought these helpful for the marketing of the film, and so they all kept quiet on the matter by strategic agreement. A more recent example of a deliberate, but initially publicly unacknowledged, literary parallel of this sort is to be found in Paramount's *Clueless* (Amy Heckerling, 1995) which withheld any reference to Jane Austen's *Emma* from its promotional materials in order not to impede its access to the teen market. In the case of *Clueless*, the lack of public acknowledgement ahead of time clearly does not indicate a lack of deliberateness in the narrative reference: it was purely a marketing strategy. Might the same be true of *Forbidden Planet*? It is possible. However, given the glamorous appeal of Mankiewicz' big-budget *Julius Caesar* (1953) which had emerged from the same studio (MGM) just three years earlier, it is difficult not to imagine that there might not have been *some* cultural kudos to be earned by a casual aside about a Shakespearean parallel in such a world at such a moment. The recent Hollywood, and even the in-house MGM, precedents for acknowledging Shakespeare as a film source would have been unlikely to have been taken as a reason to keep quiet. And even if so, keeping quiet for a further nineteen years would be a marketing strategy comfortably in excess of that which motivated Paramount's initial reticence to broadcast *Clueless*'s Jane Austen connection. It therefore remains conceivable that the lack of comment on the subject at the time indicates an innocence on the part of the production team (though not perhaps on Block's) of the narrative similarities between their film and an earlier work, however prestigious that work may be. And if the later work need not be considered an entirely *deliberate* emulation of the former, an alternative means of accounting for the parallels needs to be found.

One possible explanation for this is provided by the Jungian theory about archetypal narrative forms. Jung claimed that there is a small body of archetypal narratives which embody and so satisfy fundamental human narrative cravings. These narratives are constantly in circulation in one form or another, resurfacing repeatedly across social and temporal boundaries. By a process of unknowing transmission, they can be absorbed into a cultural awareness of the forms that stories may most pleasingly take, and so be unconsciously reworked and innocently presented as if new. An individual tale may thereby endure through constant recycling even when a particular telling of it demonstrates no conscious awareness of its affinity with, and contribution to, a wider tradition.[21] Such a theory of unknowing transmission may account for the correspondences between any or all of *Island of Lost Souls*, *Iguana*, *Forbidden Planet* and *The Tempest*. These films reproduce elements of Shakespeare's play and explore several of its themes and relationships, but without *necessarily* a conscious awareness of the illustrious dramatic tradition within which they are working.

Iguana, and most particularly *Island of Lost Souls*, may help to support the claim that *Forbidden Planet*'s relationship to *The Tempest*, though strong, need not necessarily depend upon an imputed *strategy* on the part of its producers. Stories of as fundamental and familiar a character as the one we know most commonly as *The Tempest* find representation constantly in various transmuted forms. Whether they are identified as such or not seems to depend not only upon the strength of the association, but sometimes, less predictably, upon the random accidents of critical attention.

Although the specific process of transmission of the inherited narrative tradition may not be evident in the case of *Forbidden Planet*, it seems plain to contemporary viewers that, consciously or unconsciously, the film did draw on the same story pool as *The Tempest*. What now seems plain, however, has not always been so. In the 1950s, the particular visual and cultural idioms into which the film translated the inherited narrative were sufficiently new for its Shakespearean antecedent to have been overlooked in favour of a critical absorption in its various innovative special effects. MGM's own trade advertisement for the film certainly made available a wealth of enticing, entirely non-Shakespearean material for critical comment:

> *See an electronic blaster vaporize an attacking tiger in mid-air! See an invisible demon hurl an earth man to fiery destruction! See an uninhibited beauty as she meets young earth men for the first time! See the fabulous flying saucer spaceship of 2200 AD – faster than the speed of light! See how the invisible demon smashes buildings and burns itself through steel! See Robby, the Robot, the most amazing technical genius ever devised! See two moons floating in a green sky! See the planet Altair explode into a fiery inferno! See the fabulous inventions of planet people of 2,000,000 years ago! See the thrilling romance of an earth man and a captive planet goddess! See how the final destruction of the invisible demon is accomplished! Never before on any screen! . . . Unique! Different!*[22]

It was the film's proclaimed 'unique[ness]!' and 'differen[ce]!' rather than any familiarity or derivativeness that merited comment in the early days of its release. In technological terms, the film pushed forward the barriers of what was possible in visual and acoustic film special effects in the 1950s. As 'the first sci-fi film produced for $1m',[23] it was a pioneering film. 'More Than A Year in Production!' became one of its tag-lines, to signal its high production values.[24] The generous budget and production schedule allowed the production team to experiment with daringly new effects. There was, therefore, plenty of interesting material to discuss, from the film's pioneering use of visual and aural technologies to its sexualised view of an unsocialised virgin wearing 'diamonds or a modish evening gown',[25] without critics needing to cite Shakespearean parallels to fill copy. The tone and detail of the reviews from 1956 confirm this. An example from *Screen Stories* can serve as a characteristic illustration of the enthusiasm that the film's pioneering gadgetry generated:

> By means other than positronic trans-figuration, no doubt, MGM put together the eight-foot robot which contains 2600 feet of electrical wiring. Robby's face is a series of dials and knobs which enable him to think, record, and talk. . . . An innovation in the picture to delight kids of all ages is the space jeep, a lightweight, streamlined two-seater which has amazing acceleration, no visible steering apparatus and a motor electrically controlled by a robot. . . . The space tractor is another amazing contraption, boasting an electromagnetic hoist two feet in diameter, capable of lifting a man. . . . Other examples of studio genius include a flying saucer and a 350-foot cyclorama which depicts a planet desert.[26]

It was only after the slightly dazzled interest in the film's techno-wizardry and special effects had waned that serious consideration of possible narrative parallels found the critical space, or indeed the need, to surface.

This may partially explain how *Forbidden Planet* escaped acknowledgement as a narrative parallel to *The Tempest* during the early years of its exhibition. In many ways, though, this is still an enigma. Anecdotal evidence from people who saw the film in the late 1950s and early 1960s indicates that the claim of a Shakespearean allusion in the film, once made, certainly did not jar with existing readings. It might even have confirmed, as the best ideas do, a common, although previously unformulated, impression of familiarity in the film's narrative. Nevertheless, the obviousness of the correspondence between the film and the play from *our* historical perspective renders it difficult to understand how it could have been unrecognised or ignored from an earlier one. It is perhaps this difficulty in believing that what is now widely recognised might not always have been so that has led many critics retrospectively, and misleadingly, to conjure fictional readings of the film from the 1950s in which a Shakespearean patterning was explicitly identified. The film's early reception, however, was determined by real rather than by subsequently constructed ideal spectators, and seemingly those real spectators were struck by nothing in the film sufficiently Shakespearean to merit published comment.

An enormous number of films, and narratives in other media, appear somewhere along a continuum of graduated removes from a narrative as ubiquitous as *The Tempest*. The cut-off point beyond which audiences fail either to identify the resemblance or fail to think it an interpretively useful referent varies between individual spectators and between spectating communities. *Island of Lost Souls*, however, appears as least as close to *The Tempest* on this continuum as does *Forbidden Planet*. Had *it* been picked up by an Amis figure, as *Forbidden Planet* was, at a timely moment, it might similarly have received considerable attention as a *Tempest* movie. Since it already had an obvious literary derivation in Wells' novel, however, no one felt the same need to seek out a source narrative beyond that. Thanks to the random accidents of critical attention, *Island of Lost Souls* thus escaped the centripetal process by which some popular texts receive a form of establishment validation by being read in the light of classical precedents.

The reconstruction post-production of popular texts as 'versions' of classics testifies both to a need to criticise by cited comparison, and to a more specific desire to honour a modern work by drawing it into relationship with an older one already established as canonical. It may be that through the 1960s and 1970s *Forbidden Planet* was recognised as suitable material to feed such an establishment critical urge to invest popular cultural texts with a cultural validity by attaching them to a venerable tradition. The locations of cultural validity are, however, increasingly fluid and popular texts are now a legitimate area of serious enquiry in their own right, independent of any claim to a connection with a text of established 'high' culture. In this more egalitarian climate, attributing an intention to mimic a classic to a popular text may no longer automatically be taken as enhancing its value.

MEN OF RESPECT (WILLIAM REILLY, 1991)

If the precision or deliberateness of *Forbidden Planet*'s relationship to *The Tempest* is open to question, William Reilly's *Men of Respect* (1991) leaves no room for equivocation in its relationship to *Macbeth*. Through a series of direct equivalents, *Men of Respect* transplants the action of *Macbeth* to the Mafia underworld of contemporary New York, and translates the language of the play to a New York streetwise vernacular.

It was not the first time that *Macbeth* had been made the subject of an updated gangster treatment. Thirty-six years earlier Philip Yordan[27] had already staked a claim on the same territory in his screenplay for Columbia's 1955 *Joe Macbeth* (directed by Ken Hughes). Despite its give-away title and opening words lifted straight from the play ('Not in the legions of horrid hell / Can come a devil more damn'd / In evils to top Macbeth'), it was *Joe Macbeth*'s adherence to the conventions of the gangster genre rather than to Shakespeare that determined its marketing. The film's pressbook put out by Columbia suggested that exhibitors should mount a display of old gangster films in the lobby, advertising the film as the 'Most Violent Underworld Drama Ever Filmed'.[28] *Joe Macbeth*, starring Paul Douglas as Joe, Ruth Roman as his ambitious wife Lili and, surprisingly, Sid James (of 'Carry On' fame) as Banky (Banquo), made several significant changes to the *Macbeth* story. One was to amalgamate the narrative functions of Macduff and Fleance into a

Ruth/Lady Macbeth (Katherine Borowitz) makes Mike/Macbeth (John Tuturro) consider his own self-image in *Men of Respect* (1991).

Source: *Men of Respect* © 1990 Grandview Avenue Pictures, Inc., Central City Film Co. and Columbia TriStar Home Entertainment, Inc. All rights reserved. Courtesy of Columbia Pictures.

composite character called Lennie, who, having avenged his father, wife and son, effectively then commits suicide by offering himself as a target for police marksmen.

The central plot of Reilly's 1991 mobster adaptation is appreciably closer to Shakespeare in both its detail and its pacing than was Hughes' earlier gangster spin-off. It is, however, clearly indebted to the earlier film not only in its central conception but also in some of its adjusted character names (Duffy for Macduff, Banky for Banquo, Rossi for Ross). It tells the story of Mike Battaglia (John Turturro),[29] a trigger-happy Mafia foot soldier. In accordance with a prophecy delivered by some eccentric down-and-out mystics, Battaglia is prematurely promoted to replace the Duncan-like padrino of the syndicate (Rod Steiger) whom he has himself murdered at the urgings of his wife Ruthie (Katherine Borowitz, Turturro's real-life wife). In order to secure the future of his own position he subsequently orders the death of his friend Banky Como (Dennis Farina), a good-humoured Banquo-equivalent with a penchant for cooking. Contrary to Battaglia's instructions, Banky's son Philip (David Thornton) escapes the attack. A further mystical prophecy persuades Battaglia that he is personally invulnerable, encouraging him to behave with a cavalier insouciance in relation to his fiefdom. His wife commits suicide and he is himself finally killed by Matt Duffy (Peter Broyle), out to avenge the death of his wife and son. This central *Macbeth*-imitative plot is supported by a plethora of smaller points of deliberate correspondence: the animal screech that precedes the first murder, a comedically surly porter (Stephen Wright) who takes his time to answer the knocking at the gate, Duffy's son's sassy talking, the story of a Caesarean birth as preface to the protagonist's downfall. In fact, for an adaptation that has rejected both Shakespeare's language and dramatic locale, *Men of Respect* demonstrates an unusually earnest degree of fidelity to the play, closely imitating its source both in broad sweep and in minute particulars.

Men of Respect lacks *Joe Macbeth's* perkiness in taking liberties with its source and lacks too the pervasive irony of the later black comedy *Macbeth* spin-off, *Scotland PA* (Billy Morrissette, 2001).[30] And not only does the *plot* offer a mass of Shakespearean correspondences, but large sections of the script also closely paraphrase Shakespeare's poetry (if peppered with a litany of predictable expletives to add emphatic local street colour). The film's courted proximity to the original does not, however, serve to bind the film to its source in close kinship, but rather has the self-subverting effect of throwing into relief its points of divergence. In fact, the poetry, so nearly evoked at so many points ('If it's going to get done, it'd better be done quick'; 'I've got blood on me. I'm not crying about it'; 'A little water and it's all gone. See how easy that was') tends to feel more powerfully absent than it does in a film with fewer points of correspondence. In fact, the way in which Shakespeare's language hovers nearly, but not quite said behind so much of the dialogue ('There's a gun behind every smile here'; 'Time was you shot the guy's brains out and he'd die. That was the end of it. Now he comes back at ya'; and best of all, 'Not a man of woman born can do shit to me') creates the feeling of a slickly executed improvisational rehearsal exercise. Once the actors have tried out versions of their lines in Queens' bite, as we seem to witness their doing, they might then be able to return to the cadences of Shakespeare's language refreshed in their engagements with it. The rehearsal exercise *is*, however, in this case the final performance, and the lines, often sounding like an unpolished experiment in prosaic parallelism, are only allowed to flirt in the vicinity of their far weightier Shakespearean original. When the script does allow itself to stray from Shakespeare's – for example, in the padrino's threatening and yet avuncular speech during the first banquet at the Battaglias – it can catch a tone that sounds organic to the world in which it is set. Such moments lift the film. When it then returns to something more directly imitative of Shakespeare, however, the signs of strain are once again plainly exposed. Sheila Johnston for *The Independent* rued the film's lack of 'vulgar liberties'.[31] Certainly in relationship to its script, a few more vulgar liberties might have served it well.

Although centrally riven about how to position itself in relation to its source, Reilly's film does imaginatively capture the spirit of several individual scenes from the play. The murder of Charlie D'Amico, the padrino, is one such. The nervy, breathless, fast-paced exchanges that Shakespeare scripted for Macbeth and Lady Macbeth during the night of Duncan's murder ('Did not you speak? – When? – Now – As I descended? – Ay. – Hark!' II.ii.16–18) are here captured not just in the equivalent pace of the script but also, crucially, in the shooting style. A shaky handheld camera flits nervously in a single take from Mike's hands in a basin, up to his face, across to his image in a bathroom mirror, down to his blood-drenched t-shirt, back up to his face and then jumps discernibly when a sudden noise off-camera signals someone else (Ruthie) entering the bathroom.[32] Still in the same restless shot, the camera then careers wildly between them, down to the basin to witness blood being rinsed from hands and across to the bath where blood is seen flowing out of clothes. Although everything Ruthie says attempts to keep panic at bay, the camera's crazed jitteriness undermines the effect of her words. Its erratic and uneasy restlessness destabilises the articulated assurances that all will be well and deprives the spectator of the sense that there can be any security in this world. In attuning itself to what characters might be feeling rather than to what they say, the shooting style graphically illustrates the scene's emotional truth, in direct contention with its surface rhetoric. It is noticeable that later in the film, when Mike and Ruthie visibly fall apart, the camera loses some of the edgy angst of the handheld look and tends towards a more measured shooting style. Characters now blatantly advertise their own lack of poise, Mike chewing the scenery in his Wellesian peeling cellarage, Ruthie dropping her *femme fatale* granite control as she sleepwalks around the courtyard in a pair of fancy pyjamas. In the final third of the film (until the Mike–Duffy shoot-out), the camera can spend more time simply recording the characters' manifestation of their own troubled disorder rather than needing to interpose itself to find stylistic expression for that underlying disorder.

Men of Respect is set in a *noir*-esque universe. The film's *noir* aesthetics and the supporting iconography of the *femme fatale* with which Borowitz' Ruthie is invested reference a set of well-established generic conventions. Unlike in Welles' *Othello* (1952), however, here the *noir* connotations determine not just the style of the depiction (for example, artificially high contrast lighting and lacerating shadows from venetian blinds falling on troubled characters), but also the urban, vice-ridden cynicism and moral messiness of the entirety of the world depicted. Stylistic convention is here generically of a piece with the mindset of the *noir* universe.

In discussing setting his adaptation of *Macbeth* in New York's criminal underworld, Reilly said: 'It seemed the perfect environment. The play itself is about treachery and deceit and the dark side of human nature and ambition.

All those elements are in full force in the underworld.'[33] Setting an adaptation of *Macbeth* in an underground world of *noir*, however, implies a different relationship of the protagonist to his environment from that usually encountered in *Macbeth*. Shakespeare's medieval Scotland is no prissy world of innocents. Nevertheless, in the Shakespeare play, there is a sense of a community beyond Macbeth that, though weak for a period, does not subscribe to systematic violence as the obvious route for achieving all ends. It is a world that can legitimately be outraged by the behaviour of its king and can grieve to see Scotland become a territory 'where violent sorrow seems / A modern ecstasy' (IV.iii.169–170) and where 'good men's lives / Expire before the flowers in their caps' (IV.iii.171–172).

It is against the background of, and in contradistinction to, such a world that Macbeth's reign of horror is dramatically defined. Although the world of *Men of Respect* lives to its own code of allegiance and honour, as one of its central principles it sets itself beyond the law. *All* members of the syndicate (and all characters in the film) therefore subscribe to the efficacy of violence as the means of furthering individual and collective interests. Against this world, Turturro's Battaglia can stand out not in kind but only in degree: he is bloodier than they, less scrupulous than they and more successful in his ambition than they, but not of a different order of being. Those working for Mal (Malcolm – Stanley Tucci) and for the overthrow of Battaglia are as capable of playing dirty and playing bloody as he is: it simply takes them a while to establish a rival power base that enables them to do so. Once they have rallied their forces, they dump the body of Battaglia's trusted henchman on his doorstep and ambush his deserters. The unscrupulous exercise of force is in the culture. The world of *Men of Respect* is so well versed in acts of wanton violence that the Battaglias' behaviour does not seem as dramatically disruptive of the normal codes as the Macbeths' does in theirs. The film's title (as opposed to Shakespeare's) implies a desire on the part of the film to be about a world and its behavioural code more than simply about an individual adrift from that code. The final scene in which Philip (the film's Fleance) undergoes the same initiation rite into the brotherhood of the 'Men of Respect' that we saw Battaglia undergo near the beginning of the film specifically makes that case, broadening the implications of Battaglia's story. The little smile that plays on Philip's lips as he is sworn in suggests that the cycle of ambition and violent usurpation is set to be replayed. Philip, like Battaglia before him, aspires to fulfil the prophecy made about him: the implication is that Mal's reign as padrino will be no more secure than was his father's. Using Fleance (or his proxy) to destabilise the security of the ending is not a new piece of interpretive business.[34] In this film, however, the suggestion that opportunity could make a Battaglia out of any one of these mobsters carries particular force: the *noir* context muddies them all.

Men of Respect's January 1991 moment of release did it few favours. As a gangster film it was inevitably judged against the elegant control of Scorsese's *Goodfellas* (released September 1990) and the considerable pedigree of Coppola's *Godfather III* (released December 1990). The mean streets of New York had rarely been so cinematically crowded and, in such weighty company, first-time director Reilly was unsurprisingly found wanting. Although *Men of Respect* suffers in the comparison with the work of Scorsese and Coppola, the film nevertheless has moments of stylish intelligence – particularly in its brilliantly nervy depiction of the night of the first murder. As a performance interpretation of *Macbeth*, however, it morphed the central character into a different being. In the world of Shakespeare's *Macbeth*, others may be morally innocent but it is Macbeth who is dramatically sympathetic. In the world of *Men of Respect*, nobody is either innocent or sympathetic. Since Battaglia does not soliloquise, and since little compensatory intimacy is offered in the place of the soliloquy, we are given minimal access to a touching honesty, or self-contempt, or sense of awareness of his own isolation that might make him less odious and more accessible to sympathy. In place of Macbeth's unsparing examination of the purposelessness of lived experience, from Battaglia we see only increasingly psychotic behaviour. The film, therefore, plays host to an odd mixture of faithfully transcribed imitative Shakespearean details from the play, and a central character who is more observable than knowable.

Men of Respect's painstakingly recreated details from *Macbeth* draw the play firmly into the interpretive frame as a narrative and poetic backdrop for its own contemporary drama. Reilly's drama is directly played out; Shakespeare's constantly evoked as an absence. The distance between the two is established not only by the absence of the poetry, but also by the film's transformation of the central premises which drive the play. Gone is an intimate engagement with Macbeth, and gone too the sense of a world which can still be scarred by the despotic reign of a tyrant. The metaphysical forces behind human affairs are tempered by being rendered vaguely comic, and any grandeur of action or character is punctured by both language and context. In making the drama more or less plausible in a contemporary, realistic context, the film tamed the play's account of humanity's attempt to account for itself in a universe of mysteries and rendered it bathetic.

O (TIM BLAKE NELSON, 2001)

Bathos is not just the almost inevitable result of rethinking the tragedies in a contemporary setting but is often the deliberate goal in doing so. The project frequently becomes to remove the story from the world of dukes, monarchs and generals and to contain the extent of its implications in order to make its points of connection to the world of its audience more immediately appreci-able. The psychology of the relationships, abstracted as they now are from too elevated a plane of action, may then be examined as they play out in a more localised, and often more accessible, milieu. Shakespearean comedies, play-ing from a lower social base and typically invested with more knockabout resilience, often fare better in such a translation. The tragedies are potentially more brittle, and less forgiving of such roguish interference. *Ten Things I Hate About You* (Gil Junger, 1999), a teen adaptation of *The Taming of the Shrew*, therefore starts with a public relations advantage over *O*, Tim Blake Nelson's teen adaptation of *Othello*. In terms of the weighty dignity of the original, if not of the potential complexity of the material, there is less at stake.

O updates the action of *Othello* to a present-day waspish private southern American high school whose one black student is also the star of the basketball team and hero of the school. War against the Turks is therefore converted into competitive sport against other schools, and Othello the warrior hero becomes Odin ('O') James (Mekhi Phifer) a champion slam-dunker. Desdemona is reimagined as Desi Brable (Julia Stiles),[35] the daughter of the Dean. Iago becomes Hugo (Josh Hartnett), the 'utility man' backbone of the basketball team who feels that his efforts are always overlooked in favour of those of Michael Cassio (Andrew Keegan). In a non-Shakespearean interpolation, Hugo's father (Martin Sheen) coaches the basketball team, and the warmth of his affection for O (whom he loves 'like my own son') is inevitably resented by Hugo, who feels he has to compete even for the attention of his own father. Except for a few motivational shimmies such as the jealousy about paternal affection, the film keeps closely in step with its source (including the business with the handkerchief and the scene of choreographed eaves-dropping). Like *Men of Respect*, therefore, *O* shadows the plot of its Shakespearean precursor. Unlike *Men of Respect*, however, it very rarely tries to echo Shakespearean language with any precision, preferring a vernacular more consistently organic to its world.

O had a troubled passage towards the screen. Dimension Films, a division of Miramax, had first scheduled it for release in the US on 17 October 1999. The release was postponed, and after a succession of further advertised release dates over the following two years, each of which was reneged upon in turn, the film finally made it on to American screens on 31 August 2001.[36] Circumstances beyond the film itself had conspired to turn *O* into a topical hot potato in post-production, its new-found pertinence proving to be an impediment to its release. While the film was still in post-production there had been talk of releasing it at a moment calculated to give it the best chance of being considered for the 2000 Academy Awards.[37] While controversy *can* translate into good box office, for a film that was at that stage being groomed for glory, it seems to have been thought desirable to protect it from an adverse media storm. In fact, the film might not have been exhibited at all had not Lion Gate Films bought it up in an eleventh-hour rescue deal that saved Miramax the embarrassment of keeping it on the shelf any longer.

It was the final moments of the film that had secured its controversial topicality. These depict a confused mêlée of emergency service vehicles, stunned and weeping teenagers, journalists and film crews amassed outside a high school where there has just been a clutch of fatal shootings. At the centre of the drama is Hugo, a sad, damaged teenager quietly proud of the mayhem he has caused and the attention – even, if need be, judicial attention – he will now receive as a result. In the period between production and release, this scene took on a heightened relevance for American society. The fatal shootings at Columbine High School Colorado in April 1999, at Deming Middle School New Mexico in November 1999, at Buell Elementary School Michigan in February 2000 and at Santana High School California in March 2001 left an American public traumatised. In the wake of each tragedy there was an onslaught of media analysis both about behaviourally disturbed young people and about their ready access to guns. Against such a background, the scene of high school carnage and the subsequent human and institutional turmoil at the end of O had become uncomfortably reminiscent of scenes from recent television news reports – or, as Eric Gitter, O's producer put it, those television reports had become reminscent of footage from the film.[38]

It was not the first time that the release of an *Othello* film had intersected more closely than anticipated with a contemporary media frenzy. Oliver Parker's *Othello* had opened in the United States on 15 December 1995. As played at such a moment, it could not but take on a particular topical resonance. Another story composed of the same essential narrative ingredients had until very recently enthralled the United States (and the world beyond) as it played out under the spotlight of saturation media coverge. The verdict at the trial of the black American football player, O.J. Simpson, accused of murdering his white ex-wife, had been delivered on 3 October 1995 after almost nine months of testimony.[39] The political and emotional fall-out from what became known as 'the trial of the century' was still being felt as Parker's *Othello* took to the screens. The points of intersection between the two stories were difficult to avoid. In both, the central protagonist was a black man celebrated by white society for his heroic performances in a masculine, combative endeavour (soldiery/football). Each had married a white woman (Desdemona/Nicole Brown), attracting a blaze of publicity in the process, and each had subsequently suspected her of having a sexual relationship with a white man (Michael Cassio/Ronald Goldman). After the murder, each displayed self-dramatising suicidal tendencies: Othello delivers a dramatic speech of self-exoneration before his public, choreographed suicide, and Simpson had, it seems, written a suicide note before being shown on live television holding a gun to his own head on a Los Angeles freeway. In an uncanny echo of Othello's self-portrait as 'one that lov'd not wisely, but too well' (V.ii.345), Simpson's suicide note included the claim that 'If [Nicole and I] had a problem, it's because I loved her so much'. The sentiment was reiterated later in the note: 'I loved her; make that clear to everyone.'[40] His 'make that clear to everyone' exhibits the same concern for how he will be remembered after his death that motivates Othello's comparably insistent 'set you down this' (v.ii.352) in his final speech. Neither, it seems, could contemplate suicide without having first scripted a romanticised version of his own history and stipulated that its central tenets be 'ma[d]e . . . clear to everyone', or 'set down' as authoritative.

Parker's *Othello*'s late 1995 release ensured that in its American reception, it was overwritten by the O.J. story. Roger Ebert in the *Chicago Sun-Times* saw 'the fates of O.J. and Nicole Simpson projected like a scrim on top of the screen' when he watched the film; John Dargie in the *L.A. Weekly* asked 'Why . . . is there something so creepy and so very O.J. in the initial love scene between Othello and Desdemona?' and Joe Baltake claimed that the film offered 'the O.J. trial transported to sixteenth-century Venice'.[41] The film, intriguingly ambushed by a narrative from the extra-cinematic world, had been turned into a palimpsest on which were inscribed both its own intended Shakespearean story and a related, though accidentally acquired, contemporary narrative.

The influence of Simpson upon the film may even have been reciprocated. The re-energised debate about Simpson that the film provoked helped to confirm Simpson's own sense of himself in the role in which he had been cast. In conversation with Celia Farber in 1997 Simpson's repeated testimony of love for Nicole now became a curiously unguarded speculation about what, hypothetically, his motivation would have been if he *had* murdered her: 'Let's say I committed this crime. Even if I did do this, it would have to be because I loved her very much, right?'[42] In his suicide note in 1994, the Othello resonances had almost certainly been purely coincidental. In the intervening three years, however, the Shakespearean echoes in both Simpson's story and language of expression had become a matter of considerable public comment. It is therefore difficult to imagine that by 1997 Simpson's occupation of the Shakespearean role allotted him was not now at least semi-conscious. The implication that a murder – even a hypothetical murder – could be justified specifically on the grounds of having loved someone 'very much' resummoned Othello's justification of *his* actions, made over the body of Desdemona, specifically on the grounds of having loved her 'too well'. Rather than shaking free of the parallel, deliberately or otherwise Simpson seemed to be reinvoking it.

It was a more disruptive and potentially damaging version of this same process of fusion and confusion between a cinematic narrative and a real-life story that Dimension presumably feared might happen to *O* if they mistimed its release. Their anxiety was that in the wake of the Columbine and subsequently the Santana High School shootings, the movie might touch a raw nerve and be received as a lurid revisiting, and perhaps even glorification, of teenage gun crime.

In Parker's *Othello*, some of the host of fears and prejudices unleashed by the O.J. affair were given a site on which they could be remediated and examined at a useful symbolic remove through the distancing filter of a Shakespearean narrative. The prevalence of emotive questions relating to teenage gun crime (and teenage drug use) as the backdrop for the release of *O* gave it the opportunity to operate in comparable ways. Playing host as it does to the oppositional encounter of a grand Shakespearean narrative with a banalised contemporary setting enabled it to perform a correspondingly dual role. As a high school drama the film speaks from a world recognisable to its audience and drawing upon its concerns – teenage insecurities, teenage violence, teenage drug use, interracial relationships. As an allusion to a Shakespearean narrative, it also transcends that world and references by association a set of far grander concerns – the identity and insecurities of nation-states, the cultural indeterminacies of territories and individuals, the cultural construction of notions of the monstrous. Engaging in the stuff of its contemporary world, the film invites the direct inscription of topical concerns upon it. However, pointing to a world beyond itself also allows the film to function as an arena in which the topical could be considered from within the safely *other* territory of a Shakespearean tale. That is, if the film felt immediately relevant to extra-cinematic life when viewed, it could upon post-flicks reflection be reclassified as 'Shakespearean' and therefore to some extent removed from the more worrying world of actualities.

Even without the availability of this distancing filter, however, the nature of the film renders it difficult to make sense of the twitchiness it generated pre-release.[43] Nelson, the director, suggested in interview that its delayed release could be accounted for by the fact that it had fallen victim to the media's 'facile rhetoric' about violence.[44] Certainly, the film seems to offer a catalogue of means to contextualise teenage gun crime and drug use morally, pitting it *against* achievement, *against* justice and even finally *against* cool.[45]

The voice-over narrative of Hugo as he is driven away at the end of the film is not the victory speech of a seductively glamorous anti-hero, but rather the hollowly articulated delusions of a needy child. The media-hungry cries for attention of the transparently pitiable Suzanne Stone (Nicole Kidman) in Gus Van Sant's *To Die For* (1995) are detectable in his final speech. It would, therefore, be a stretch to see the film as celebrating the devastation Hugo has caused. The teenification of the story diminishes all the characters (except perhaps for Desi, whose instinctively feminist will to protect herself from humiliation makes her considerably more feisty than her Shakespearean counterpart). It is, however, Iago whose dimensions suffer most in the translation. An adult Iago who can outwit and outmanoeuvre those around him, and whose motive for wanting to do so is curiously, frustratingly opaque, can elicit a combination of admiration and fear. The response that a teenage Iago whose specified motive is clearly appreciable (feeling unloved by his own father) is most calculated to elicit, by contrast, is a pitying sympathy for his vulnerability and attendant psychosis. Josh Hartnett's summary judgement on his own character was that 'He's missing a lot of love.'[46] Hugo may be slick and clever in his dastardly schemes, but his youth and transparent neediness invite a pitying concern that would be unthinkable in relation to Shakespeare's Iago, whose villainy is too persuasive, and too appealing perhaps, for us to *want* it to be amenable to redemption.

The thorough demystification of the causes of Hugo's hate is symptomatic of the clarification of motives in most Shakespearean updates.[47] In O, not only is Hugo's motivation rendered transparent, but the extravagant turn in O's behaviour in the latter stages of the film is also given a concrete explanation, in this case by his being on a drug-induced high. In the film's squeamishness about having O reach a murderously excessive frame of mind without artificial stimulus, it presents a character who is clearly not Othello.

In fact, the film even satirises an audience's expectations that O *could* be Othello. When in bed with Desi, her fingers (and the camera with her) seek out and caress a deep scar on his back. The camera's careful attention to the scar teasingly prepares its Shakespeare-aware audience for the exotic tale and the rhetorical flourish to come. It was, after all, with extravagant stories about the heroic 'dangers [he] had pass'd' (I.iii.168) that Othello wooed Desdemona. As if to confirm the association, and to add to the anticipatory drum-roll, Desi says of O, 'You do have the best stories'. The tale as related here turns out to be one of underprivilege and of having to bear the marks of underprivilege: O reports that he was born by caesarean section and because his 'Mom couldn't afford a good doctor', the knife cut him deeply in the womb. Seeing that Desi, the child of a privileged home, has been caught by the romantic allure of this tale of a humble background, O laughs and corrects his own story. He had been toying with her: actually, it transpires, the scar is simply the result of a skate-boarding accident. The flirtation with a glamorously deprived and yarn-spinning hero who has risen to glory from unpromising beginnings gives way to the bathos of his self-revelation as simply another all-American kid. Half offering a tale that is then revoked to be replaced by something more prosaic in this way both satirises the play's explicit celebration of Othello's rhetoric and simultaneously asserts the film's own rejection of a claim to an elevated register. The scene of the variant accounts of the scar is delicately handled in a pleasingly offhand manner. Nevertheless, in hinting at a direction in which it might have gone but then decisively and humorously renounces, the scene epitomises the film's own broader processes. The film as a whole, like O's account of how he came by his scar, alludes to a grander narrative only to snatch it away and replace it with something less articulate and more mundane. Having had two histories about its origins related, the scar becomes partially defined by the history *not* its own as well as by the literal version of how it came to be. And just as the scar subsequently becomes both that from a skate-boarding accident and simultaneously *not* that from a back-street surgeon's knife, so the film itself is defined both in terms in what it is and in terms of what it is not. Like any adaptation, it is indelibly inscribed with its point of departure, with the thing it is not.

The film's self-definition as 'not *Othello*' is microcosmically insisted upon in O's self-definition as himself not Othello. His name, Odin James (a further reinvocation of OJ) most specifically references Odin, the Norse god of war and poetry. War and poetry, significant forces in Othello's life, are significant absences in Odin's. The vigorously contested basketball matches are his substitute for war, and American teenspeak his substitute for poetry. His name Odin is, therefore, partly the tokenist compensation for key points of omission and substitution in the film. Having his used name, and the title of the film, as 'O' also combines the salacious associations of Pauline Réage's de Sadian and sexually violent *Story of O*[48] and the theatrical history of Shake-speare's Globe as 'wooden O' (*Henry V* Prologue Chorus). The film positions itself at the intersection between sexual scandal and an eminent theatrical history, its title pointing simultaneously in both directions. The Globe's sobriquet derives from its shape. The film's architecture, by contrast, seems to be a territory in which O's name can find repeatedly insistent expression. The sweeping ovals of the stairwell and gallery at which the camera gazes up intermittently throughout the film prominently display the imprinted no-menclature. The angle of the shot makes it difficult to decode the on-screen image immediately as a stairwell: what it indisputably is, however, is a large O. Time and again his name announces itself as part of the fabric of his world. Spectators at the basketball games hold up thin balloons twisted into the shape of an O as their small-scale tribute, and even the camera wants to participate in the hymning of him, itself swirling in clearly defined circles, describing his name. O's name is not only imprinted upon his environment, but is expressed in the very texture of the film.

The losses incurred in translating *Othello* into a contemporary American high school movie are probably generically greater than those incurred by appropriating *The Taming of the Shrew* in a similar cause. Nevertheless, the film's scrupulous and unabashed documenting of those losses in its nimble advertisement of the ways in which O is not Othello helps the film to establish its own territory and so sidestep much purely comparative criticism. Moreover, in the central conceit of its title in combination with its concomitant shooting style, it stands as a benchmark for other adaptations, for in this film a theatrical and wooden O has been formally displaced by a thoroughly cinematic one.

FURTHER READING

Richard Burt, *Unspeakable ShaXXXspeares: Queer Theory and American Kiddie Culture* (London: Macmillan, 1998).

Richard Burt, *Shakespeare after Mass Media* (New York and Basingstoke: Palgrave, 2002).

Ruby Cohn, *Modern Shakespeare Offshoots* (Princeton, NJ: Princeton University Press, 1976).

Christy Desmet, 'Introduction', in Christy Desmet and Robert Sawyer (eds), *Shakespeare and Appropriation* (London and New York: Routledge, 1999), pp.1–12.

Tony Howard, 'Shakespeare's Cinematic Offshoots', Chapter 17 in Russell Jackson (ed.), *The Cambridge Companion to Shakespeare on Film* (Cambridge: Cambridge University Press, 2000), pp.295–313.

Douglas Lanier, *Shakespeare and Modern Popular Culture* (Oxford, Oxford University Press, 2002).

Robert F. Willson, Jr, 'The Selling of *Joe Macbeth*', *Shakespeare on Film Newsletter* 7, 1 (December 1982), pp.1, 4.

NOTES

1. Hector Berlioz, letter to Joseph-Louis Duc, 1846, trans. David Cairns. Quoted in John Gross (ed.), *After Shakespeare* (Oxford: Oxford University Press, 2002), p.295.

2. Brian McFarlane, 'A Literary Cinema? British Films and British Novels', in Charles Barr (ed.), *All Our Yesterdays* (London: BFI, in association with the Museum of Modern Art, New York, 1986), pp.120–1.

3. Henry James, writing in 1907, and quoted by E.P. Kuhl in 'Shakespeare and the Founders of America: *The Tempest*', *Philological Quarterly* 41, 1 (January, 1962), p.142.

4. Jack Williamson, *H.G. Wells: Critic of Progress* (Baltimore, MD: Mirage Press, 1973), p.78.

5. H.G. Wells, *The Island of Dr. Moreau* (Harmondsworth: Penguin, 1962), p.109. (Hereafter Wells.)

6. Wells, p.112.

7. Wells, p.86.

8. There have been two subsequent films made of Wells' novel: *The Island of Dr. Moreau* (Don Taylor, 1977) starring Burt Lancaster and Michael York and *The Island of Dr. Moreau* (Richard Stanley and John Frankenheimer, 1996) starring Marlon Brando and Val Kilmer. The parallels with *The Tempest* are no further enhanced in these films.

9. Wells, p.118. Other changes in the direction of *The Tempest* included giving the beast-men the opportunity, Caliban fashion, to express directly to their creator their resentment about the 'pains' that had been taken over them.

10. In the original draft of the filmscript Altaira's virginity was emphasised by some considerable discussion of the myth of the unicorn and the virgin. This was cut in shooting. See the unpublished continuity script, deposited for copyright purposes in the Motion Picture Division Reading Room of the Library of Congress (hereafter LOC): call no. LP6177. 26B.

11. The monster makes a brief appearance in the film, dragged out of invisibility by being caught in the cross-beams of the visiting spaceship's perimeter fence. It was produced in a special animated sequence by a tense collaboration between Arthur Lonergan, art director to the film, and Joshua Meador, on loan from Walt Disney.

12. F.R., *New York Times*, 6 March 1956. On file in the LOC.

13. *Monthly Film Bulletin* 23 (June 1956), p.71, and an unreferenced review clip on file in the LOC.

14. Bosley Crowther, *New York Times*, 4 May 1956. On file in the LOC.

15. Kingsley Amis, *New Maps of Hell* (London: Gollancz, 1961), pp.29–30. *New Maps of Hell* was originally delivered as a series of lectures at Princeton University in 1959.

16. Douglas Brode, *Films of the Fifties* (New York: Carol Publishing Group, 1976), p.183.

17. James Robert Parish and Michael R. Pitts, *The Great Science Fiction Picture* (Metuchen, NJ: Scarecrow, 1977), p.137.

18. Philip Strick, 'Space Invaders', in Ann Lloyd (ed.), *Movies of the Fifties* (London: Orbis, 1982), p.34.

19. Steve Rubin, 'Retrospect: *Forbidden Planet*', *Cinéfantastique* 4, 1 (Spring 1975), p.7.

20. Will F. Jenkins, 'Forbidden Planet', *Screen Stories* 55, 4 (April 1956), pp.40–1, 60–3.

21. See C.G. Jung, *The Archetypes and the Collective Unconscious*, 2nd edn (London: Routledge, 1968), and especially *Civilization in Transition*, 2nd edn (London: Routledge, 1970), para. 847.

22. *Motion Picture Herald*, 10 March 1956. On file in the LOC.

23. Jay Robert Nash and Stanley Ralph Ross, *The Motion Picture Guide* (Chicago: Cinebooks, 1986), vol. III, p.899.

24. See, for example, the whole-page MGM advertisement for *Forbidden Planet* in *Screen Stories* 55, 4 (April, 1956), p.3.

25. Ibid.

26. Ibid., p.62.

27. Among Yordan's many other filmscripts is included the *King Lear* spin-off *Broken Lance* (Edward Dmytryk, 1954).

28. See Robert F. Willson, Jr, 'The Selling of *Joe Macbeth*', *Shakespeare on Film Newsletter* 7, 1 (December 1982), p.4.

29. Turturro was at that stage known for his gritty stage work as well as his roles in *Miller's Crossing* (Coen Brothers, 1990) and *Barton Fink* (Coen brothers, 1991).

30. *Scotland PA* (Billy Morrissette, 2001) wryly relocates the principal action to a fast-food restaurant ('Duncan's', subsequently renamed 'Mcbeth's' (*sic*)) in an unpromising backwater of rural Pennsylvania in the early 1970s.

31. Sheila Johnston, *Independent*, 28 February 1992, p.18.

32. *Men of Respect*'s director of photography was Bobby Bukowski. Many of the film's triumphs are his.

33. Columbia Pictures Production Information, viewed on microfiche (as 'Pressbook') at the British Film Institute.

34. See, for example, the omen-laden close-up on Fleance (Alistair Henderson) at the end of the BBC/TimeLife *Macbeth* (Jack Gold, 1982).

35. *O* was the first Shakespeare adaptation in which Stiles appeared (although not the first released). After making *O*, Stiles also played 'Kat' in *Ten Things I Hate About You* (Gil Junger, 1999) and Ophelia in *Hamlet* (Almereyda, 2000). *O*'s director, Tim Blake Nelson, appeared as the flight captain in Almereyda's *Hamlet*.

36. The film was released in Britain on 13 September 2002. On the subject of the film's delayed release, see Rebecca Traister, 'The Story of O, Weinstein Style: High-School *Othello* Is Held Up', *New York Observer*, 13 November 2000, p.1, and Sharon Waxman, 'Studio Keeps a Lid on "O" After School Shootings', *Washington Post*, Saturday 10 March 2001, p.C01.

37. See Traister (2000), p.1.

38. Nelson reports that Gitter called him in the editing room on the day of the Columbine High School shooting and said, 'Have you turned on the news? It feels exactly like our footage.' Quoted by Traister (2000), p.1.

39. Barbara Hodgdon has deftly enumerated some of the parallels that may be drawn between Shakespeare's Othello and O.J. Simpson as part of her rich consideration of representations of blackness in productions of *Othello*. See Barbara Hodgdon, 'Race-ing *Othello*, Re-engendering White-out', in Lynda E. Boose and Richard Burt (eds), *Shakespeare the Movie* (London and New York: Routledge, 1997), pp.23–44. See also Ellis Cose, 'Caught Between Two Worlds: Why Simpson Couldn't Overcome the Barriers of Race', *Newsweek*, 11 July 1994, p.28.

40. The suicide note was read at a news conference on behalf of Simpson on 17 June 1994 and reprinted the following day in the American dailies. See, for example, *New York Times*, 18 June 1994, late edition.

41. Roger Ebert, *Chicago Sun-Times*, 29 December 1995. John Dargie, *LA Weekly* review, 27 December 1995. Dargie is quoted in Lynda E. Boose and Richard Burt, 'Totally Clueless?: Shakespeare Goes Hollywood in the 1990s', in L.E. Boose and R. Burt (eds), *Shakespeare the Movie: Popularizing the Plays on Film, TV and Video* (London and New York: Routledge, 1997), p.15. Joe Baltake, 'Pared-down "Othello": Is It Really O.J.'s Tale?', *The Sacramento Bee's MovieClub*, 29 December 1995, available online at: http://www.movieclub.com/reviews/archives/95othello/othello.html. The parallel has spawned its own more explicit dramas too. Maarten van Hinte's play (from John Leerdam's idea) *O.J. Othello* had its UK première in the Observer Assembly Ballroom at the Edinburgh Fringe in August 1998.

42. His conversations with Celia Farber, which took place over several months during the summer and autumn of 1997, were published as a question-and-answer interview under the title 'Whistling in the Dark' in *Esquire* magazine, February 1998, p.54. The line 'if I did do this, it would have to be because I loved her very much, right?' became the subject of much comment at the time.

43. There was some suggestion that Miramax's co-chairman Harvey Weinstein's public support for Al Gore and Joe Lieberman's campaign for more regulation in Hollywood may have proved an unhelpful impediment in the film's trajectory towards the screen. Harvey Weinstein, whose areas of personal responsibility did not specifically incorporate Dimension Films, has denied any personal involvement in decisions about the film's release.

44. Quoted by Traister (2000), p.1.

45. Despite its hip soundtrack and cool casting from the Hollywood teen pack, it is not a film riven in its attitude towards the violence (or the drugs) it presents. As first conceived, the film was yet more explicit in its distaste for the drugs it includes. The black drug-dealer Del's speech about black dependency on white money and the insidious relationship of drugs to dependency of all sorts (a scene included as an extra on the region one DVD) was cut in post-production. Even without this speech, however, the film is not morally neutral on the subject.

46. Hartnett interview on region one DVD.

47. The most blatant example of the delineation of a clear motivation to explain that which was more ambiguous in a Shakespeare play is the introduction of the incest theme in Jane Smiley's novel *A Thousand Acres* and in Jocelyn Moorhouse's 1997 film adaptation of the novel. The Goneril and Reagan figures in that retelling of the *Lear* tale are capable of being vicious specifically because they have been sexually abused in childhood. In Shakespeare, no cause is offered to account for their spite.

48. Unlike the O of *The Story of O*, however, who is the victim of sexual violence – if in time a willing victim – Mekhi Phifer's O is the perpetrator of a sexually violent act in the film.

PART II

Moment and Context:

How History Works on Story

In 1954, Paul Dehn wrote:

> *I suppose I have seen about eleven Shakespearean films and I find that if I put them in the right order, about as little emerges in the way of profitable conclusion as would emerge from a row of historically juxtaposed beans.*[1]

It is the contention of Part II that thinking about the chronology of Shakespeare films yields considerably more interesting results than Dehn's allusion to 'a row of historically juxtaposed beans' might suggest. Any classic work continues to accumulate new meanings as it is freshly encoded and decoded in succesive generations, a process Yuri Lotman has referred to as 'the complex . . . ability of an artistic text to amass information'.[2] The nature of the 'information' amassed in the text will inevitably vary depending on the moment at which it is examined.

The four chapters of Part II explore a range of ways in which film texts emerge from, are expressive of and engage with the priorities and predispositions of their own production moment. Considering how the dramatic material of *A Midsummer Night's Dream* and *The Tempest* has reinvented itself across time to suit the altered contexts of production and reception inevitably makes of each drama an illuminating signpost to the processes of cultural change. Kenneth Branagh's films play to a contemporary agenda, and themselves contribute to the aspirations of others of his moment. The films considered in the final chapter are in their own irrepressibly individual ways shot through with the ironic self-awareness that has characterised the intellectual and cultural climate of the 1990s and early 2000s. The set of possible relationships between a text and its contexts of production and reception is always intricate and elusive. It is one of the purposes of Part II to try to map some of those engagements.

NOTES

1. Paul Dehn, 'The Filming of Shakespeare', in John Garrett (ed.), *Talking of Shakespeare* (New York: Hodder and Stoughton, 1954), p.49.
2. Yuri Lotman, *The Structure of the Artistic Text*, trans. Gail Lenhoff and Ronald Vroon (Ann Arbor: University of Michigan Press, 1977), p.25.

CHAPTER FIVE

Historically Juxtaposed Beans (I):

A Midsummer Night's Dream on Film

A dramatic text gathers plenty of critical baggage as it bowls through history. Among its accretions is its history in performance, a cumulative history which can decisively affect the nature of the text then handed on to successive generations. From the perspective of later interpreters, the accumulated history of performance, and reception, become so inextricably identified with well-known texts that they necessarily become part of what constitutes the broader, all-encompassing 'source'.

The presence of a composite performance legacy 'in' the inherited text complicates any simple notion of a pure source and disrupts a putative line of direct, unimpeded influence from author to interpreter. Contemporary makers of a Shakespeare film therefore inherit not only the raw Shakespeare text(s) from which to develop their own performance interpretation, but also the history of earlier stage and screen performances of the same text. The influence of a text's performance history may be felt even when film-makers may not consciously be able to identify the origin and history of a specific interpretive idea, or even in some cases be aware that it need have a history that predates them. The unknowing reprise of inherited ideas is made possible by the gradual percolating of production and performance ideas through creative communities across generations in ways that can obscure and anonymise their beginnings.

This chapter and the next follow the cinema's contribution to the transmission across the century of two Shakespeare plays, *A Midsummer Night's Dream* and *The Tempest*, in order to observe the adjustments of meaning and emphasis the core tale has undergone in each case. In relation to each case study I illustrate the processes of interpretive layering, of retrospective imitation, tribute, reaction and collaborative reference, whether conscious or unconscious, at work in the films. I also suggest ways in which the historical moment and political context of particular productions have brought interpretive agenda to bear upon the inherited material, nudging it in some directions rather than others.

The films of A Midsummer Night's Dream to which I will make reference in this chapter are: the 1909 American silent Vitagraph production which took the striking step of replacing Shakespeare's Oberon with a powerful female fairy called Penelope; an almost unknown 1913 Italian silent film directed by Paulo Azzuri; the famous big budget 1935 Warner Brothers Max Reinhardt/ William Dieterle co-production starring James Cagney as Bottom and a young Mickey Rooney as Puck; Celestino Coronado's 1984 film adaptation of Lindsay Kemp and David Haughton's stage production which reinterpreted the text to a flamboyantly gay agenda; Adrian Noble's 1995 stage-inspired film with the Royal Shakespeare Company which recasts the entire action of the play as the dream of a young boy; and the 1999 Twentieth Century Fox version directed by Michael Hoffman, starring Michelle Pfeiffer, Kevin Kline, Rupert Everett and Calista Flockhart.

*

In 1866, Henry Morley wrote:

> *Every reader of Shakespeare is disposed to regard the 'Midsummer Night's Dream' as the most essentially unactable of all his plays. It is a dramatic poem of the utmost grace and delicacy; its characters are creatures of the poet's fancy that no flesh and blood can properly present – fairies who 'creep into acorn-cups,' or mortals who are but dim abstractions, persons of a dream.*[1]

The anxiety in the nineteenth century was that in production the stage might over-concretise the ethereal fairy world of the play and so destroy its delicate beauty. In 1817 William Hazlitt had lamented that when A Midsummer Night's Dream was performed, '[t]hat which was merely an airy shape, a dream, a passing thought, immediately becomes an unmanageable reality', concluding that the 'boards of a theatre' and the 'regions of fancy' were not at all the same thing.[2] Many critics felt that the very process of producing this play necessarily diluted the particularity of its charm, since 'no flesh and blood' could 'properly present' the conjurations of the imagination.

The cinema, of course, like the stage, also removes the play from the pure 'realm of fancy', converting purely imaginary forms into visible ones whose precise character is dictated by the designing fantasy of another. Unlike the stage, however, the cinema does not deal in anything so coarsely material as actual human bodies, rather itself presenting 'dim abstractions, persons of a dream'. It offers not flesh and blood but the mere projected memory of flesh and blood, a collection of insubstantial shadows flickering on a screen. Little wonder, perhaps, that the play might hold an appeal for film-makers eager to demonstrate the fluency of their medium for the evocation of the magical and the insubstantial over the more mundane stuff-in-trade of the stage. As pioneer film-makers of fantasies from Georges Méliès and Robert Paul onwards believed, form and content had the opportunity to coalesce with peculiar harmony when fluidly transmutable projected moving images rendered fluidly transmutable magical kingdoms – that is when magical moving pictures told stories explicitly about magic.

With wise-after-the event hindsight, we might even read some of the nineteenth-century stage's strivings for effects appropriate to the fairy quality of the play as part of the cumulative anticipation of the new medium that would in due course take up the baton in finding representation for Shakespearean fairies and other non-Shakespearean magical worlds. In Samuel Phelps' famous 1853 production of A *Midsummer Night's Dream* at Sadler's Wells, for example, the designer Frederick Fenton hung a green gauze across the proscenium arch in order to filter the impression of substantiality and disturb the clarity of focus with which the fairies could be seen. This, as Morley said, had the effect of 'subdu[ing] the flesh and blood' of his actors. The crude fact that real substantial actors were present in the same physical space as that occupied by the audience was nicely obfuscated.[3] Phelps' erection of a literal 'fourth wall' between actor and audience (even as here a gauzy fourth wall) made explicit the partitioning of the actors into a separate world that the audience were invited to view through the framing window of the proscenium arch. In its gauziness, the screen also constituted, in effect, a fixed lens through which the audience could view actors, a lens that both introduced a colour filter and subdued the crisp clarity of focus with which the scene could be viewed. In its effects on spatial separation, framing and focus, it testified to a desire for a new sort of relationship between actor and audience – a relationship with some correspondences to that which in due course the new medium would usher in.

VITAGRAPH'S *A MIDSUMMER NIGHT'S DREAM* (J. STUART BLACKTON AND CHARLES KENT, 1909)

That medium, once in existence, has appropriated A *Midsummer Night's Dream*, as might perhaps be expected, partly as an excuse for show-casing the special effects possible in its new dream-like kingdom of insubstantial shadows. The American Vitagraph Company, which was responsible for a string of Shakespearean adaptations before the First World War, produced the first filmed version of the play, directed by J. Stuart Blackton and Charles Kent in 1909. From the vegetation and weather conditions visible in the surviving film, it seems to have been shot in the summer. Nevertheless it did not open until 25 December 1909. Such a delay was unusual in a period in which films were typically moved through the cycle of production, distribution and exhibition with extraordinary, commercially-minded speed. The Christmas release of *A Midsummer Night's Dream* almost certainly represented a strategic deferral on the part of the company, to increase the impact of a seasonally festive, prestige film by bringing it out at a seasonally festive, holiday moment. This marketing ploy might even have been successful in maximising takings; certainly the film drew plenty of favourable critical attention through late December 1909 and early January 1910.

The trade papers particularly commended Vitagraph on the location shooting and use of natural scenery in its *Midsummer Night's Dream*. The woodland scenes, shot in the southern part of Flatbush near the old Greenwich village, are visually appealing. Attractive, well-dressed characters stumble in and out of picturesque, sunlit, cheery copses. And the film proudly vaunts its capacity to create illusions of a sort beyond the scope of the theatre. By a series of simple stop-motion sequences, for example, young Gladys Hulette's skipping, tripsy Puck appears and disappears with arresting suddenness. And when instructed to collect the magic flower, by the use of a magic wire and some careful frame composition, Puck is shown flying over a spinning globe. None of the Vitagraph Shakespeare productions had its genesis in a stage production. Rather they were all conceived as autonomous pieces of cinema. The use of outdoor locations, superimposition and other forms of trick photography were all part of the company's bid to stake a claim for the cinema as an art form distinct from, rather than dependent upon (or palely imitative of) theatre. By 1909, and in the hands of such confidently imaginative cinema producers as Vitagraph, silent Shakespeare films were no longer consistently peddling themselves as mere mute recordings of theatrical material, or of acclaimed theatrical performances. Rather, as here, they had gained sufficient confidence to offer themselves as a separate art form whose neglect of the spoken word was amply compensated for by an impressive range of other representational and performative strengths.

Although no contemporary comment upon it survives, either from Vitagraph itself or from any of its early spectators, the aspect of the film that most elicits comment now is the seemingly extraordinary decision to substitute a feminine fairy called 'Penelope' for Shakespeare's fairy king Oberon. Despite her long floaty dress, Penelope orchestrates events in the wood with all the authority of an Oberon (and may even have been titled 'Oberon' in some early prints).[4] The presence of Penelope in Oberon's place cannot help but raise a question about the relationship that is then to be inferred between Titania and Penelope. Certainly a simple intertitle stating that these two female fairies were 'friends of old' would have been sufficient to dismiss the shadow of Oberon from consideration in this respect. But the film offers no explanation for its curious substitution, and does not take any other steps to disambiguate the relationship between Titania and Penelope. Since the jealous lovers' quarrel between the two principal fairies in the wood is maintained despite the exchanged gender of one of them, it is therefore difficult entirely to avoid wondering whether a same-sex love might not be being delicately suggested in Vitagraph's version of the story. As Oberon does in the play, so here Penelope punishes Titania for her part in their quarrel by a form of sexual humiliation, offering a monstrous substitute in the form of Bottom to share her bed. And as Shakespeare's Titania does, so too this Titania is subsequently delighted to abandon the sleeping ass to be reunited with the fairy consort (here Penelope) who first caused her torment. Penelope and Titania clasp each other in delighted relief at the end of the woodland sequences, and take their final exit by walking out of frame still entwined, without removing their fixed gaze from each other's eyes.

Of course, it is possible that Vitagraph simply found itself with a superfluity of able actresses on its books in the summer of 1909 and wishing to use as many of them as possible in its latest film, created an extra role for one of its favourites. It is not known who the actress is who plays Penelope, but if Vitagraph found itself with an opportunity to cast a prominent actress for the film, it would surely have wanted to cast her in a prominent a role – a function which Oberon certainly fulfils.

But there may also have been reasons beyond the pragmatics of casting that influenced the creation of Vitagraph's 'Penelope'. Fairyland in general had been understood in the nineteenth century as a female domain. In practice this meant that not only Puck and Ariel were regularly cast as women (or girls), but from 1840 onwards, in a trend started by Madame Vestris, Oberon was too. Imitators of this particular piece of cross-gender casting included Augustin Daly in his 1895 production at Daly's Theatre and Herbert Beerbohm Tree in his famous 1900 production at Her Majesty's Theatre. The Atlantic posed little obstacle to theatrical gossip and if, for example, Julia Neilson's Oberon in Tree's 1900 production had some currency in late Victorian England, as it did, talk of this would certainly have reached the United States. Vitagraph may therefore simply have done for Oberon what Asta Nielsen and Svend Gade were subsequently to do for Hamlet (as discussed in Chapter 2). In Hamlet's case, it was as if the feminising of the role by a succession of actresses had reached a point of sufficient orthodoxy for the final little step in the feminising of the character then to be undertaken with comparative ease. Thus it was that Hamlet was tipped over from being a part suitable to *be played by* a woman to being a part that *was* a woman's. And in similar fashion, it may be that Vitagraph's decision to present Titania's lover-rival as a woman was inspired by a succession of female Oberons on the stage.

Viewed in this light, Oberon's intriguing transmutation into Penelope may be less of a dramatic leap from understandings of Oberon in the early years of the twentieth century than it might seem in the early years of the current one.

Nevertheless, watching the film now, it is difficult to imagine that those involved in the Vitagraph production would not have been conscious of the daring interpretive possibility that the presence of Penelope presented.[5] Spectators at the time may have been too wholesomely schooled or decorously blinkered to recognise or comment upon it. However, Vitagraph seems to have dramatised an idea which could itself have been lifted straight from one of Shakespeare's festive comedies, namely that patterns of attraction do not always conform to society's dominant (heterosexual) organisational principle.

LINDSAY KEMP'S *A MIDSUMMER NIGHT'S DREAM* (CELESTINO CORONADO, 1984)

After the 1909 Vitagraph production, *A Midsummer Night's Dream* inspired little further thinking on the theme in cinematic form until 1984 when Lindsay Kemp's company was to return to it with an explosion of overt gay energy. In Celestino Coronado's film adaptation of Lindsay Kemp and David Haughton's stage production, many of the design excesses of high camp are energetically embraced: excessive costuming, extravagant make-up, protracted dance routines, narrative-suspending operatic performative moments. The Kemp/Coronado film is in essence a performance art piece which incorporates song, dance, mime and the spoken word. The role of Titania is played, with considerable panache, by 'The Incredible Orlando', a drag queen, and this transgender casting invests the encounters between Titania and Oberon with a homoerotic charge. The Changeling Boy becomes explicitly an object of desire for both Titania and Oberon, and although the actor (François Testory) is clearly a young adult rather than a child, he is so delicately thin, and he plays the part with such a wide-eyed, exploitable, youthful innocence, that his highly sexualised abduction by a predatory Oberon hints disquietingly at a paedophilic dynamic to their engagements. The love juice applied by Puck in the wood causes Lysander to awake and desire Demetrius, and Hermia to awake and desire Helena. Thus Puck's sense of the arbitrariness of the pairings in the Shakespeare play ('Yet but three? Come one more, / Two of both kinds makes up four.' III.ii.337–338) here becomes the basis for a more sexually experimental joke about conservative expectations in relation to couplings. In the freedom of the woody dreamworld, 'Jack' does not just have 'Jill'. Rather both 'Jack' and 'Jill' enjoy the bisexual, experimental free-for-all that this instantiation of the wood makes possible.

The film as a whole advertises its project to invert the more conservative ways in which Shakespeare in general, and perhaps this text in particular, has been traditionally understood. It explicitly broadcasts this interest when the mechanical playing not Thisbe but, in this adaptation, Juliet (Christian Michaelson) is heard to cry 'Oemor, Oemor'. The word is as baffling to his on-screen auditors as it is to his off-screen auditors, until it transpires that he has his copy of the rehearsal text upside down and so, with a logic all and only the film's own, is calling 'Romeo', read backwards. This process of inverted reading, illustrated with a clunking literalness in Juliet's mistaken orientation of the text, is central to the whole Kemp/Coronado interpretive undertaking. Shakespeare's text is itself being turned upside down, with the result that it is persuaded to yield its campest and gayest possible meanings. In terms of the amount of sense it is able to make of the play, the result occasionally feels a little insecure. However, there *is* certainly fruitful ground within the play for a playfully experimental intervention of this kind, as is entertainingly demonstrated in the film's exaggeration of the dramatist's apparently cavalier lack of concern about which particular mortal ends up with which particular fellow so long as the overall patterning comes good. The film's indulgently heightened approach to colour, sound, design and performance makes for a strained viewing experience. Nevertheless, by its selective and exaggerated concentration on the currents of sexual ambiguity, experimentation and aggression in the play, the film does usefully draw attention to something in the play that had been absent from critical readings until the 1960s.

WARNER BROTHERS' *A MIDSUMMER NIGHT'S DREAM* (MAX REINHARDT AND WILLIAM DIETERLE, 1935)

If the idea of a same-sex love between Titania and her fairy lover, delicately and sympathetically suggested in the 1909 Vitagraph production, was taken up, regendered and exaggerated to a point of wild excess by Lindsay Kemp, a far more direct link of a commercial kind can be made from the Vitagraph film to the Warner Brothers' production of 1935. Ten years earlier, in 1925, Warner Brothers had bought up the Vitagraph studio and distribution network. In this buy-out they inherited not just the increasingly out-of-date materials and equipment of a film company now in decline, but along with them a set of aspirations to produce prestige cinema, an aspiration made explicitly manifest in Vitagraph's earlier Shakespearean, biblical and other 'high culture' productions. Warner Brothers was not a studio with a single generic allegiance. Its output in the 1930s, for example, included a series of James Cagney gangster films, the wonderfully over-the-top Busby Berkely musicals, the Errol Flynn swashbucklers and some fairly formulaic melodramas. But alongside such box-office gold mines as the gangsters and the musicals, the studio also sustained its commitment to producing the occasional prestige picture – including the biopics *The Story of Louis Pasteur* (1936) and *The Life of Emile Zola* (1937) (both directed by William Dieterle) – in the hope of raising its cultural profile by attracting a different kind of publicity. In doing so, it inadvertently flew the flag for the priorities of the far smaller company it had swallowed, the now defunct Vitagraph.

The première of the Warner Brothers' 1935 *A Midsummer Night's Dream* was telling in this regard. A more dazzling, high-profile, well-attended première could scarcely be imagined. It was as lavish as anything that glamorous Hollywood of the glamorous 1930s could offer. The studio's huge publicity machine had been swung into action to promote a film which did not make, and perhaps could not have been expected to make, a profit. But the film was evidently thought to merit the investment in a whole series of other, less easily quantifiable, terms. Its returns would come in terms of prestige for its own in-house stars and so, by association, for the studio itself, and this, it must have been hoped, would translate into box office further down the line. The film marks a significant moment in the history of Shakespeare film. For the first time, the two huge industrial going concerns of 'Shakespeare' and 'Hollywood' had forged a serious alliance. In due course both would be well served from the trade-off of cultural validity for mass appeal that their union entailed. It was not Warner Brothers, however, who would benefit from this.

The co-director of the film, the German theatre director Max Reinhardt, was no newcomer to Shakespeare, nor to this play. He had first produced *A Midsummer Night's Dream* on the German stage exactly thirty years earlier – a production which drew such plaudits for Reinhardt himself that on the basis of it he was appointed head of the Deutsches Theater in Berlin, the leading German theatre of the time. Over the next three decades, Reinhardt was to revive and adapt his *Dream* stage pageant in about fifteen different versions.[6] He worked with different designers on these productions, and as a result the wood near Athens took on a range of identities, sometimes of a more literal, sometimes a more symbolic character. A number of these productions achieved international acclaim as they toured to Salzburg, Vienna, Munich, Prague, Budapest, Stockholm, Oxford, Florence, and across America. In 1927 Reinhardt's *Dream* became the first German production ever to play on Broadway. Seven years later, in 1934, an enormous production was mounted both at the University of California at Berkeley and at the Hollywood Bowl, which 150,000 people paid to see. It was on the back of the success of this that Reinhardt then joined forces with his former pupil William Dieterle, already on the payroll at Warner Brothers, to start work on a film version.

Reinhardt's original fantasy casting for the film had included Charlie Chaplin as Bottom, Greta Garbo as Titania, Clark Gable as Demetrius, Gary

Cooper as Lysander, John Barrymore as Oberon, W.C. Fields as Flute/Thisbe, Wallace Beery as Lion, Walter Huston as Theseus, Joan Crawford as Hermia, Myrna Loy as Helena and Fred Astaire as Puck.[7] Such a cross-studio cast, had it ever been assembled, could not have but resulted in the most extraordinary film. In the event, however, none of these stars was signed, and so the Chaplin/Garbo/Astaire *Dream* sadly never came into being. Warner Brothers did, however, demonstrate its whole-hearted support for the project by giving over to it some of the biggest stars from its own stable: James Cagney as Bottom, Mickey Rooney as Puck, Dick Powell as Lysander, Joe E. Brown as Flute, Victor Jory as Oberon and, launching a new star career, Olivia de Havilland as Hermia. Thus the Warner publicity machine, with its ubiquitous marketing slogan for the film 'A Dream Come True', had plenty of stardom to peddle as the sweetener for a little Shakespeare.

Notwithstanding its slight commercial link to the Vitagraph lost empire, the Warner Brothers' *Dream* has more in common with a 1913 Italian silent film of the play directed by Paulo Azzuri than it does with its predecessor American production.[8] And it is, of course, perfectly possible that Reinhardt and/or Dieterle might have seen this Italian film at some stage in its European distribution. Azzuri's Puck, with clear correspondences to Mickey Rooney in the Reinhardt/Dieterle production, is a diminutive boy, arrogantly imperious in style. Like Rooney, this Puck seems to spend much of his time perched in a tree laughing.[9] As in the Reinhardt/Dieterle Hollywood extravaganza, Azzuri's fairyland is populated by myriad diaphanous, dancing feminine fairies who balletically appear and disappear, all in double exposure. In the Reinhardt/ Dieterle production, a troop of ethereal dancers with gauze wings awake from the mist and dance around a tree in upwardly spiralling circles until their fairy path magically peels away into the distance where the fairies disappear at the vanishing point, all seen in soft focus. In 1913, such a version of fairyland was still in keeping with its moment. By 1935, however, this vaseline-lensed vision of fairy loveliness might already have begun to seem a little bland, or even passé.

As early as 1914, Harley Granville Barker had made a decisive move away from balletic, ethereal fairy spirits in his stage production at London's Savoy Theatre. His fairies – complete with gilded faces, golden shavings for hair, angular head-dresses, 'peg-top' baggy trousers, and, according to *The Times*, looking like 'Cambodian deities' – moved not in ethereal, flighty ways, but rather with a weighty deliberateness by adopting, as one invited guest scribbled in his programme, 'Eastern attitudes'. The fairies' movement in- volved, again according to *The Times*, 'fall[ing] into stiff postures in corners'.[10] Such descriptions must have pleased Cecil J. Sharp, Granville Barker's choreographer, whose wish was to avoid anything that was merely 'pretty in a tiresome, superficial sort of way'.[11] Gone were the little girls with wings

A troop of ethereal dancers offers a sentimental vision of fairy loveliness in the Warner Brothers' 1935 *A Midsummer Night's Dream*.

on wires. These fairies were substantial beings, and they remained planted firmly on the boards throughout. Their references to their own lithe speed as they moved about the stage with a stylised stiffness cannot but have introduced an element of irony into the depiction. The reviewer for *The Daily Mail* was unimpressed with these new disjunctures between the *claims* fairies made about themselves on the one hand, and what an audience was *shown* on the other. He grieved over the absence of the traditional lovelinesses and agility he evidently felt he had a right to expect:

> *Out of sheer cussedness, [Mr Barker and Mr Norman Wilkinson, the designer] have banished children from the fairy glades and peopled them with sinister-looking figures of Indian brass, heavy and expressionless, their faces immove-able under a brass grease paint. Peas-blossom, Cobweb, Moth, and Mustard Seed . . . too are all brass, with brass faces and corkscrew curls of brass, unlovely, unrecognisable, except as 'the fierce vexations of a dream'.*[12]

Here, perhaps, was the rub. Changing the fairies could not but help change the nature of the dream, and in an attempt to speak on behalf of the nation, *The Daily Mail* was reluctant to relinquish the *beautiful* version of the *Dream* that theatre-goers had been able to share for at least the past hundred years. If the dream were to change, a common heritage would be lost: then, as perhaps now, *The Daily Mail* flexed its conservative muscle in opposing change.

The fairies in some of Reinhardt's own earlier stage productions had been 'no longer the depressing ballerinas of old-fashioned performances' but rather wore 'green wigs and green tights'.[13] When it came to making the film, however, such experimental thinking about the occupants of fairyland was rejected and it was in essence the aesthetics of the Hollywood Bowl production that determined those of the film. An edgier design aesthetic might have worked for Reinhardt's more limited and cultured audiences in Vienna or Berlin, or indeed for Granville Barker's in London, but for the masses that the new medium could reach, and predominantly American masses at that, something less challenging and more immediately appealing was required.

If Granville Barker's production had, as *The Tatler* reported, been 'impregnated by the note of Futurism', Reinhardt and Dieterle's film was impregnated by a note of nostalgia.[14] In effect, the Reinhardt/Dieterle film resummons the subjects of Victorian fairy paintings in a piece of retrospective sentimentality. The prominent presence of Mendelssohn's incidental music to *A Midsummer Night's Dream* makes clear this conscious sentimentality. This suite had been considered a little passé as early as 1914, as Sharp's comments make clear: 'We of the present generation are no longer under the influence of the wave of German Romanticism which swept over this country sixty or seventy years ago, and, therefore, his music comes to us as an echo of a past age, the expression of an ideal which is not ours.'[15] If this had been true of the Mendelssohn in 1914, by 1935, it unequivocally represented a past age. And it was exactly this nostalgic ideal that was finally embraced in the Warner Brothers' film, as it had not been in many of Reinhardt's earlier and more experimental stage productions. The combination of Mendelssohn and an uncompromising return to prettily balletic female fairies with gauze wings made this plain.

In keeping with such sentiment, and drawing additionally upon a tradition of melodrama, the iconographies of the film's two principal fairies are placed in stark, and starkly gendered, contrast to each other. Titania's retinue is characterised by its white, fragile, delicate femininity; Oberon's by its black, muscular, predatory masculinity. The power disparity in the organisation of this fairy kingdom is illustrated with particular force when one male fairy spirit picks up a female fairy, drapes her over his shoulder with exaggerated precision and carries her pliant form off into the ether. In an effect retained from the open-air stage production in Oxford, her balletically dancing hands flutter her tremulous surrender to his winningly executed abduction, until their image is extinguished at the vanishing point.[16] This is Victorian sentimentality, and the dark sexual mores of melodrama, rolled into one complexly composite image.

At the opening of Reinhardt's much reproduced speech 'Of Actors', he had claimed that 'It is to the actor and to no one else that the theatre belongs'[17]. What he meant by 'the actor' in this context was impressively elastic. Even allowing for this, however, his practical film-making suggests that his ideas about the role of the actor in the cinema differed markedly from his thinking about the centrality of the actor in the theatre. *A Midsummer Night's Dream* is certainly not a film that belongs exclusively to the actors. No matter how pleasing Cagney and Rooney and the rest might be, the special effects and trick photography resources of a major film studio were now on hand and these were not to be ignored. In fact Reinhardt and his technical team were so taken with the wizardry of the cinematic resources available to them that they made these clearly visible to spectators at many points in the film. At the impressively imposing entrance of a rather sinister-looking Oberon and his retinue of black-clad bat-spirits, for example, a twinkling sequined filter interposes itself between the spectator and the action, a filter that then remains in place for much of the rest of the woodland scenes. The introduction of such 'casket filters' was the innovation of cinematographer Hal Mohr, an important late-comer to the production team who went on to win the Academy Award for *A Midsummer Night's Dream*'s photography. Mohr had a net made of very fine steel wires, sprayed cobweb material on to it and blew on some sparkling flitters. These were only visible when directly illuminated, so he placed tiny bulbs around the edge of the camera that he could turn on and off, thus alternately illuminating the sparkly effects and rendering them invisible. Then he shot through a disk to magnify the star-like quality of the radiating sparkles.[18] The effect generated is striking. It throws a sheen of magic across fairyland, in the process also alerting us to the mediated character of our vision by advertising the fact of a lens between us and the scene viewed.

It is not, however, only its visual artifice to which the film draws our attention. Its soundtrack too alerts us to its functioning within the narrative. In 1927 Warner Brothers had, of course, been responsible for the first commercial sound film, *The Jazz Singer*. Although by 1935 it was no longer sufficient to parade the mere fact of a soundtrack in order to impress, it was still perhaps worth reminding the audience from time to time of the significance, and sophistication, of a soundtrack's operations within the film. During Lysander's conspiratorial tryst with Hermia in Athens prior to their flight, the soundtrack plays the 'cello melody from the Mendelssohn suite, as arranged for the film by the noted Viennese composer Erich Wolfgang Korngolg. As the young lovers are disturbed, they spring guiltily apart and the music stops. Lysander (Dick Powell), however, then recovers his dignity by nonchalantly starting to hum the same tune we have just heard on the sound track and this in turn is shortly afterwards then taken up once again by a full orchestra on the soundtrack. Such playful baton-passing of a theme tune in and out of the narrative is evocative of the style of the Warner Brothers' musicals, to which this film alludes in several particulars, not least in its casting of one of the stars of those musicals, Dick Powell. The agility of the theme to hop in and out of the narrative has the effect, here just as in such moments in musicals, of alerting us both to the separateness from the visuals of the film space occupied by the soundtrack, and simultaneously to its crucial integration *into* the operations of the film. There is little that is self-effacing, either visually or aurally, about this film's construction. The film, it seems, with great good humour, is encouraging a degree of self-consciousness about spectatorial and auditory position that is far from inappropriate in relation to the rendering of a Shakespearean comedy – this one, perhaps, in particular.

THE ROYAL SHAKESPEARE COMPANY'S *A MIDSUMMER NIGHT'S DREAM* (ADRIAN NOBLE, 1995)

. . . he awoke and found it truth.[19]

If Reinhardt and Dieterle are caught up in a retrospective sentimentality about Victorian spectacular staging and Victorian conceptions of Shakespearean fairies, Adrian Noble's 1995 film of *A Midsummer Night's Dream* is caught in its own, more precisely targeted act of nostalgic tribute to an earlier stage production. Peter Brook's landmark Royal Shakespeare Company production of 1970 made a decisive intervention into the performance history of the play, of a type that Granville Barker's 1914 production with his stiffly weighty fairies might perhaps also have made had its influence been more widely felt, or the community more receptive to his progressive thinking. The moment in which Brook mounted his production was, by contrast, extremely receptive to his project. Part of the reason for this was that Brook's thinking about the play was inflected by the work of Jan Kott, the popular Shakespearean who had drawn attention to the blatant and troubling sexual energies of much of the play. Kott's book *Shakespeare Our Contemporary*, first published in English in 1964, was referred to by Alfred Harbage in the Annual Shakespeare Lecture of the British Academy in 1969 as 'the most fashionable book of Shakespearean commentary of the past decade'.[20] Thus in translating some of Kott's ideas about the play into theatrical practice in 1970, Brook was working *with* the critical grain of his moment.

Brook had rejected romantic pictorial staging, taking as his set a laboratory-style space in a three-sided white box designed by Sally Jacobs. He wanted this set, he said, to act as an opening into which the audience could pour their imaginations.[21] Characters appropriated the vertical axis of the available playing space as well as its more board-bound horizontal counterparts by making many of their entrances and exits to and from the box on swings, trapezes and stilts. Meanwhile the magic of the wood was represented through the performance codes of the circus – juggling, plate-spinning, acrobatics.[21] The exposed sexuality of the play in Brook's production was an innovation on the Royal Shakespeare Company stage.[23] Bottom's phallus, as evoked by a fairy's forearm thrust between his legs, became a crucial part of his assinine identity and, presumably, of his appeal for Titania. Titania's bed was a womb-like nest of red feathers to which she and her donkey consort retired.

Noble's production itself had started life on the Royal Shakespeare Company stage and makes reference to its celebrated predecessor in several respects. Like Brook, Noble organised his ascents and descents on machinery, this time not on trapezes but on colourful umbrellas surrounded by light bulbs, in and out of an almost entirely blank performance space with wooden stage boards for floor. The film is dominated by frontal camera work and its editing lacks pace. The result has widely been felt to be a film that mimics the theatrical in its own forms of presentation.

About Brook's production, Robert Speaight had written:

> He persuaded you to forget a century of theatrical tradition, with its conventions and its clichés; and commanded you into a frame of mind where the very notion of magic, of supernatural agency, had to be created afresh. You could, if you chose, harbour a reminiscence of Alice in Wonderland, but of nothing else.[24]

Noble's significant addition to the Brook conception was a little boy (Osheen Jones) in his pyjamas who was dreaming the entire action of the play. The opening shot of the film shows the boy asleep in bed, having fallen asleep still clutching the book he had been reading – an illustrated edition of *A Midsummer Night's Dream*. Like Imogen in *Cymbeline*, the boy's bedtime reading inspires his night-time experiences. He wakes up into his own dream and his pyjama-ed figure is then present in each scene, voyeuristically observing the action summoned by his own dreaming mind. Part of his journey into his own dream territory is via a 'down-the-rabbit-hole' experience. If, as Speaight suggested, *Alice in Wonderland* was hovering as a peripheral idea in the Brook production, it was moved far closer to the centre in Noble's.

It was not, of course, the first time the play had been configured not just as *a* dream, but as *the* dream of an identifiable character. As early as 1913, the Deutsche Bioscop loose film adaptation of the play (now lost) had presented the action of the play as the dream of an old gentleman. Judging from what we know of the particular film-makers involved, his dream was almost certainly of a liberally sexual nature; 'a gross and nasty distortion,' as Ball writes with distaste, 'ill met by moonlight or any other time'.[25] In Lindsay Kemp/Celestino Coronado's 1984 production, the colourful, campish revel emanates directly from Puck's dream, in which he casts himself as the sexually titillated voyeur of the encounters of the other characters. The trend is also discernible in academic criticism. In 1985 Thomas MacCary reconfigured the dream as that of Theseus as he considers his future nuptials, 'and its resolution as his attempt to deal with own fears and desires'.[26] But most significantly in relation to Noble's production, in 1988 Allen Dunn found the play to be 'a drama of young adulthood, of accession into the adult order or socially sanctioned sexuality'. So whose dream was being explored in the play? asked Dunn:

> [W]ho would imagine that a quarrel over the possession of a child would not only disrupt a marriage but throw the entire world into a state of disorder? The fantasy is clearly that of a child; in this case I will argue it is the fantasy of the Indian Boy himself.[27]

The dreamer of the dream has been recast as the Changeling boy whose fantasy about how much he is wanted by competing adults and whose concomitant anxiety about the strife that he is causing are translated into narrative form. It is with Dunn's thinking about the play that Noble aligns himself most closely.

The little boy dreamer in Noble's *Dream* is positioned as a separate voyeur for most of the action, moving unobserved but observing through a strange adult tale being played out in a childlike world. But when Puck recounts the story of the Changeling Boy, the little boy then finds a place for himself in the story *as* that child over whom the adults seem to be fighting. In his dream, he imagines himself as the highly treasured child wanted by all the parental figures around him. As the camera takes its inspiration from his mindworld, we too briefly see him in the guise of the turbaned and exoticised child of Puck's story. The boy's watching self in pyjamas smiles broadly at the image of his other self in a turban. He is both entertained by the curiousness of this image and, presumably, emotionally reassured by its significance.

Since it is a little boy's dreamworld we enter by watching the film, much of what we encounter there has its roots in childhood stories. The model of a white rabbit on the boy's mantelpiece near his bed seems to inspire his subsequent down-the-rabbit-hole experience; the umbrella floating upwards remembers *Mary Poppins*; the upturned umbrella-boat bearing its two passengers out to sea by the light of the moon is reminiscent of popular illustrations for 'The Owl and the Pussycat'; the motorcycle silhouetted in front of a giant moon is deliberately evocative of *ET*; the magically flying vehicle from which the passengers wave down at the world below recalls *Chitty Chitty Bang Bang*; the reappearance of the mechanicals in altered guises as the fairies mimics the way in which Dorothy's friends and acquaintances in Kansas are recast in heightened versions of themselves as her friends and foes in the land over the rainbow. Thus the boy's dreaming mind weaves together a tapestry of childhood stories. These act as points of reassuring security in a world which in other respects takes him to new, and sometimes disturbing places as it enacts a rite of passage.

The film asserts that it is the 'slumber[ing] here' (v.i.411) of the little boy that has made these visions appear. As the film draws to a close, *our* acknowledgement of the little boy as the creator of the fantasy is also then shared by the characters of his creating. The seal is put upon this acknowledgement when, at the end of the film, the characters lift him above their heads and twirl him around, apparently pleased at the comfortable narrative resting place to which he has finally managed to steer them. Having been the solitary little figure with his eye either literally or metaphorically pressed to the keyhole for most of the film, he finally finds his own peace by emerging from the voyeuristic shadows to be acknowledged as a participator in the story and warmly absorbed into the wider community.

His journey towards this safe, communal place of acceptance has not been without its traumas. The most disturbing encounter he has witnessed on his emotional odyssey is that between Titania (Lindsay Duncan) and Bottom (Desmond Barrit). The queen of the fairies and her new-found lover are given a romantic send-off as the deep red, womb-like padded upturned giant umbrella in which they sit silhouetted against the moon is put out upon the water. But the image of the floating umbrella does not retain its stylised romance for long, being soon violently disrupted by the noisy and basic copulation of its passengers, accompanied by loud orgasmic donkey brays from Bottom. It is a sexual encounter stripped of all romantic veneer.

There is, as Kott pointed out, simmering below the surface of many of the play's interactions a pervasive brutality and a violent sexuality. Just as the wood snatches at the clothing of the mechanicals, so, emotionally, it pares away the vestiges of civilised decorum from all the characters caught within its spell. Being in a context of unchecked psychological and sexual expression, the play suggests, may bring to light some truths about humanity which are far from pretty. It is these truths that surface intermittently in Noble's production.

As revealing as any other single element from the play in determining a film's interpretive slant is its treatment of Titania's seduction of Bottom. In the play Titania imperiously instructs her fairies about the nature of the hospitality her guest-prisoner is to receive:

> *Come, wait upon him; lead him to my bower.*
> *The moon, methinks, looks with a watery eye,*
> *And when she weeps, weeps every little flower,*
> *Lamenting some enforced chastity.*
> *Tie up my love's tongue, bring him silently.* (III.i.190–194)

The first and last lines of her five-line speech contain specific instructions to her attendants. In between these two lines, however, Titania seems to be taken by a momentary digression as she muses on the weeping moon and the corresponding weeping of 'every little flower'. Despite appearances, there is nothing whimsical or diversionary about these lines. On the contrary, they refer very much to the business in hand. The moon is associated with chastity through the figure of the goddess Artemis. 'Enforced' means here not 'insisted upon' as it might now, but rather 'forced' or 'violated'. The moon, and with her the flowers, are therefore weeping in sorrow for the forcing of someone's virginity. The lyrical surface of Titania's lines does little to obscure the graphic revelation of her plans for Bottom. 'Tie up my love's tongue, bring him silently' she says immediately afterwards, and Bottom is led away. The audience is left in little doubt as to whose impending fate it is that has caused the chaste moon and flowers to weep.

In the Reinhardt/Dieterle film, Titania (Anita Louise) delivers these lines as if sentimentally transported by her own love for 'every little flower'. The *seeming* digression from her dealings with Bottom (James Cagney) is allowed to be an *actual* digression that here concerns only the botanical mystery of flowers that weep. The deep threat latent in the lines is thus left unexhumed. And indeed this is entirely apt in the context of this production since Bottom's fate seems to be limited to sleeping beside the fairy queen beneath a cobweb veil in a bower strewn with petals. In this respect and others, the film offers us a sanitised rendering of the play, or, more accurately, a version that largely predates its *desanitising*. An exposure of its potential murky depths, and the related sounds of enthusiastic copulation, had not yet entered the frame.

Noble by contrast, is working at a time when it had become almost habitual for the Royal Shakespeare Company to find ways of drawing attention to Shakespearean bawdy in explicit, and explicitly visceral ways. Making use of Kott through the mediation of Brook, he takes pleasure in the brute sexuality he finds in his source, bringing this to the fore. In such a playworld, it is understandable that the little boy's eyes should open wide at some of the images conjured by his dreamlife.

Although the drama played out in Noble's film is the boy's private dream fantasy, the boy himself makes efforts to pass it off as someone else's responsibility. In the toy theatre, for example, he pushes the tiny figure of Helena towards Oberon (Alex Jennings) and Puck (Barry Lynch) for them to do with as they will. He does not wish to believe this is exclusively his vision. Indeed, who in Act II of *A Midsummer Night's Dream* would want to feel responsible for Helena's fate? Rather he prefers to believe this story is governed by forces beyond himself, so that he can then simply take pleasure in following it as a disinterested observer. In this, he acts as a surrogate for our own relationships to the action of the drama. We too are happy to believe we are following a strange story that has been dreamt up for us by another. However, just as the very title of *As You Like It* denies us the luxury of believing ourselves distanced from the direction in which *that* fantasy tends, so *A Midsummer Night's Dream* enjoys reminding us of the proximity between being, as Puck says, an 'auditor' and an 'actor', that is, between being simply a member of the audience and being an agent of the drama. The play manœuvres us in stages into acknowledging our own agency, our own unwitting involvement in events. Puck concludes this evolving argument with a flourish when, in the Epilogue, he persuades us that the whole action has emerged from *our* dream life, that whatever is capable of offending in it is the product of *our* fantasy world:

> If we shadows have offended,
> Think but this, and all is mended,
> That you have but slumber'd here,
> While these shadows did appear.   (V.i.409–412)

If we see perversity and brutality in the wood and identify it as emerging from the ugly depths of liberated imaginations, we are asked to consider whether those imaginations might not in fact be our own.

Making the action of the drama into the dreamlife of the little boy, as Noble does, or indeed of any other visible figure in a production, therefore represents something of a 'get out' for the audience since it identifies an external figure upon whom responsibility for the direction of the action can be thoroughly offloaded. If these shadows offend, we can think that not we but the little boy has 'but slumber'd here'. Thus in a film which is superficially more shocking than many other productions of the play, its real core of potential offence for an audience has been removed.

FOX SEARCHLIGHT'S *A MIDSUMMER NIGHT'S DREAM* (MICHAEL HOFFMAN, 1999)

There is little to offend either superficially or fundamentally in Michael Hoffman's 1999 *A Midsummer Night's Dream*, in which the action of the play is transplanted to turn-of-the-century Tuscany. Those who have taken exception to it largely did so on the grounds that it lacks bite, that it is anodyne or that it seems to return the play to a realm of frothy sentiment. The emotion of the film is, however, more interestingly and thoughtfully modulated than such a judgement would suggest.

In several respects this film was Fox Searchlight's late-in-the-day response to the film that its older competitor studio, Warner Brothers, had produced sixty-four years earlier. Hoffman's use of the Mendelssohn suite from the opening moments of his film could not help but make the deliberateness of the association with the Warner Brothers film immediately apparent. Later the soundtrack diversifies into a range of gloriously over-the-top moments from Italian high opera, some of which disruptively introduce narrative cross-currents to the Shakespearean narrative being played out, others of which serve as interesting counterpoint to it.[28] But in showcasing Mendelssohn on the soundtrack at such an early stage, Hoffman was nostalgically attaching himself to the 1930s filmic rendering of the play which had itself already been caught up in its own act of conscious nostalgia. Inevitably for its late twentieth century moment, the double layering occasionally gave the Hoffman film a slight ironic distance from too consistently sincere an engagement in his own sentimentality, and this was most clearly signalled in the deliciously laconic moments of observation shared by Puck (Stanley Tucci) and Oberon (Rupert Everett). What is remarkable in a film of its moment, however, is that some sincerity was sustained at all. Anachronistically, this film did not seek to deconstruct its own purposes at each turn. Rather it was able to enjoy at least some of them with a sincerity that was a welcome change from contemporary trends. Even as he carved out his own unique interpretive space, therefore, Hoffman was unembarrassed simultaneously to signal his conscious, and in several respects unironised, alignment with the Reinhardt tradition. From tiny details – such as the indication in the screenplay that Bottom should run to the pond to study his reflection[29] as if in tribute to James Cagney's comparable self-examination, or the little horns discernible on Puck's head recalling those that had earlier been on Mickey Rooney's – to a central understanding of the play as more interested in the power of love to elevate and redeem than to distort and debase, the Fox film is far closer to its Warner Brothers' predecessor than it is to the more sexually troubled, and more self-aware, screen productions that have emerged in the interim.

The thread of continuity between the two films is discernible not merely studio to studio, but also director to director. Like Reinhardt, Hoffman had been living with the play for years before he made his film, having already both acted in and directed it for the stage. And although the resulting film met with a tepid response at the box office and some bruising treatment from Shakespeareans, there is in it a maturity of thinking about the play which testifies to a process of reflection that has evidently not been rushed.

Through the 1990s, Kenneth Branagh had wooed and won a market for Shakespeare films. Nevertheless, as box office returns repeatedly show, there is still a marketing hurdle to be negotiated in mounting a Shakespeare production for a mass market. Fox in 1999, like Warner in 1935, therefore needed big-name stars to dilute the mere fact of Shakespeare with popular audiences. And just as Warner consciously traded upon the associations that their stars brought with them to their Shakespearean roles, so too Fox was able to make carefully strategic casting decisions in order to extract maximum mileage from the previous role associations of its cast.

This is most obviously detectable in the casting of Helena. In 1999 the actress Calista Flockhart was entirely identified across the world of Western popular culture with the eponymous heroine of the hit American situation comedy *Ally McBeal*. Such was the prevalence of the programme that Ally's central characteristics – her dreadful luck with men, self-definition as the hapless, spurned lover and self-castigations about her own romantic incompetence – could not help but inform a reading of Calista Flockhart's other roles. Such firmly established character credentials were not easily to be sloughed off. In many ways, the very presence of this actress in *A Midsummer Night's Dream* offered an efficiently communicated thumbnail portrait of Helena through the imported Ally screen persona. Helena, like Ally in the first few series of the show, is self-pityingly obsessed about her disastrous love-life, convinced she will never get it together with 'the one' (Demetrius/Billy), engaged in an undignified rivalry with a woman she considers her friend (Hermia/Georgia) and willing to compromise her principles in pursuit of the man of her dreams. In fact the description of her character's relationship with Demetrius that Flockhart supplied for Fox's press promotions might as easily have applied to that of Ally with Billy: 'People call Helena obsessed, but I like to think of her as hugely determined. I think she knows that, somewhere inside him, Demetrius loves her and she just has to get his attention . . .'[30] As if in confirmation of the correspondences in her thinking about the two roles, on screen as Helena, Flockhart's over-breathy delivery of the lines, obsessively fidgety hands and hyper-mobile eyes conjure Ally at every turn. The resulting character elision is almost certainly as interpretively useful for those spectators who appreciate clear signposts to navigate the emotional landscape of the drama as it is distracting for those who do not.

Michelle Pfeiffer's ethereal beauty worked particularly well in her role as Titania, and the sheer appeal of her look in the film in itself earned the production a tie-in advertising deal for shimmering cosmetics with Maybeline.[31] Although she looks every inch the fairy queen, however, her lack of experience with Shakespeare is plainly evident in her nervously over-emphatic verse-speaking. From the perspective of the production, a little verbal awkwardness, however, must have been more than amply compensated by the significant box-office draw that the fact of her presence in a movie represents. By contrast, some of the British actors, such as Anna Friel and Dominic West, whose screen presence lacks the electrifying charisma of Pfeiffer but whose cadencings of the Shakespearean line sound assured and organic, were cast partly to give the film some cultural ballast. Kevin Kline as Bottom, however, nicely combined established Hollywood appeal (*A Fish*

Calista Flockhart's performance as Helena in Hoffman's 1999 *Dream* is evocative of her performance as television character Ally McBeal.

Source: William Shakespeare's A Midsummer Night's Dream © 1999 Twentieth Century Fox.

Called Wanda, French Kiss) with significant experience in acting Shakespeare on the stage (he had at this stage already played Henry V, Richard III, Benedick and Hamlet twice). In *A Midsummer Night's Dream*, Bottom sits on the cusp between communities, forming the only point of direct encounter between the otherwise distinct mortal and fairy worlds. Similarly, in the film Kline represented the most obvious point of encounter between the two distinct casting pools – Hollywood and classical acting. Both in the character's position in the narrative, and in the actor's position in the cast, therefore, Kline's performance as Bottom constitutes the central pivot of the film.

As Hoffman reports,[32] it was the part of Oberon that he had first discussed with Kline. When subsequently asked if he would consider playing Bottom instead, Kline inadvertently confirmed his suitability for the part by countering with the suggestion that he could play Theseus, Oberon *and* Bottom – an aspiration entirely fitting perhaps for an actor who once in role was going to have to voice his desire to play Pyramus, Thisbe *and* the lion. Just as Peter Quince (Roger Rees) – here an unprepossessing trade union foreman amidst a company of honest comrades – contains Bottom's actorly aspirations by casting him as Pyramus and only Pyramus, so Hoffman was able to channel Kline's extraordinary talents into the part of Bottom alone. Deprived of the more aristocratic end of the play's spectrum of characters, Kline embraced instead the emotional range that could be found within Bottom. As he said in a promotional interview for the studio, not only does Bottom have the instincts of a ham actor, but also 'the soul of an artist. . . . He loves to escape the reality he's in, to discover something more noble and more beautiful about himself.'[33] And it is in this discovery of something 'more noble and more beautiful' about Bottom that Hoffman's production distinguishes itself most profoundly from Noble's. Whereas Noble graphically demonstrated the bestialising effect of Bottom's encounter with Titania, Hoffman and Kline's collaboration suggested that Titania's gently amorous and gently erotic attentions, though short-lived, touched and transfigured Bottom in ways that would enrich him for life.

The Titania–Bottom encounter is, in this production as in so many others, a telling indicator of the tone of a production as a whole. Pfeiffer's Titania still issues the imperious instructions of a dominatrix: 'Out of this wood do not desire to go. / Thou shalt remain here, whether thou wilt or no.' (III.i.145.6) But here this lacks the purchase of a dark sexual threat since the scene dissolves immediately into a farcical abduction sequence in which Bottom's feet are magically encircled by a vine, he is hoisted aloft upside down and

Titania's (Michelle Pfeiffer) gently eroticised attentions have a transfiguring and lasting effect upon Bottom's (Kevin Kline) life in Hoffman's 1999 film.

Source: *William Shakespeare's A Midsummer Night's Dream* © 1999 Twentieth Century Fox.
All rights reserved.

dropped into Titania's aerially suspended bed. If this is the fulfilment of a fantasy of Bottom's, it is a fantasy with a sense of self-deprecating comedy at its core. Without being over-coy, the film also handles the sexuality with a far lighter touch than had become habitual. There is still some play (not without delicacy) on the stereotypically impressive phallus of the ass. The community of female fairies allows itself to giggle with good-natured discretion at the sight of Bottom's sexual arousal (discreetly out of frame). But here this is gently alluded to as an entertainingly wholesome part of a larger scene. The more forthright sexuality of the Kemp/Coronado and the Noble productions is absent from this vision of fairyland.

Kevin Kline's agreement to cede the part of Oberon to concentrate on a nuanced portrayal of Bottom left the part of the fairy king open for another. The look of Oberon was to be drawn directly from Moreau's brooding Apollo in *The Muses Leaving Their Father Apollo*. It was Rupert Everett ('Who more moody or languid?' said Hoffman)[34] who was cast as this brooding god, although in the film he was to become more Bacchus perhaps than Apollo. In stark contrast to Victor Jory's powerful black knight riding on horseback through his fairy domain in Reinhardt and Dieterle's film, Everett is a pensive, languid Oberon who can scarcely exert himself even to raise a quizzical eyebrow at the extravagant behaviours he finds around him. He mostly observes the action impassively, just occasionally rousing himself sufficiently from decadent inactivity to exchange a glance with Puck in shared bafflement at mortal folly. And the observation of these two boyish voyeurs provides a comic locus for our own. By themselves registering very little, they are able to concentrate and release our own gently amused responses.

The Tuscan hillside town (called Athens) from which the lovers flee is riddled with prophetic references to the magical world they will in due course encounter. A stone sculpture, for example, alludes to the Puck who subsequently appears in the wood. Puck is an impish version of the little stone man sitting astride a giant stone tortoise in the ornamental alcove where Hermia and Lysander plan their flight. This figure comes fully to life in the wood when Puck himself is shown riding a giant tortoise. And the image of Puck on tortoise-back plays to one of the sustained jokes of the film. Unlike a host of athletic and agile Pucks who proudly boast their ability to put a girdle round the earth in half an hour, this Puck cannot be induced to hurry. His claims to lithe speed are always ironised. By giving him a stylised lethargy, Stanley Tucci effectively does for Puck what Simon Russell Beale did for Ariel in Sam Mendes' RSC production of *The Tempest* in the 1993–94 Stratford season. Hoffman's screenplay had allowed for moments of dramatic haste from both Puck and Oberon,[35] but most of these were excised in shooting, as the humour that could be found in inactivity was developed. Nor was the joke limited to the province of Oberon and Puck. When Theseus (David

Strathairn) selects his evening's entertainment, for example, the screenplay suggests that the camera should dwell in turn on each hopeful acting troupe rehearsing, including the Pyramus and Thisbe crew. But in the film, the frantic rehearsal bustle and activity of their rivals is comically contrasted with the despondent stillness of Quince's company. They sit glumly depressed at their prospects, comically static in the midst of an array of wildly over-active luvvies.[36] The comic languor that characterised much of fairy life in the wood seems here to have been carried by the mechanicals backs into Athens. The lines of influence between town and wood evidently work in both directions.

Hoffman's interest in the points of continuity between the two worlds of the play is made manifest in both domains.[37] During the film's opening sequences in Tuscan Athens, satyrs in street clothes sporting horns under their hats and little satyr feet, can be discerned pilfering shiny things from the kitchen and carting off their spoils to adorn their woodland fairy kingdom. Equally, at the end of the film Puck places his cap over his little horns and strolls off into the night, 'just an ordinary goblin in a little Tuscan town'.[38] Thus the film encourages us to see what Theseus refuses to see – that the magical can be found in among the ordinary, that fairy possibilities might conceivably be enlivening any street corner. As Bottom gazes from his bedroom window in the closing moments of the film, he glimpses one particularly bright star amidst a dancing cluster. The seemingly personalised twinkling of this star reminds him of the privileging attentions that Titania gave him and persuades him that the most ordinary things can be made full of magical meaning if looked at through believing eyes. Bottom's tiny smile at his window makes it clear that he is capable of being lifted out of the disheartening mediocrity of his own world by such a belief.

A sense that magic is spun from the stuff of ordinary life is one of the central impulses of the film. A bicycle is an item of fearsome mystery to Puck, a turntable a thing of magical enchantment to Titania, the nightsky a significant memory for Bottom. A sense of awe about the world can be provoked by the most humdrum or unpromising materials, and it is often only perspective that distinguishes the mundane from the mysterious. Thus as the lovers wake up after their night in the enchanting, perplexing wood, they are discovered by Theseus and his hunting party under a perfectly innocent tree at the bottom of an ordinary hill below their own familiar home town. In daylight there is nothing troubling and little mysterious about this world. The wood that had tormented and confused them is nowhere in sight, having been presumably merely a construct of the night that helped them to enact and resolve their own fears and dilemmas. As a realm of the imagination, it need not – cannot perhaps – be subjected to daylight scrutiny.

Even the mechanicals' performance of Pyramus and Thisbe, so often simply the stuff of pitiable farce in performance, finds a route through its own rather unprepossessing component elements to touch its audience almost in spite of itself. Flute/Thisbe's comic falsetto gives up on his lines 'A tomb must cover thy sweet eyes', and the sudden lowering of the voice into a more sensible register has the effect, equally suddenly, of introducing a note of seriousness to proceedings. Having failed to sustain the falsetto, Flute entirely abandons his pretence to be Thisbe, taking off his wig and speaking the rest of his lines with a quiet sincerity directly to his audience. The excessive hamming from Flute and the derisive merriment from his audience are both abruptly cut short. Actor and audience alike find themselves stilled and sobered by the simple truth of the words that are now rescued from ridicule and allowed instead to focus the mortality of the whole community. A shiver runs through his on-screen audience. The power that can be found in theatre can, it seem, emerge even from earthen vessels, even, that is, from crude mechanicals. Once again, the everyday is transformed into the magical by a willingness on the part of the perceivers to participate in a collusive act of belief. Thus the film's insistence upon a process by which the ordinary may be transfigured through the faith of the onlooker ultimately comes to rest in its proper home, as a metaphor about the processes of drama itself.

The dominant interpretive trends in relation to *A Midsummer Night's Dream* on stage and film in the 1990s have tended to take this dramatic material towards 'the dark pool of the unconscious'. Ironically, this is the very place where Hoffman claims he found his fairies.[39] Other productions, however, suggest that pools of the unconscious can get considerably darker than anything in evidence in Hoffman's film. If anything, this film restores the play to a more optimistic world view than has been its customary territory in the last thirty years It is literally and emotionally a film about mischief, and takes pleasure in dramatising a mischievous look at the world. Simultaneously it allows itself to express the imagination's power to transfigure even patently unsatisfactory lives. Stanley Tucci said of *A Midsummer Night's Dream* that it is a comedy that is 'incredibly beautiful and poignant',[40] and in Hoffman's hands, this is discovered to be true. It is a reading of the play that had been starved of oxygen for some time.

*

When he revived his production of *A Midsummer Night's Dream* at His Majesty's Theatre in 1911, Beerbohm Tree had written of it that it 'presents a picture of pure love unsullied by any grossness of sensual passion'.[41] In this Tree was speaking not just for himself but for his age. A 'grossness of sensual passion' was not something that Victorians had found in the play. On the contrary, romantics in the nineteenth century consistently found a delicate beauty and poetic sweetness in the wood near Athens, and in the action of the play as a whole. The play was read most frequently as a celebration of the redemptive power of the imagination.

It is noticeable, for example, that both silent films considered in this chapter – the Vitagraph from 1909 and the Azzuri from 1913 – present the wood as a tame and pleasant place, that takes on none of the more troubling properties or atmospheres that would later come to dominate its character in performance. Azzuri's wood, for example, seems more like an ornamental garden than a place genuinely capable of alarming. After their flight from Athens, his Lysander and Hermia are found not in some bare laboratory space in which, freed from other distractions, they can come face to face with their own unconscious fears and desires, nor even in a knotty, tangled clearing surrounded by dark imposing trees. Rather, Azzuri's lovers are found leaning fetchingly on the balustrade of a picturesque little bridge over a pleasant stream. Far from being a place in which crawling serpents, or yet more literally, warped sexualities, might feasibly threaten to take over, this wood seems to testify without embarrassment to the civilised forces that have constructed it. Later woods would parade less obviously their orderly running and good maintenance. But for the moment at least, the rural idyll could survive intact, and with the added benefits of humanly constructed technologies to make streams crossable while keeping dresses clean. The idyll was rural without being too inconveniently or disruptively so.

Interpretations of *A Midsummer Night's Dream* on both page and stage have undergone a shift over this century. The play has moved from being an exquisitely delicate ballet of tripping fairies and momentarily wayward lovers bathed in ethereal moonlight and frolicking entertainingly in an Arcadian retreat to being a more tonally mixed exploration of the power of the imagination. Imagination as explored in the play is now understood to have the power not only to liberate but also to ensnare as the brutality and perversity of its own darkest repressions surface. Things encountered in one's environment or in oneself in the wood no longer tend to be picturesque. It has become a wood that takes its visitors to dark places. As the *Evening Standard* said of the Renaissance Theatre Company's stage production in 1990, it 'might just as easily have been Transylvania in a Dracula film as . . . the leafy Athenian woods'.[42]

However, the trend away from playfully treated ethereal themes about waking and sleeping and towards a more tortured journey into the world of sexual taboo, has been bucked in Michael Hoffman's far more delicately sexualised and warm-hearted vision of fairyland and human possibility. It will be for future releases to show whether there is now a desire to reclaim the dream world of the play from savagery and return it to a slightly more *delicately* sexualised fairy dream world, or whether the Hoffman film represents only a blip on an interpretive landscape.

FURTHER READING

Charles W. Eckert, *Focus on Shakespearean Films* (Englewood Cliffs, NJ: Prentice-Hall, 1972), pp.42–52.

Leonhard M. Fiedler, 'Reinhardt, Shakespeare and the *Dreams*', in Margaret Jacobs and John Warren, *Max Reinhardt: The Oxford Symposium* (Oxford: Oxford Polytechnic, 1986), pp.79–95.

Russell Jackson, 'Shakespeare's Comedies on Film', in Anthony Davies and Stanley Wells (eds), *Shakespeare and the Moving Image* (Cambridge: Cambridge University Press, 1994), pp.99–120.

Russell Jackson, 'Shakespeare's Fairies in Victorian Criticism and Performance', in Jane Martineau (ed.), *Victorian Fairy Painting* (London: Royal Academy of Arts, 1997), pp.38–45.

Jay L. Halio, *A Midsummer Night's Dream: Shakespeare in Performance* (Manchester: Manchester University Press, 1994), Chapter 3, pp.48–69.

Michael Hattaway, 'The Comedies on Film', in Russell Jackson (ed.), *The Cambridge Companion to Shakespeare on Film* (Cambridge: Cambridge University Press, 2000), pp.85–98.

Michael Hoffman, *A Midsummer Night's Dream* (London: HarperCollins, 1999).

Mark Thornton Burnett, 'Impressions of Fantasy: Adrian Noble's *A Midsummer Night's Dream*', in Mark Thornton Burnett and Ramona Wray (eds), *Shakespeare, Film, Fin de Siècle* (London: Macmillan, 2000), pp.89–101.

Gary Jay Williams, *Our Moonlight Revels: A Midsummer Night's Dream in the Theatre* (Iowa City: University of Iowa Press, 1997).

NOTES

1. Henry Morley, *The Journal of a London Playgoer* (London: George Routledge and Sons, 1866, reprinted 1891), p 56

2. William Hazlitt, *Characters of Shakespeare's Plays* (Cambridge: Cambridge University Press, 1915), p.105.

3. Morley (1866/1891), p.57.

4. See the synopsis of the film given in *The Bioscope*, 3 March 1910, p.47. This names one of the fairy lovers 'Oberon'.

5. A knowledge of the colourful private life of some of the breeches-role actresses who had previously played Oberon does nothing to render such a radical reading less plausible: there was perhaps already something a little sexually suspect about some of the associations of the role and its players. Madame Vestris, for example, had several well-publicised relationships with women.

6. For accounts of Reinhardt's stage *Dreams* see J.L. Styan, *Max Reinhardt* (Cambridge: Cambridge University Press, 1982), pp.54–61, and Leonhard M. Fiedler, 'Reinhardt, Shakespeare and the *Dreams*', in Margaret Jacobs and John Warren (eds), *Max Reinhardt: The Oxford Symposium* (Oxford: Oxford Polytechnic, 1986), pp.79–95.

7. See Gottfried Reinhardt, *Der Liebhaber: Erinnerungen seines Sohnes Gottfried Reinhardt an Max Reinhardt* (Stuttgart: Deutscher Bücherbund, 1973), p.264.

8. The Azzuri production was picked up by Warner Features for its American release.

9. At one point, when standing on the ground, the Italian Puck even laughs so much that he makes himself fall over. This too is evocative of Rooney, who also falls over with laughing and whose on-set antics became so vigorous that he even broke a leg during shooting. He then had to be pushed along on a bicycle by unseen stagehands with only his upper body visible above strategically positioned bushes.

10. 'Golden Fairies at the Savoy Theatre', *The Times*, 7 February 1914. On film at the Theatre Museum, Covent Garden. See *The Sketch*, 11 February 1914, p.168 and the annotated invitation held in the Theatre Museum, Covent Garden.

11. The production's composer and choreographer, Cecil J. Sharp, explicitly committed himself to a rejection of movements that were 'meaningless, or pretty . . .'. Cecil J. Sharp, *A Midsummer Night's Dream: Songs and Incidental Music Arranged and Composed by Cecil J. Sharp for Granville Barker's Production at the Savoy Theatre, Jan: 1914* (London: Simpkin, Marshall, Hamilton, Kent & Co. Ltd, Novelloe & Co., Ltd, 1914), p.15.

12. 'Did Shakespeare Mean This?', *The Daily Mail*, 7 February 1914. On file at the Theatre Museum.

13. This was the response of Ernst Stern, one of Reinhardt's designers. See Ernst Stern, *My Life, My Stage*, trans. Edward Fitzgerald (London: Gollancz, 1951), p.63.

14. *The Tatler* 660 (18 February 1914), p.197.

15. Cecil J. Sharp (1914), pp.11–12.

16. See Felix Felton's report of the open-air production in 'Max Reinhardt in England', *Theatre Research* 5, 3, edited by Hans Knudsen (London, 1963), pp.134–42. The description of 'a slowly narrowing spotlight following the undulation of her hands to a pinpoint of light in the darkness' is on p.142. (Felton played Bottom in the Oxford production.)

17. See, for example, Fiedler in Jacobs and Warren, p.89.

18. For the details of Hal Mohr's contributions to the finished film, see his interview with Leonard Maltin reproduced in Leonard Maltin, *Behind the Camera: The Cinematographer's Art* (London: Signet, 1971), particularly pp.124–6.

19. John Keats, writing about Adam's dream, in 'Letter to Benjamin Bailey' (22 November 1817). Reproduced in H.E. Rollins (ed.), *The Letters of John Keats* (Cambridge: Cambridge University Press, 1958), Vol. I, p.185.

20. The Annual Shakespeare Lecture of the British Academy (1969). Reproduced in Alfred Harbage, *Shakespeare Without Words* (Cambridge, MA: Harvard University Press, 1972), pp.3–23. This quotation, p.8.

21. Glen Loney, *Peter Brook's Production of William Shakespeare's 'A Midsummer Night's Dream' for the Royal Shakespeare Company: The Complete and Authorised Acting Edition* (Stratford-upon-Avon, 1974), p.32.

22. For a detailed account of the production see Jay L. Halio, *A Midsummer Night's Dream: Shakespeare in Performance* (Manchester: Manchester University Press, 1994), Chapter 3, pp.48–69.

23. For all its iconoclasm, Brook's production was not the first to remove decorousness from representations of sexual desire as expressed in the wood. The Actors' Workshop production of the play in San Francisco in 1966 (itself inspired directly by Kott), for example, had included a light bulb flashing on and off in Demetrius's codpiece. See Robert Speaight, *Shakespeare on the Stage* (London: Collins, 1973), p.240.

24. *Shakespeare Quarterly* 21 (1970), p.448.

25. Robert Hamilton Ball, *Shakespeare on Silent Film* (New York: Theater Arts Books, 1968), p.177.

26. W. Thomas MacCary, *Friends and Lovers: The Phenomenology of Desire in Shakespearean Comedy* (New York: Columbia University Press, 1985), p.148.

27. Allen Dunn, 'The Indian Boy's Dream Wherein Every Mother's Son Rehearses His Part: Shakespeare's *A Midsummer Night's Dream*', *Shakespeare Studies* 20 (1988), pp.15–32. These quotations, pp.19, 20–1.

28. I am grateful to Tony Davies for an interesting correspondence on the subject of the score to this film. As Helena talks to Hermia about the unhappy love triangle in which she finds herself the loser, for example, we hear Alfredo from Verdi's *La Traviata* singing to Violetta in the presence of her established lover, the count. The evocation of another love triangle serves to reinforce the universality of the phenomenon.

29. Michael Hoffman, *A Midsummer Night's Dream* (London: HarperCollins, 1999), p.87.

30. See www.foxsearchlight.com/midfinal/html/piazza.html

31. Images of Michelle Pfeiffer's Titania and her fairy retinue in their shimmering sparkly facial make-up were used post-release to advertise Maybeline cosmetics, appearing on make-up counters across the United States in the two-month period post-release. Maybeline presumably wished to trade upon the same images of idealised fantasy and beautiful escapism that animate the film.

32. See www.foxsearchlight.com/midfinal/html/piazza.html

33. Ibid.

34. Ibid.

35. For example, 'Puck races back into the clearing'. Hoffman (1999), p.61.

36. See Ibid., p.97.

37. Blaine Greteman wrote persuasively on the points of parallelism and continuity between Athens and the wood in his draft Oxford MPhil thesis (2001). In relation to this film, it is also something that Hoffman himself makes explicit in the published screenplay.

38. Hoffman (1999), p.114.

39. Ibid., p.viii.

40. Ibid., p.4.

41. Herbert Beerbohm Tree, *Some Notes on A Midsummer Night's Dream, produced at His Majesty's Theatre (for the second time) on Easter Monday, April 17th, 1911, by Sir Herbert Beerbohm Tree* (London, 1911).

42. Michael Shulman, *The Evening Standard*, 22 August 1990. On file at the Theatre Museum.

CHAPTER SIX

Historically Juxtaposed Beans (II):

The Tempest on Film

. . . some secreted island, Heaven knows where![1]

The variety of spectacle, displays of magic, richness of language and bubbling political subtexts to be found in *The Tempest* might be thought to have rendered it appealing as a source for cinematic adaptation. Curiously, however, the far longer and wordier *Hamlet* has been repeatedly and enthusiastically adapted for the cinema, whereas the industry has tended to fight shy of *The Tempest*. Appropriately in relation to material deriving from such a fantastical source, the small clutch of film adaptations that have emerged are all quirky or idiosyncratic in some way. As are their makers.

Since two *Tempest* films from the silent era have already been discussed in Chapter 1, this chapter restricts itself to a critical production history of *The Tempest* on film in the sound era. It considers the ways in which one Shakespearean dramatic narrative has been moulded and adjusted to suit both the medium of translation and the altered contexts of production and reception. Considered chronologically as a small collection of films which share, or which seem to share, a common Shakespearean source, these films bear interestingly both upon each other and upon their own production moments. The five film projects that will be considered are: Fred McLeod Wilcox's *Forbidden Planet* (MGM, 1956), Michael Powell's unrealised plans to film *Magic Island* (1969), Derek Jarman's *The Tempest* (1979), Paul Mazursky's *Tempest* (Columbia, 1982) and Peter Greenaway's *Prospero's Books* (1991).

*

The Tempest's strange island territory and curious collection of characters marked by political, social and sexual anxiety have throughout the play's history of performance and adaptation lent themselves naturally and repeatedly to being assimilated into other cultures free from any specific historical context. Despite its cultural versatility, however, *The Tempest* cannot be cut loose completely from its origins. It dramatises contemporary debates from the early seventeenth century about exploration, the New World, political and dynastic schemings, the ethics of colonialism, the role of language-learning in the establishment of empire. It gives expression to topically-charged fantasies about how to build the perfect society and how to redeem society from its own worst inclinations. It incorporates linguistic echo of letters from the newly settled Americas about shipwrecks and adventures that had taken place there, copies of which were in circulation in London by 1610, and it dramatises the ongoing debate about how to colonise the natives of a discovered land.[2] For the play to make geographical sense, Prospero's island has a narrative requirement to be in the Mediterranean (somewhere between Tunis and Naples). Superimposed upon this literal geography, however, is a poetic geography which, while finally eluding the co-ordinates of any map, would in some respects have reminded early audiences of topical tales from the New World. The play's themes, interests and pools of reference repeatedly evoke the newly settled Americas. As such, in its own moment, the play was evoking a space at the geographical and imaginative edge of the currently known, and knowable, world. Prospero's island constituted a peripheral space, as far removed from the comfort of familiar civilisation as could be imagined ('[t]en leagues beyond man's life' [II.i.241–242]), in which disconcerting and strange things, half-remembered both from classical mythology and from travellers' extravagant tales, might reasonably be expected to happen. In this way it managed to combine being the landscape for a universal fairytale with what A.D. Nuttall has referred to as 'an air of circumstantial actuality'.[3] Even in its moments of purest fantasy, it resonates with the anxieties and aspirations of its own first production moment.

The requirement that Prospero's island be seen as a risky, peripheral dramatic location at a complete remove from the civilised centre, has set an interpretive challenge to those who wish to reproduce the drama for a modern context. A space needs to be found to represent Prospero's 'uninhabited island' that is capable of generating in a modern cinema spectatorship a degree of fear and wonder comparable to that which the allusion to the New World presumably would have inspired in a playhouse (or Blackfriars) audience of 1611. This territory cannot, of course, allude to the same specific space (the Americas) as it partly did in 1611 and be able to generate the same degree of anxious excitement. A new peripheral space, therefore, needs to be found appropriate to each new interpretive context. As even the remote corners of the world have been demystified in the popular imagination, increasingly charted, explored and known through a range of media, evoking a territory capable of generating such resonances has inevitably become an increasingly tricky project.

MGM'S *FORBIDDEN PLANET* (FRED MCLEOD WILCOX, 1956)

In Chapter 4, I questioned how necessarily deliberate we need to consider the narrative and thematic parallels between Shakespeare's *The Tempest* and the 1956 popular American science fiction film *Forbidden Planet*. Here that question is put to one side in order to examine more simply the *effect* of the points of correspondence when considered as part of the ongoing narrative of films which deliberately or otherwise fall within a tradition of *Tempest*-evocative narratives.

The action of *Forbidden Planet*, like that of *The Tempest* in 1611, is located at the remote borders of what can be conceived in its contemporary world. By the 1950s the borders of the imaginable world had expanded dramatically, being no longer found in remote and incompletely explored regions of the Earth, whose proportions were by then largely known and whose furthermost regions no longer seemed so inaccessible in the popular imagination. The borders of a distant Universe were still, however, convincingly beyond the imaginative horizon. In its isolation and distance from the inhabited centre, the film's location on the planet Altair-4 functions as an end-zone territory in its own right. That is, it is sufficiently removed from a sense of the known to generate a sense of mystery and for strange and marvellous things to be expected to occur there.

Like Prospero's island, however, it is clearly not intended simply to demonstrate its *removal* from the world familiar to its first audiences, but rather it also tries to evoke, if in exaggerated and stylised form, hints of the latest discoveries and advances current in its contemporary world. In his review of the film for the *Hollywood Reporter*, Jack Moffitt identified the contemporaneity of many of the film's scientific devices:

> [H]aving dipped into Sir George Thomson's 'The Foreseeable Future' I was able to recognise every scientific gimmick used in the film as being related to some theory that is at present advanced by reputable researchers. The electric rays sent forth by the human brain have, for instance, already been measured in laboratories.[4]

The central concern with a huge, and potentially hugely destructive, source of power in the film must also have had an obvious resonance for 1950s audiences living in a post-Hiroshima world. Moreover, news bulletins of pioneering explorations in space were arguably as exciting in the period and as rich a resource for fictional elaboration and fantasy as pioneering tales of the New World had been in the early seventeenth century. There are, therefore, correspondences in contemporary status between Shakespeare's 'uninhabited island' and *Forbidden Planet*'s distant star.

The isolated scientist Morbius (Walter Pidgeon) sees his daughter Altaira (Anne Francis) transfer her allegiances from him to the all-American young hero Commander Adams (Leslie Nielsen) in *Forbidden Planet* (1956).

Source: *Forbidden Planet* © Turner Entertainment Co. A Warner Bros. Entertainment Company.

The Tempest is made up of a series of archetypal narrative elements: a bitter rivalry for power between brothers; a suitor being tested by his future father-in-law; an externalised tussle between the nobler and baser parts of a single person played out through the agency of distinct characters in the world beyond; a tale of familial loss and restitution. As *The Tempest* has been passed on from one generation to the next, there have inevitably been adjustments of attention and emphasis in its narrative elements to suit the new medium and context. Gilbert Murray has referred to 'the gradual shaping and reshaping of a primitive folk-tale' in its passage through history as a process in which that core tale is constantly, and necessarily, 'modified and expurgated, re-felt and rethought'.[5] Part of the modification *The Tempest*'s 'core tale' has undergone (deliberate or otherwise) in the case of *Forbidden Planet* is the concentrated intensification of the identification between the civilised colonial and the creature of unbridled instinct, between, that is, the story's 'Prospero' and 'Caliban' equivalents. In *Forbidden Planet*, it is this one element of the tale that is played out on an unignorably large scale, eclipsing in the process some of *The Tempest*'s other narrative tropes.

In the Shakespeare play, Prospero's sense of dispossession at having been robbed of his dukedom is mirrored in Caliban's parallel sense of dispossession from *his* kingdom. Equally, Prospero's bitter eloquence about the crimes of the man who has usurped him finds a distorted echo in Caliban's complaint at the unfair treatment he has received at the hands of *his* usurper. And Prospero's consequent desire to punish those who have wronged him finds its cruder equivalent in Caliban's desire for bloody retribution on the man he feels has wronged *him*. The discernible parallel in situation and attitude between Prospero and Caliban is, needless to say, not one that Prospero himself is eager to own. Seeing the less noble aspects of his own personality crudely manifest in another does, however, give Prospero the moral luxury of expressing his contempt for these things as exemplified in another, and punishing them severely at a convenient remove from himself. As a result, he can almost atone for his own base instincts by scape-goating a proxy. By such a reading, Prospero's acknowledgement in the final moments of the play of Caliban as 'this thing of darkness' (V.i.275) and, importantly, as *his*, may indicate a recognition that he cannot continue to disown those impulses that tend towards violent retribution. The partial identification between Prospero and Caliban implied in the play, however, becomes in the film a complete identification between their equivalent characters. This identification is rendered explicit since master and creature become in this telling of the tale two conflicting expressions of the same person, id and super-ego of the same troubled psyche.

For *Forbidden Planet* to work as a narrative relative of *The Tempest*, the film's 'monster from the id' must be seen as fulfilling the play's Caliban function: the unruly force that the central character, Dr Morbius (Walter Pidgeon), must battle against and attempt to subdue. Despite its psychoanalytic terminology and central interest in Morbius's inner turmoil, the film's concern with the theme of inner conflict extends to a societal as well as to a psychological level. The psychological schism within Morbius which gives rise to two competing expressions of his psyche – one (the monster) driven by instinct, the other (the civilised man) governed by notions of honour and social taboo – becomes by this scheme a microcosmic representation of a political schism detectable in a society divided against itself. The film therefore both explores the effect of one man's aggression on himself as a divided individual, *and* turns that divided individual into a metaphor for the opposing forces of good and evil, order and anarchy, in the world. In its toying with two possible levels of meaning through a single narrative, the film as a whole, therefore, like the name and character of its central character Morbius, has something Möbian about it.[6]

Successive interpretive communities have assigned to Caliban a specific topical identity in order to find representation for the force which, in their contemporary terms, seems least amenable to reason or nurture. The particular symbolic character attached to that subversive 'Caliban' force can, therefore, be telling about the fears and preoccupations prevalent in the production context. Certainly in the case of *Forbidden Planet*, turning the image of a character divided against himself into a metaphor for a society similarly divided allegorises some of the pressing concerns of the film's production moment.

In early 1947 the House Committee for the Investigation of Un-American Activities was reformed as the Committee for Un-American Activities, and the first of what would be many investigations into Hollywood personnel was launched. The fear was that Communist sympathies were being allowed to infiltrate America's most influential mass medium. In two key speeches given in February 1950, Senator Joseph McCarthy warned of the epidemic spread of Communism and of its purchase on every level of American life.[7] Playing upon American paranoia, he presented the Soviets not as a force which might attack from their own distinct territory, but, worse, as one which was insinuating itself into the heart of American society, operating as an internal cancer: 'When a great democracy is destroyed, it will not be because of enemies from without, but rather because of enemies from within.'[8] He cited particular examples of the contaminating Communist influence percolating into American institutions – even, as he said, into the State Department. In his investigations into Un-American Activities, McCarthy created a culture in which everyone should suspect everyone else, and, in the most paranoid cases, perhaps even themselves, in the communal fight to preserve American 'honesty and decency' against the Red threat.[9]

Hollywood, as the centre for the mass dissemination of popular culture, became a particular focus for investigation and 'cleansing' action. Blacklists were assembled and suspect actors and directors found themselves unable to get work. In response, there was what Daniel Manny Lund calls 'a brief initial stiffening of the studios' collective spine' in opposition to the censoring of their output.[10] *The Day the Earth Stood Still*, for example, a science fiction film from 1951, may be seen as illustrating this early resistance to the political pressure under which the industry was placed. In this film a Martian lands in Washington DC in order to warn Earth about its imminent elimination by the peace-keepers of the Universe unless the opposing powers on Earth can themselves come together in peace. In response, the Americans first of all open fire on the interplanetary delegate for peace, and then declare co-operation with Russia impossible on any terms. The extravagant warmongering of the Americans and their crippling paranoia (filtered as these things are through the perceptions of a peace-loving Martian) are shown to be both ridiculous and dangerous to the future of the whole planet.

The House Committee was, however, uneasy about such implicit criticism of American fears and military attitudes. The political pressure was increased and Hollywood to a large extent submitted. Communism was acknowledged a threat: the imagination of America should be warned. Subversion from within became a prevalent theme in America, and its attendant anxieties formed the spring for many of the American science fiction films that emerged in the 1950s. *Forbidden Planet* seems to represent part of that collective abdication from political challenge that overtook Hollywood once the studios buckled under McCarthyist pressure. Political expediency and a desire to reflect the thinking of its moment, by now itself profoundly affected by the Red scare, combined to make an adherence to the dominant ideology seem attractive. H.L. Gold, the editor of *Galaxy Science Fiction* throughout the 1950s, made this considerable claim for the genre: 'Few things reveal so sharply as science fiction the wishes, hopes, fears, inner stresses and tensions of an era, or define its limitations with such exactness.'[11] A consideration of science fiction films of the 1950s such as *The Thing* (1951), *The Day the Earth Stood Still* (1951), *This Island Earth* (1955) and *Forbidden Planet* (1956) would certainly seem to substantiate this claim in relation to 1950s America. Indeed, throughout the 1950s and 1960s science fiction films were frequently read in politicised, allegorical terms.

In the emergence of *Forbidden Planet's* inimical force *from within*, a submerged reference may legitimately, therefore, be discerned to McCarthy's alarmist warnings about Communists as the 'enemies from within'. The parallel suggests itself for behavioural as well as definitional reasons. First, this particular science fiction 'enemy from within' is hostile to the representatives of America, sabotaging equipment and killing personnel. In attacking the spaceship's captain, Commander Adams (Leslie Nielsen), in particular, it is waging war against the epitome of the American hero – square-jawed, upright, just. Secondly, in a culture nervous about the Soviets' development of the Atom Bomb, the monster's efficiency in exploiting sophisticated technology to generate its own powerfully destructive energy may well have invited comparison. Perhaps any representation of *an* enemy of America was likely to be associated directly or indirectly by establishment thinking with *the* enemy, Communism. This one, not unlike the McCarthy alarmist caricature of Communism, is particularly anxiety-provoking by virtue of being invisible to the naked eye. American films of the mid-1950s were faced, as Phil Hardy expresses it, with 'the conflicting demands of needing to alarm and reassure their audiences simultaneously'.[12] In its presentation of an enemy that was evil, dangerously powerful, and difficult to locate, but which could, eventually, be dragged out into the open and overcome by the all-American hero with his steadfast values of honesty and decency, *Forbidden Planet* perhaps succeeded in doing both.

The Tempest offers an oblique comment on some of the latest political developments of its moment, in particular dramatising a contemporary colonial discourse. As well as being a fairytale, it is, therefore, a play with a highly topical, and politicised, charge. *Forbidden Planet* also manages to synthesise two narratives. The first is a representation of a mythic, and Shakespeare-evocative tale about a powerful father and naïve daughter stranded in a remote place, visited by a group of men from the world they have left behind and troubled by a monster driven by instinct. The second is an allegory about some of the latest concerns of *its* own moment. In its discovery of a diegetic point of fusion for a pre-existent dramatic narrative on the one hand and a commentary on its own moment on the other, it constitutes a highly Shakespearean dramatic project.

MAGIC ISLAND (MICHAEL POWELL, 1969–79, UNMADE)

In 1969, Michael Powell planned to make a film adaptation of *The Tempest* with James Mason as Prospero and, initially, with Mia Farrow as Ariel.[13] The title for the proposed film was never settled upon definitively, but one suggestion was *Magic Island*. The proposed production remained in play, in variously transmuted forms, for ten years. On a couple of occasions it came within an ace of being made: locations were secured and shooting schedules drawn up. In the event, however, the funding was not finally forthcoming and, to Powell's great disappointment, the film was never made. It has, however, left a paper trail of production documents, including a complete shooting script, in its wake, from which illuminating clues can be gleaned about the film it might have been.[14]

Powell's production notes make it clear that the look of the proposed film was to have imitated the bizarre and tormented landscape of the Hieronymous Bosch painting, *The Garden of Earthly Delights*. In the side of a mountain within this peculiar and fantastical landscape was to have been Prospero's cell, the nerve centre of operations. Eerily, the cell was to have been shaped like a giant skull within which Prospero was to have been permanently fixed for the duration of the action. The skull, therefore, had to be literally entered in order to encounter him. At first glance it might seem as if Prospero's 'head' would have been on offer as a piece of architectural and anatomical scenery to be explored. However, the surviving shooting script reveals that there was no proposal to have anything within the skull which would make Prospero any the easier to fathom. The 'head' is discovered to be hollow, bar a series of pulleys and machinery and a whirr of mechanical activity. It is, in fact, more mechanised and less personal than the painterly landscape of the world outside. Like the Wizard of Oz, the film's head symbol teases the (proposed) spectator with the *possibility* of revelation about its central protagonist's inner life, and then not only reveals little but even suggests there may be no such thing as an inner life there to be revealed. Caliban and Ariel, as the other inhabitants of the skull, provide the extent of the intimations about Prospero's character, which remains – as perhaps it does too in the Shakespeare play – in other respects impenetrable. It is, that is, a skull in function as well as appearance – a vacated space that points to its distinction from being a fleshed-out head.

The proposed production was to have made its sympathies clear in relation to Prospero and Caliban. In his 1904 stage production at His Majesty's Theatre, Herbert Beerbohm Tree had choreographed a final scene in which Caliban (played by Tree himself) was left on a rock as the courtiers sailed back to Naples. In the final moments, Caliban stretched out his arms 'in mute despair' as the ship sailed away leaving him to his lonely island kingdom.[15] This was a Caliban who was finally grateful to have been exposed for a while to the civilised benefits of empire and who was correspondingly aware that he would be bereft without them. The final scene was very much in tune with the political thinking of its imperial moment. Powell too decided to give Caliban the final moment of *his* production. In acute tonal contrast to Tree, however, as the ship sailed away Powell's Caliban was to have been seen capering on the beach that is once again his exclusive domain, accompanied on the soundtrack by the film's 'joyous' play-out music.[16] Tonally, it could not have been more different from Tree's 'mute despair'. Whereas the mainstream American studio film *Forbidden Planet* had killed off its monstrous force in its closing moments to demonstrate the restoration of order to the world, this British independent film-maker, by contrast, wanted to give a victorious Caliban the final celebratory shots of his film. Caliban's skittish dance on the sands of his own island kingdom as the credits rolled would have served as a piquant illustration of a significant critical shift: a production which pays heed to and finally rewards the voice of the colonially dispossessed emerges from a very different political wellspring than does a production motivated by the need to subdue the unruly insurgent. Power, it seems, was to have been more subversively located in Powell's production than it had been in either Tree's stage production or in MGM's *Forbidden Planet*.

Although Powell's intense efforts to launch his *Tempest* project sadly never succeeded, his work was not entirely lost in the broader context of this production history. For even unmade, as it was to remain, Powell's abortive *Tempest* has left an imprint on its world. At the very least, Powell's publicly registered interest in the play brought it back into circulation as potentially fertile material for cinematic adaptation. And in fact its interpretive and stylistic legacies are still being felt in later films. Others were able to benefit from the suggestion that the play, so rich in its language, in its opportunities for spectacle, and in its reflections on the processes of artistic construction, might offer interesting possibilities for cinematic adaptation.

THE TEMPEST (DEREK JARMAN, 1979)

In the same year, 1979, that Powell told *Film Comment* that he had still not 'wholly abandoned' his plan to make a film of *The Tempest*, Derek Jarman, an admirer of Powell's work, went into production with his own low-budget version of the play, suggesting in interview later that the project had in some sense been 'inherited' from Powell.[17] Jarman's *The Tempest* emerged from a group of film-makers who were not, and would not have wanted to be, inside the mainstream British cultural establishment. They represented a challenge in a range of ways to the dominant cultural and political expectations of their time, and were attempting to create a set of new cultural conventions in their ostentatious flouting of conservative ones.

The budget for the film was a modest £150,000. Beginning a consideration of Jarman's film with a focus on its budget is no idle distraction. In a semi-flippant aside during an interview with *Cinema Papers*, Jarman himself said, 'We shouldn't talk about aesthetics, as money is all that matters!'[18] His aesthetic choices *were*, to a large extent, determined by his constrained finances. It is also true, however, that being an outsider who did not easily find favour with potential backers[19] formed part of the platform from which Jarman operated artistically. It was his status as a gay, anti-establishment critic of mainstream political culture that invested his work with its confrontational edge. It was only possible to be that voice of challenge to the system from outside the system, a position which afforded Jarman both a certain vocal freedom and an ongoing financial headache.

In part, Jarman's film was a reaction against, in Samuel Crowl's words, the 'stale, safe atmosphere'[20] of the BBC/Time-Life Shakespeare productions launched two years prior to the release of Jarman's *Tempest*. The series certainly did encapsulate some elements of a middlebrow, establishment approach to Shakespeare that Jarman resented. His film joyously constitutes a transgressive appropriation of Shakespeare that is one in the eye for those who sought to cater to more temperate, conservative sensibilities. The things against which Jarman may be seen as reacting in his *Tempest* film are, however, more extensive than that which can be represented by the BBC/Time-Life series alone. In adapting *The Tempest* for the cinema 'as seen through the eyes of Derek Jarman' (as announced in the film's title sequence), Jarman was taking dramatic material from the heart of establishment culture and reconceiving it in terms that were radically and extensively anti-establishment.

His cast was as improbable and alternative as might be expected given this central project. And many of them shared Jarman's own fascination with the possibilities of mysticism and magic. Heathcote Williams, for example, for whom Jarman had to procure an Equity card in order to enable him to play Prospero, was himself a member of the Magic Circle and in 1970 had written *AC/DC*, a play concerned with extra sensory perception and 'interlocking psychic vibrations'.[21] As ever, the team he gathered about him was composed not of industry 'norms' but of like-minded individuals. Jack Birkett (Caliban), Toyah Willcox (Miranda) and Karl Johnson (Ariel) had all worked with Jarman on his previous film, *Jubilee* (1978), in which John Dee conjures an angel called Ariel who enables Queen Elizabeth I to be given a sobering tour of modern English urban life.

Jarman's central interpretive decision was to submerge the entire action of *The Tempest* into the complexities and confusions of Prospero's dream world. Prospero both starts and ends the film asleep, and the otherwise very spare soundtrack intermittently includes sounds of the breathing of a fretful sleeper as an attempt to remind us that everything we see is part of the dream of the central character. Since the whole action is to be seen as emanating from the unconscious mind of the dreamer, Prospero, the film therefore deliberately offers itself as an insight into the workings of that mind. And entering this Prospero's mindworld *is* psychologically revealing, in ways that the discovered pulleys and Oz-esque machinery inside Powell's skull were clearly not intended to be.

The film opens with black and white footage of a large yacht caught in a storm (originally shot on super 8 mm), intercut with colour shots of a sleeping Prospero tossing restlessly on a bed (shot on 16 mm).[22] The words from the first scene of the play are whispered urgently as a voice-over, all of them in Prospero's voice. His sleep is increasingly disturbed. We see alternately the inside and the outside of his fevered brain, still distinguished schematically for us at this stage both by film-gauge and colour. Far from his deliberately conjuring up this sea-storm, as Shakespeare's Prospero does, *it* seems rather to be assaulting *him*, in his dreams. Prospero is seen as in some sense a prey to his fantasies, rather than their organising agent. Eventually, his sleep is so disturbed that he sits bolt upright in bed, eyes open. The storm of his dream continues around him. As was subsequently also to be the case for Adrian Noble's little boy in his *A Midsummer Night's Dream*, this semblance of awakening marks the moment at which he himself becomes a protagonist in his own dream. From this point onwards Prospero starts trying to exercise some control over the course it will take. Surprisingly, perhaps, for *The Tempest*, the story created by his unconscious mind seems in this interpretation to be more a nightmarish embodiment of fears than a fantasy of wish-fulfillment.

Prospero's anxiety finds expression in his many complicated and time-consuming attempts to create his magic spells. As an earnest, ahistorical amalgam of Renaissance magi – Cornelius Agrippa, John Dee, Giordano Bruno, Paracelsus, Fludd – this Prospero spends much of the film absorbed in covering the floor and walls with his cabalistic chalk markings, in making extravagantly complex astrological calculations, and in reading his instruments that measure spiritual activity. Jarman's Prospero cannot rely on an art of rhetoric, or on an airy raising of the magic staff, in order to achieve his desired effects. Rather his magic requires much thought and effort.[23]

Given Jarman's wish to believe in the efficacy of cabalistic activity, it is striking that the magic in the film is much more noticeable for its elaborate processes than for its achievements. It generates an atmosphere, but it materially effects very little: the spiritual business, and busy-ness, scarcely ever translates into metaphysical occurrence. For all Prospero's urgent calculations and desperate attempts to subdue the world to his control through his magic, it seems to remain worryingly unsubdued for much of the time. And the things that do happen are often clearly the result of natural circumstances, not of supernatural intervention. For example, Ferdinand (David Meyer) arrives naked on the beach, following the shipwreck, and sits hugging his knees and rocking through cold. Ariel (Karl Johnson) whispers 'Full fadom five thy father lies . . .' (I.ii.399) in a characteristically energyless and lack-lustre tone, but the voice stops before Ferdinand sees a castle in the distance. The camera follows him as he stands up and walks shivering towards the silhouetted castle on the horizon. Still bent over with cold he staggers through an outer courtyard and once inside gravitates naturally towards the fire that is burning in the kitchen, where he curls up and goes to sleep. He may choose, poetically, to tell himself that it is the 'heavenly music' that has drawn him thither, but the film shows that the real draw was the more mundane prospect of warmth. There is here, as elsewhere, a natural explanation for what might else have been considered magical. Repeatedly the potential magic or mystery in a situation is punctured. There is, for example, no magical banquet offered to the courtiers. The harpy is only a harpy in the imagination of the guilty – to the film spectator it is just Ariel standing on a table in his usual worker's overalls. Similarly, the dogs only exist in the imagination of the hounded – to the film spectator, the suggestion of the chase is created by Ariel walking in small circles barking noisily.[24] There is, therefore, often a noticeable irony in the magical language used to describe a world which seems largely (although not entirely) oblivious to magic processes.

The harpy scene and the scene of the hounding are indicative of one of the strategies of the film as a whole. Jarman's uncostumed presentation of Ariel as the harpy reminds us that it is the conscience of the beholders that makes a harpy of the voice of accusation. Prospero's reliance upon the guilty

Karl Johnson plays a lacklustre Ariel in white overalls to Heathcote Williams'
anxiously industrious Prospero in Jarman's *The Tempest* (1979).
Source: The Tempest (1979). Reprinted by permission of Don Boyd.

imaginations of his enemies of old to see a screeching harpy may well have
been inspired by budgetary considerations: it was, after all, a strategy that
excused him from the need to generate expensive costumes or effects.
Whatever its original spring, however, its effect is to play nimbly with the
dynamics of the harpy scene in the play.

In *The Tempest*, Shakespeare offers us a group of educated Renaissance
courtiers who, finding themselves shipwrecked *en route* from Tunis, are a little
unnerved by an awareness of classical parallels for their own story. They are,
for example, shown joking, in slightly strained fashion, about 'widow Dido'
in Act II Scene 1 (lines 73–82). The reference testifies to their familiarity with
Virgil's *Aeneid*. Their own departure from Tunis might even have reminded
them of Aeneas's flight from Carthage. The fact that they are one and the same
place ('This Tunis, sir, was Carthage.' II.i.80) seems worth insisting upon, as if
to leave no room for evading the possible analogy between travellers from
Tunis (Alonso and company) and travellers from Carthage (Aeneas and
company). The courtiers' subsequent shipwreck would have done nothing to
lessen the uncomfortable sense of correspondence between their own fate and
that of Aeneas. Their knowledge of the *Aeneid* Book III (lines 209–249) would
have told them that Aeneas was shipwrecked in the Ionian sea. And having
been shipwrecked, he and his men then found themselves swooped upon by

harpies who ruined their food while accusing them of trying to usurp a realm not rightfully theirs. The appearance of an accusing harpy figure following a shipwreck might, therefore, even have accorded with Alonso's, Sebastian's and Antonio's sense of what could reasonably be *expected* next in a narrative such as theirs. In specifically sending such a harpy, Prospero therefore seems to trade upon a shared pool of classical learning in order to unsettle his 'guests' further: suspecting one was living out an Aeneas-evocative story would, after all, scarcely be a consoling thought.

Thus the Virgilian harpy of accusation may be considered partly a construct in the minds of the guilty. Karl Johnson's lack of additional costuming at this point in Jarman's film nicely illustrates this possibility. He does not need to look like a harpy to be understood as one: the strong expectation that such a figure would at some point appear as the mouthpiece of their guilt is sufficient to render him harpy-like in the minds of the guilty. Ariel's very unharpy-like appearance is, moreover, an exaggerated reminder that any stage performance requires the imaginative collusion of the audience in order to make it happen as a theatrical event. Showing Ariel's minimalist stage performance within a film, however, also demonstrates a confidence in the imaginative collusion that a cinema audience will bring to the work. That audience is expected to weigh the discrepancy between how it perceives, and how the on-screen audience perceives, the humble figure on the table and then to appreciate why Ariel (and Jarman) do not have to employ elaborate winged costumes and tones of screeching accusation in order to conjure a harpy in the minds of these particular guilty characters.

In both the harpy scene and the scene of the hounding with dogs Jarman exploits his audience's understanding of how theatrical as opposed to cinematic illusions typically work, in order to alert them to a deliberate self-limitation in his cinematic style at this point. An emaciated figure in white overalls standing on a table is to be understood as an arresting, accusatory harpy, and the same overalled figure walking in circles barking and panting is to be understood as a pack of hounds chasing miscreants. The film's magic is therefore most forcibly enacted in the minds of the audience, as they are invited to transform what is into what might be.

Jarman's Prospero has only an erratic control over his world. The storm alarms him, Ariel unnerves him and Miranda deceives him. The action of *The Tempest* becomes the arena in which Prospero the dreamer plays out his deep-seated fears about himself and his world. He explores them in his dream by translating them into a story for which he tries to effect a successful outcome. Freud described the process of finding narrative dream form for a primal fear as *secondary revision*. The dream narrativising of the fear can be relied upon to distort that fear, claimed Freud, thus obfuscating its own initial impulse.[25] In as far as this Prospero's dream *is* still decodable, despite the distorting influence of the story, it seems to testify, among other things, to a desperate desire to feel in control, and an appalling sense of being largely unable to be so.

Locating the action of *The Tempest* in Prospero's dreamlife was new to the cinema, although not to literary criticism. In 1967 D.G. James had written: 'we may best render the total impression [the play] makes on us by saying that Prospero in truth never left Milan, and that the island and all that we see happen on it was a dream of Prospero's only'.[26] Discussed in these terms, the action of *The Tempest* might have been considered a pleasurable dream, satisfying Prospero's lust for revenge, dynastic aspirations *and* his need to think well of himself. However, neither James nor Jarman saw it that way. James saw it as clarifying a 'half-realised anxiety'[27] in Prospero about his divided duties; Jarman made it a mix of nightmare and fantasy, presenting Prospero frequently as the victim of his own imaginative vision. Since the drama in both emerges directly from Prospero's unconscious mind, its shape, tone and progress inevitably become a direct insight into the anxieties of that mind.

In some of his earlier draft film treatments, Jarman envisaged Prospero as having even less dignity and control than he does in the finished film. At the opening of one early draft, for example, Prospero is imagined 'manacled and under restraint' in the charge of 'the immaculate figure of Ariel' who wears mirrored sunglasses.[28] Jarman refers to another set of plans in a diary entry from January 1975, quoted in *Dancing Ledge*:

> *I've made a script of it. Prospero's a schizophrenic locked into a madhouse –*
> *Bedlam. He plays all the parts – Miranda, Ariel and Caliban; the King of Naples,*
> *the Duke of Milan and the rest of them visit him and watch his dissolution from*
> *behind the bars. It works very well, but uses less than one third of the play.*[29]

In this proposed film version Prospero was to exhibit 'all the classical clichés of madness, head against the wall',[30] the action of the envisaged drama arising entirely from his dementia: 'The pursuit of his cabalistic studies has isolated him and left him unfit to govern. Confined in his cell he is prey to delusions of power (temporal) and regrets, but he is able within himself to stage a form of redemption.'[31] The predatory nature of his mindworld is thus much more obvious in this early treatment. In the actual film, it is a subtler process to portray Prospero as in some ways still the victim of the vicissitudes of his mind, although no longer obviously insane. Heathcote Williams' Prospero is prey no longer to the delusions of the mad, but to the vexed fantasies of the terrified.

Undermining Prospero's authority was in keeping with Jarman's attitudes more generally. In *Dancing Ledge* he wrote: 'I distrust all figures of authority, including the artist.'[32] His distrust sprang in part from his sense of himself, and of the gay community more generally, as, frequently, a victim of authority simply on the grounds of sexual identity. It was fundamental to his conception of the world that '[h]omosexuals have . . . a struggle to define themselves against the order of things'.[33] *The Tempest* can be read as illustrating some of the pain involved in defining oneself 'against the order of things'. Jarman depicts the island as a gay world where Caliban's lament that Prospero once loved him, Caliban's subsequent profession of self-abasing devotion to Stephano, and Ariel's eager question about whether his master loves him all are given an erotic inflection. At the film's centre, however, is the depiction of an individual deeply unhappy about his world and himself.

In many renderings of *The Tempest*, the way in which Caliban is represented is crucially important in identifying what can most alarm Prospero. In Jarman's film, however, the whole world, not simply Caliban, is a direct reflection of Prospero's mind. The focus for what Prospero finds most threatening need no longer therefore be so exclusively focused on Caliban since everything presented is shown to emanate from his hallucinating mind.

Caliban, taken in isolation, presents no great threat in this production: he is more mooncalf than monster, effete and ineffectual: 'a bald North Country prole, half slobbering idiot, half sly lecher'.[34] His effect on his environment, however, is considerable. Trinculo and Stephano first appear on the beach, having been washed in by the tide. In a parody of Robinson Crusoe, they find Caliban's footprints in the sand where he has been gathering driftwood for Prospero's fire, and with exaggerated and drunken hilarity try to walk in his footsteps. The image provides a literal representation of one of the film's central metaphors, for in this production Caliban's desire to 'people[] . . . [t]his isle with Calibans' (I.ii.352–353) is fulfilled: more and more characters effectively start to walk in his footprints. Initially, Caliban is the only sexually suggestive and overtly camp influence on the island. Gradually, however, he has a widening circle of influence, as his earthy enjoyment of his own sexuality is reflected in increasing numbers of places by increasing numbers of people. First of all Trinculo and Stephano frolic on the beach with him. Then they giggle and ride their way piggy-back through the mansion, self-transvestising on their way. Finally, in the masque celebrations at the end, the whole world seems to break out into an only slightly more co-ordinated version of Caliban's skittish dance when forty sailor boys perform an ostentatiously gay hornpipe. It is thus in an idealised form of Caliban's, not of Prospero's, image that the world is made anew.

Although so much of the rest of the world is drawn towards the camp Caliban persona, however, Prospero the dreamer is aggressive in his insistence that Caliban is distinct from him. He tries to assert his otherness from this giddy imbecile, punishing him personally and viciously for misdemeanours.

Prospero does not acknowledge 'this thing of darkness' (V.i.275) his at the moment at which any Shakespeare-aware audience would expect it. The shot, however, cuts almost immediately after this point to Prospero asleep, reminding us that Caliban is very much *his*, created, like the rest of 'the baseless fabric of this vision' (IV.i.151), entirely by *his* unconscious mind. A verbal acknowledgement is therefore unnecessary. Caliban is punished, it seems, because he represents the thing Prospero most wants to keep distinct from him, and most fears he cannot.

The unconscious mind of Prospero the dreamer has constructed a story in which a deep-seated fear has been given a tangible representation. The story partly establishes a contest between the influence of Caliban on the one hand, and that of his own dream persona on the other. His dream shows that the more the world seems to resist his influence, the more it seems to submit to Caliban's. Prospero's dream becomes increasingly saturated in gay images as the plot continues to elude his firm control. At the conclusion of the drama, however, as Caliban figures proliferate, demanding recognition, Prospero's attitude changes. In summoning the delightful Elisabeth Welsh 'Stormy Weather' number and, significantly, the sailors' crazed hornpipe, he demonstrates that his hostility to the Caliban influence in his own mindworld has abated. The darkness and stasis of the film before this point is banished in an eruption of bright colour and energetic movement. That element of his imagination that has been conjuring camp images of a cramped and unproductive nature, repressed by his own sense of taboo, is finally allowed free rein to express itself in an outburst of unrepressed camp imagery. Whereas, therefore, the scene of reconciliation with the courtiers is unremarkable, happening in the dreary world *before* the party, Prospero's reconciliation with the homosexual part of his own imagination, whose spring he has labelled Caliban, is the lively and colourful climax of the film. The tonal character of Shakespeare's masque is here gloriously inverted. Whereas the entertainment scripted by Shakespeare's Prospero formally validates chastity by promoting sexual deferral, in the sailors' dance Jarman's Prospero licenses a dionysian celebration of sexuality. It is not just, therefore, at establishment Shakespeare that Jarman is cocking an impish snook in his remade *Tempest*.

Peter Davies has characterised the process of coming out for some gay men as 'a single moment of recognition of one's "true" self, a gestalt shift in which the label of the derided other is applied to one's self'.[35] Derek Jarman's *The Tempest* seems for most of its duration to depict the internal fight *against* 'applying the label of the derided other . . . to one's self'. By this interpretive scheme, Prospero's level of personal viciousness towards Caliban can then be taken as an expression of the strength of his desire to see a disparity between them. As Nicholas de Jongh, among others, has pointed out, 'psychiatrists of the 1950s argued that the vehement persecutors of homosexuality tended to be men who were unconsciously projecting their own homoerotic desires upon others'.[36] As early as 1950, Mannoni had characterised the tension at the heart of the Caliban–Prospero relationship in terms of a repressed homosexuality: '[Caliban] is rather in the position of a repressed homosexual among overt homosexuals, a situation which, as is well known, is liable to give rise to hatred, either conscious or unconscious.'[37] Whereas Mannoni's analogy cast Caliban as this creature of repression, Jarman suggests that the prime hatred lies not in Caliban but in Prospero, and represents him – consciously or otherwise – as the character at war with himself over his sexual identity.

In its final stages, however, the film shows a joyous abandonment of this internal fight. For the majority of the dream Prospero the dreamer has been conjuring images of strife with which his dream persona has had to contend. At the end, with a welcome explosion of energy and colour for the masque-celebration, his dream persona actively chooses to provide a celebratory image of men as objects of sexual attraction. Prospero no longer needs to try desperately to subdue his environment to his control as he has ceased to interpret it as a threat. He can therefore allow himself to enjoy the sailors' dance. At the opening of the film his sleep had been very troubled: at its close he sleeps peacefully. Through the narrativising activities of his unconscious mind, he has, it seems, been reconciled to his enemy from within, and so ceased to think of it as inimical.

COLUMBIA'S *TEMPEST* (PAUL MAZURSKY, 1982)

In Paul Mazursky's *Tempest*, both Shakespeare's language and cultural context are translated into a contemporary vernacular. Whereas Jarman 'sailed as far away from tropical realism as possible' in making of Prospero's island an 'island of the mind', Mazursky specifically sought out just such island realism for the location of his film.[38] In this instantiation, *The Tempest* becomes a drama not about encounters between conflicting forces within a given character, but rather about the relationships between conflicting people in a given context.

At the centre of many Mazursky films – *Bob & Carol & Ted & Alice* (1969), *Alex in Wonderland* (1970), *Blume in Love* (1973), *Willie and Phil* (1980), *Moscow on the Hudson* (1984), *Down and Out in Beverley Hills* (1986) – is an angst-ridden hero caught between possibilities embodied by different places, or by competing lifestyles, or by more than one woman with rival claims on him. It is difficult to imagine that a preoccupation with drifting, purposeless men unwilling to, or incapable of, making active determinations about their own lives would have led Mazursky naturally to *The Tempest* as a suitable inspiration for his cinema. The play, in contrast to the Mazursky narrative model, is structured tightly around Prospero's steadily gathering 'project', and is given a discernible forward pulse by the constantly enumerated hour of the day and reiteration of the pleasure with which Prospero observes the development of his evolving (if undisclosed) plans. One of the curiosities offered by the film, therefore, is observing how the naturally antithetical concerns of the play and the director might encounter each other.

From Mazursky's attempt to coax the play into some degree of compatibility with his own cinematic preoccupations, *Tempest* emerges by turns minutely attentive to, and extravagantly negligent of, its Shakespearean precursor.[39] Although kings and princes are replaced by gangsters and architects, the play's general character scheme is preserved. Miranda (Molly Ringwald) retains her own name and role; Alonso, King of Naples, becomes Alonzo (Vittorio Gassman), head of a corrupt American business empire;[40] Caliban is transmuted into Kalibanos (Raul Julia), a local Greek islander and Ariel into Aretha (Susan Sarandon), a free-spirited young woman willing to give herself to serve somebody else's vision; Prospero becomes Phillip (John Cassavetes), a New York architect on the run from professional bullying and domestic humiliation; and Antonio is feminised as Antonia (Gena Rowlands), Phillip's unfaithful wife; Trinculo becomes Mr Trinc (Jackie Gayle), a comedian and favourite of Mazursky's Alonzo; Sebastian (Anthony Holland) keeps his name but is now a camp and unprincipled quack doctor; Ferdinand is rerendered as college kid Freddie (Sam Robards); and slightly improbably, Gonzalo is transformed into a dizzy blonde called Dolores (Lucianne Buchanan) who, with obvious Gonzalo correspondences, chatters senselessly and daydreams about everything turning out well for the good of humanity.

In addition to this cast, closely parodying that of *The Tempest*, at many given local moments the film transcribes tiny details from the Shakespeare play. In imitation of Caliban's self-abasing show of servitude to Stephano, 'I'll kiss thy foot; I'll swear myself thy subject' (II.ii.152), Kalibanos, in a flurry of apology to Phillip, says, 'Hey, Boss . . . Kalibanos kiss your feet'. In flippantly summary imitation of Gonzalo's Utopian dream for the island, Dolores, rescued from a magical shipwreck, looks about her admiringly and says, 'We could start an ideal society. Just think, no more wars, no more poverty. No more traffic jams . . .', and in imitation of Ariel's assertion that were *he* human his 'affections / Would become tender' (V.i.18–19) towards the courtiers, in Mazursky's film Aretha says to Phillip, 'It's time to forgive'. There are many such examples of moments of deliberate echoing of the Shakespeare play that can trigger an odd spark of recognition in the spectator familiar with the play. In the context of a 1982 film described by its director as 'a *contemporary comedy*' (my italics),[41] however, these transcriptions of local details of the Shakespeare text can seem incongruous and even disruptive of the film's own diegetic integrity.

Amassing imitative detail in this way certainly does not cumulatively add up to an evocation of the spirit of the Shakespeare play. What these small-scale expressions of homage to, in Mazursky's words, 'the things in the play',[42] do, rather, is to establish a relation between the film and its dramatic precursor that is not easily accounted for within a standard grammar of 'adaptation'. By calling attention repeatedly to the particular terms in which *The Tempest*'s dramatic tale is told, these incongruously recreated details draw the play firmly into the comparative territory as a significant referent for the film without ever becoming a direct pattern for it. *The Tempest* operates in relation to Mazursky's *Tempest*, therefore, in a way similar to that in which Powell, for example, had envisaged the Bosch painting operating in relation to his proposed film: not as a straight source, but as a text which when held in the same interpretive frame can usefully illuminate the contemporary text under consideration. Viewed in this context, the film's project may be seen as finding a way of clearly invoking, without actually reconstructing, the mythic tradition of *The Tempest* as a thematic backdrop for its own contemporary drama. A deliberately ambivalent diegetic territory emerges from this process in which the two conjured narratives – Mazursky's directly played out, Shakespeare's intermittently alluded to – may resonate with, and comment upon, each other.

The twin narratives within the film are, for the most part, appreciably distinct from each other. This distance is established primarily by the film's transformation of the central premises which drive the play. Crucially, for example, the central protagonist's exile on a remote Greek island is more sabbatical than banishment, a willed escape from the complexities and betrayals of New York, not the result of a high-level conspiracy and enforced exile. Moreover, the betrayal which leads him to it is not political but sexual; not a usurping brother, Antonio, hungry for power, but an unfaithful wife, Antonia, enjoying some extra-marital attention. The drama is thereby domesticated, and the action played out on a smaller scale than the play. It is perhaps for this reason that three different contemporary reviewers, consciously or otherwise picking up each other's terms, separately referred to the film as a tempest in a teapot,[43] presumably to characterise the film as a containment, a diminishing and a domestication of the forces in the play.

Despite being voted most popular film at the Toronto Film Festival on 21 September 1982, *Tempest* was not, in general, well reviewed. It was described as a 'pokey, vacuous, self-indulgent doodle' by Gary Arnold in *The Washington Post*, as 'an overblown, fancified freak of a film' by Vincent Canby in *The New York Times*, and as 'a disaster of sufficient magnitude to require the services less of a critic than of a coroner' by Andrew Sarris in *Voice*. Kenneth Turan in *California Magazine* found, in addition, that 'its endless, agonizing ditherings on borrowed Shakespearean themes' resulted in a 'pointlessness' from which it could not recover.[44] This degree of journalistic hostility was in large measure the result of unfavourable comparisons made between the film and the Shakespeare play. The film was clearly advertised as a reconception of the play and, therefore, such comparisons were both inevitable and, presumably, part of the critical attention which Mazursky and Columbia's marketing strategists had actively sought. On many levels, as was repeatedly pointed out in review, the film dilutes and tames the dramatic material it inherited, rendering it ordinary and inconsequential, and as a stand-alone piece it emerges fractured and incoherent. It is, however, by no means without interest in its reflections on the play, but these received almost no attention. Raul Julia, for example, was given enthusiastic reviews for his entertaining and astute performance as Kalibanos, but Kalibanos's crucial function in the drama went largely unmentioned.

Two years before Mazursky's film was released, Jarman had shifted the Prospero–Caliban relationship on to a psychological plane, implicitly making Caliban the camp tendency within the central protagonist with which he had to be reconciled before he could know any peace. Mazursky places the Caliban figure back in the external world as a cultural other whose interests are often antagonistic to those of the Prospero figure. In so doing, he repoliticises the relationship. As many stage Calibans have been over the past three decades (although no other screen Calibans), Kalibanos is on offer here as an exploited, displaced native of specific and knowable origin.[45] He is the developing world's impoverished, uneducated local who, paradoxically, attempts to reclaim some personal power through opportunistic sycophancy to the tourists and travellers from the First World. His efforts to exploit his American visitors through touristic selling and sycophantic flattery are small-scale, crudely expressed and honest in their transparency. By contrast, the Americans' exploitation of him for expert knowledge of the area and for manual labour is of a subtler order. The contemporaneity of the architecture of this relationship is interestingly able to revivify, in geographically inverted form, the colonial assumptions inherent in the Prospero–Caliban relationship that Shakespeare offers us.

Where Shakespeare displaced European courtiers to a space thematically and poetically evocative of the New World, Mazursky displaces rich Americans to an island in the Old World inhabited by one lone European. Thus the East to West Renaissance colonialism of the Americas that obliquely comes under scrutiny in the Shakespeare play is inverted in the film. The inversion of the demographic flow is, of course, illustrative of the transatlantic shift in the locus of colonial power that has taken place since *The Tempest* was written. Aptly enough, the imperialist premise governing the interactions between Prospero and Caliban in the play is revisited in the 1980s in ways that accord with a transformed political geography.

   Reversing the colonial demographic movement of Europeans to the Americas, and examining the cross-cultural engagement between them in specifically identifiable terms makes central to the film's dramatic project a discourse about colonialism contemporary to its own production moment. In its New World representation of the underdeveloped stasis of the Old World, it also inadvertently mirrors Renaissance colonial representations of the New World. Early European travel writers had romanticised the lifestyle of the Hispanioli and Amerindians into a vision of enviable rustic purity, the exact counter to what was seen as the cluttered and corrupt sophistication of contemporary European civilisation. The New World came to represent both how things were believed once to have been in a mythic European world before the decadence of commercial progress and individualised ambition upset the balance of created orders, *and* where things could, from this flawed starting point, be built anew. Karen Kupperman has described the aspirations of European colonisers of the Americas at the beginning of the seventeenth century:

> *Many people of all walks of life looked back nostalgically, and with a good deal of romanticism, to a settled past where everyone had a place in society and money meant less than place. This nostalgia had an impact on colonialism. Gentry or aristocratic colonial leaders . . . came to America looking for a chance to recreate such a society . . .*[46]

The New World provided for Renaissance Europe a territory – both real and conceptual – on which all expressions of societal idealism, nostalgic longing and contemporary desire could be pinned. It was described repeatedly as a *tabula rasa*, a virgin territory, offering a means of redeeming the Old World by providing the site for an alternative societal pattern.

   It is in strikingly similar terms that Mazursky's Phillip sees his Greek island. The nostalgic longing he vests in it is given an additional layer of poignancy by his sense of his own ethnicity. Phillip is a Greek-American who, like many children of *émigrés* to the affluent West, nurtures an idealised notion of the ancestral homeland as a rustic idyll where the simple things in life may be enjoyed away from the distracting clutter of an overdeveloped materialistic world. The return to Greek territory gives a specificity to the nostalgia that the Renaissance world indulged in its thinking about the New World. Their nostalgia was really about the way the Old World might once have been, displaced to a reading of the way the New World currently was. Phillip's nostalgia is genuinely about trying to recapture the world of his ancestors, and, what's more, in the appropriate territory. His backwards glance towards his antecedents is generous in its temporal sweep as is evidenced, for example, by his abortive attempt to rebuild a Greek amphitheatre on the island.

   In his elision of a poetic dream (of recapturing a Golden Age) and a political experiment (to create a Utopia), Phillip is clearly indebted less to

Shakespeare's Prospero than he is to Shakespeare's Utopianist Gonzalo. Like Gonzalo, Phillip has come from a place in which the particular expression of absolute authority, Alonzo, has been self-serving and corrupt. Phillip's Utopian dream is, like Gonzalo's, constructed in specific reaction against the imperfect old order. In *his* new society, however, Phillip has the opportunity to attempt to put into practice those things about which Shakespeare's Gonzalo can only airily hypothesise for the distraction and amusement of the assembled courtiers. Unsurprisingly, perhaps, Phillip's practical experiment to eradicate hierarchical power structures proves to be as riven against itself as is Gonzalo's articulation of a Utopian fantasy. That fantasy, as Antonio and Sebastian take pleasure in acerbically pointing out, paradoxically depends upon Gonzalo's being king of the isle to be able to decree that there should be 'no sovereignty' (*The Tempest*, II.i.152). Similarly, Phillip's rhetorical antipathy to the term 'boss' is shown to be emphatically adrift from his own uncompromising, even oppressive, occupation of the role of boss.

Mazursky's film deliberately queries the premises upon which a Utopianism may be developed, and repeatedly exposes as hollow Prospero's claims to have built Paradise on the island. Everything about the island – from its stones to its personnel – is expected to assist Phillip in indulging his dream. It is Kalibanos's refusal neatly to exemplify the pastoral purity that Phillip wishes upon him that reveals most clearly the romantic inadequacy of the dream. Both Aretha and Miranda increasingly revolt against it too though, and Phillip's own troubled dreamlife suggests that even for him it is not proving to be the restorative haven he had hoped. It becomes evident that Phillip can really know no peace until he abandons his deluded Arcadian dream and returns to New York, whose flaws he is willing to admit. In the published filmscript there is no provision for such a return, the final scripted scene being a long shot of the island gradually disappearing from sight, a point of view shot from the departing boat. The return is clearly in prospect but is not shown. In production, however, Mazursky clearly did not want to leave Phillip there at the end of the film. He therefore inserted a final dialogue-free scene in which Phillip, Antonia and Miranda, reunited following the shipwreck, are seen arriving together by helicopter back in New York. As they emerge from the helicopter, Phillip lingers to give an extravagant wink straight to camera. This is the nearest thing he has in the entire film to a soliloquy: for all its hokeyness, it suggests a level of ease and self-confidence about himself that would have been unthinkable on the island.

For the majority of the film, the desire to rediscover the simple life by deliberately rejecting the stultifying structures of an overdeveloped world, and renouncing the corrupting paraphernalia of 'progress' seems anachronistic in tone. The film depicts an idealistic desire to escape from the hollow values of an urban rat race and to return to a set of romanticised values by living communally on a rural island retreat. Such an aspiration would usually be considered more characteristic of the 1960s than of the 1980s. Dolores, for example, is presented as an entertainingly stereotyped 1960s advocate of world peace and universal love. The film, however, is ultimately not persuaded by, but deeply suspicious of, such aspirations. In demonstrating the failure of the attempt to live up to these romantic ideals, and the joy involved in finally abandoning them to return to city life, the film adopts a thoroughly 1980s attitude of cynicism about the sentimental delusions of a previous generation. It is symptomatic of that moment that it should be not the attempt to live out an Arcadian myth, but rather its abandonment in the return to the capitalist city, that merits the film's sense of celebratory closure.

The film emasculates much of the dramatic material inherited from the Shakespeare play by trying to render the action plausible in a modern world. Phillip is presented as a believably real man – weak, fallible, insecure. He is accompanied by his believably real daughter, Miranda – obstreperous, pubescent, bored – and by a nearly believably real local, Kalibanos – opportunistic, materialistic, sympathetically engaging. This almost colloquial plausibility announces the film as a very different drama from the play, and by contrast throws into stark relief the magical anti-realism of the play. Returning to it from the Mazursky film, for example, emphasises those elements of the play which remove it from the plane of ordinary people and realistic contexts. Its fairytale resonances are therefore heightened: it seems yet more intensely an extended narrative trope about ideals and the relation of power to the enactment of ideals. The play is not muddied by the indecision of the central character, by the unco-operativeness of his daughter, or by a constant, fruitless quest to summon up a purpose to give direction to an otherwise aimless life. The shift in genre from fantasy to realism that Mazursky executed in constructing his movie from a collection of situational, thematic and linguistic elements in the play brought with it a whole set of ordinarinesses of person and place on to which a later world of magical storms and efforts at conjuration could not then cogently be pasted. As Joy Gould Boyum of the *Wall Street Journal* wrote, 'Mazursky can't settle on what he wants'.[47] The result of this discernible ambivalence is finally a film riven between options: of genre, of approach to Shakespeare, even perhaps of target audience. Unlike Phillip, who lacks a central purpose, Mazursky perhaps had too many.

PROSPERO'S BOOKS (PETER GREENAWAY, 1991)

By the time Peter Greenaway came to make his film adaptation of *The Tempest*, the Shakespeare text he inherited had, of course, already been inflected by those film-makers and other interpreters who had preceded him. In the credit sequence for *Prospero's Books*, Greenaway even explicitly signalled his awareness of his own involvement in the ongoing process of textual transmission. A lengthy tracking shot follows an old book being passed carefully from hand to hand, read by some on the way and simply passed on by others. The *Tempest* book that was passed on to Greenaway by his predecessors was by no means a 'neutral' copy, but rather had accumulated a history of critical and performance meanings by having been handled and creatively 'interfered with' by a series of active interpreters before him.

Some of the specifics of the cinematic interpretive legacy Greenaway received are discernible in the finished product. When, for example, in 1980, one interviewer expressed disappointment to Jarman that his Prospero had not broken his staff, Jarman wryly replied that Prospero had instead broken his piece of chalk.[48] Moreover, one of Jarman's early draft treatments reveals that he had at one stage intended to have Prospero playing *all* the parts, as if living out a private, mad drama in his mind.[49] The legacy which Greenaway received is evident: his Prospero also abdicates his power not by breaking a magic staff but by breaking his writing implement (in this case a quill), and his Prospero actually does play all the parts, until a late stage in the drama speaking everybody's lines for them. It seems that, consciously or otherwise, Greenaway picked up the baton from Jarman on some of the options he chose not to pursue. Such interpretive relays by undeclared (or even unwitting) collaboration with a predecessor are an integral part of the processes of textual transmission.

Like Jarman, Greenaway chose to subsume the entire action of the play into the mind of Prospero. However, in *Prospero's Books* the action does not emerge from the unconscious dreamlife of Prospero, but rather is composed as a drama by conscious imaginative effort. In fact, Greenaway configures Prospero as a scholarly Renaissance doge, an amalgamation of Shakespeare's Prospero and Shakespeare himself (and a more distant allusion to the creative presences in the film of both Greenaway and Gielgud as well), composing *The Tempest* and scripting himself into his own play as its central powerful protagonist. As this Prospero-dramatist figure composes the play's dialogue from the calm haven of his Renaissance scholar's writing cell, he tries out lines in his head and on paper. The words he writes conjure the action that is then played out in the world beyond his study; enacted before his, and our, eyes in a bombardment of complexly organised visual data. All other characters in the play are, therefore, his imaginative constructs, and the action and dialogue are seen to follow the whims and determinations solely of his dramatic imagination. The reluctance of the frame to resist splintering into multiple inset windows of associated or duplicate imagery testifies to the richly hyper-textual processes of that dramatic imagination.

The film is structured around a series of non-Shakespearean interpolated descriptions of twenty-four books, descriptions which puctuate the progress of the Shakespearean drama.[50] These interjected documentary style descriptions are almost the only moments of escape which the film offers us from the boundaries of Prospero's oppressive imagination: they constitute a temporary stepping outside of his mindworld partly for the purpose of trying to explain its inner workings. The nature of the series of books is the result of Greenaway's speculations about the specific books from Prospero's Milanese library which Gonzalo might have thrown into the boat at the moment of eviction. These books, Greenaway reasons, have been Prospero's only reading for twelve years and have therefore helped to shape the man he is by the beginning of the play. Observing his passions, fears and interests has led Greenaway to ponder what in literary terms might have nurtured these in his time abstracted from society:

> *Prospero is a character who is very complex, constantly changes his moods. . . .*
> *And each time this character change happens, we as it were bring forth a book*
> *to explain how it happens. By reading this book . . . we can understand that*
> *Prospero is the man that he is.*[51]

The lines of responsibility and possession can therefore be seen as running from the books to Prospero as well as from him to them. The film could therefore as aptly (if not as elegantly) have been called *The Books' Prospero* as *Prospero's Books*. He, that is, is as much their creature as they are his possessions.

Until a late stage in the film, all the parts are spoken – in various modulations and with some overlaid electronic sampling – by the Prospero-dramatist figure who is scripting the drama. In Ariel's eleventh-hour intervention into the course of the action, however, Prospero's vocal monopoly is finally broken as Ariel expresses his disapproval of the 'revengeful humiliation' forced on Prospero's enemies.[52] Having found his own voice, Ariel then uses it to divert the plot. In reply to Prospero's question about the welfare of the captured courtiers, he hisses:

> *Confin'd together*
> *In the same fashion as you gave in charge,*
> *Just as you left them; all prisoners, sir* (V.i.7–9)[53]

His virgin voice is erratic in strength and volume, but he has gained some autonomy in daring to use it. He claims even more in then presuming to write in Prospero's book, from the pages of which he himself has sprung. Three expressions of Ariel – a child, an adolescent and a grown man – huddle together around the book, carefully writing one line each of their collective entry in it, and so reshaping the drama:

> *Your charm so strongly works 'em,*
> *That if you now beheld them, your affections*
> *Would become tender.*   (V.i.17–19)[54]

The sight of the child Ariel's higgledy-piggledy, untutored handwriting in these last three words is one of the very rare moments in the film in which a spark of warm human interest is allowed to collapse the cool subject–object distance normally maintained in the film by its extraordinarily beautiful imagery and manicured design. Even Prospero is affected by it, for he then needs no ruminative, or indulgently teasing, 'Dost thou think so, spirit?' (V.i.19)[55] to commit himself to a reformed course of action. Ariel's borrowing of the quill is, at this stage in the film, a startling image, since the quill, and all it represents, has until this point been so exclusively Prospero's domain. The transfer of the quill potently illustrates, therefore, the momentary vacillation in the drama's power dynamics. Ariel has taken the initiative, which, in the terms of the film, places him temporarily in the role of playwright. Following this daringly critical intervention from one of its characters, Prospero cannot return to writing his play. Seeing his role as author momentarily usurped by another enables him to relinquish it permanently. He breaks the quill, shuts the book and steps down from his writing cell: from this point onwards the play is left to make itself and Prospero himself contributes to it as just another participant player.

Prospero's abandonment of authorial control colours the way in which the remaining story must then be understood. Greenaway has presented the story as one constructed by a single designing mind, to whose preferences and priorities it can thereby be seen to testify. But at a late stage this author then abdicates control. There is, therefore, a clearly advertised juncture in the film at the moment when the drama seems to escape from being played out exclusively inside Prospero's mind. The force of Prospero–Shakespeare's imaginative conjuring of the fictional island territory seems to have invested it with its own strange reality. It is a world now capable of luring its creator away from his desk and into the mêlée of its own terrain.

Interposing a juncture of such structural significance in the film has the effect of offering a rationale for some of the indeterminacies and irresolutions that Shakespeare left at the close of his drama. Since characters at the end of the film are no longer trapped inside Prospero's composed drama, they can no longer be required to perform according to the dictates of his determining fantasy. Readings of the play that would make of it a drama of forgiveness and reconciliation are always problematised by the obstinate refusal of Antonio and Sebastian to declare themselves reformed. Greenaway, however, interprets the material as a drama not about forgiveness and reconcilation but about control and the ceding of control, and by such a reading, Antonio and Sebastian's refusal to be reformed makes perfect sense. They take advantage of the removal of the advertised control to deny their would-be author a fully harmonious conclusion. They do not even acknowledge Prospero's grudgingly uttered, and far from fully persuasive, words of forgiveness ('For you, most wicked sir, whom to call brother / Would even infect my mouth, I do forgive / Thy rankest fault . . .' V.i.130–132). The drama, in Greenaway's vision of it, is now subject to the whims and wickednesses of a *collection* of characters, newly plucked from a realm of puppetry to be granted their own self-determining personhood. Appropriately, therefore, it loses a sense of unilateral determinations and its characters, more like real-life people, amble haphazardly towards something that is far from being a full resolution. These final moments of the play therefore join with the descriptions of the twenty-four books in existing beyond the bounds of Prospero–Shakespeare's own imagination.

Shakespeare's plays are frequently caught in a creative dialectic between the vastly popular and the intensely learned. In the dizzying density of its artistic references, *Prospero's Books*, by contrast, is caught up in an exclusively scholarly self-referential discourse. The lowly and popular are consistently excised,[56] or transmuted into something more coolly appreciable. Moreover, the sense of a tremendous time pressure under which Prospero is operating in order to accomplish all that is necessary, becomes lost in a far more dilatory approach to action. In fact, the whole film feels more like an extended masque than a drama in which the sequence of action matters crucially. The film has, therefore, modulated the tone of the play significantly. As an adaptation of Shakespeare's *The Tempest*, it powerfully and interestingly releases some of the play's possible meanings – notably the sense of the play as a self-referential comment on the processes of artistic creation, and the plot-turning significance of the crucial moment when Ariel dares momentarily to displace Prospero as moral arbiter. In doing so, however, the film performs an act of usurpation of its own, robbing the words to which it seems so attentive of their power, in the very domain in which they used to hold supremacy. They, like Caliban, are supplanted by a wizardry with which they cannot compete, although *their* usurper is not a human magician but an irrepressible graphic paintbox. As the words are contained within frames, and reified as technologically complex design artifacts, they are also largely defunctioned as agents of meaning. Daringly for a Shakespearean project – and surprisingly, perhaps, given the proliferation of words seen and heard in the film – meaning has been largely wrested from the domain of the verbal. The domain of the painterly and the artistically allusive in which it has been broadly resituated forms part of the subject of discussion in Chapter 8.

*

Finding a territory equivalent to Prospero's 'uninhabited isle' has set film-makers an interpretive challenge. A frontier space needs to be found that can resonate with a sense of fearful and wonderful possibility in ways that correspond to the effect that the allusion to a mythically reconceived version of the New World presumably would have had for a London playhouse audience of 1611.

In Percy Stow's 1908 silent film version of *The Tempest* (discussed in Chapter 1), there was no sense that this was a land at a dramatic and dis-concerting remove from the civilised centre. It was a pleasant, and knowable, territory that oscillated between the sunny English countryside and stage sets of a rocky place. Subsequently, *The Tempest's* island territory has been variously reconfigured as a planet at the futhermost reaches of the Universe, a mythic, tormented painterly landscape, a troubled dreamlife, a sunny Greek island and the densely bookish, highly stylised world conjured by a power-obsessed dramatist. It is perhaps noticeable that only one of these film-makers – Mazursky – has chosen to try to represent the requisite anxiety-provoking space by locating the drama on an actual island, and doing so only succeeded in rendering banal the play's excitingly peripheral zones of mythic and imaginative extravagance.

Despite the blip that Mazursky's film represents in many ways, there is a skeletal trend detectable in these film adaptations of *The Tempest*. Over the course of the century, Prospero's island, as represented in film interpretations, has become decreasingly a geographical space in which external conflicts may be played out *between* people, and increasingly a psychological space in which internal conflicts may be played out *within* one character. Where, therefore, *Forbidden Planet* had suggested that the tale's Caliban character could emerge directly from the fantasy life of the central powerful protagonist, Jarman suggested that not just Caliban but *everything* in the tale emerged directly from there. Whereas Powell had planned to offer a hollow skull and invite us to peer inside it, Jarman and Greenaway each offer a far more intimate and re-vealing tour of a human psyche. Cinema's preference for a more psychological reading of the play in part testifies to its own particular fluency in rendering a subjectivised world. It is also, however, simply indicative of where the uncharted spaces of the world have, in the past thirty years, increasingly been considered to lie. The psychological world, unlike its material counterpart, still offers spaces to be explored and in which to be awed and bemused. The frontier, that is, has moved inwards.

Caliban has been the most obvious pointer to cinema's interest in Prospero's unconscious, and the internalising of the Caliban figure on film predated the internalising of the whole action. In most cinema adaptations, he has tended to be presented less as the externally identifiable other (whose alterity must be battled against and subdued), and more as the troubling force within (against which the Prospero figure must contend, and to whom he must finally be reconciled in order to secure his own inner peace). How that inimical force has been identified – as mindless savage, as repressed incestuous desires, as a Communist threat, as a self-destructive xenophobia, as a homosexual tendency, as an unruly, untutored libido, as a contempt for culture – enables each production to synthesise a reinterpretation of the Shakespeare play with a comment on its historical moment.

In 1916, Ashley Thorndike wrote of the play's island as a place where we may encounter:

> music and moonlight and feeling, and also fun and mischief and wisdom. There, in tune with the melody and transfigured by the charm of the moonlight, we may encounter the nonsense of drunken clowns, the mingled greed and romance of primitive man, the elfishness of a child, the beauty of girlhood, and the benign philosophy of old age.[57]

It is not to such things, however, that contemporary productions of *The Tempest* typically draw attention. The significance of the comedy and low-life skittishness has, for example, been diminished, Ariel has become less elfish and more angular or embittered, and the play as a whole has become darker – a disquisition on the problems of empire, or an angst-driven journey into a troubled psyche. Cinema has played a part in this shift of interpretive attention in relation to *The Tempest*. The contemporary substitutes for actual islands found by film-makers suggests that a discernible shift has taken place in where we locate the precarious and disconcerting margins of our lives. As Linda Williams suggests, monsters are indeed no longer things which jump out of the closet: 'instead, the body is the closet from which the monster jumps'.[58]

FURTHER READING

Douglas Bruster, 'The Postmodern Theatre of Paul Mazursky's *Tempest*', Chapter 2 in Mark Thornton Burnett and Ramona Wray (eds), *Shakespeare, Film, Fin de Siècle* (Basingstoke: Macmillan, 2000), pp.26–39.

John Collick, *Shakespeare, Cinema, Society* (Manchester: Manchester University Press, 1989), pp.98–106.

Peter Greenaway, *Prospero's Books* (London: Chatto & Windus, 1991).

Derek Jarman, *Dancing Ledge* (London: Quartet, 1984).

Douglas Lanier, 'Drowning the Book', in James C. Bulman (ed.), *Shakespeare, Theory and Performance* (London: Routledge, 1996), pp.187–209.

Paul Mazursky and Leon Capetanos, *Tempest: A Screenplay* (New York: Performing Arts Journal Publications, 1982).

Kenneth S. Rothwell, *A History of Shakespeare on Screen* (Cambridge: Cambridge University Press, 1999), pp.204–11.

Christel Stalpaert (ed.), *Peter Greenaway's 'Prospero's Books': Critical Essays* (Ghent: Academia Press, 2000).

NOTES

1. William Wordsworth, *The Prelude; or, Growth of a Poet's Mind; an Autobiographical Poem* (London, 1850), BK XI, p.141.

2. See, for example, Paul Brown, ' "This thing of darkness I acknowledge mine": *The Tempest* and the discourse of colonialism', Chapter 3 in Jonathan Dollimore and Alan Sinfield (eds), *Political Shakespeare: Essays in Cultural Materialism* (Manchester: Manchester University Press, 1985), pp.48–71, and Alden T. Vaughan, 'Shakespeare's Indian: The Americanization of Caliban', *Shakespeare Quarterly* 39 (1988), pp.137–53.

3. A.D. Nuttall, *Two Concepts of Allegory* (London: Routledge, 1967), p.138.

4. Jack Moffitt, ' "Forbidden Planet": Class A Science-Fiction Picture', *Hollywood Reporter* 138, 43 (12 March 1956), p.3.

5. Gilbert Murray, *The Classical Tradition in Poetry* (London: Oxford University Press, 1927), pp.235, 237.

6. Dr Morbius's name is evocative both of *morbus*, the Latin word for disease, and *möbius*, the mathematical phenomenon whereby a twisted strip in circular form appears to have two surfaces but upon closer inspection is discovered only to have one. Both resonances are illuminating about Morbius's personality. The cancerous effect he has upon his environment forms the basis for the film's plot, and what initially seem to be two distinct presences in the film prove by the end to be differing expressions of the same central psyche. Morbius is therefore both the linguistic and psychological fusion point for *morbus* and *möbius*.

7. McCarthy first gave his landmark speech on 9 February 1950 at the McLure Hotel in Wheeling, West Virginia. He repeated a version of it on the Senate floor on 20 February 1950, submitting a copy for Congressional records. The speech is reproduced in, for example, Brian MacArthur, *Twentieth-Century Speeches* (London: Viking, 1992), pp.239–42.

8. MacArthur (1992), p.240.

9. Ibid., p.242.

10. Daniel Manny Laud, 'Writing Film History', in Sari Thomas (ed.), *Film/Culture: Explorations of Cinema in its Social Context* (Metuchen, NJ: Scarecrow, 1982), p.52.

11. H.L. Gold, quoted in Kingsley Amis, *New Maps of Hell: A Survey of Science Fiction* (London: Gollancz, 1961), p.64.

12. Philip Hardy (ed.), *Science Fiction* (London: Aurum, 1991), p.xv.

13. For a detailed analysis of the surviving shooting script and discussion of this unrealised film, see Judith Buchanan, ' "Like this insubstantial pageant faded": Michael Powell's *The Tempest*', *Film Studies*, 1, 2 (March 2000), pp.79–90.

14. I am grateful to Michael Powell's widow, Thelma Schoonmaker Powell, for giving permission for me to consult these unpublished documents.

15. From Tree's tonally charged stage direction for the final tableau in *The Tempest: As Arranged for the Stage by Herbert Beerbohm Tree*, Souvenir Edition for the 50th performance in the run (London: J. Miles & Co., 1904), p.63.

16. Shooting script (unpublished), p.99.

17. Ian Christie, *Arrows of Desire: The Films of Michael Powell and Emeric Pressburger*, 2nd edn. (London: Faber, 1994), p.99.

18. Anne-Maree Hewitt, 'This Jarman Man', *Cinema Papers* 65 (September 1987), pp.12–14.

19. Jarman did, however, acquire various private sponsors, of which the most prominent was Don Boyd who financed *The Tempest* through his wholly owned company and *War Requiem* out of his own pocket.

20. Samuel Crowl, 'Stormy Weather: A New *Tempest* on Film', *Shakespeare on Film Newsletter* 5, 1 (December 1980), p.1.

21. *AC/DC*, first performed at The Royal Court Theatre, May 1970; playscript (London: J. Calder, 1971).

22. It is in keeping with Jarman's disparagement of the concept of single authorship that he appropriated this Super 8 found footage of a sea storm and, having transferred it to 16 mm, incorporated it as part of his own creative project. The cut-in found footage both created a contrast between the texture of Prospero's dream world and the texture of our observation of his dreaming presence, *and* made literal the sense of the artist as an organising agent of material, rather than as its exclusive creator. In *Jubilee* (1978), he had used some of his own earlier Super 8 footage from *Glitterbug*, on that occasion enjoying the contrasts in grain that juxtaposing footage shot on different gauges offered. A notion of the collaborative artist was politically more attractive to Jarman. In 1991 Colin MacCabe even reported that it was Jarman's avowed ambition 'to make a film which would be produced entirely by his collaborators'. Colin MacCabe, 'Edward II: Throne of Blood', *Sight and Sound*, 6 (October 1991), p.14.

23. Jarman's interest in the work of Frances Yates, explicitly detailed in several of his pre-production documents, is revealing about his concern with a living hermeticism eager to establish its roots in hermetic tradition. Unpublished draft treatments and production notes for Jarman's production are held in Special Materials at the British Film Institute (hereafter BFI).

24. An earlier draft treatment of the play had, more ambitiously, stipulated that at this point 'strange figures clad in leather with savage dogs hunt Stephano, Trinculo and Caliban'. See The Derek Jarman Special Collection, held in Special Materials, BFI. Item 19: typescript treatment (1976). In shooting, however, budget and time restrictions pushed the scene towards a much more spare and suggestive style.

25. For an accessible discussion of secondary revision, see Anthony Storr, *Freud* (Oxford: Oxford University Press, 1989), p.33.

26. D.G. James, *The Dream of Prospero* (Oxford: Clarendon Press, 1967), p.149.

27. Ibid., p.150.

28. The Jarman Special Collection. Item 12: (June 1976).

29. Derek Jarman, *Dancing Ledge* (London: Quartet, 1984), p.140.

30. The Jarman Special Collection. Item 16: MS notes and sketches (Autumn 1974).

31. The Jarman Special Collection. Item 16: (Autumn 1974).

32. Jarman (1984), p.241.

33. Ibid.
34. Philip French, *The Observer*, 4 May 1980, p.15.
35. Peter Davies, 'The Role of Disclosure in Coming Out Among Gay Men', in Ken Plummer (ed.), *Modern Homosexualities* (London: Routledge, 1992), p.75.
36. Nicholas de Jongh, *Not in Front of an Audience: Homosexuality on Stage* (London: Routledge, 1992), p.50.
37. O. Mannoni, *Prospero and Caliban: The Psychology of Colonization*, trans. Pamela Powesland (London: Methuen, 1956), p.75.
38. Jarman (1984), p.186.
39. In describing the play's structural role in relation to this particular film, I prefer the phrase 'precursor text' to the more obvious 'source text'. This seems more appropriate to this analysis given the oblique nature of the indebtedness of Mazursky's film to Shakespeare's play.
40. Shakespeare's Alonso and Mazursky's Alonzo may be distinguished from each other by the spelling of their names, taken from the First Folio and Mazursky's credits respectively. Vittorio Gassman in the part of Alonzo in this film is, as the most famous postwar Italian stage Hamlet, himself a resonant Shakespearean reference.
41. Mazursky described the production as 'a contemporary comedy with dramatic overtones'. See Columbia Pictures' unpublished Preliminary Production Notes (1982), p.1. Copy consulted at the Library of Congress Motion Picture Division Reading Room.
42. Columbia Press Pack (1982), p.2. Copy consulted in the Motion Picture Division Reading Room at the Library of Congress.
43. Andrew Sarris, 'Tempest in a Teapot', *Voice*, 17 August 1982, p.45; David Sterritt, 'Tempest in a Critical Teapot', *The Christian Science Monitor*, 26 August 1982, p.19; 'Despite the title and the storm scene, a more appropriate title might have been "Teapot".' Quoted from Gary Arnold, 'Tempest: Steady Drizzle', *Washington Post*, 24 September 1982, C3.
44. Arnold (24 September 1982), C3; Vincent Canby, 'A Prospero for Today', *New York Times*, 13 August 1982; Sarris (17 August 1982), p.45; Kenneth Turan, quoted in Rita Kempley's article, 'Tempest: Apologies to the Bard', *Time Life*, 24 September 1982, W/E p.15.
45. Of particular interest in this respect is Aimé Césaire's *Une Tempête* (Paris, 1974), a rewritten stage play which makes Caliban specifically into a black man of the developing world who eloquently complains about his subjugation to Prospero, the 'Enlightened', white European.
46. Karen Ordahl Kupperman, *Settling with the Indians: The Meeting of English and Indian Cultures in America, 1580–1640* (London: J.M. Dent, 1980), pp.8–9.
47. Joy Gould Boyum, *The Wall Street Journal*, 20 August 1982, p.20.
48. Samuel Crowl, 'Stormy Weather', *Shakespeare on Film Newsletter* 5, 1 (December 1980), p.6.
49. The Derek Jarman Collection. Item 16: MS notes and sketches (Autumn 1974). See also the Jarman interview in *Film Directions* 2, 8 (1979), pp.14–15, in which he discusses this earlier production idea.
50. Numbers are, as always in a Greenaway film, significant. The twenty-four books which punctuate the action may be taken as alluding both to the hours of the day which must be marked off before the drama (which obeys the neo-classical unities) can end, and to the traditional cinema projection speed (24 frames per second) which determines the nature of the product we are viewing. Peter

Greenaway's time working for the Central Office of Information inculcated in him a passion for ordering systems and categories for processing and presenting information, a passion which repeatedly finds expression in his films.

51. Greenaway, interviewed on BBC 1's *Omnibus* (September 1991).

52. Greenaway, *Prospero's Books: Film-script* (London: Chatto & Windus, 1991), p.9.

53. Ibid., scene 88.1, p.148.

54. Ibid., scene 88.1, p.148 and 88.3, p.150.

55. The line is in Greenaway's script (scene 88.1, p.148), but cut in the film itself.

56. For example, the following lines are cut: Sebastian and Antonio's quibbling word-play, II.i.10–55; Stephano and Trinculo's banter, II.ii.25–36, 41–58, 61–65, 67–90, 92–100, 106–117, 120–136, 142–147, 150–159; Stephano and Trinculo's drunken ramblings, III.ii.1–39; Ariel's teasing of Stephano and Trinculo, III.ii.43–50, 61–85; Stephano and Trinculo and Caliban's drunken singing, III.ii.109–132.

57. From Ashley H. Thorndike's 'Introduction' to Rudyard Kipling, *How Shakespeare Came to Write the 'Tempest'* (New York: Dramatic Museum of Columbia University, 1916), p.2.

58. Linda Ruth Williams, 'Movie Nightmares', *Sight and Sound*, May 1993, p.32.

CHAPTER SEVEN

Boxing with Ghosts:

The Shakespeare Films of Kenneth Branagh

In December 1935, Richard Watts complained in *The Yale Review* about American screen actors' poor standards of Shakespearean verse-speaking. The problem, he said, was that 'the [American] cinema actor . . . simply doesn't possess the sort of voice or voice-training that equips him for the poetic drama'. This difficulty could perhaps be overcome, he suggested, 'by bringing a few more boatloads of English actors to Hollywood'.[1]

This idea was not new. The desire to import English acting talent to add gravitas to American screen presentations of Shakespeare had begun in the silent era, predating the need for nuanced verse-speaking. In 1916, for example, D.W. Griffith had invited the spectacular actor–manager Herbert Beerbohm Tree to California to make *Macbeth* for Triangle-Reliance under his broad supervision (although directed by John Emerson). Tree was evidently flattered by the way he was fêted on his arrival and, as he reported after his first day of shooting, very taken too by the 'pictorial possibilites' of 'this strange new art'.[2] For all his enthusiasm, however, he was not the easiest man to direct. Even on set, he was self-consciously a Shakespearean, and insisted on reciting large chunks of text for the camera, even though not a word he said would be audible in the film. Weighing courtesy against economics, the production team decided to shoot sparingly in order to save their filmstock and, where necessary, simply to pretend to their exalted guest that the cameras were still rolling for the duration of his declamations. An English respect for linguistic fidelity was even then, it seems, coming into conflict with an American concern to give pace and autonomy to the movie. Nevertheless, Tree's name, reputation and even nationality were thought useful for selling the film.[3]

It was not the most auspicious start to transatlantic Shakespearean cinematic collaborations. This notwithstanding, in the sound era the selective use of British Shakespearean actors to enhance American Shakespeare films has become almost habitual. Perhaps most famously, Joseph Mankiewicz imported an array of British actors to Hollywood to add cultural ballast to his impressive MGM production of *Julius Caesar* (1953). Mankiewicz's film not only sports a transatlantic cast but also makes purposeful use of it within the film. The Roman subversives are played by British actors: James Mason (Brutus), John Gielgud (Cassius), Deborah Kerr (Portia), Edmond O'Brien (Casca). Those loyal to imperial Rome, by contrast, are played by Americans: Louis Calhern (Julius Caesar) and Marlon Brando (Mark Antony). The pattern of American and English accents within the film therefore narrates its own mini-drama about distinct communities as opposing forces. Beyond that, the accent pools pitted against each other also alludes tangentially to the story of the two national film industries in the 1950s. Shakespeare's idealistic political subversives take their stand against the might of imperial Rome but cannot finally defeat it. Similarly, the smaller, idealistic British film industry of the 1950s could rail at the presumptuous power of Hollywood, and even have its moment in the sun now and again with an occasional successful release. Ultimately, however, Brutus-like, it was doomed to fail in any endeavour to topple the power base of its tyrannical competitor. Emerging as this film does directly from that tyrannical competitor, it is perhaps no surprise that it should have cast the British as the insurgents: to have done otherwise would have been to spike its own metanarrative. To the film's credit, however, tribute is paid to the integrity if not the political acumen of those insurgents. Hollywood took its hat off to its small-fry British cousin even as it squeezed it to within an inch of its life. The eloquence of the schematised casting of the British and Americans therefore transcends the bounds of the film's own surface narrative.

But Hollywood could not scoop all the honours for Shakespeare films. Laurence Olivier's films of the 1940s and 1950s introduced a standard of Shakespearean verse-speaking that would have pleased even Watts, and in so doing, Olivier partially reclaimed Shakespeare from Hollywood for the British film industry. His *Hamlet* (1948) even won the Academy Award in 1949 for best actor, best art direction (black and white), best costume design (black and white) and best picture. Staking the national claim decisively, Olivier cast his films exclusively from a pool of well-known English actors.

For the casting of his first Shakespeare film, *Henry V* (1989), Kenneth Branagh followed suit. It was not, therefore, until Branagh's second Shakespeare film, *Much Ado About Nothing* (1993), that the demographic flow of acting talent that Watts had suggested might rescue Hollywood's engagements with Shakespeare was actually reversed. For *Much Ado*, Branagh assembled what Richard Briers has described as 'a mongrel company with pedigree', an eclectic mix of British and American actors.[4] Branagh has not had to watch boatloads of British actors set sail for Hollywood to bolster Shakespearean film-making there. Rather, for *Much Ado*, and his subsequent Shakespeare films *Hamlet* (1996) and *Love's Labour's Lost* (2000), he has instead attracted box-office American stars to come and add commercial weight and screen glamour to his British Shakespearean productions. The result has both given a transatlantic flavour to some of his cast lists and, by inverting the direction of the talent drain called for by Watts, adjusted the power balance implicit in the two film industries, in relation to Shakespeare films at least. Branagh's Shakespeare has even been used as a rallying call for the British film industry more generally, the charity première of *Much Ado* in 1993 provoking unprecedented cries of 'Up the British Film Industry' from the enormous crowd gathered outside the Empire Leicester Square.[5] Branagh has both acted and directed in Hollywood in non-Shakespearean productions, and received funding from American companies such as Samuel Goldwyn and Miramax for his Shakespearean ones. Nevertheless, he has clearly branded his Shakespeare films as British products, and in addition to doing the pre- and post-production work for his films in England, has made his allegiances plain by also summoning American actors to Europe for all the principal photography.

Branagh, like Mankiewicz before him, is fully conscious of the implications of casting from an international pool, and even on occasion alludes to the processes of cultural encounter within his own productions. In his *Hamlet* (1996), for example, Branagh cast Charlton Heston as the first player, thus creating a memorable scene as his own Hamlet directs Heston's first player in the formal lament for the fall of Priam. Both a dying Priam and a grieving Hecuba are here given fleeting appearances among the burning ruins of Troy in the persons of John Gielgud and Judi Dench respectively. If we peep *through* character for a moment and allow ourselves to see the actors inside the roles, as the mechanisms of cinema constantly invite us to do, the overall shape of the scene is even more striking. A young British film director directs a big-name American movie star in narrating the demise of *the* standard bearers for English classical acting, among the ruins of their city. The iconic American movie star displaces these English classical actors both literally in frame, in transfixing close-up, and symbolically, in the economics of Shakespearean production more generally. The cries of Dench's Hecuba are tellingly inaudible. She is quite literally silenced that Heston may tell us movingly of her plight. Thus the scene as a whole mock-dramatises Branagh's own direction of big-name American movie stars in roles that signify the displacement of traditional English classical actors. In a casting strategy that had already aroused considerable attention, and a raised eyebrow or two, in the British press, Branagh had included Denzel Washington, Keanu Reeves and Michael Keaton in his cast for *Much Ado*. The cameo moment of Heston's impressive silencing and displacement of Gielgud and Dench in *Hamlet* grandly mock-allegorises the implications of just such a casting.

In Branagh's 1990 Renaissance Theatre Company's touring production of *A Midsummer Night's Dream*, Branagh himself played Peter Quince. In rehearsing his acting troupe, Quince had converted himself with comic suddenness into a parody of a self-fancying film director, 'with von Stroheim jodhpurs and megaphone'.[6] It is tempting to imagine that in playing Quince in this way, Branagh was poking fun at his own filmic ambitions, or perhaps more precisely at the way in which, by 1990, those ambitions were being perceived by a British press notoriously ambivalent about home-grown success. At the moment of instructing the first player in *Hamlet*, Branagh again positions himself temporarily as a film director, and this time as one with a genuine star to direct rather than a bunch of hokey amateurs. In *Hamlet*, however, the reference functions more as a canny, and even self-deprecating, reflection on the implications of Branagh's own directorial and casting decisions than as the entertaining cartoon it had been in *A Midsummer Night's Dream*. The celebration of a star screen persona at the cost of English classical acting, as enacted in Heston's lament for Gielgud, cannot of course be taken altogether seriously in relation to Branagh's own work; although he speaks Shakespeare with the greatest possible degree of naturalism, and even colloquialism, he always retains a sense of the poetry. Like his Peter Quince, however, the illustration does demonstrate a delicious self-awareness about how he might be perceived.

Small moments of personalised inscription of this sort crop up intermittently in Branagh's *Hamlet*. However, each time we think we identify an autobiographical reference in aspects of the film, we have to realise that Branagh is himself ahead of us. Our detection of something of Branagh in Hamlet is a little after the fact since Branagh had been detecting something of Hamlet in himself for years. As a teenager he saw Jacobi as Hamlet for the Prospect Theatre Company. He subsequently played the part himself as a twenty year-old at RADA, played Laertes to Roger Rees' Hamlet for the Royal Shakespeare Company in 1984, and Hamlet again for the Renaissance Theatre Company in 1988 ('Errol Flynn with a PhD'),[7] this time directed by Jacobi. The role stayed with him. It is no surprise, perhaps, that in 1989 it was a 'Hamletian angst' that he sought in his portrayal of Henry V.[8] The prevalence of Hamlet as a referent for his own life and work returned irrepressibly to the fore when he played Hamlet in a radio production in 1992, and again later the same year in Adrian Noble's production on the Barbican stage for the Royal Shakespeare Company. By the time he took his Hamlet to the screen in 1996, he was, by his own admission, a man obsessed, and feeling his own Hamletian qualities keenly. When subsequently asked in an interview for *The Times* whether he was a depressive, for example, he answered: 'Sure, big-time. It's hard to get out of. Deep, deep, deep and wide-ranging. *Hamlet* sums up clinical depression, which is possibly why I'm so obsessed with the play.'[9]

Stephen Berkoff proffers an explanation for the particularly personal hold that the part of Hamlet can exert on actors: 'Since Hamlet touches the complete alphabet of human experience every actor feels he is born to play it. . . . [W]hen you *play* Hamlet, he becomes *you*. When you play Hamlet, you play yourself and play the instrument which is you.'[10] Simon Russell Beale, who played Hamlet at the National in the 2000/01 season and subsequently on tour, has commented upon the accommodating versatility of the part that allows itself to bend to the personality of the actor: 'You bring whatever you are to the role, and it accepts you.'[11] For Branagh, as for many actors who have played the role, Hamlet has been absorbed fundamentally into his own self and become an intellectual and emotional filter through which to experience and make sense of the world.

Nevertheless, Branagh's engagements with Hamlet are different only in degree and not in kind from his engagements with his other roles. As part of his preparation for several parts, he has concentrated on the character's correspondences with his own life. For example, when preparing for his season as Henry V in the Royal Shakespeare Company's 1984 season, he talked up to himself the points of coincidence between his life and Henry's: 'Henry was a young man, and so was I. He was faced with an enormous responsibility. I didn't have to run the country and invade France, but I did have to control Brian Blessed and open the Stratford Season.'[12] Identifying some points of connection, however tongue-in-cheek, proved helpful for Branagh and his Henry was widely acclaimed. It is interesting to note that in theorising the process of assuming a role, he does not, as some actors do, first seek to map the distinctions between his self and his role in order then to discover ways of bridging the gap between the two. Nor does he have to reach into what Simon Callow has referred to as the bank of 'muscular memory' in order to resummon a vaguely analogous experience from the past which, reinvoked, can then invest a performance with authenticity.[13] Rather, Branagh enjoys the process of fusing his immediate self with the character and allowing a composite persona to emerge from the engagement. The analogous experiences for which he seems to reach are not locked in the mists of time, but are now – coterminous with the act of playing. Little wonder we often suspect we detect something about Branagh in the roles in which we see him. That seeming transparency is something he nurtures, often advertising the processes of self-disclosure – or at least a courted *semblance* of self-disclosure – every bit as much as the processes of self-obfuscation in his work.

And it is not only in Branagh's Shakespearean work that this tendency is manifest. It is no surprise, for example, that the part of Sir Ernest Shackleton in the two-part big-budget Channel Four film *Shackleton* should have appealed.[14] The Antarctic explorer's goal – to reconquer territory where someone else's flag had already been planted (that of the Norwegian Roald

Amundsen) – finds its own resonance in Branagh's early decision to make a *Henry V* for the cinema even after Olivier had famously stamped his pioneering mark on it. Moreover, Shackleton's efforts to fund his British Imperial Trans-Antartic Expedition have clear points of correspondence with Branagh's own working method and experience in launching his Renaissance Theatre Company. Driven by a passionate belief both in himself and in the romance of the project, and supported by a group of underpaid fellow enthusiasts, Shackleton personally door-stopped potential investors, committed himself to making his vision for the expedition accessible not just to experts in the field but also to the general public, and was even given a royal blessing in private audience with the king. Branagh's entrepreneurial acumen in finding funding for seemingly risky endeavours, charisma in attracting other talented people to work with him, determination to render *his* chosen passion accessible to a broad audience and own well-publicised interviews with royalty[15] add an only minimally submerged autobiographical piquancy to his performance as Shackleton.

In writing *Much Ado About Nothing*, Shakespeare evidently had his actors very much in mind. So much so that in writing the part of Dogberry, he entered the names 'Dogberry' and 'Kemp' (variously spelt) interchangeably in speech-headings.[16] Will Kemp was the comic actor for The Lord Chamberlain's Men in the 1590s and was not only potently present 'in' his roles once these took the stage, but seems to have been informing them even at the stage of composition. When Shakespeare thought of his fictional creation Dogberry, he thought also of his real actor Kemp: both seem to have been part of the character he committed to paper and his variable speech headings testify to this.

It is, perhaps, this sort of Dogberry/Kemp composite presence of role and actor combined that Branagh brings to his performances as Henry/Branagh, Benedick/Branagh, Hamlet/Branagh and Berowne/Branagh. Or, perhaps it would be more accurate to suggest that it is this sort of composite presence not that he necessarily intentionally generates, but rather that in his case we insist on detecting in his performances (which accounts more modestly only for reception). Writing in *The Sunday Telegraph* in response to Branagh's stage Hamlet of 1992, John Gross stated: 'Hamlet doesn't seem an obvious part for Kenneth Branagh. You might even say that he doesn't look like Hamlet. Certainly the pale cast of thought isn't the first thing you associate with his cheerful features.'[17] There is, it seems, a particularly keen desire to see a correspondence between Branagh the man and the roles he plays, and to lament its absence if it is not immediately obvious. Branagh's personal visibility within discussion of his roles is perhaps testimony as much as anything to his own prevalence in discussions of Shakespeare film more generally: his unrivalled profile in relation to this body of films makes his own self hard to ignore, especially perhaps in the nature of the performances he offers.

HENRY V (1989)

It was in his film version of *Henry V* that Branagh was at his most personally visible. The correspondences between the man and the role on that occasion easily transcended those that Branagh had himself identified when he played the part on the Royal Shakespeare Company stage. The facts about Branagh's precocious ambition and achievements are well known. He won the RADA Bancroft Gold Medal at 21. He played Henry V for the RSC at 23. He formed the Renaissance Theatre Company at 24. He persuaded Derek Jacobi, Judi Dench and Geraldine McEwen to direct for the first time at 25. He made a film of *Henry V* at 27. He published his autobiography at 28.[18] He was, that is, as ambitious a young hothead as Henry V himself.

In the first act of Shakespeare's play, Henry's youth is jeered at by the French. When it became clear that Branagh was contemplating making a film version of *Henry V*, to be more in keeping with the times than Olivier's much revered 1944 masterpiece then seemed, Branagh too was lampooned for his youthful presumption. In the drama the young pretender (Henry V) cheekily takes on the established, older authority (King Charles VI of France) and beats him on his own territory at the battle of Agincourt. In real life the young pretender (Kenneth Branagh) was seen to be challenging the established authority (Laurence Olivier) by producing a new film version of *Henry V* to rival the 1944 cinematic classic. The move, like Henry's claim on France, was both impudent and, in the event, impressively successful.[19] And just as in the play the mockery of the French is silenced by the subsequent success of Henry's military campaign, so many of Branagh's detractors softened the charges of hubris once they had seen the film. For this insistently biographical reading to work most neatly, Olivier himself would have been needed generously to fall on his sword by playing the part of the French King, whose role it is to be challenged by and cede to the young pretender. Although everywhere evoked by it, Olivier is not, however, literally present in the film.[20] As Peter Donaldson first pointed out, in Olivier's absence, Paul Schofield – 'the last of the greats of the old school' according to Richard Briers (Bardolph)[21] – stands eloquently for that theatrical tradition that is being taken on with such aplomb in the film.[22]

The scale of Henry's ambition is made the plainer in the film by Branagh's emphasis on his youth. In the first draft of the screenplay (dated January 1988), Branagh had proposed that the opening shots of the film would show Henry 'as a "silent watcher" on the shore, looking out to sea, solitary and pensive'. As accompaniment to this moody, reflective opening, Richard II was to have been heard in ghostly voice-over delivering the speech which begins:

> *For God's sake, let us sit upon the ground,*
> *And tell sad stories of the death of kings.*   (*Richard II* III.ii.151–152)[23]

This haunting opening was excised over rewrites of the screenplay, and in the film itself Branagh chose to delay his own entrance. Instead he made it a set-piece of significant dramatic impact, and one which played explicitly upon his youth.

The scene was shot on his first day of shooting, 31 October 1988, when, as Branagh reports in his autobiography, he was understandably anxious to seem up to the task in front of the assembled cast and crew. The finished scene, and his own role in it, makes it a bravura beginning to a film career. Branagh gives himself as Henry the glamorous entrance to his council chamber of a revered warlord – shot from a stature-enhancing low angle, grandly cloaked, back-lit, silhouetted.[24] The camera preserves a sense of the hallowed mystery of his presence by withholding the sight of his face over a sequence of several shots. Following his silhouetted entrance, the camera shoots from over his shoulder as he moves along the line of his counsel members, each of them nodding to him in turn with cautious, uncommitted deference. When he reaches his own throne he turns as if finally to receive the camera's gaze, but still the camera fights shy of his presence, cutting coyly away instead to show his nobles' reaction to the entrance of their king. So self-aggrandising is the sequence that when Judi Dench (who played Mistress Quickly) saw the rushes, she is reported to have said, 'Who do you think you are?', to which Branagh is said to have replied sardonically, 'The film is not called *Mistress Quickly the Fourth*'.[25]

The aggrandising effect, however, is not sustained. Once the nobles are seated, the camera finally settles its gaze upon the ruler, only now to show a figure who, having discarded his cloak and taken his seat, looks like nothing so much as a little boy drowning in a throne patently too big for him. The bathos is humorous: the more so for following such a dramatically drum-rolled entrance and deliberate build-up of expectation by the strategic withholding of his image. By first enhancing and subsequently puncturing so thoroughly the power of his own screen presence, Branagh is toying both with his character's role in the drama and, more obliquely, with his own in the film. Henry is a young man trying to grow into the mantle of political warmongering, carefully watched by a world of nobles more experienced than himself. Branagh is a young man trying to grow into the business of film acting and directing watched by a world of industry professionals significantly

This film poster image for Branagh's *Henry V* (1989) signals a bravura beginning to a film career. Branagh gives himself the glamorous entrance of a revered warlord, only subsequently to puncture such hubris with gentle, self-ironising humour.

Source: Reprinted by permission of Britannia Films Limited.

more experienced than himself, while being constantly compared with a man hailed as the greatest actor of the century. Both Henry and Branagh are present in the figure we see on screen. It is, as so often, difficult to eliminate the real-life presence of its star from a reading of the film. The image of a human face on screen has, from the earliest days of the medium, been experienced as offering a sense of privileged access to the actor, with whom one instinctively feels more intimately acquainted than is typically possible in the theatre. This sense of privileged access is, of course, ultimately illusory. Nevertheless, in Branagh's case its illusory quality is tempered by his own purposefully autobiographical engagements with some of the roles he plays. This is certainly the case in his *Henry V*, in which his own visibility in the role provides part of the force of his performance. The composite presence that emerges in this version of the boy venturer adds interpretive interest to the film.

Comparisons between Branagh's film and Olivier's are inevitable and Branagh's film has thrived partly on the enhanced publicity that the prevalence of the comparison has brought in its wake. Olivier was a key figure in England's self-configurations during the Second World War. By the time he gave his famous performance as Henry V in the 1944 Two Cities production, he was already firmly established as the emblem of English nobility, resolution and victory at time of war. As the narrator of Humphrey Jennings' propaganda documentary *Words for Battle* (1941) and of David Lean's *This Happy Breed* (1944), Olivier was the voice of decent, honourable Englishness and resolve. Yet more pertinently, as Nelson in Alexander Korda's 1941 film *Lady Hamilton* (opposite Vivien Leigh's Emma), he had already spearheaded another famous historical English military victory. In a process that would later be applied to the battle of Agincourt in *Henry V, Lady Hamilton* specifically brought to the fore the battle of Trafalgar's points of comparison with the contemporary 1940s struggle. In Olivier's bulldog rendering of Nelson, he speaks out against weak-willed appeasement of a cruel European dictator (a suggestively composite Napoleon/Hitler) and himself becomes the agent of European liberation from that dictator. And as if that were insufficient to make the film's topicality unmissable, Olivier even imitates the idiosyncratic speech patterns of Churchill in Nelson's address to the House of Lords. (It is, perhaps, no surprise that, as Roy Jenkins reports, *Lady Hamilton* should have been Churchill's favourite wartime film.)[26]

There was reportedly a prime ministerial flavour to some of Olivier's real-life off-screen work as well. Part of his war work involved delivering Shakespearean speeches such as 'Once more unto the breach, dear friends' (III.i.1ff) as a crowd-pleasing morale booster and, according to Anthony Holden, this too he did in grandiloquent Churchillian vein. A uniformed Lieutenant Olivier would end his flag-waving roadshow 'with an impassioned exhortation to work and fight for victory'.[27] Through such rabble-rousing performances a nexus of incontrovertibly British institutions – Churchill, Shakespeare and Olivier himself – could join forces in weighty defiance of the foe.

The patriotic character of Olivier's presence was even strategically protected by the Ministry of Information, which was keen to keep his propaganda credentials untarnished. To this end, they refused to release him from his work with the Fleet Air Arm to play the blimpishly endearing but ultimately ineffectual General Clive Wynne-Candy in Powell and Pressburger's controversial *The Life and Death of Colonel Blimp* (1943).[28] The MOI found the 'ambiguous quicksands' of the proposed film 'wantonly provocative' at such a moment.[29] It was far from being the sort of unambiguous tub-thumper for which they thought the validating stamp of Olivier's presence ought to be reserved, despite his own wishes in this respect. Although they could not ban the film entirely (contrary to Churchill's private instructions), they could, and did, block the production's access to Olivier. 'I do not think that there is anybody in the Admiralty,' wrote Churchill's Minister of Information in 1942, 'who would be ready to authorise [Olivier's] release for this film.'[30]

Thus it was that, as *Henry V* went into production, the national treasure that Olivier's cinematic presence constituted had deliberately been kept unsullied by anything that interrogated or problematised the patriotically propagandist agenda of the MOI. As *Lady Hamilton* had done, *Henry V* drew once again upon a glorious precedent from English military history as a means of depicting the European enemy as defeatable and the English as worthy victors. In terms of lasting influence, *Lady Hamilton* pales alongside *Henry V*, lacking as it does that incontrovertible bastion of weighty English value, Shakespeare, to add gravitas to the film and secure lasting iconic status for Olivier's performance. Moreover, by the time that *Henry V* was released, it had been overtaken by events: thus the sight of Henry's men dragging cannon up Normandy beaches revisited the images associated with the D-Day landings from only a few months earlier. The film's own particular glories as a viewing experience were intensified by the peculiar (and unrecoverable) intimacy of its connection with its moment of release. As Alexander Walker wrote in the *Evening Standard* in 1989, Olivier's film 'remains sealed inviolately in the wartime euphoria of the D-day invasion that paralleled Henry V's invasion of France, and additionally preserved like a Grade One listed monument in the post-war cultural patrimony of Britain'.[31]

Necessarily for his moment, Olivier took *Henry V* partly as a vehicle through which to glamorise the processes of war – making it colourful, pageant-like, sunlit, clean and based on moral certainties. The idealised, mythic quality of the world to which Olivier introduces us is emphasised in the film's opening sequence – the aerial pan across a model of Elizabethan London. This sequence both echoes and transforms the opening sequence from another Two Cities film, *This Happy Breed*, released in early summer 1944, just a few months before *Henry V*. The opening shot of *This Happy Breed*, accompanied by Olivier's voice-over narration, is, similarly, an aerial pan across London, centrally taking in the Thames in its visual sweep. The London to which Olivier's voice introduces us here is, however, the drab, contemporary, industrial and somewhat bomb-damaged city of 1944. The close parallels of shot construction and subject of the opening sequence of *Henry V* with the opening sequence of its predecessor film from the same stable therefore cannot help but throw into heightened relief *Henry V*'s abstraction from the desultory stuff of real life. The black and white contemporary London of *This Happy Breed* has been overwritten by the technicolor model of a beautifully clean and unsullied London in *Henry V*. The striking correspondence of the aerial shot across the river and rooftops points up keenly the tonal distinctions in the cityscape depicted: the London to which we are introduced in *Henry V* is one that has been healed of its scars. As is clearly signalled from its opening moments, therefore, this was in every way to be a film about ideals.

Olivier's film had been released on 22 November 1944, less than six months after the D-Day landings. The moment of release confirmed the topical parallels being drawn between the 'few, [the] happy few' (IV.iii.60) of the drama and the few to whom the many owed so much in the world beyond the movie theatre. Fully conscious of and in control of the parallels, Olivier generated an unequivocally righteous war in which there was no room for doubt about the nobility or justice of the cause. By entirely cutting the scenes of English ignobility – the traitors at Southampton, Henry's graphic threats of rape, pillage and murder made to the people of Harfleur, the reference to Bardolph's hanging for having robbed a church – Olivier presented a cleaned-up English force of whom it was easy to be proud. Olivier also strategically omitted the Chorus's closing words in which he points out that the English very soon after were to lose their hard-won French lands through mismanagement. This telling of the tale had no room for savage undercut.

In making a film from the same source play, Branagh has consciously dared us to judge him, in Walker's word, by Olivier's 'Imperial measure'. The judgements made have been many and varied. What is a point of consensus, however, is that whereas Olivier was at pains to sanitise war, Branagh sought to muddy those processes in every way. Whereas for the battle of Agincourt Olivier stopped shooting whenever the sun went behind a cloud, Branagh stopped shooting whenever the sun came out. He wanted his medieval warfare to be messy and grim, and stripped of the consolation of pleasing aesthetics. There were no penants flying or gleaming suits of armour here. Rather the scene is dominated by the sickening squelch of quagmire and blood. And just as Branagh's world was physically messy, so was it morally so.

Olivier's screen image had been strategically protected from any unpatriotic sullying during the war years. His presence was therefore uncompromised as he raised his sword against the continental foe in Two Cities' 1944 film of *Henry V*.

Source: London Features International Ltd.

Henry V is, of course, a play that can lend itself neatly to fervently patriotic treatment and to a passionate belief in nationalist ideals: the stirring rhetoric of the set-piece speeches can be gloriously seductive in this respect.[32] Branagh, however, is not entirely seduced. He found in *Henry V* a play far more riddled in moral ambiguities than Olivier's strategically selective interpretation had suggested.[33] In this, Branagh partly drew upon Adrian Noble's stage production of four years earlier. That production, as Branagh himself had said, consciously tried to capture something of contemporary anxieties about war: 'Everything brought up by the Falklands is there – the futility and messiness of war, the women left behind, the children . . .'[34] About Olivier's *Henry V* Branagh said: 'the movie is resolutely of its time, reflecting values, politics and even acting styles that have undergone great shifts. I was convinced that a screen *Henry V* for the nineties and beyond must reflect our very different world . . .'[35]

Whereas Olivier's *Henry V* (1944) was a study in ideals, Branagh's film (1989) dealt in some of the messier realities of war.

Source: Henry V (1989). Reprinted by permission of Britannia Films Limited.

The differing acting styles of Olivier and Branagh not only reflect their separation in time, but also emphasise the difference in their interpretive concentration. Whereas Olivier gives us the portrait of a king with public duties to perform, Branagh gives us the portrait of a man with personally costly, and even personally sullying, decisions to make. Olivier's set-piece speeches are marvellous exercises in Shakespearean declamation and his quieter moments still carry a self-consciousness of himself as a public figure, an archetypal king and the stuff of which legends are made. Branagh, by contrast, is here, as elsewhere, master of the conversational aside, and manages to inject an almost casual intimacy even into some moments in his big speeches. Branagh's less mannered portrait of Henry in comparison with that of Olivier must have been helped by his relatively unknown screen status at the moment of making the film. Olivier's self-consciousness as an international star of stage and screen was by contrast already secure when he made his *Henry V* and is even entertainingly elided with an allusion to an earlier Shakespearean star actor – Richard Burbage – in the tiring house (backstage) scene at the Globe. Unlike Olivier's, Branagh's Henry is a self-critical figure in the drama – a man with a private as well as a public self and one who feels keenly the tension between the two. It was, as Branagh himself has said, a 'Hamletian angst'[36] he nurtured in his portrayal of the boy king.

In both Olivier and Branagh's appropriation of the Shakespearean drama to capture a truth about a contemporary mood, they were following Shakespeare. Like all canny historians, Shakespeare used history partly as a springboard for commenting upon, and causing others to reflect upon, the present. His telling of the glorious tale of Henry V and the events of 1415 was therefore undoubtedly infused with some of the preoccupations of its 1599 moment of composition. The Chorus at the beginning of Act V illustrates the topicality of the piece with particular clarity when he discusses Henry's triumphant return to London:

> But now behold, . . .
> How London doth pour out her citizens . . .
> As, by a . . . loving likelihood,
> Were now the general of our gracious empress,
> As in good time he may, from Ireland coming,
> Bringing rebellion broached on his sword,
> How many would the peaceful city quit
> To welcome him! much more, and much more cause,
> Did they this Harry.

(Act V Chorus 22, 24, 29–35)

The simile the Chorus chooses to illustrate the reception given to Henry is drawn from close to home. In 1599 London was itself preoccupied with a war on foreign soil. The war in Ireland, which had been dragging on for years, had become a drain on the nation's emotional and material resources. In a city wearied by the news of a series of indecisive battles, *Henry V*, which narrates the story of a decisive English triumph, must have played partly as a highly topical exercise in wish-fulfilment. And of course the pluck of the English army, the charisma of its leader and the victory against the odds dramatised in the play can only have enhanced its appeal. The 'general' of the 'gracious empress' (Queen Elizabeth I) referred to by the Chorus was the Earl of Essex. Essex's military expedition left London for Ireland in the spring of 1599 and it was warmly hoped that he would be able to put an end to the war by finally securing the decisive victory. The Chorus's expressed optimism about Essex's campaign both helps to date the play to the summer months of 1599 (since by the autumn it was known there were further disappointments to contend with) and also reminds us of a contemporary obsession at the time of its first performances. In deliberately drawing out the points of political intersection between the dramatic tale told and the moment of its telling, Olivier and

Branagh form part of an interpretive tradition to which Shakespeare himself subscribed. They, like the players Hamlet describes, are the 'abstracts and brief chronicles of the time' (II.ii.527) giving expression to truths contemporary to the moment of production in each case.

It is the role and figure of the Chorus that constitutes the most interesting challenge to would-be adaptors of *Henry V*. It is he who sits outside the drama and draws attention repeatedly to the fact that the story-telling vehicle for this particular tale is specifically a play. Through references to theatrical architecture ('this unworthy scaffold . . . this cockpit . . . this wooden O' Prologue 10,11,13), resource limitations ('four or five most vile and ragged foils' Act IV, Chorus 50) and requests for an imaginatively collusive audience ('On your imaginary forces work' Prologue 18), the play is famously saturated in an awareness of its own theatricality. The challenge this poses to film-makers is how to retain a sense of the self-referentiality of the play in a medium beyond the play's sphere of reference. In 1944 Olivier neatly side-stepped the problem by setting his film initially in the Globe playhouse of 1600. He thus deliberately eschewed some of the realism and effects possible in the cinema and started by grounding his production in a sphere of interesting but circumscribed representational practice where both on- and off-screen audiences still had to participate in a game of let's pretend. The Globe setting also had the advantage of explicitly reminding an audience of the Renaissance filter that constantly shapes and influences this dramatisation of a medieval past.

As his first draft screenplay testifies, Branagh also initially intended to have the Prologue spoken from inside a theatre. A match was to have been struck 'in an empty, darkened theatre. The Chorus stands in the centre aisle of the stalls near the stage surveying the eerie scene of torn seats, musty balconies with torn hangings, broken chandelier.'[37] In the October 1988 version of the screenplay, however, this proposed setting was jettisoned and replaced, as Branagh's directions say, with 'a deserted film studio sound stage' complete with all the paraphernalia, props, sets and lights shortly to be pressed into service for the making of the film.[38] Thus the theatrical self-consciousness of the play was converted specifically into a cinematic self-consciousness.

Despite the transference of medium, the appeal for the imaginative participation of its audience in order to conjure its illusions was still entirely apt – especially perhaps since Branagh's budget was a modest £4.5 million. The production's financial limitations imposed an obligation on Branagh to limit the scale of his visual ambitions, and shun any effects of too spectacular or grand a character. He managed, however, to convert an obligation into a purposeful aesthetic. The battle, for example, trades not upon epic sweep as Olivier's does, but upon a stylish synecdoche, asking the audience to infer a broader context from a selection of smaller details, sample encounters and reaction shots. As discussed in Chapter 1, this was, of course, a narrative device for depicting a battle that had already been traded upon by Shakespeare films of the silent era. Nigel Andrews, writing for the *Financial Times*, allowed himself a slight sneer at Branagh's film for its poverty: 'one keeps suspecting that Henry's army is really a band of thirty-odd British actors rhubarbing away in a bid to persuade us that they are several hundred. We are not convinced.'[39] The play's Chorus had specifically asked its theatrical audience to 'make imaginary puissance' (Prologue 25) so that they could infer two mighty armies from the 'brawl ridiculous' (Act IV, Chorus 51) on show. The suggestion of under-resourcing made in relation to a film adaptation of this particular play therefore seems particularly mean-minded since the drama explicitly broadcasts its desire to conjure much more than it actually shows. Andrews' criticism that he was unconvinced by the size of the army therefore boomerangs somewhat as it exposes his reluctance to play the dramatic game according to the rules laid down by the Chorus.

At the battle of Agincourt, Derek Jacobi's Chorus strides across the English line in trench coat and long scarf, a cross between a Doctor Who time-traveller and a front-line battle reporter risking his life to file a despatch home. His evident modernity once again bridges the gap directly from our own moment to a medieval world. As it had done in the Prologue, the omission of an intervening Renaissance filter telescopes the time frames present in the drama. Unlike Olivier's Chorus, Branagh's no longer serves as the explicit reminder that what we are watching is already a Renaissance revisionist view of a glorious medieval past. Without this intervening filter the narrative mechanism is more streamlined, but the compression of time frames skips one of the layers of retrospection that interestingly complicates the operations of nostalgia and the stylisations of history within the Shakespearean drama.

The Chorus's presence on the battlefield, among the English troops, is one of the few moments in the film that has survived from the many such moments Branagh had originally intended for him. In earlier versions of the screenplay, although unobserved by the actors, the Chorus was to have been habitually integrated into the space of the action. In the council chamber near the beginning of the drama, for example, 'a figure emerges from the outer reaches of the hall. Dressed in anonymous black, apparently invisible to the lords who sweep by him as he watches all. It is the Chorus. Lit by the flame of a torch he speaks directly to the camera, casting glances at the activity around him.' Again, at the Boar's Head, as Pistol, Bardolph and Nym 'move out of shot and up the stairs a familiar hand comes into shot to pick up one of the breakfast flagons and drink from it. We follow the cup to reveal the face of the Chorus.' It was to have been the Chorus too whose physical presence negotiated some of the location changes. It was he, for example, who was to have shifted the scene from the Boar's Head to Southampton: 'As the next speech begins [the Chorus] moves away from the musty smoking room dawn of the Boar's Head away to his right where another room in another hostelry, this time by the sea, is filled with full morning light. All the nobles from the council are there. . . . The Chorus wanders unseen amongst them.' Then at the end of the traitor scene, 'From a corner of the room the Chorus emerges to close the window shutters after the king's departure, creating a blackout.' Shortly afterwards, as Henry's troops march into Harfleur, a very partisan and involved Chorus is there, 'Calmer now, sharing the relief of the rest of the English.'[40] In fact, the desire to absorb the Chorus seamlessly into the spaces of the action persists throughout the January 1988 draft of the screenplay. Bruce Sharman, the producer, wrote a series of questions besides these directions in his copy. Sharman's pencil scorings suggest he was unpersuaded by Branagh's initial idea about the intimacy of the Chorus's relationship to the rest of the action: '?Is it better with a cut?'; 'V/o?'; 'Should it not be left to the camera, as if Chorus was our director, with cuts??' Sharman's suggested amendments extract the Chorus from too close an involvement with the tale he narrates, and through strategic cutting largely divorce him from the space in which the drama is played out. This voice seems to have been listened to for the final version. With only a couple of exceptions – the most noticeable of which is his striking presence in the line at Agincourt – the Chorus is given sufficient distance and separation to be more of an impassive observer than a partisan participator, more of a removed commentator than an agent in the drama who might feasibly himself feel 'relief' at Harfleur.

In some ways it is a shame that in the revision the spatial elision between the teller of the tale and the tale told was necessarily sacrificed. Especially since with it, we seem to have lost a variety of other touches that hinted at a theatrical fluidity to the playing space, and a spatial coherence in the fictional world of the drama. Indeed this earlier version even made provision for some less than immediately obvious mergings between characters. For example, as Mistress Quickly stared out of the window of the Boar's Head, the note reads: 'We move very close in on this tired face until it seems to blur into that of an old man, a face at a window, staring wildly from a room filled with light and noise and merriment. This haunted expression belongs to THE KING OF FRANCE.'[41] And thus, through an implied association between characters destined to feel loss, the shift to the French court is negotiated. The *Henry V* film Branagh made is rich and interesting. The film he did not finally make, with its ghostly voice-overs from *Richard II*, Renaissance uses of space, spookily omnipresent Chorus and unexpected elisions between characters, sounds, if anything, yet more so.

MUCH ADO ABOUT NOTHING (1993)

Following the release of *Henry V*, Branagh's mailbag suggested that the naturalness of the acting was one of the things that the public had most enjoyed about the film. This, Branagh said, was 'depressing testament to the usual expectation of incomprehensible booming and fruity declamation' when people went to see a Shakespeare play.[42] The desire to eschew an acting style that was in any way precious was one of the guiding principles of his stage work with the Renaissance Theatre Company and has continued to inform his Shakespeare performances on stage and screen. A similar desire to allow other considerations to bend to the need for clear and lively story-telling has equally been felt in his work. His priorities both about acting style and about the priorities of the story show a concern for the needs of a popular audience, and (which is in many ways the same thing) an interest in box office.

The opening moments of *Much Ado* illustrate his concern to make his work both absorbing and accessible. As the voice of Emma Thompson (Beatrice) is heard reciting the words from Balthasar's song 'Sigh no more, ladies, sigh no more / Men were deceivers ever' (II.iii.62ff.) in an amused and gently ironic tone, the words she speaks appear on screen on a black background. Each line builds up phrase by phrase across the centre of the screen before vanishing so that another can replace it. By offering the text both aurally *and* visually for the first few moments, the film gently acclimatises the audience in stages to the sound of Shakespeare. This strategy pays dividends once the audience is then launched into more fluent exchanges of Shakespearean dialogue, now deprived of the supporting visuals to aid comprehension. The gradual process of incremental immersion that Branagh offers us is fun in an old-fashioned 'sing-along' way for those familiar with Balthasar's song, and considerate as a helpful opening for those lacking experience in listening to Shakespearean language.

A large measure of the delight to be found in the film derives from the energetic, biting and flirtatious banter that crackles between Beatrice (Thompson) and Benedick (Branagh). Benedick laughs at the 'shallow follies' of lovers (II.iii.10). Beatrice says she will not take a husband 'till God make men of some other metal than earth' (II.i.55–56). The comedy lies in watching the self-deceptions and intellectual games of two consummate performers as they declare themselves immune to the ravages of love, only to find themselves tricked into grudgingly admitting their love for the other. In their antagonism to romantic cliché and sentiment, and in their taste for unsparing exchanges of wit, they prove well suited to each other. And of course on the film's first release, an extra layer of mild comedy was added to the jokes about the advisability or otherwise of marriage by the

knowledge that Emma Thompson and Kenneth Branagh had already themselves succumbed in this respect.

Shakespeare's play *Much Ado* takes as its subject a military community in an
off-duty moment. In the leisured calm after the wars, soldiers become lovers.
As 'soft and delicate desires' displace 'war-thoughts' (I.i.283, 281), and the
'tabor and . . . pipe' replace the 'drum and . . . fife' (II.iii.13–15), the men's
established allegiances to each other are tested by their newly emerging
allegiances to women. In the terms of the play, the life of a soldier is
characterised by a shared pride in jocular camaraderie, masculine courage
and a sense of honour. The life of a lover, by contrast, is the stuff of jokes –
peace-loving, domestic, tame, emasculating.

Branagh captures the drama of the transition from men as soldiers, with
allegiances to each other, to men as potential lovers, with a more complex
set of emerging allegiances, in the choreography of their return from the
wars. They ride over the hill in glamorised slow motion (an allusion to
John Sturges' 1960 Western *The Magnificent Seven*). Their company's internal
structures are then temporarily laid aside as they rip off their smart military
jerkins and leather trousers, and bathe with happily chaotic glee at their own
nakedness and that of their companions. The structures are, however, then
quickly reasserted as they put their uniforms back on and march into the villa,
now clean and in tight formation once again. An aerial shot down on the
courtyard shows the ceremonial choreography that governs their first encounter with their hosts, pregnant with expectation on both sides: the soldiers,
spearheaded by Don Pedro (Denzel Washington), march into the villa's
courtyard from one archway to be met by a mirroring formation dominated
by women, though spearheaded by Leonato (Richard Briers), from another.
The camera does not retain its aerial position for long but descends to narrate
the two groups' encounters with each other from their level. The formality
of the moment is held briefly as Leonato greets Don Pedro. It then collapses
joyfully as both groups splinter and become muddled up with each other
across the military–civilian divide. From this point until the film's next formal
moment – the disrupted wedding of Claudio and Hero – Don Pedro, Claudio
and Benedick all advertise their desire to integrate into the community of their
hosts by shedding their military jackets in favour of a series of more relaxed
waistcoats. Don John, Borachio and Conrade, however, who resent and seek
to poison the bonhomie of life in Messina, choose not to exchange their
jackets for other garb, preferring to retain the outward forms of their soldiery.
In the military life, at least, everyone's position is known and secure, and
personal success is not dependent on anything so contemptible as beauty,
charm or rhetorical wit. Their refusal to relinquish their jackets partly
proclaims their insecurity in the face of a subtler set of rules of engagement
than the ones to which they had been accustomed in the wars. The *Magnificent*

Seven allusion is apposite in this respect. These are men who, like Sturges' gun-toting posse, feel keenly their separation from the world of domestic attachment and responsibility.

Don Pedro and Claudio's desire to put aside soldierly allegiances and to allow themselves to be temporarily influenced by a competing set of demands is, however, then put to the test. When Don John suggests that Hero (Kate Beckinsale) may have been less than chaste, a choice has to be made. They make it with impressive speed. There is an immediate reaffirmation of the bonds of male friendship in collective contempt for, and unbridled aggression towards, the woman. For all the film's pervasive gaiety, Branagh does not temper the degree of male aggression that Hero's supposed crime unleashes. The violence done to her at the altar by both her lover and her father is shocking, the more so perhaps for following so many shots of her skipping girlishly down hillsides, giggling innocently with her female companions and shooting modestly coy glances at Claudio. Claudio throws Hero to the ground, overturns benches and knocks down the floral wedding tributes. As women cling to each other in hurt incomprehension, and men finger their swords as a reassuring reminder of their own power in the face of supposed female inconstancy, the latent misogyny of the community as a whole is horribly exposed. Don John's presence in Messina has been poisonous, but the function of his poison has been to act as a catalyst, exposing that which is ugly or morally suspect in the characters around him. In the grip of their fear, the beautiful Claudio and the dignified Don Pedro are ready with troubling haste to devise a plan for shaming Hero, before they have even been offered any proof of her infidelity. And the kindly Leonato, Hero's father, shouts abuse at his daughter as a lascivious wanton merely on the report of others. Moreover, he repeats and intensifies the brutality of Claudio's attack by himself taking Hero by the hair and throwing her again to the ground. The words and actions of these male characters reveal an acute anxiety about female sexuality which seems temporarily to have eluded their commodifying ownership and control.

In their willingness to believe the worst of Hero, in their violence of language and action towards her, and subsequently in their apparent callous indifference to the news of her death, neither Shakespeare's Don Pedro nor his Claudio emerges unstained. Equally, Shakespeare's Leonato, who upon reflection and counsel from the friar, transfers blame for the outrage from Hero to Claudio, had himself publicly abhorred his daughter's 'foul-tainted flesh' (IV.i.143) before having heard a single word from her on the subject of her alleged guilt. Shakespeare's text can, therefore, sustain at the very least a moral ambivalence about Don Pedro, Claudio and Leonato and this ambivalence can take the drama to dark places.

Branagh's casting for these three roles, however, contributes to the neutral-ising of the offence of the community as a whole by putting unquestionably benign forces in places where the text may be read more equivocally. The tone of the film is, therefore, part influenced by the generosity of the view of character suggested by these castings. Denzel Washington's screen presence tends to the noble, Robert Sean Leonard's to the delicately innocent and Richard Briers' to the sympathetically kindly, bumbling and familiar (though three years later Branagh was to interfere significantly with Briers' image by encouraging him to be a strategically politicised and thoroughly unpleasant Polonius). Individually and collectively, these three actors seem born to be let off the hook.

It is Keanu Reeve's scowling villainy as Don John that makes possible the exoneration of the others. This is a Don John who takes an evident delight in his own villainy, as he scampers along the underground passageways of the villa, laughing maniacally at his own dastardly schemes. His performance is so excessive that it tips beyond the point at which his much advertised menace might actually persuade. His is a villainy of cartoon proportions whose primary function seems to be to amuse.[43]

In a world of unquestioning misogyny, an excessively villainous Don John is a moral convenience. The blame for the near-catastrophe of the broken nuptials may eventually be neatly placed on him, and castigating him implicitly exonerates the others. By receiving both the explicit condemnation of his fellow characters and the implicit condemnation of the production as a whole, he provides an easy fall guy. The effectiveness of his villainous scheme is wholly dependent upon an inherently prejudiced attitude in the others that makes them initially so eminently suggestible and subsequently so violent in response. However, this production prefers to isolate the crime of Don John (and his associates Borachio and Conrade) than to point with any emphasis to the more prevalent cultural prejudice that makes his villainy effective. The final joyous dance through the villa and into the gardens, in whose giddy swirlings even the camera participates, is, in this production, therefore, delightfully free of any lingering cloud hovering over any of the principal characters. The thorough vanquishing, and as thorough scape-goating, of Don John, enables the others to emerge without blemish.[44] Branagh's interest is not in the ways in which this play can point to the more mixed tone of the endings of Shakespeare's late plays (particularly *The Winter's Tale*, with which it shares narrative elements). Rather he prefers to celebrate the harmonious giddiness that can surface when the comic spirit is allowed to triumph absolutely. The long shot of the communal dance through the villa that ends as an aerial shot down on the hordes of actors and extras dancing with abandon in the gardens of the villa puts the seal on this triumph. It is also, perhaps, characteristic of the benevolent vision of the film as a whole that even its villainy should be as much a source of visual pleasure (Reeves looks tremendous) and of gentle amusement for its audience, as of anything more sinister.

Balthasar's song, with which the film both begins and ends, blithely recommends that the best thing for women to do in life is, simply, to *'convert[] all your sounds of woe'* into a far merrier *'Hey nonny, nonny'* (II.iii.68–69). The violence and extremity of the male responses to Hero's 'guilt' ensures that there needs to be some drastic *'converting'* before the women in this film can voice anything as frolicsome as a *'Hey nonny, nonny'*. Benedick discovers that Beatrice is not short of her own 'sounds of woe': her instruction to him to 'Kill Claudio' (IV.i.288), uttered with a deadly seriousness, comes from a deep rage in her about the treatment her cousin in particular has received, *and* about being female in such a world generally. Nevertheless, the film's uncompromising comic vision ensures that even such sounds may be dissipated. By rendering the real perpetrators of the play's misogyny immensely likeable, by showing that the wrongs committed may be swiftly and easily rectified, the forgiveness of the women willingly and unreservedly bestowed, and the consciences of the men free of any hint of self-accusation, this production betrays a hugely generous view both of humanity and of what comic form can overcome. By the time the *'hey nonny nonny'* is sung lustily at the close of the film, it is without tonal competition.

HAMLET (1996)

At the end of *Much Ado*, a snowstorm of confetti is dropped from the upper galleries of the villa on to the dancing figures below. The falling confetti with which *Much Ado* ends is then reprised near the beginning of Branagh's *Hamlet* when a confetti snowstorm is thrown from the upper galleries of Elsinore's central palace chamber on to the court, assembled to witness the nuptials of their King and Queen. It is a striking moment of visual excess in both films. Whereas in *Much Ado*, however, it contributes to the sense of joyously heady abandon, in *Hamlet* its effect is more sterile: a calculated piece of visual theatre to complete a choreographed moment in the formal life of the Elsinore court. The slight visual echo from the earlier film, therefore, reminds us incidentally of a range of things *this* community and *this* wedding decidedly are not. Unlike for the community of *Much Ado*, the driving principle of the Elsinore court is always strategy not instinct. And more tellingly yet, the celebratory confetti shower here marks the troubled opening, not the happy conclusion, of a drama.

The wedding is not, however, the opening shot of the film. Branagh's decision to include the entire text[45] – a first for any filmed Shakespeare – places the opening scene with the night watch as they discuss the appearance of Hamlet senior's ghost. The ghost (Brian Blessed) takes possession of and animates his own statue from its plinth in the forecourt of the castle. A close-up on the carved name 'HAMLET' on this plinth closely mimics the title sequence of Kozintsev's Soviet *Hamlet* (1964), which also begins with a close-up on the word 'HAMLET' chiselled into a block of stone. In Kozintsev's film, the moment is given an additional gravitas by the portentous accompanying Shostakovich soundtrack. Branagh's advertisement of a retrospective allusion to a previous production of *Hamlet* in the opening moment of the film is only the first of a litany of such references to the production history of this and other Shakespeare plays on both stage and screen. Even while carving out its own interpretive space, therefore, one of the things this film offers is a condensed summation of Shakespearean performance history, a cumulative tribute to many of the achievements of past productions.

Not only does directing Charlton Heston (First Player) in a lament for the death of John Gielgud (Priam) in the ruins of his classical city, for example, comment savvily on the fate of British classical acting in the face of box-office American movie stars, it also references a moment from an earlier Shakespeare film. In Stuart Burge's 1969 film of *Julius Caesar*, Heston (as Mark Antony) had already delivered a highly rhetorical lament over the dead body of Gielgud (as Caesar). The replay of a Shakespearean Heston mourning the loss of a prematurely silenced Gielgud releases a series of retrospective performance references in the film. The presence of Gielgud as an old-guard Caesar in Burge's 1969 production, for example, had in turn connected that film with Joseph Mankiewicz's dramatic *Julius Caesar* from 1953, in which a younger Gielgud had played not a weathered Caesar but a hot-headed Cassius. Branagh's use of Gielgud as a dying Priam in *Hamlet* is thus strategic in serially tapping a network of performance memory. In addition, a connection to the British theatrical tradition of this play is established most obviously through the film's casting, which includes John Gielgud (as Priam) and Derek Jacobi (as Claudius), both of whom had played Hamlet on the stage to critical acclaim. In addition Richard Briers (as Polonius) had played the part at RADA ('perhaps not the best but certainly the quickest Hamlet'),[46] and Michael Maloney (as Laertes) was already under contract to play it the following year.[47] Being surrounded by such a cast must have kept very alive the sense of being part of an evolving performance tradition.

Virginia Woolf is reported to have said that were a man to make notes on his readings of *Hamlet* every year of his life, by its end he would have written his autobiography.[48] Branagh, by contrast, in performing his own screen *Hamlet*, so full of retrospective reflection on many aspects of the play's theatrical and cinematic heritage, produces in the process an oblique biography of the performance history of the play itself. Stephen Berkoff describes the experience of assuming a dramatic role that the greats have inhabited before you as a constant process of 'boxing with ghosts', the ghosts of past inhabitants of the role seeming reluctant to cede place for the newcomer.[49] For Branagh, however, these ghosts are substantial beings. He includes past Hamlets in the cast for his production, allowing us to see in the frame with him the actual forms of some of the ghosts with whom he might be thought to be 'boxing'. It is tribute not only to his talent but also to the courage of these castings that he was rewarded by receiving from Jacobi on set the symbolic mantle of *the* Hamlet of his generation in the form of Forbes-Robertson's acting edition of the play (discussed in the introduction).

That it was Jacobi who gave this to him must have carried a particularly special charge for Branagh. Seeing Jacobi's Hamlet as a teenager had been the original inspiration for Branagh to act and Jacobi was now symbolically appointing him his successor. Jacobi's presence in the film as Claudius, the surrogate father who declares Hamlet 'the most immediate to our throne' (I.ii.109) but whom Hamlet is instructed to usurp, thus forms an interesting counterpoint to the narrative being played out off-screen. A curious cross-current to this is the far closer family resemblance discernible between Hamlet and Claudius in this production than that between Hamlet and Hamlet senior. Brian Blessed's enormous ghost has a broad face and sports a thick brown beard. Jacobi's Claudius's trim beard and hair, by contrast, are the same striking peroxide blond as Branagh's Hamlet, and his face shape and skin tone have also been widely felt to suggest some genetic affinity. The flashback to the happy family group of Hamlet, Gertrude (Julie Christie) and Hamlet senior triggered by the ghost's sad tale is, therefore, fractionally disrupted by the presence of Claudius at the edge of the frame – a man far more plausibly the biological father of this Hamlet than the king is.

The possibility that Hamlet's paternity might be subject to doubt, and that Gertrude's relationship with Claudius may, therefore, have had a long history, had some critical currency in 1996.[50] When Laertes storms back from Paris to avenge his father's death shouting, 'That drop of blood that's calm proclaims me bastard' (IV.v.117), his words make us reflect again upon the possible meanings of Hamlet's inactivity in the face of his own dead father. Laertes, the true son, springs into action to avenge his father's death. Hamlet, however, is somehow less able to occupy the role of filial avenger with the same alacrity. Does the apparent calmness of Hamlet's blood in the face of his father's killer proclaim him the bastard that Laertes is not? The film does not engage with this possibility with any detailed attention, and even shows us a comparison in sustained close-up of the ghost's wildly bright blue eyes (enhanced by coloured lenses) and Hamlet's own blue-grey eyes, as if thereby to assert something about their kinship. Moreover, the significance of the ghost's role as father (in name at least) is broadcast when the 'HAMLET' of the title sequence is revealed to refer not to the young prince but to the dead king's statue. Nevertheless, the production's hair and make-up departments deliberately constructed a resemblance between Claudius and Hamlet in ways calculated to make us wonder whether the dead king's relationship to Hamlet might not be a paternity in name only.

Off-camera, Jacobi implicitly appointed Branagh his acting heir through the bestowing of the acting edition that had been passed from one Hamlet of distinction to another across the century. On-camera, the distinctive look of the characters of Claudius and Hamlet specifically draws attention to the question of the inheritance from this (surrogate) father to this (surrogate) son. As ever with Branagh, it is difficult to avoid falling across some truth about the man's career in the fortunes of his screen character. His gift for reducing the gap between himself and his role, between, as it were, Kemp and Dogberry, has the habit of making itself felt.

LOVE'S LABOUR'S LOST (2000)

As with all three of his previous Shakespeare films, Branagh's film of *Love's Labour's Lost* (2000) had its genesis in a stage production. Branagh had played an over-the-top King of Navarre in the 1984 RSC production, and warmly acknowledges a debt to Barry Kyle, the director, for some pieces of stage business imported from that production into the film.

Branagh gives the film a specific generic identity – its title sequence announces it is a 'romantic musical comedy' – and sets it in 1939, with impending war as a backdrop to the far more frivolous action. Thus the film draws in touches of melancholy through the associations of a moment when time is precious and leisure, even for the leisured classes, is under threat. As Adrian Lester (Dumaine) sings and dances his graciously acrobatic way through George Gershwin's 'I've got a crush my baby on you' in a beautiful circular library, the camera pans past a newspaper whose headline reads 'International Crisis Deepens'. The juxtaposition between Dumaine's emotional decadence in Navarre's all-male academy on the one hand, and the pressure of external circumstances that will eventually close in on these pleasantly silly young men on the other, is felt keenly.

Those external circumstances become unignorable by the end of the film when the Folio's closing line 'You that way, we this way' characterises a parting made necessary by the outbreak of war. These words (Armado's in the Folio) are here not only appropriated by Berowne (Branagh) but also written across the sky by the aeroplane that carries away the Princess of France and her attendant ladies. The appearance of the aerodrome and the style of the take-off is deliberately evocative of the end of *Casablanca* (Michael Curtiz, 1942). The reference suggests that this really is a farewell, that having waved off the women, there is nothing left but 'a beautiful friendship' for the men who remain.

But Branagh's *Love's Labour's Lost* then subverts the poignant implications of its own nod to *Casablanca*, and indeed abandons its Shakespearean source by adding a coda to the story. This coda finds a route back from the sadness of parting. The play advertises its consciousness of having subverted comic convention by deferring romantic resolution when Berowne says, 'Our wooing doth not end like an old play; / Jack hath not Jill' (V.ii.866–867). Branagh, however, prefers that the drama *should* 'end like an old play' and so steers the action towards a place in which 'Jack' may indeed have the 'Jill' the play would deny him. Thus, after a montage sequence taking us through the fates of the various principal characters during the war, the lovers are then gloriously reunited during the celebrations to mark the end of the war. The subsequent freezing of their celebratory meeting into a black and white still photograph allows us to infer something lasting about this reunion. The Shakespeare play, unusually for a comedy, suggests that the sort of romantic high spirits depicted in the play cannot last, and that the only plausible ending for such encounters is, therefore, in the short term at least, to find a civilised way of parting. Branagh, with his tongue firmly in his cheek, speculates that his coda may be reinstating the spirit of the 'lost' Shakespeare play *Love's Labour's Wonne* – a playful justification for the happy ending to which he was in any case committed.[51]

The altered tone of the ending represents an emotional calculation on Branagh's part about what a movie audience warms to, even sometimes in spite of its own better judgement. 'It seems corny and hokey and suddenly it catches up with you and there are tears in your eyes,' says Branagh.[52] The hardened critic Nigel Kennedy, writing in the *Financial Times*, had said something very similar about *Much Ado*: 'If . . . you feel there can be no final excuse for turning a Shakespearean play into a star-studded Tuscan travelogue, I suggest that you go to see the film and get mugged by its magic as I did.'[53] Branagh is unembarrassable about catering for a public taste that prefers quick bright things to be brought together than to confusion at the close of a drama. The smile this generates may be obvious, even 'hokey', but a smile nevertheless.

The black and white newsreel insert sequences from 'Navarre Cinetone News' that punctuate the action were another part of the calculation about how the film might work best upon an audience. The first cut of the film did not include these. It was shown in an early preview to an audience in Wimbledon and generated an uncomfortable laughter, apparently at (not with) the film's sheer silliness. In response, Branagh decided to include the pastiche newsreel inserts not only as a compressed mechanism for moving on the story, but, more importantly, to signpost more clearly the film's self-consciousness about its own silliness. With these newsreel sequences spliced in, Branagh apparently felt happier that in subsequent previews audience laughter was more sympathetically distributed across the film's intentionally comic moments. Audiences were, it seems, released to enjoy the silliness more once it was made plain to them that there was something self-ironising about what was on offer. The newsreel-style shots were accompanied by a voice-over (Branagh's), evocative in pace and phrase of voice-overs from the late 1930s. Branagh's voice-over is particularly reminiscent of the exaggeratedly clipped, pukka tones of E.V.M. Emmett's narration to the 1939 propaganda film *The Lion Has Wings*, which explicitly celebrates the frivolous leisure activities of the British in comparison with the high-stepping bellicose drills of the Nazis. The reference to a film that explicitly, even farcically, counterposes harmlessly decadent frivolities with marching troops is particularly apt for the wilfully politically negligent flavour of the Navarre Branagh seeks to evoke.

The opening of *Much Ado* had demonstrated a concern to introduce an audience to the peculiarities of Shakespearean language in easily digestible units. In *Love's Labour's Lost*, an only very loosely disguised follow-up class in Shakespearean linguistic appreciation is offered. Berowne stands in the circular library with his back to camera and starts to tap out an iambic rhythm with his feet. He turns and breaks into blank verse, keeping with exact precision to the rhythm he had been tapping:

> Have át you, thén, afféction's mén-at-árms.
> Consíder whát you fírst did swéar untó.   (IV.iii.286–287)

His three companions join in by tapping their replies in turn. Thus the structure of the line is first shown in its extreme and decontextualised form as a pure iambic rhythm. Then it is primatively contextualised by having words added to it with exaggerated rhythmic precision. Finally, as the baton passes back to Berowne, the stress patterns are allowed to shed their deliberate tee-tum tee-tum tee-tum tee-tum tee-tum-ness and become rhythmically a little more naturalised, while still retaining the imprint of the underlying iambic structure. Branagh's exposure of the building blocks of the iambic pentameter line is thus playfully offered as an educative game in scansion.

The speech he then delivers, now romantically underscored, is about the transformative power of love. Even this heady transport, however, is kept within the metrical bounds just advertised:

> And when love speaks, the voice of all the gods
> Makes heaven drowsy with the harmony.   (IV.iii.340–341)

As if by auto-suggestion, however, the word 'heaven' then launches him into the Irving Berlin song: 'Heaven, I'm in Heaven'. The scansion game transmutes as iambic pentameter is thrown over in the pursuit of other rhythms, accompanied now too by melody and harmony. Throughout the film, the slimmest of linguistic excuses can catapult the characters into a song and dance routine. Berowne's opening line to Rosaline (Natascha McElhone) 'Did not I dance with you in Brabant once?' prompts her to respond, a little improbably via Jerome Kern, 'I won't dance, don't ask me', and the next number is under way. The transitions into song make little pretence to any organic relation to the action from which they spring. More, they provide brief fantasy moments outside the plot where characters can indulge the passions and fantasies that they must otherwise keep in check. Their intention is in part, therefore, skittishly to point up an emotional subtext to the action. Branagh said that life on set in the making of this film was characterised by switches 'between the disciplined and the lunatic'.[54] If this was true of the process of making the film, it is also true of the film that emerges from this process.

Musicals offer a stylised system of communication, releasing characters from the need to communicate with each other in naturalistic ways. The principal male characters in this drama have, of course, already stylised their own positions, and their own feelings, by adopting their ludicrous project to abstain from worldly pleasures and devote themselves to ascetic academic pursuits for a year. Their unsustainable vows involve them almost immediately in compromising the honesty of their communications with the world. In order to live up to the pretentiousness of their endeavour, their patterns of speech emerge self-consciously and poetically ornate. The self-indulgence of these men is felt not only in the way they live, but also in the way they speak: these are four young men rather taken with their own powers of lyricism. The additional layer of codification ushered in by finding themselves singing from time to time therefore simply emphasises the lack of linguistic directness that already characterised their dealings with each other. This is a world in which communication is rarely transparently unmediated. If any Shakespeare comedy is to be turned into a musical (and in the Restoration, of course, several were), it is at least possible to argue why making it this one might draw attention to something inherently amenable to such a treatment in the fabric of the play and in the nature of its characters.

Moreover, in a world in which men are frequently frustrated by their inability to dictate the terms, the dance numbers allow male fantasy to exact a level of co-operation from their female companions that is rarely achieved off the dance floor. Typically, for the purposes of the film the women submit to the rules for the duration of the dance, allowing themselves to be twirled and lifted and led, but return to their feistier and more savagely ironic selves once the dance has finished.

The exception to this pattern is the Irving Berlin number 'Let's face the music and dance' when the masks are switched and the men are fooled into dancing with the wrong partner. The highly sexualised nature of this fantasy moment allows the women temporarily to abandon ladylike propriety and play the dominatrix: steamy, erotic, tawdry. The fast-paced cutting shows us flashes of flesh being grasped by lustful hands. The number exposes us temporarily to the unbridled passion the characters might like to express if they did not feel obliged to be so strategically contained in their overtures to each other. It is a moment whose tone is dramatically out of keeping with the drama that surrounds it, exaggerating the disjunction between dramatic action and musical numbers that has characterised all the segues into song. As the sexualised fantasy moment cedes to the main action of the drama once again, we find the women smugly enjoying a cigarette. They hold their cigarette holders elegantly aloft, but the self-indulgent smoking is, presumably, intended as a sexually suggestive joke about what has passed in the previous fantasy scene. The men's vow of celibacy undertaken at the beginning of the drama is thus implicitly exposed as sham in this production.

Branagh wanted the film to be an act of tribute to musical films of the 1930s and 1940s rather than a hubristic attempt to compete with them. On the first day of rehearsal he had the entire cast watch *Top Hat* (Mark Sandrich, 1935). But then in his address to the cast, he said: '[Fred and Ginger] are geniuses and we're not. But if we can capture the twinkle in the eyes and feet of those performers, then we'll recapture something that gives people a lot of joy.'[55] The musical tributes in this film extend beyond Fred and Ginger to Esther Williams, Judy Garland, Gene Kelly, and more. Shakespeare has to jostle for position with songs by Cole Porter, George and Ira Gershwin, Jerome Kern and Irving Berlin. There is a joyously inclusive sweep in the film's imitative attention, and an energy in its execution. And, in fact, a hint of the Fred and Ginger twinkle in the eye is captured in some of the numbers. Unfortunately, however, that twinkle does not reach the feet: with the exception of Lester as Dumaine, the film's casting would have needed to be quite other for this to have been so. The result is an uneven film: good-hearted and bravely perky, but unconvincing as a musical and largely unilluminating as a parody.

*

In addition to his own four Shakespeare films produced to date, and to the two that had, before the tepid response to *Love's Labour's Lost*, been thought to be in the pipeline (*Macbeth* and *As You Like It*),[56] Branagh has also appeared as Iago in Oliver Parker's *Othello* (1995). Because Branagh's name has become so universally identified with filmed Shakespeare, it is perhaps more difficult in his case to dissolve a sense of Branagh the man even while observing the most finely tuned performance. As Iago in *Othello*, it is neither his impudent, youthful ambition that percolates from Branagh's life into his performance role (as it had been in *Henry V*), nor a loose enactment of his love life (as it was in *Much Ado*), nor (as it was to be in *Hamlet*) a sense of his own power to direct the lament for the passing of previous greatness as he himself takes possession of the territory of popular classical star of his generation. Rather, as Iago in Parker's *Othello*, his capability of making the cinematographic and directorial decisions about the drama of which he is a part provides a point of confluence between his life and his role. Iago's clear dictation of the lens through which Othello is to perceive things identifies him as a version of an internal cinematographer. It is his Iago who explicitly instructs the spectator to 'look', and indeed how to 'look', at Othello when he is standing ruminatively by the shore and it is Iago who determines how Othello should look both at others (most obviously when he blocks the encavement scene to suit Othello's angle of vision), and at himself (most obviously when he helps Othello to dress in front of the mirror). Casting Branagh as Iago and configuring Branagh's Iago as the man who determines who will see what, from what angle, and in what clarity of focus, Parker incidentally alluded to the contained talent, the silent and unacknowledged director, that he had on his set in the person of Kenneth Branagh. Rita Kempley, in her review of the film for the *Washington Post*, speculated that Branagh's role in this production might have been more extensive than this: 'Kenneth Branagh doesn't just steal the show; one suspects he might have sat in the director's chair as well.'[57] Needless to say, he did no such thing, and is on record as saying he enjoys the freedom from responsibility that acting in someone else's film from time to time affords him.[58] Nevertheless, his profile has often accidentally displaced Parker from the director's chair in retrospective discussions of the film, as it is erroneously assumed that his presence in it makes it *his* film.

The *Othello* picture created was, despite Kempley's speculations, not Branagh's but Parker's, as at the end of the film Parker cannily reminds us by his final superior angle down upon a disempowered Iago whose intimate and knowing glances at the camera have finally been tamed. Perhaps partly because he is not the film's director, for the UK release Branagh had his image removed from the advertising posters. It was not his production and he clearly wished to minimise the errors of authorial ascription made about it. The impression that Iago has some control over the cinematic images we see is, of course, ultimately a mere ironic ruse on the part of the real director. The actor behind Iago, however, still had the power to pluck his still image from the advertising hoardings to signal that for all his respect for Parker, these particular cinematic images did not bear his authorial signature.

In fact the sort of control that Branagh has been able to exert over his own career and self-projections is extraordinary. The Renaissance Theatre

Company he ran for seven years gave him a platform from which to operate with an enviable degree of autonomy. He used it to flex a muscle at the Royal Shakespeare Company in 1992, from whom he had parted in 1985, partly over a dispute about pay and a perceived autocratic style in the management's treatment of actors. When the RSC subsequently invited him back to appear as Hamlet in Adrian Noble's production in 1992, he arranged for a note to appear in the theatre programme: 'Kenneth Branagh appears by arrangement with the Renaissance Theatre Company'.[59] Publicly acknowledging a debt to an unsubsidised company was a new humbling for the RSC and a clear assertion of Branagh's ownership of his own career. After all, to all intents and purposes he himself was the Renaissance Theatre Company, by arrangement with whom he was announced as being able to appear.

FURTHER READING

Samuel Crowl, 'Fathers and Sons: Kenneth Branagh's *Henry V*', Chapter 10 in *Shakespeare Observed: Studies in Performance on Stage and Screen* (Athens: Ohio University Press, 1992), pp.165–74.

Samuel Crowl, 'Flamboyant Realist: Kenneth Branagh', Chapter 13 in Russell Jackson (ed.), *The Cambridge Companion to Shakespeare on Film* (Cambridge: Cambridge University Press, 2000), pp.222–38.

Anthony Davies, 'The Shakespeare Films of Laurence Olivier', in Russell Jackson (ed.), *The Cambridge Companion to Shakespeare on Film* (Cambridge: Cambridge University Press, 2000), pp.163–82.

Peter S. Donaldson, 'Taking on Shakespeare: Kenneth Branagh's *Henry V*', *Shakespeare Quarterly* 42 (Spring 1991), pp.60–71.

Donald K. Hendrick, 'War is Mud: Branagh's Dirty Harry V and the Types of Political Ambiguity', Chapter 3 in *Shakespeare the Movie: Popularizing the Plays on Film, TV and Video* (London: Routledge, 1997), pp.45–66.

Russell Jackson, 'Kenneth Branagh's Film of *Hamlet*: The Textual Choices', *Shakespeare Bulletin* 15, 2 (Spring 1997), pp.37–8.

Douglas Lanier, '"Art Thou Base, Common and Popular?": The Cultural Politics of Kenneth Branagh's *Hamlet*', in Courtney Lehmann and Lisa S. Starks (eds), *Spectacular Shakespeare: Critical Theory and Popular Cinema* (London: Associated University Presses, 2002), pp.149–71.

Ramona Wray and Mark Thornton Burnett, 'From the Horse's Mouth: Branagh on the Bard', Chapter 11 in Mark Thornton Burnett and Ramona Wray (eds), *Shakespeare, Film, Fin de Siècle* (Basingstoke: Macmillan, 2000), pp.165–78.

NOTES

1. Richard Watts, Jr, 'Films of a Moonstruck World' *The Yale Review* 25, 2 (December 1935), pp.311–20. Quoted in Charles W. Eckert, *Focus on Shakespearean Films* (Englewood Cliffs, NJ: Prentice-Hall, 1972), p.50.

2. *Pictures and the Picturegoer* 9, 105 (19 February 1916), pp.483–4.

3. See Robert Hamilton Ball, *Shakespeare on Silent Film* (New York: Theater Arts Books, 1968), p.233. It is a nice irony that it should have been Tree whose adherence to Shakespeare's language brought him into conflict with those more willing to sacrifice language in the pursuit of spectacle. In the London theatre world it was for precisely such trade-offs – language for spectacle – that Tree himself was often known. Since the film cameras of the time were clunkingly noisy when rolling, it seems likely that the story of 'pretending to shoot' is apocryphal.

4. 'A Bit of Ado for Emma and Ken', *Daily Mail*, 6 May 1993. Review on file at the Theatre Museum, Covent Garden (hereafter Theatre Museum).

5. The charity première was on 26 August 1993 and was reported by, for example, Tom Leonard in 'Stars Make Much Ado about Branagh', *The Evening Standard*, 27 August 1993. On file at Theatre Museum.

6. See for example, Michael Coveney's review in the *Observer*, 19 August 1990. On file at Theatre Museum.

7. Paul Taylor, *The Independent*, 21 December 1992. On file at Theatre Museum.

8. William Leith's interview with Branagh, *The Times*, 16 September 1989. On file at Theatre Museum.

9. Interview with Noreen Taylor in *The Times*, 15 March 2000, pp.6–7.

10. Stephen Berkoff, *I Am Hamlet* (London: Faber, 1989), pp.vii–viii.

11. Simon Russell Beale interviewed by Ned Sherin, on *Loose Ends*, BBC Radio 4, 6 January 2001.

12. The 17 September 1989 instalment in *The Observer* of the serialisation of Branagh's autobiography, *Beginning.* On file at Theatre Museum.

13. Simon Callow, *Being An Actor*, new edition (Harmondsworth: Penguin, 1995), p.173.

14. *Shackleton*, written and directed by Charles Sturridge, was first aired on the British terrestial Channel 4 on 1 and 2 January 2002.

15. Branagh consulted Prince Charles about the responsibilities of royalty as part of his preparation for playing Henry V. Prince Charles has been a staunch supporter since.

16. The names appear interchangeably in the 1600 Quarto edition of the play (probably prepared for publication from Shakespeare's own manuscript).

17. *The Sunday Telegraph*, 27 December 1992. On file at Theatre Museum.

18. Finding time to write about directing the film for his autobiography, while actually directing the film illustrates both the determination and the calculation which have characterised Branagh's career.

19. It was a critical success, and has come good financially over time through the staggered market of video rental and sales. Five years post-release, however, it still had at least £1 million to recoup. For news of its finances see, for example, 'Luvvies Labour Lost', *Time Out*, 13 April 1994 and *The Times*, 3 April 1994, both on file at Theatre Museum. See also Russell Jackson's introduction to *The Cambridge Companion to Shakespeare on Film* (Cambridge: Cambridge University Press, 2000), p.4.

20. For those who see Branagh's career as in some ways shaped by and responding to that of Olivier, Olivier's subsequent death in July 1989, occurring as it did just ahead of the 11 August release of *Henry V*, must seem symbolically timely: the mantle had been passed.

21. Richard Briers, interviewed by Sue Lawley for *Desert Island Discs*, BBC Radio 4, Sunday 22 December 2000.

22. Schofield's surrogacy for Olivier was first noted by Peter Donaldson in 'Taking on Shakespeare: Kenneth Branagh's *Henry V*', *Shakespeare Quarterly* 42 (Spring 1991), p.61.

23. First Draft Screenplay of *Henry V*, p.1. Manuscript dated January 1988 and catalogued as Item 1 (Bruce Sharman's copy) in Branagh Special Collection, held at the British Film Institute.

24. This was immediately referred to by Anthony Lane as Branagh's 'Darth Vader entrance'. See 'The Current Cinema', *The New Yorker*, 27 November 1989, p.105. The phrase 'Flamboyant Realist' as a label attached to Branagh also had its origins in Lane's article. It too has reappeared since, including in the title of Samuel Crowl's essay on Branagh in Russell Jackson (ed.), *The Cambridge Companion to Shakespeare on Film* (2000), pp.222–38.

25. *Time Magazine*, 13 November 1989, p.46.

26. Roy Jenkins, *Churchill* (Basingstoke and Oxford: Macmillan, 2001), p.664. See also Clive Coultass, *Images for Battle: British Film and the Second World War 1939–1945* (London and Toronto: Associated University Presses, 1989), p.66.

27. See Anthony Holden, *Olivier* (London: Weidenfeld & Nicolson, 1988), p.172. Olivier's wartime speech-making is also discussed by Anthony Davies in 'The Shakespeare Films of Laurence Olivier', in *The Cambridge Companion to Shakespeare on Film* (2000), p.166.

28. See the protracted correspondence between Michael Powell and the MOI about the proposed film and Olivier's proposed role in it, in Ian Christie (ed.), *The Life and Death of Colonel Blimp* (London: Faber, 1994), particularly pp.40–1.

29. Ibid., pp.32, 36.

30. See Brendan Bracken's letter to Powell, 7 July 1942, reproduced in Christie (1994), p.41.

31. Alexander Walker, 'The King Sneaks In', *Evening Standard*, 25 May 1989. On file at Theatre Museum.

32. Olivier is not the only film-maker to have appropriated *Henry V* with a clearly nationalist agenda. Penny Marshall's skittish but passionately American film *Renaissance Man* (1994), for example, employs the play, without irony, as a twin advertisement – for the universal relevance of Shakespeare and simultaneously for the United States Army. The filmic rendering of this particular play to a nationalist agenda did not end with Olivier and, as *Renaissance Man* shows, is not limited to Britain.

33. Nevertheless, it is perhaps worth noting that even Branagh baulks at some of the ignobilities with which Shakespeare invests Henry. For example, Branagh's Henry at no point orders the killing of the prisoners – something Shakespeare has him do twice.

34. Branagh, quoted in the *Evening Standard*, 3 May 1985. On file at Theatre Museum.

35. Kenneth Branagh, 'Hallowed Ground', *Vogue*, September 1989, p.330.

36. *The Times*, 16 September 1989. On file at Theatre Museum.

37. First Draft Screenplay of *Henry V* (January 1988), p.2.

38. Second Draft Screenplay of *Henry V* (October 1988), p.2.

39. Nigel Andrews' report on the Cannes Film Festival, *The Financial Times*, 20 May 1989. On file at Theatre Museum.

40. First Draft Screenplay of *Henry V* (January 1988), pp.12, 17, 18, 24, 39.

41. Ibid., pp. 27–8.

42. Branagh, quoted in 'Beatrice and Benedick in Close-up', *The Sunday Telegraph*, 25 July 1993, Review Section, p.9.
43. Reeves' Don John, along with Brian Blessed's infectiously laughing Antonio, yields more amusement than that more standard centre of humour in the play, Dogberry. Michael Keaton's zanily eccentric performance in the role as a deeply unhinged man with an imaginary horse, feels like an experiment that was admirably pursued without quite coming off.
44. Moments of irresolution or tension sometimes characterise the close of contemporary productions of this play. The nearest this production comes to such a moment is when Don Pedro declines to participate in the dance, although even then he warmly salutes those who do. Branagh's text consultant, Russell Jackson, has reported how Denzel Washington was asked by Branagh before the scene was shot whether or not he thought his character *would* participate in this final dance. Washington was wearing a wool jacket and a pair of leather trousers on a hot day, and was aware that the scene would probably take a long time to shoot. He assessed the situation and then said that he thought it would be truer to his understanding of Don Pedro's character if he did *not* participate in the dance. As a result he took the afternoon off while the rest of the cast sweated it out in the sun. (Russell Jackson's plenary paper to the 'Shakespeare on Screen Centenary International Conference', Málaga, September 1999.) Don Pedro's absence from the final dance is a salutary reminder that points of interpretive interest in a finished film have often been determined by entirely pragmatic considerations.
45. Branagh uses the complete 1623 Folio and adds to it the extra passages included in the Second Quarto. This creates a very full text. This compositely inclusive text had also been used for Adrian Noble's stage production in 1992. Branagh considered it the best story-telling vehicle.
46. Richard Briers, interviewed by Sue Lawley for *Desert Island Discs*, BBC Radio 4, Sunday 22 December 2000.
47. Maloney had also played Rosencranz in Zeffirelli's 1990 film of *Hamlet*, in which Mel Gibson played Hamlet. Simon Russell Beale was the second grave digger in the film and went on to play Hamlet for the National in the 2000/2001 season. Like all major plays in the repertoire, it often witnesses cast recyclings.
48. I have not myself been able to find this in Woolf directly: it may be an attributive myth. It is indirectly cited in Michael Hoffman's introduction to *William Shakespeare's A Midsummer Night's Dream* (London: HarperCollins, 1999), p.ix.
49. Quoted from *Shakespeare's Villains*, Berkoff's one-man touring show of Autumn/ Winter 2000/2001. Seen at York Theatre Royal.
50. See Steve Sohmer, 'Certain Speculations on Hamlet, the Calendar and Martin Luther', *Early Modern Literary Studies* (online) 2, 1 (April 1996), particularly paragraphs 38–49. See www.humanities.ualberta.ca/emls/02–1/sohmshak.html
51. Director's DVD commentary.
52. Ibid.
53. Nigel Andrews, 'Much Ado about Glamour', *The Financial Times*, 26 August 1993. On file at Theatre Museum.
54. Director's DVD commentary.
55. Quoted in *Premiere* (US), November 1999, p.122.
56. According to David Lister, writing in *The Independent*, Branagh put back plans for *Macbeth* and *As You Like It* after *Love's Labour's Lost* failed to draw an audience. See *The Independent*, 31 January 2001. On file at Theatre Museum.

57. Rita Kempley, *Washington Post*, 29 December 1995. Available on line at: www.washingtonpost.com/wp-srv/style/longterm/movies/videos/ othellorkempley_c03fe2.htm

58. Mark Thornton Burnett and Ramona Wray (eds), *Shakespeare, Film, Fin de Siècle* (Basingstoke: Macmillan, 2000), p.168.

59. The acknowledgement appears beneath the cast list on the centre page spread of the RSC *Hamlet* programme. The production's opening night at the Barbican was 12 December 1992.

CHAPTER EIGHT

Leaves of Brass and Gads of Steel:

Cinema as Subject in Shakespeare Films, 1991–2000

Nor Fire, nor cankring Age, as Naso said
Of his, thy wit-fraught Book shall once invade.[1]

In early March 1995, a quartet of Danish film-makers drew up a manifesto in Copenhagen that spelt out their agenda for redeeming cinema. Later that month they presented their charter publicly in Paris as part of the celebrations to mark the centenary of the Lumières brothers' first public screening of moving pictures. One hundred years on, they said, it was time to reject the sophisticated illusionism and flashy technical resources of contemporary cinema and return the medium to a vehicle of truth-telling. The concentration was to be on the characters and the story and the location. Nothing else – not the camera, not filters, not effects, not unmotivated sound or light sources, not digital interventions, not studio sets, not self-advertising directors – should be allowed to distract from the 'honesty' of the tale or its telling. Their rejection of much of the standard grammar of Hollywood production was distilled into a set of 'rules' formalised in a document they humorously called the 'Vow of Chastity'. The Vow, signed by Lars von Trier and Thomas Vinterberg on behalf of the collective, committed them all to renouncing the decadent pleasures of cinematic wizardry. In a frame of mind that managed to be almost self-satirising in its high-blown expression, but nevertheless entirely serious in intention, they called the movement Dogme95. Their project to pare away the extraneous and distracting clutter of cinematic production in order to recover the power inherent in simplicity and self-denial was both dogmatically conceived and (fairly) dogmatically adhered to in the four films that emerged from the original Copenhagen signatories.

The last of the four original Dogme films was *The King is Alive* (Kristian Levring, 2000), shot in line with Dogme principles from a hand-held camera and using only natural light. The film tells the story of a group of white

European and American tourists whose tour bus runs out of fuel in a disused mining outpost in the Namibian desert. Stranded there, without any obvious hope of rescue, they are in need of a project to help stave off madness. Struck by the tonal appropriateness of *King Lear* to their present situation, one of their number Henry (David Bradley), who was himself once an actor, writes out sections of the play from memory so that they can stage an *ad hoc* production. He casts Gina, a giddy young American (Jennifer Jason Leigh), as Cordelia and eventually takes on the role of Lear himself. When Gina subsequently dies, the other tourists hold an improvised funeral rite over her body, composed entirely of lines from *Lear*. The Shakespearean words, initially adopted as material for a communally distracting game, have become the material of a communally consoling ritual. Over the course of the film the nature of what it means to 'quote' someone else's words shifts. Shakespearean lines start being used not to 'represent' someone else's character but to give expression to one's own. Lear's agonies over the body of Cordelia and Henry's over the body of Gina ('I know when one lives, and when one is dead: / She's dead as earth.' V.iii.259–260) become indistinguishable. In stages, the tourists-turned-actors have appropriated the play not as a means of forgetting themselves and their situation, but as the vehicle for expressing their own aspirations and fears in circumstances that have stripped them of those things upon which they would otherwise have relied for self-definition.

The cinematography for *The King is Alive* has an elegance which derives directly from the operatic grandeur of the desert scenery it depicts. The striking ambience in many scenes depends upon the naturally golden sheen of desert light. The film demonstrates how natural beauty can translate directly into cinematic beauty without cosmetic interventions. The self-denial that lies at the heart of the film production[2] has an obvious echo too in the production of *Lear* we see in rehearsal. There are, of course, minimal resources, and effectively no audience for this production. Since the characters can only use what is to hand, bar an empty oil drum or two, their principal resource is simply themselves. This is a production that must do without lights, costume department or purpose-built stage. The enforced minimalism of the characters' *Lear* mimics the elected minimalism of their Dogme creator. This reflexivity was deliberate. As Levring said in interview:

> *I wanted to do something where Dogme and the story were interlinked – the whole idea of putting on a play without a theater, without props. I wanted these things to come together. . . . Everything was chosen from that point of view – even* King Lear *was chosen from that point of view. The play is about a man who loses everything, and that's very much what it's like when you're doing a Dogme film and that's very much what's happening to the characters.*[3]

The film therefore not only accords with Dogme principles but also itself enacts the implementation of the Dogme agenda.

Dogme's challenge to its signatories was to work to principles that would set them apart from the mainstream of contemporary film production. Even in their will to be set apart methodologically, however, their inclination to explore their own working practices in their films is thematically of its moment. In this chapter four Shakespeare films of the 1990s and early 2000s are considered: *Prospero's Books* (Peter Greenaway, 1991), *William Shakespeare's Romeo+Juliet* (Baz Luhrmann, 1996), *Hamlet* (Michael Almereyda, 2000), *Titus* (Julie Taymor, 2000). Each makes its own construction and medium status part of its subject and here I give detailed attention to the reflexive processes of each film. *Prospero's Books* and *Titus* are less immediately accessible upon a first view than the other two and so these receive more extended attention. I will conclude by asking whether such self-absorption is indicative of an age whose ironic self-awareness has stymied any possible interpretation that turns the gaze outward to a world beyond the (movie) theatre. If, on the other hand, the prevalence of self-reference in these films (which for sheer ubiquity surpasses even that of Shakespeare) is not the sign of an interpretive exhaustion, to what purposes is it put?

PROSPERO'S BOOKS (PETER GREENAWAY, 1991)

The self-advertising artifice of cinema against which the Dogme directors wished to define themselves is exemplified *in extremis* in Greenaway's *Prospero's Books*. Where Dogme rejected conspicuous style, Greenaway made conspicuous style the focus. Where Dogme renounced digital intervention, Greenaway showcased the new digital technology. Where Dogme concentrated on story and character, Greenaway made story an irrelevance and smothered character in excessive costumes while literally depriving all but one of a voice. Where Dogme sought to minimise the mediation in an audience's access to character, Greenaway sought to advertise those layers of mediation in extravagant ways. Where Dogme directors wanted to capture something 'honest', Greenaway maintained that no cinematic image can pretend to 'honesty', so it is ultimately more truthful to exaggerate and broadcast the artifice than to minimise it. For Greenaway, the artifice is the film.

But for all their points of dramatic opposition, both use their films as the means of discussing their own processes and import. *The King is Alive* dramatises a story about mounting a production without resources, even as it puts itself through a comparable process of self-limitation. *Prospero's Books* dramatises (or perhaps it would be more accurate to say 'sequentially pictorialises', for there is little conventional drama in the film) the story of its own production. The central character sits in his Renaissance scholar's writing cell quietly eliding the functions and associations of Prospero, Shakespeare, Gielgud and Greenaway. The film's principal conceit is that we are watching the processes of composition of *The Tempest*, into which the depicted scholar-playwright seems to be scripting himself as the central protagonist. As he composes his drama, the words that he tries out in his head and those that he commits to paper are made public as the substance of Greenaway's film. Thus there is a proliferation of words not just heard but also seen.

The overlapping encounter between words heard and words seen gives Greenaway the opportunity to explore a set of playful and shifting relationships between the two communicative systems. The occasional contradictions between them helps to suggest that what we are witnessing is not the rehearsed delivery of a text already complete, but rather the gradual emergence of a text from the (stylised) throes of a creative process. The opening word of the play, 'boatswain', for example, is written and uttered many times by the Prospero-Shakespeare figure of the film, sometimes appearing with no punctuation, once with a question mark and once with an exclamation mark, as if the dramatist were still trying to establish what sort of dramatic charge it could most effectively carry. And later textual variations extend beyond the possibilities of punctuation to the replacement of words. At one point, for example, the character Prospero is heard saying to Ariel, 'Thou shalt be as free as mountain *air*' (my emphasis). There is no textual precedent for 'air' here, which in context, therefore, assumes the role of an experimental pre-Folio draft of the lines. Almost immediately afterwards, however, the shot cuts to the Prospero-Shakespeare dramatist, sitting alone in his writing cell, savouring out loud the lines he has just had his own character speak in role. Rolling the words around on his tongue, he now says, 'Thou shalt be as free as mountain *winds*' (I.ii.501–2, relineated) (my emphasis). On reflection, Prospero-Shakespeare has emended 'air' to 'winds', and so brought it into line with the authorised Folio version. Other variations further illustrate this process of emending the text on the hoof. For example, the deliberate textual adjustment from a spoken version ('Of the mariners, say how thou has dispos'd . . .') to a written version ('Of the king's ship, the mariners, say how thou hast dispos'd . . .' I.ii.224–5, relineated) also brings the text more closely into line with the First Folio. These adjustments make explicit the sense (albeit an artificial, strategic sense) of spontaneous, improvised composition. Prospero-Shakespeare is trying out provisional sound and ink patterns to see what most pleases his eye and ear. As variants are considered and discarded, the text is refined in stages into the known and revered First Folio version. The process we are made privy to in this film, therefore, is the passage of the provisional into the monumental.

Being made privy to the processes of composition recalls a far earlier Shakespeare film that similarly culminated in the emergence of a Shakespearean monument. Georges Méliès' *Shakespeare Writing Julius Caesar* (1907) depicted Shakespeare seated in his study making several unsatisfying attempts to write the assassination scene from *Julius Caesar*. In despair at his blocked imagination, he leaves his desk and papers, paces around the room and then sits in an armchair leaning his head on his hands in the hope of regaining his inspiration. It is while he is sitting in this armchair that his thoughts then take life and are played out before him as the Capitol scene. Finally, after the conspirators have stabbed Caesar and Caesar falls, the scene loses its Roman flavour and returns to being purely Shakespeare's private study once again. Méliès' Shakespeare is left alone once more, evidently delighted by the scene that his muse seems to have delivered to him in neatly finished performative form.

The view of authorship Méliès skittishly proposes in this short film is essentially Romantic in origin. It was Byron who insisted that no books or pens should appear in his portraits since they suggested the prosaic, humdrum trade of books as opposed to the inspired spontaneity of the imagination. Méliès' Shakespeare is in this sense Byronic. It is only by leaving his desk

Gielgud's Prospero is presented as a painterly Renaissance doge in *Prospero's Books* (Peter Greenaway, 1991). The design of his writing cell is a direct visual quotation from Antonello da Messina's painting 'St. Jerome in his Study'.

Source: *Prospero's Books* (Peter Greenaway, 1991).

and resting his head on his hands in his armchair, free from all other literary clutter and bookish distraction, that his inspiration can then flow unfettered and his natural genius can find expression. Greenaway's configuration of the Shakespearean dramatist, by contrast, is anti-Byronic, working to a pattern that is ostentatiously learned. Unlike Méliès' Shakespeare, he does not need to leave his books in order to compose. Rather he immerses himself in them the more to write, advertising at every turn his art's dependence on literary study.

Greenaway modelled the look of Prospero's writing cell on Antonello da Messina's painting *St. Jerome In His Study* (*c.* 1456, The National Gallery, London). This is a portrait of the saint that shows him in left profile, sitting reading at a raked lectern in a study alcove, viewed with a dispassionate detachment through a framing architectural portal. The visual quotation occupies a privileged place among the film's exhausting supply of other artistic and architectural allusions since it sits at its very heart, at the material

Antonello da Messina's 'St. Jerome in his Study', oil on lime, 45.7 × 36.2 cm, *c.* 1456 (The National Gallery, London). This is the most prominent in a series of Jerome-related references in *Prospero's Books*.

Source: Saint Jerome in his Study by Antonello da Messina. © National Gallery, London.

and intellectual centre of operations. Prospero's study is the visual and narrative anchoring device to which the film constantly returns. Its role is of central importance as the material place from which the rest of the film's action is dramatically conjured. And that same study is also the place that must at some point be abandoned by Prospero if he is to cede his god-like control of the destinies of others, 'abjure' his 'rough magic' and attempt to reintegrate with the rest of fallible humanity. The film's incisive moment in this respect comes when Greenaway's Prospero steps down from the cell, amidst the flurrying montage of closing books. His decision to learn to engage with his world as a participant rather than as an all-determining author and voyeur is thus demonstrated in action by his breaking his quill, closing his book, and leaving his desk and study. The writing cell, both as a place lovingly inhabited, and subsequently as a place resolutely forsaken, thus constitutes the nerve-centre of the film. And its particular design, directly imitative of *St. Jerome in His Study*, evokes a series of pertinent associations.

Prospero's appropriation of Jerome's study space, clothes and writing pose, signalled through the mediation of da Messina, is supported in the film by a series of references to other artistic traditions associated with Jerome (including the broad-brimmed cardinal's hat[4] and the assumption of the quill by a cherubic Ariel[5]). The cumulative effect of these references is to evoke the saint as a shadowy presence behind Gielgud's scholar playwright throughout the film. The iconography of the robed figure we see studiously engaged at the writing desk in Greenaway's film effectively makes a palimpsest of him: in him both Prospero and Jerome may be simultaneously discerned. The cluster of allusions to Jerome in the film is undoubtedly decadent. In context, however, these allusions are both pertinent and purposeful.

Jerome's life and reputation provide useful referents for a reading of Prospero. Jerome was a fourth-century curmudgeonly scholar and translator. He was known as an avid collector of both sacred and secular texts and even took his books with him when he went as a religious hermit into the Syrian desert for several years. He was astonishingly productive in his work, translating Hebrew and Greek biblical texts into Latin, and making discriminations about the validity and authenticity of the available texts in their various states of corruption. Part of Jerome's bibliographic legacy was a tidy version of the Bible in a language accessible to the educated that was known initially as 'nostra tralatio' ('our translation') and whose later name, the 'Vulgate', reinforced its associations of communal popular proprietorship. In fact it is Jerome's discriminations about the form in which the Scriptures should become authoritatively settled that have largely determined the shape of the Bible we have received from history.

The fact that Jerome is known to have played a determining role in the selection and validating of (biblical) texts for the edification of generations to come lends significance to the process upon which we see Greenaway's dramatist studiously engaged in his Jerome-like writing cell. Prospero-Shakespeare's discarding of variants in *Prospero's Books*, and determinations about the text that will remain, contributes to the establishing of a monumental text (the First Folio) which will, in its own way, become an article of faith for later generations. The eventual product of Prospero-Shakespeare's judicious textual selections in this film, like the product of Jerome's earlier textual selections, is a book that has been canonised and appropriated by establishment systems. Like the Vulgate, it has taken on a status that makes it part of a shared cultural heritage, communally 'ours' in some properly vulgar way. In the published film script there is even a daring suggestion that a conflation between these two texts (Christian Bible and Shakespeare First Folio) may even have been intended. On Greenaway's skeletally drawn schematic chart of the twenty-four books, reproduced in the filmscript, the final book is shown entombing a line-drawn image of the crucified Christ who lies literally caught and embedded within its pages. There is both an elision implied in the image between two 'sacred' texts (Bible and Shakespeare's First Folio) and a yet more radical suggestion that the First Folio has, literally, subsumed the matter of that earlier sacred text (swallowing its subject within its own capacious pages). Indeed, in doing so, it may also have supplanted that earlier work in some cultural functions from the perspective of later generations. The drawing of the Christ figure swallowed and fixed by Greenaway's final book, in its range of possible suggestivenesses, is self-consciously audacious.

The canonised Folio, produced before our eyes in the course of *Prospero's Books*, does not suffer the fate of the other books from Prospero's prized library. It is one of only two to escape the bibliographic purge that constitutes the culmination of the film. For most of the film the desire to destroy books is presented as a dangerously subversive force, which the imaginative mind of the dramatist chooses to embody principally in his darker creations, Caliban and Antonio. Visually, the film can even be read as telling a simply schematised tale of the good and the bad, identifiable by their reverence or otherwise for books. Caliban grossly defiles them and, in Milan, Antonio orchestrates their burning. By contrast, Miranda's rapt absorption in *The Book of End Plants* may be taken as evidence of her goodness.

The end of the film, however, mocks the suggestion that the destruction of books desecrates all that is most valuable in life. Following Ariel's daring critical intervention in temporarily appropriating the quill to write in the book, Prospero cannot return to writing his play. Seeing his role as author momentarily usurped by another enables him to relinquish it permanently. He breaks the quill, shuts the book and steps down from his writing cell to participate in the world beyond. His decisive closing of his book seems

The final book on Greenaway's line-drawn chart, reproduced in the published screenplay, has swallowed the Gospel subject within its pages. The audacious implications of this image are explored in *Prospero's Books* partly through the elision between St Jerome and Prospero-Shakespeare, each of whom produces a canonical text of some 'religious' significance.

Source: From *Prospero's Books* by Peter Greenaway, published by Chatto & Windus. Reprinted by permission of The Random House Group Ltd.

to trigger an extended montage of many other books snapping, or being snapped, shut. The books replace one another in the frame at a dizzying rate. The speed of the sequence, and the sharp clap on the sound track accompanying each percussive book closure, create both visually and aurally the impression of applause, and suggest a causal relationship between the two elided acts. Are we hearing and seeing applause *because* the books are being abjured, *because* they are being shut with an irreversible finality? Is the rejection of books finally being celebrated? Although Greenaway describes the film as 'a project that deliberately emphasises and celebrates the text as text', it still seems to present the rejection of books as laudable and, at the last, lauded.[6] At odds with Greenaway's claim, the film seems to celebrate text less as text and more as design artefact – one amidst an array of others. As text, as printed words, it proves expendable. This inversion of what has seemed to be, and what Greenaway announces as, the value system promoted in the film is confirmed in the penultimate sequence when Prospero and Ariel themselves become supremely systematic destroyers of books. As the books are one by one annihilated, the prolonged pyrotechnic display, and accompanying celebratory Michael Nyman soundtrack, proclaims itself the climactic destination of the film's narrative.

In spring 1994, a conference was held at Yale University entitled 'Beyond Gutenberg'. Edward Tufte, known for his graphic design of digitised information packages, delivered a nostalgic paper about the culture of the book. In the course of his paper he held up a beautiful old volume which had been Ben Jonson's copy of Euclid. By this emotive gesture in such a context, he drew attention to the limitations of digitisation by reminding his audience of the beauty, the unique sensuality and the ability to accumulate meaningful associations of books.[7] In *Prospero's Books*, Greenaway makes a similar gesture by offering twenty-four old and beautiful volumes for the sensory appreciation of his spectatorship. Unlike Tufte, however, Greenaway is not, as becomes obvious, ultimately offering these books to be viewed in a spirit of nostalgia. In the course of the film, they undergo increasingly violating treatment. They are defecated upon, triumphantly slammed shut and finally destroyed by fire and water. The film, itself an extravagantly flamboyant celebration of cinematic and digitised technology, therefore ends in a pyrotechnic orgy of book destruction. In such a film, the place of hard-copy literature cannot but look insecure. From the perspective of the end of the film, the books seem to have been showcased less to highlight their irreplaceable distinctness than to testify to their own demise. There is almost a sense of satisfying teleology about their fate. The scene, after all, is notably lacking any hint of the elegiac or regretful.

In effect, the bibliographical purge at the end of the film literalises the film's unacknowledged metaphor: for words as agents of meaning are consistently devitalised by the film's design, and in the end dramatically and triumphantly destroyed by it. The arrival of the spectacularly showy technology (the Graphic Paintbox) that Greenaway pioneers in *Prospero's Books* gives him an appropriate platform from which to narrate the demise of the book. *Prospero's Books* is a film that not only presides over the progressive neglect, rejection and eventual destruction of the book, but also self-consciously celebrates its own ascendancy specifically at the book's expense. The Shakespeare Folio and the text of *The Tempest* are allowed to survive, but only, as it were, within the confines of the film which becomes their guardian and vehicle of transmission. In the closing sequence of the film, Ariel jumps on to and then out beyond a piece of parchment. Though it cannot hold the energetic Ariel, this book fragment remains behind as the film's final cinematic simulacrum: parchment on screen can look persuasively weathered but it neither smells like parchment nor crinkles to the touch. This is a film which glories in reminding us what a book is and can do, only then to present itself as the gleeful agent of its displacement.

WILLIAM SHAKESPEARE'S ROMEO+JULIET
(BAZ LUHRMANN, 1996)

Whereas in Greenaway's *Prospero's Books* Shakespeare's authorship is part-dramatised and part-effaced by an array of competing authorial agents, a paradoxical relationship to the source play and its authoring is flagged in the very title of Baz Luhrmann's *William Shakespeare's Romeo+Juliet*. The unprecedented authorial designation in the title – *William Shakespeare's . . .* impishly appears to authenticate the film as authoritatively Shakespearean, as the film that, in effect, Shakespeare's protocinematic imagination might prophetically have written. However, the replacement of the familiar *Romeo and Juliet* in the second half of the title with the funkier *Romeo+Juliet* equally impishly problematises this effect, unstitching the semblance of Shakespearean authenticity courted by the inclusion of Shakespeare's name. Through the intrusive 'plus' sign in its title, the film symbolically insists upon its distinction from its Shakespearean source and specifically upon its right to a hip contemporaneity not limited by that source. In this contradictory play of Shakespeareanness and unShakespeareanness, the title emblematises the dialectic of the film as a whole which enjoys the contradictory pull, the appeal and the rejection, of those elements in the play that its history in the theatre has enshrined as iconic.

The theatre's role as part of the precursor territory for the film is implicitly the subject of exposition in the film. If *Prospero's Books* in part narrates the demise of the book and the ascendancy of digital technology as the favoured means of recycling Shakespeare, Baz Luhrmann's film joins the fray to narrate the waning of a public performance space as the enduring site for presenting Shakespeare. It is the dramatically derelict ruined theatre on the seedy beachfront (whose surviving proscenium arch still proclaims the words 'The Sycamore Grove') that stands for such a space in the terms of the film.[8] It was Luhrmann's intention that this structure should act as a memorial to a grandly ornate movie theatre.[9] In its afterlife as a ruined shell, however, it has been transmuted into a found theatrical space, complete with high arch and platform stage. It not only resembles the ruins of a theatre, but the improvisatory uses to which it is put confirm its specifically theatrical identity. Here local youths claim it as their own, giving a heightened charge to aspects of their own lives by rendering them performative in ways that correspond to the impressive scale of the stage and the grandeur of its framing.

The theatrical ruin is first introduced approximately ten minutes into the film. In order to appreciate the drama of its effect in the context of the film as a whole, and its tonal contrast with everything that precedes it, it is worth documenting the film's opening sequences.

The film opens on a newscaster (Edwina Moore) delivering the play's prologue from within the bounded space of a television screen. For a brief moment the story of the feuding families and the star-crossed lovers seems narratable, containable, amenable to tidy, newsworthy summing-up. As the newscaster finishes speaking, however, the shot speed-zooms directly *into* the graininess of the screen, exploding the sense of narrative and visual containment implied by the televisually framed opening and breaking apart its frame borders into a far more expansive world. The film now bursts explosively into life, resisting fixity or containment in the manic freneticism of its scene-setting title sequence. As a dizzying onslaught of images maps a dramatic urban landscape (a contemporary world of heightened aesthetics shot principally in Mexico City but called Verona Beach), the newscaster's words from the prologue are now heard again. No longer delivered with the dispassionate detachment of a news anchorwoman, they are now spoken in emotionally laden tones in portentous male voice-over. Just as televisual space has ceded to a version of cinematic space, so a television news voice has given way to a cinematic trailer voice. All the sensationalism and drama inherent in the story that a journalistic training has held at bay is now allowed uninhibited expression. Simultaneously, amidst the whistle-stop tour of character and setting, lines from the prologue are intermittently flashed up on the screen as a series of attention-grabbing newspaper headlines. For all the crazy pacing of the visual introductions and the headily operatic insistence of the soundtrack, the processes of immersion in Shakespearean language are therefore gradual, and surreptitiously repetitive in ways that help acclimatise the ear gradually to the non-naturalistic nature of the language.

From the pace and pizzazz of the title sequence, a wipe then transports us into the film narrative proper, to a gang shoot-out at a petrol station between the boys from the house of Montague (Hispanics) and the boys from the house of Capulet (white trash beach bums). This shoot-out comically pastiches stylistic aspects of a Sergio Leone spaghetti Western (sustained close-ups on the still, steely face of Tybalt accompanied by a twangily spare Morricone-esque melody on guitar with breathy, reedy pipes). In its free-wheeling filmic tributes, the scene also mimics the stylish fight choreography of a John Woo film (extreme slow motion shots of a character diving sideways firing simultaneously from two guns). This is a film which signals clearly and early the pleasure it wishes to take in its own cinematic identity and which aligns itself – in appropriately ironic vein – with a glamorous heritage of savvily self-aware action films. The shoot-out cedes to a city-wide helicopter/ car chase accompanied once again by the heightened and insistent strains of a soundtrack imitative of Orff's 'Carmina Burana', and it is this sequence that in turn leads into the scene which is to be of central interest here.

The tone changes dramatically as Romeo (Leonardo DiCaprio) is introduced. He is discovered at dawn on the beach sitting ruminating beneath the 'Sycamore Grove' arch. This is the first of three appearances of the ruined theatre in the film. Sentimentally lit by the dawn light, he sits perched on the edge of a broad stage lost in an indulgent reverie as, in internalised voice-over, he rehearses his paradoxical platitudes about his love for Rosaline ('O brawling love, O loving hate . . . O heavy lightness, serious vanity' I.i.174– 176). It is a moment that iconises the particular variety of fragile, almost androgynous, sex appeal that characterised its star. In comparison with the eye-dizzying speed-zooms and ferocious velocity of the editing in the title sequence, the obsessive swish pans of the shoot-out, and the visual and acoustic excess of the chase, Romeo's reverie beneath the ruined theatrical arch cannot but seem both wordy and static. This is, in effect, the first moment of peace in the film. Taken by the poeticism of his own lacklustre words, Romeo even jots them down in a notebook for future reference. And having thus 'scripted' them, he has the opportunity to 'perform' them soon afterwards in conversation with Benvolio further up the same beach.

The shots of the ruined theatre are given more potential symbolic weight than any single image that has preceded them by virtue of the fact that for once the camera is allowed a moment of pause. This is not merely another fleeting contributor to an atmospheric collage of architectural impressions, as previous locations have been. The lingering of the shot works in concert with Romeo's own lingering to suggest there might be something more significant about this place than any yet encountered. As narratively employed within the film, the ruined symbol of a theatre is first introduced as the location in which tired phrases may be recycled by the linguistically indulgent. It also subsequently comes to stand for the site in which dramatic writing destined in time for a more vibrant performance arena may first be tested. In illustration of this, we hear Romeo's words twice: once in voice-over as they emerge from within the proscenium arch and then again a few minutes later – no longer now in space designated 'theatrical' – as he tries them 'for real' on his cousin. In response to Romeo's string of rehearsed oxymorons, Benvolio (Dash Mihok) can scarcely suppress a snigger. It is a laugh that is partly prepared for by Shakespeare. Its significances are, however, here transformed. In the first analysis, this Benvolio's snigger serves as a lightning conductor for potential

The ruined sea-front arch has a desolate symbolic force in *Romeo+Juliet* (1996). It stands like an architectural abortion, a monument to its own evisceration.

Source: '*William Shakespeare's Romeo and Juliet*' © 1996 Twentieth Century Fox. All rights reserved.

embarrassment among an audience. That is, any potential discomfort about the use of heightened language in the context of a hip movie is diffused by being anticipated on screen. More specifically, however, Benvolio's response also implies that there is something contrived-sounding and inauthentic about such phrases when voiced away from the willed artifice of theatrical playing space. Such words cannot simply be transferred from one space to another unadapted, as Romeo has literally attempted to do, without in the process striking the ear as embarrassingly self-conscious. The moment is neatly illustrative of a thesis consistently adhered to in the film as a whole, which itself fearlessly and radically transforms words originally penned for theatrical space.

The particular speech that Luhrmann tracks in its symbolic pretence of crossing performance media from theatrical to filmic space is, however, the most self-consciously contrived and unfelt of any in the play, illustrating as it does Romeo's indulgent wish to believe himself in love. To single out this speech to illustrate theatrical language's inability to make the transfer to film unaltered without then sounding overblown, therefore, unfairly weights the dice against approaches to adaptation less radically transformative than Luhrmann's tends to be. Reminding an audience how forced or silly heightened language can seem in the unsparing linguistic exposure of cinematic space is consistent with Luhrmann's agenda, which is partly to minimise just such heightened linguistic effects. True to the implications of the gentle derision which greets Romeo's naïve attempt to carry words unadjusted from one performance space to another, the showcasing of Shakespearean language in Luhrmann's film is kept strategically economical. It is noteworthy, for example, that the standard theatrical trailer for the film used none at all. This was a film bursting with editorial energy, hip sound, engaging young faces and stunning cinematography: its script was not considered helpful, or even necessary, for its marketing. The hope was to circumvent innate fears of Shakespeare in the movie-going public by rendering his language peripheral to the film's operations. It was a marketing strategy that evidently paid off: the film's box office has comfortably exceeded that for any other Shakespeare film made to date.[10]

The ruined theatre's second appearance is as the space in which the Montague revellers assemble in preparation to crash the Capulet party. They use it as their warm-up arena for the real action, and here, crucially, they take the (Queen Mab) tabs that will propel them forcibly into a *mélange* of drug-induced impressions at the party itself. Using theatrical space as the antechamber and rehearsal space for the unfettered cinematographic hedonism of the party once again establishes a clear hierarchical relationship between the two performance arenas. The theatre is necessary as a point of rehearsal and departure. It is, however, clear that it must be left for the drama really to begin and, from Romeo's point of view, for a supposed love to be replaced by a real one. Remaining in theatrical space keeps his love artificial and phoney. By contrast, leaving it enables him to encounter the real thing.

The symbolism of the ruined theatre becomes most explicitly delineated, however, in its final appearance. In all its visual drama it stands within the iconographic scheme of Luhrmann's film almost like an architectural abortion, a monument to the fact that the life has been ripped from its middle. Given the desolate force of the structural shell that remains, it is no accident that it is in this space that Mercutio too is eviscerated. It is here that he takes the wound to his middle and then self-consciously performs his own death. Once he has taken his final bow, he himself becomes another forlorn monument to something once vital and now gone as the innards seep from his gaping stomach. His body is left, dramatically framed by the desultory theatre arch until, with deliberate stylisation, the lights are brought down on them both. The symbolic scheme is brutally clear: a human lifeless form is left encased by an architectural one. Meanwhile the living action now continues elsewhere, in a world beyond the theatre, in a medium where old words can yet be revivified by being rethought for new contexts (if, in this instantiation, through slightly uneven central vocal performances).

This public performative arena is a form, the film's iconography seems to declare, whose moment is passed and whose power to move or to signify now depends upon its status as a ruined monument. And, as if to reinforce the point, following Benvolio's embarrassment at Romeo's use of heightened language in the early stages of the film, the cousins subsequently stroll off to a seedy pool hall along the front. The name across its door is 'The Globe Theatre', its presence on Verona Beach serving as a piquant reminder of a more traditional acting arena that, with a baroque flourish, this film consigns to faded has-been status. Benvolio's snigger at the *un*topicality of what the film has implicitly labelled *theatrical* forms of language perhaps even extends to the film itself. Certainly it is a film that energetically relishes exploring those aspects of film-making – speed of editing, variety of shooting styles and shooting speeds, split-screen imagery, visual scope and grandeur of effect – which set it apart most clearly from theatre.

And yet it is not just *theatre*'s demise over which the film presides, for the ruined space upon which the lights are brought down was once, apparently, itself a *movie* theatre. The ruined space therefore has a double identity and, for those able to see through the apparently theatrical character of the ruin to its authorially determined history as a cinema, the elegy for it implicit in the film takes on another layer of meaning. What might be the purpose of having a ruined movie theatre haunt a key space at key moments in a film that so flamboyantly celebrates its own specifically cinematic energy? At a first take, the image can seem wonderfully inappropriate. Cinema is far from derelict in this film. Placing it as a noble ruin among the washed up and unwanted on a seedy beach can, therefore, seem perverse. However, if the movie theatre is taken not as the general representative of cinema, but more precisely as the representative of a public arena in which films are viewed communally, its demise may be seen as more topically pertinent. Such a socialising architecture is in ruins before the film opens as if in acknowledgement that the primary reception context of films is no longer communal movie theatres but rather the isolated and isolating space of private living rooms. This same space is, of course, evoked by the television screen with which the film both opens and closes. It is the viewing space implied by this television screen – the domestic living room – that symbolically puts paid to theatrical movie-going, that consigns it to its status as a noble ruin. Economically and sociologically it has supplanted it. The relative buoyancy of the rental, sell-through and pay-to-view market for films in comparison with their life on theatrical release may even, therefore, be seen as obliquely allegorised in pictorial terms in the ruination of the movie theatre.

The elision between cinematic and theatrical public space that the ruined monument ultimately represents offers itself as a composite foil to the more private spaces of reception and consumption which Luhrmann's film rightly seems to foresee itself inhabiting. The two 'houses' upon which Mercutio calls down a 'plague' as he stands beneath the theatrical arch carries an additional frisson of disturbing meaning in the context of this double-duty performative space. The eloquence of the lights being brought down simultaneously on Mercutio's dead body and on the scarred architecture of the cinema-cum-'found theatre' contains the film's comment – half victory dance, half monody – upon its own capacity to thrive in comparison with cultural forms that necessarily depend upon communal public space. These, suggest the visuals of the desecrated beachfront, have no future. As the prostitute's suggestive dance for a lone man further along the same beach also implies, spectating pleasures have become socially fractured, solitary. As literally configured by the small screen at the beginning and end of *Romeo+Juliet*, a cinematic world no longer needs a communally receptive audience in a designated public place in order to be summoned into being. It is in fact now more usual, as the elegiac symbolism of Luhrmann's film perhaps forecasts, for that cinematic world to have been wrested from public space and resited in a domestic context where a television screen must serve as its vehicle of delivery. While home movie-viewing thrives, public performative arenas – both theatres and cinemas – are left to crumble in spaces no longer fashionable, memorials to their own outmodishness. In graphically literalised, hyperbolic form, Luhrmann's film shows us one such.[11]

HAMLET (MICHAEL ALMEREYDA, 2000)

At the close of Luhrmann's *Romeo+Juliet*, the remnants of the narratively and stylistically explosive drama are reeled back in and squeezed once more into the space of a television frame as the newscaster appropriates the Prince's final words ('A glooming peace this morning with it brings . . .' V.iii.304–309). In the sanitised context of the newsroom, the story is once again subsumed into a form that makes it sound amenable to tidily summative phrasing and neat narrative packaging. It is an impression that sits oddly with the heady passion that has characterised the story that precedes it.

The figure of a newscaster that bookends *Romeo+Juliet* as the uninvolved voice of narration and commentary was, in effect, to stage a come-back four years later as the voice of summation (in place of Fortinbras, with a few additional lines from the Player King) at the end of Michael Almereyda's *Hamlet*. The film, independently made, was humbler and less technically ambitious than its Bazmark predecessor. Orson Welles had famously shot his *Macbeth* (1948) in twenty-one days, describing it as a rough charcoal sketch of the play. It was with the same 'spirit, roughness and energy' that Almereyda said he wanted to make his *Hamlet*. Accordingly, it was shot on small, mobile, agile super 16 mm cameras, 'fast and cheap' in a New York that is to be taken as a media-saturated version of Elsinore.[12]

Almereyda imagines his Hamlet (Ethan Hawkes) as a present day disaffected teenager and would-be film-maker, trying to impose shape and purpose on the myriad images by which he finds himself assailed in present-day, corporate Manhattan. Ophelia (Julia Stiles) is a surly, depressive but ultimately grimly bully-able waif of a teenager, resentful but silent in the face of the infantilising treatment she receives from her father (who insists on tying her shoe-laces and turns up at her apartment carrying balloons). Her will to find a point of fixity in a baffling and bruising world leads her to an interest in photography and developing. These two quietly 'alternative' and vulnerable-seeming teenagers are ranged against the slickly presented business world that the adults of the 'Denmark Corporation' inhabit: expensively dressed, materially smug and capable of significant brutality. Hamlet slouches through this self-congratulatory world, aware of himself as an introspective misfit in it, and advertising his resistance to its codes and values by parading his obtrusive woolly hat among the expensive suits and studiedly casual weekend wear. He does not, however, move unarmed through their midst, but rather wields his pixelvision video camera as a consoling form of self-defence. The world of Manhattan/Elsinore is already caught and replayed obsessively within a series of frames generated by its own taste for surveillance systems. Hamlet contributes to its removal from too direct an engagement with the real by adding his own stream of screened images to its mediated character.

The memory of a person caught on film has, since the earliest days of photography, been thought to have something ghostly about it. Like a ghost, it is an image that exists in separate space from the person it represents and, like a ghost, it can survive even when that person dies. The tenacity with which the inhabitants of Almereyda's corporate Elsinore adhere to photographic, ghostly images of each other – often in preference to the more substantial counterparts of those images in the real world – is partly symptomatic of a pervasive anxiety about the violence that potentially (and actually) characterises real encounters in such a world. Mediated versions of each other, by contrast, are sufficiently sanitised and distanced to be reassuringly incapable of direct brutality. Such captured, ghostly visions of life even become the medium of ironic exchange in this Elsinore. Thus 'The Mousetrap' to which Hamlet invites the court is a filmic montage of found footage and manipulated images from other sources,[13] and the 'herbs' distributed by this Ophelia in her distraction are the very literal 'remembrancer' of polaroid photographs. The formalised 'giving' of these particular ghostly, unreal images to the authority figures in this world ironically inverts the habitual relationship these characters adopt to such images. More usually, images of others are surreptitiously and proprietorially 'taken' (ostensibly to ensure their own security). In fact, so pervasive is the ghostly image in this world (on security cameras, on photographs, on old home movies, as seen in reflective surfaces) that when a 'real' ghost (Sam Shepard as Hamlet senior) arrives, his identity may mark him out as otherworldly but his appearance is not in itself sufficient to do so. Being a shadowy figure on a security screen does not, that is, distinguish him from the range of other shadowy simulacra around him. Instead, he must choreograph a demonstration of his own otherworldliness, which he wryly does by disappearing into a canned drinks machine. In life, Hamlet senior had been erased by the ambitions of his brother and his thrusting corporate capitalism: in death he near-allegorises the animating force of his own extinction by allowing himself to 'be disappeared' by the pervasive representative of just such a thrusting corporate capitalism – a Pepsi dispenser. Trace projections, photographic and cinematographic memories may be the preferred version of messier personhood among the characters in this world, but the real ghost in their midst is able to demonstrate how much more organically *his* is this medium by economically finding some oblique humour in it.

When characters do step out from behind their security-inducing cameras, monitors, telephones and wire-taps to face each other in shared space, their engagements can be far from pretty, as is illustrated, for example, in Ophelia's forcible eviction from the Guggenheim Museum or in Claudius's thuggish assault on Hamlet in the public laundry. Claudius's expensive coat and Armani tie are too thin a civilised veneer to contain the simmering, primitive brutality that lies beneath. Hamlet's obsessive attachment to his camera and to his film-making is perhaps even understandable in such an environment: it helps to abstract him from too frequent or too direct an engagement with an abusive world.

Almereyda's own film-making history has a touch of his Hamlet about it. In 1992 he had himself shot a downtown love story entitled *Another Girl Another Planet* on a pixel 2000 camera (a film he later transferred to 16mm for the festival circuit). In fact, it is Almereyda's own camera that Hawkes' Hamlet is seen using in the film for his video diaries. However, despite the peripheral echo between protagonist and director in their shooting format, independence and modesty of operation, Almereyda's own film-making has considerably more panache and control than does that of his Hamlet. Hamlet's films are improvisatory, magpie-ish and a little indulgent. It is part of the condition of his youthfulness that his films should be characterised as much by angularity and attitude as by disciplined design. Almereyda's film, by contrast, is more controlled and its acts of appropriation and reference more purposeful.

Nevertheless, Hamlet's film-making (and film-viewing) offers an eloquent counterpoint to the film that contains him, and Almereyda's film is able to trade upon Hamlet's filmic self-inscriptions to help delineate his character with efficient economy. Hamlet's willed status as a misfit raging against the system finds expression in his choices of hero. Given his desire to define himself against his moment, these are drawn from a fairly predictable pool. The inevitable photographs of Che Guevara and Malcolm X on his wall, and James Dean's performance in *Rebel Without A Cause* (Nicholas Ray, 1955) – a film from the 'dissenting mainstream' which Hamlet watches admiringly – establish the romantic tradition of the disaffected and militant rebel with which Hamlet wishes to align himself. In addition, Hawkes thought Hamlet had some kinship with Holden Caulfield or Kurt Cobain.[14] The sheer number of character parallels in play makes of this Hamlet's malaise almost that of an era rather than merely that of a solitary individual at odds with his generation. Levity may not be part of his repertoire, but an earnest sense of spiritual connection to an artistic and political tradition of resistance is. Even the brief film clip of John Gielgud as Hamlet addressing the skull – for all its gestural preciousness as viewed in the context of a contemporary teenage world of woolly hats and public laundries[15] – does place Hawkes' Hamlet in a community of Hamlets, adding a historicised layer to his voice. It also pithily showcases the skull that the sterile and over-sanitised world of this gleaming Manhattan would not otherwise easily be able to supply.

Appropriately for a version of Elsinore, Almereyda's Manhattan/Elsinore is a world whose abundance of surveillance cameras and listening devices necessarily collapses the theoretical distinction between public and private space. So unstable is any notion of privacy in the Elsinore Shakespeare scripted that not only might there be (and frequently is) a spy or an eavesdropper behind every pillar or arras, but even the established theatrical convention of the inaudibility to other characters of a soliloquy is brought into question. Thus when Polonius says to Ophelia, 'You need not tell us what Lord Hamlet said, / We heard it all' (III.ii.181–182), the obsessively intrusive character of the place just allows for the possibility that the 'all' Polonius claims to have heard really *is* all. It is not impossible that this might even include the 'To be or not to be' speech delivered shortly after he and the King have put themselves strategically into hiding specifically to listen to Hamlet.[16] In stage *Hamlets* personal privacy can, therefore, be compromised in ways that even breach theatrical conventions. By comparison, film versions can offer the central protagonist the intimate privacy of the interior monologue whose freedom from prying intrusion remains inviolate. Like many film Hamlets before him, Hawkes' Hamlet often soliloquises in voice-over. He, therefore, has the luxury of enjoying the privacy of the inside of his own head as the one space that remains immune to the variety of surveillance systems – spies, cameras, wire taps – by which he is surrounded.

Yet more pervasive than the CCTV cameras in Almereyda's Manhattan/ Elsinore are the plethora of mirrors, screens and other glistening surfaces that inhibit the perception of depth in anything. The very fabric of this world seems to conspire with its inhabitants to protect its secrets by reflecting back to the onlooker little beyond his or her own image. The pursuit of profundity in a world of gleaming reflective surfaces is necessarily frustrating. Nevertheless, the films this Hamlet makes in his desire to capture and make sense of his world – if at a mediated remove – are grainy, black and white, and self-consciously 'arty' in ways that seem to court a stylish profundity. In his dying moments, through a series of subjectivised flashbacks, he even tries to remake scenes from the film that contains him in his own black and white, narratively more opaque and suggestive mode. Brief selected images from the film – the ghost, Gertrude's weeping face, Laertes in the churchyard, Claudius hitting him in the public laundry, kissing Ophelia – are thus replayed but now stylistically transformed, drained of colour, clarity and context. Fleetingly, we see Hamlet's own eye in the midst of these remade images as the force that has teasingly transformed intelligible narrative into something more stylishly abstract and enigmatic. His attempt to appropriate his own story and retell it in a tradition more akin to an abstruse art-house style is as telling about his profound sense of dis-ease amidst the world of corporate Manhattan as are any of his disillusioned words. That his dying impulse should be to recast his own story in an exaggeratedly expressionist aesthetic is perhaps appropriate for a disaffected young man whose most replayed cinematic image in life had been of himself with a gun held alternately to his temple and in his mouth. In his obsessive freeze-framing and reviewing of this image he had seemed to be assessing the artistic efficacy of the pose as much as the psychological necessity to pull the trigger. The question seems to be less whether he should kill himself and more whether the *image* of his killing himself is artistically pleasing. Unlike Shakespeare's Othello, who in his dying moments appears to want to rewrite the substance of his own story to make it accord more readily with what he would like to believe to be true, Almereyda's Hamlet seems intent on changing only the style of the telling of his.

The line the film takes as its opener is Hamlet's 'I have of late, but wherefore I know not, lost all my mirth' (II.ii.295–296). It is a fair warning of the priorities of this Hamlet who not only announces that he has 'lost all [his] mirth', but who clearly has. And Hamlet's lack of mirth is symptomatic of the tonal priorities of the film as a whole. The loss of the gravedigger scene, for example – perhaps the most obvious locus of humour in the play – emblematises the loss of skittishness in the film more generally.[17] It is, however, noticeable that Hamlet's comment on his own mirthlessness is not here, as it is in Shakespeare, a line spoken to Rosencrantz and Guildenstern, but rather to himself, or rather to a camera he has turned upon himself.

Ethan Hawkes' Hamlet is introspective, angst-ridden, self-regarding.

Having denied us a Hamlet given to wryness at the wretched way the world is, the film gives us instead a character not just driven by earnest anxiety but even a little vainly self-regarding about his own meaningfully angst-ridden state. Hawkes plays this youthful self-obsession and sense of being romantically pitted against the stream of things with conviction and control, but his character lacks the tonal range that Shakespeare's Hamlet gives us. This is a Hamlet whose engagements with the world tend to be either pained or brooding and a large proportion of which happen at one remove, through the mediation of his camera.

It is the film's triumph that it allows its protagonist sufficient space to pursue his particular artistic choices without either patronising him for the clichéd character of his attitudinal impulses or itself slipping into a comparable aesthetic. Conventionally enough, the *narrative* tension in the film is between Hamlet and Claudius who seem to occupy different worlds – the private and melancholic versus the public and unctuously corporate. The *stylistic* tension of the film, however, is between two competing modes of film-making, exemplified by Almereyda and his youthful alter-ego protagonist. It is Almereyda's luxury that his film can incorporate the interesting but indulgent self-regard of Hamlet's filmic experiments while still distinguishing itself clearly from them. Hamlet's style of film-making is a contrapuntal force and flattering foil to Almereyda's throughout the film. When he dies, the edgy, narratively obtuse style than has been his trademark dies with him and Almereyda's film is left to offer a swift conclusion of the aftermath in its own more conventional linear narrative form. As if to highlight the stylistic contrast, Almereyda even cedes to the *most* conventional of screen narrative forms by leaving the drama's summation to be told as a piece of packaged broadcast news. In context, the newscaster's slick presentation of plain narrative, literal-minded accompanying visuals and simple moralising about the story told seems like a sympton of the banalising world against which this Hamlet had sought to define himself. Almereyda generously sustains the illusion that in the absence of Hamlet there is no one left in this world to generate interesting visual metaphors about the way things are or to tell odd tales oddly. In the context of such a film, however, this is clearly a willed illusion. Until the final sequence, in which Almereyda seems deliberately to disengage the film's imaginative energy and retreat into automatic narrative mechanisms, his own metaphorical imagination has been consistently interesting and his narrative instincts considerably affecting.

TITUS (JULIE TAYMOR, 2000)

It was as an exciting and daring theatre director that Julie Taymor was known in 1998 as she went into pre-production with *Titus*. One of her innovative and adventurous stage productions had been *Titus Andronicus* in an off-Broadway production in 1994. Her sense of affinity with the impulses and dilemmas of the play was in part rooted in the contemporaneity of the play's examination of violence. As she turned her attention to the subsequent film, however, the creative process the play itself metaphorises might well have had an additional resonance for her. The question the play asks repeatedly – what to do with poetic language in a context that primarily values spectacle? – is one with which she too necessarily had to engage. The specific problem of balancing language against dramatic action is, after all, as pertinent for a theatre director turned film-maker as it must have been for the playwright with poetic ambitions who wrote *Titus Andronicus*.

Titus Andronicus, written and first performed in the late 1580s or early 1590s, was first published in quarto in 1594. The previous year Shakespeare had published *Venus and Adonis*. He prefaced this narrative poem with the dedicatory epigraph: *Vilia miretur vulgus: mihi flavus Apollo / Pocula Castalia plena ministret aqua* ('Let the common hordes admire base things: for me may golden-haired Apollo provide copious draughts from the Castalia spring'). The admiration of the multitude was the province of the public stage: the Castalia spring was sacred to the Muses and therefore where poets might gain inspiration. The opposition the epigraph implicitly establishes between the public stage and private poetry is telling about the two sides of Shakespeare's own professional life in 1593 when he was arguably more poised between being a poet and a dramatist than he would be at any subsequent point in his career. His announced contempt for the admiration of the masses in comparison with the more elevated delights of poetry adheres to the conventional contemporary hierarchies applied to poetry and the stage. In the context of the writing for the stage Shakespeare had himself recently produced and would produce again, however, it cannot but read disingenuously. For in this period, in between drinking at the Castalia spring, he was not himself above pandering to the tastes of the 'vulgus' in the public playhouses.

Titus Andronicus is full of 'vilia', of the very basenesses against which Shakespeare declares himself high-mindedly opposed in his preface to *Venus and Adonis*. One of the subjects at issue in the play is the relationship of word to spectacle, of tongue to hand, of language to action, and implicitly of poetry to the stage. The play offers a series of graphic metaphors to dramatise the encounter between these things. The most potent of these is to be found in the sensationally silenced figure of the once poetic Lavinia. Later Shakespeare plays would less controversially be carried by their dramatic poetry – that is by poetry that adds charge to the action rather than, as occasionally seems to be the case in *Titus Andronicus*, stalling, compromising or competing with its dramatic imperatives. In this early tragedy the poetry can sometimes appear to resist a responsiveness to dramatic context. Poetry and action intermittently bump against each other in extreme and unreconciled forms – most notably in Marcus's beautiful but painfully extended mythological ramble when faced by the newly mutilated Lavinia (a speech that poses a significant challenge for both actors in performance). And the play itself even seems invested with a self-consciousness about the percussive choreography of the encounter between its poetry and action. This self-consciousness is perhaps most evident in Titus's absurdist instruction to Lavinia to carry his desmembered hand in her mouth, and the absurdist spectacle that results when she then does. In the fiercely anatomical symbolic scheme of the play, the carrying of a dismembered hand in a silenced mouth can be seen as expressive of the dramatic peculiarities that can arise from attempting to merge action and language. The scene, in all its unsettling ludicrousness, is almost a comically self-aware performance treatise on the potential for clumsiness in the encounter between tongue and hand, poetry and action in this play. The dialogue into which Shakespeare's competing professional allegiances as poet and dramatist explicitly enter in *Titus Andronicus* is certainly both a peculiar and an intimate one.

The potential disempowerment that could be felt by an aspiring poet writing for the stage finds its intense embodiment in Lavinia (identified by

Marcus with 'the Thracian poet' Orpheus (II.iv.51) and known in her previous life for her poetic recitations). The excision of the poetic Lavinia's tongue to furnish a play with grotesque spectacle might even be read as a crudely cartooned self-portrait of a writer who knows the convention of valuing the rarified realm of poetry but who here finds himself writing for the 'vulgar hordes' of the public stage. In the silenced Lavinia, Shakespeare finds an exaggerated metaphor for the process of forfeiting poetry to spectacle, refined linguistic abstraction to concrete visual demonstration. Equally, those same processes of forfeit and exchange, of the sacrifice of language in order to embrace new forms of arresting spectacle, were part of the adjustments Taymor herself had to make in negotiating the shift from theatre to film. The silenced figure of the film's Lavinia (Laura Fraser), whose forms of expression have been necessarily translated from a primarily verbal to a primarily visual plane, is therefore hyperbolically expressive of the creative processes to which each of her authors – Shakespeare and Taymor – have, in turn, had to submit themselves.

When Shakespeare's Lavinia is finally empowered by writing the names of her attackers in the sand, Titus looks at her scorings and says:

> . . . *come, I will go get a leaf of brass,*
> *And with a gad of steel will write these words,*
> *And lay it by: the angry northern wind*
> *Will blow these sands like Sybil's leaves abroad,*
> *And where's our lesson then?* (IV.i.102–106)

He cannot bear to see Lavinia's painfully articulated words expressed in so transient a medium as marks in the sand. In preserving her testimony by scoring it with a gad of steel into a leaf of brass, Titus rescues it from evanescence and secures for it a form of permanence. In so doing, he symbolically plucks it from the realm of theatre whose identity depends upon its ephemerality and relocates it a medium that endures.

In Taymor's film, Titus's lines about defying the transience of the moment by fixing Lavinia's testimony in a permanent form are omitted. In the new cinematic context, of course, these words have effectively been made redundant since the entire film inescapably enacts the project to make the transient permanent. Taymor's 1994 Theatre for a New Audience stage production of *Titus* in St Clement's Church off-Broadway, with a cast of twelve accompanied only by two trumpets, had drawn plaudits for its stylised control and unflinching but purposeful engagement with the play's violence.[18] As is the way with pieces of theatre, however, when the run came to an end, the production survived only as a paper trail of recollection and review: it is both a stage production's beauty and its sadness that it has no substantial identity beyond that. Taymor's return to the play four years later, armed now with a film crew and a correspondingly enhanced budget, represented her equivalent of Titus's reaching for a leaf of brass to memorialise in lasting form the precarious expression of an important truth. The runes of the stage production are detectable throughout the film – not only in the presence of Harry Lennix as Aaron (the one actor to make the transfer with Taymor from the stage production), but also in many design decisions first conceived for the stage production.

The most startling of these are the 'Penny Arcade Nightmares', a series of insert fantasy sequences that punctuate both productions, designed to give stylised and mythologised form to the subjective realities of the characters' minds.[19] The prominence and particularity of the boy Lucius's role in the film is another.

In the film, as in the stage production, the boy becomes the mediating eyes through which the drama is seen. The ease of his transfer from stage to screen – complete with his accompanying paraphernalia of 1950s kitchen table and collection of miscellaneous toy soldiers – creates a sense of contiguity between the two performance spaces. The wolf motif on the back of his jacket when he visits the woodcarver's shop in the film joins the film's extensive network of evocations of wild animals that repeatedly literalise the animal imagery of the play. This particular wolf motif with strapped-on udders, however, also directly reproduces the image of the wolf-that-suckles-the-baby-that-founds-Rome that Taymor had designed for the stage production's publicity poster.[20] The boy's presence on screen at this moment thus curiously serves partly as an anachronistic advertisement for the production now gone. As the character whose movements within the world of the film are most fluid, it is perhaps appropriate that it should be he who carries into Taymor's film the billboard for the stage production: his spatial promiscuity within the space of the film almost allows for the possibility that he might also have arrived within its frame boundaries from a space beyond.

The only other character able to rival the boy for an ability to slip between worlds in the film is Aaron (whose actor is another interloper from theatrical space). Aaron's spatial freedom is, however, symbolically curtailed when he is buried in a pit and staked to the earth in the final moments of the film: a more resolute image of stasis is difficult to imagine. By contrast, the extent of the boy's transgressive, even potentially frame-breaching, mobility is confirmed in these final moments as he makes a daringly touching bid to break out of the prescribed spaces in which he – and Aaron's baby – have been placed. It is, in this case, an overwhelming sense of compassion which emboldens him to express his lack of respect for thresholds of containment with such gently expressed but nevertheless irresistible defiance. His strategic exit out of the barbarising amphitheatre arena into an unspecified world of promise beyond therefore epitomises the boy's ability to slip not only material but also emotional boundaries: neither the symbolic solidity of the enclosing amphitheatre nor the collective force of the Goths' desire for 'just' vengeance is now sufficient to hold him.

Taymor repeatedly remembers both the tenor and the detail of the earlier stage production in the tenor and detail of the film. In the processes of transcription for the screen, however, the cinematic gads of steel have also made their own interpretive interventions felt. One of Taymor's interventionist transformations is to take the suggestion of a performativity to the violence in her stage production of it and turn it into the driving impetus of her film. There is plenty of justification for this in the Shakespeare play. Shakespeare's Aaron insists that he has executed a series of *coups de théâtre* almost as an installation artist ahead of his time, carving grief-inducing slogans in Roman letters 'on [dead men's] skins, as on the bark of treees' (V.i.138) and then propping up the corpses, thus decorated, outside their friends' door. In doing so, he turns cruelty into art, and moreover demands for his handiwork an audience of the most morbidly interested variety. Similarly, Tamora and Titus trade acts of vengeance, seeking from the other each time appreciation for the artistry of their latest move and counter-move. Aaron, aware of the competitive game upon which Titus and Tamora are engaged, even concedes that, in response to Titus's 'weapons wrapp'd about with lines', were the empress present '[s]he would applaud [his] conceit' (IV.ii.27, 30). There is incumbent upon them each an acknowledgement of the imaginative artistry and mythological symmetry with which vengeance is exacted. If Lavinia has been used 'worse than Philomel', then Titus will be revenged 'worse than Progne' (V.ii.194–195). As the climax to the show, Tamora and Titus each dress up as part of a theatrical performance laid on in large part for the other's benefit – Tamora as Revenge and subsequently Titus as a cook. And in his role as cook, Titus does not merely chop up Chiron and Demetrius: he goes to the extravagant creative lengths of baking them into pastries that they may be served up with an appropriate flourish. In the Rome of *Titus Andronicus*, it is not enough to perform a barbarous act: that act has to be shaped, sculpted, given artistic design and purpose. Even torture is imbued with its own artistry. Titus and Tamora, therefore, each require the other not only to be a worthy enemy but also a worthy audience for an artistically conceived performance of vengeance.

The play's depiction of violence as a performance in need of an audience permeates Taymor's film to such an extent that Hopkins' Titus even allows himself briefly to register his appreciation for the artistry of his own death just before being impaled by a candelabra. It is repeatedly an attention to cruelty as art and violence as performance that Taymor seizes upon as fertile dramatic material for her adaptation. At its opening, as at the opening of the stage production, a young boy (played now by the ever fragile-seeming Osheen Jones in a partial recapitulation of his role as the young observer in Adrian Noble's *Midsummer Night's Dream*)[21] conjures a world of violence through his games with toy soldiers at his kitchen table. The game starts conventionally enough – as innocuous or as dangerous as any little boy's game with his toy soldiers may be considered. However, as his imagination creates ever greater torments to inflict upon his soldiers and for them to inflict upon each other, the game escalates, quickly escaping the control of its playmaster. As it breaks the boundaries of play, the game's disturbing implications start to be played out as grown-up war in the world around the boy. Scared by the explosions and accompanying dust clouds now invading his playspace, he takes cover under the table. From here he is subsequently rescued by a leather-clad figure who carries him down an enclosed staircase (referred to by Taymor – once again part-evoking Noble's film – as a 'down the rabbit hole experience')[22] and, by a spatial logic particular to the film, out into an enormous Roman coliseum. In the middle of the coliseum the boy's salvation is celebrated as he is held aloft for the appreciation of the galleried multitude. The multitude to which the scared boy is offered, however, is in this case visually absent. Their cheers are audible but the amphitheatre galleries are visibly empty.

Taymor's specific purpose in showing us empty galleries was to suggest a theatre populated by generations of ghosts, by the collective history of voices whose cheers have responded to, and sometimes determined, life and death for those in the amphitheatre. The ghosts, that is, were to be taken as emphatically present as part of the scene. As she expresses it: 'When you take away the visual presence of the audience, their vocal presence becomes all the more deafening.'[23] The inverse of this, however, cannot be ignored: when you include the vocal presence of an audience, its visual absence becomes all the more eerily conspicuous. And, by my reading of the scene, its visual absence takes on a significance in the context of this film that adds another layer of interpretive interest to the evocation of the ghosts.

For spectators aware of the film's specific prehistory as a stage production, and of Taymor's history as a theatre director, the empty galleries cannot but be seen as a reflection, conscious or otherwise, upon the current production's distinction from theatre. Cinema, unlike theatre, is in part defined by the dislocation between its playing space and its reception space, between the place and moment in which the actor acts and the place and moment in which the audience responds. The visual absence of the coliseum audience at this point, therefore, advertises one of the defining symptons of the medium within which Taymor is now working. The spectacular close-up on, and subsequent zoom-out from, the boy's eyes in the opening shot of the film demonstrates with effective economy one of the ways in which *this* production is no longer theatre (in which medium an audience member's focal length is necessarily fixed by the placement of his or her seat in relation to the stage). The empty galleries, presented soon afterwards, serve partly to refine that insistence on the production's distance from a live production. The sense that there is an audience implicit in this playing space, but one which cannot be seen, graphically illustrates the separation between actor and audience, the necessary sacrifice of shared space, that is part of the process of adapting a play from stage to screen.

Olivier's *Henry V* (1944) explores a theatrical space and the symbiotic relationship established between actors and a physically present audience in its opening and closing scenes, expanding out of the confines of this theatrical world for the intervening action.[24] The opening of Taymor's film explores the (literal) architecture of this relationship while removing one of the key players: in *her* chosen theatrical space there is no audience visually present. Since Taymor was fully accustomed to the physical presence of an audience for her theatre work, the strategic absence of an audience from this theatrical space documents one of the key effects the transmediation has wrought upon the material. Whereas, however, Christian Metz proposes that it is one of the conditions of cinema to pretend not to know that it is being seen,[25] the amphitheatre's absent audience reminds us, if anything, how implicitly present we, the *off-screen* audience, are throughout this film. And our self-consciousness about the processes of our own spectating is rendered the more acute by the presence of multiple proxies for us in the film itself.

The most obvious of these spectating proxies is the boy, who, having been carried into the auditorium, then becomes young Lucius through whose impressionable eyes much of the drama is seen. As Titus's grandson, he is the inheritor of a series of lessons about the uncompromising pursuit of vengeance and the performative relish with which it may be exacted. Mostly in the film, he is witness to things being done to other people. He is initially catapulted into the drama, however, by means of something being done to him – an act that, whatever its motivation, feels like a cross between a rescue and an abduction. The associations of the auditorium in which he is held aloft are clear: the Roman coliseum is the archetypal theatre of violence. His own fear at being offered up for the appreciation of the galleries establishes the context of theatrical exhibition within which future troubling events in the drama he is to witness are to be understood.

The performability of cruelty is explicitly enacted later in the film in the scene in which the heads of Titus's two executed sons are delivered to him accompanied by his own severed hand (III.i). The scene is stage-managed by the same leather-clad clown figure who had plunged the boy Lucius into the midst of a performance arena at the film's opening. He now pulls up outside Titus's house in his ramshackle sideshow wagon pulled by a three-wheeler (reminiscent of Zampano's in Fellini's *La Strada* (1954), a film also evoked

It is in the coliseum that the young boy (Osheen Jones) becomes Titus's (Anthony Hopkins) grandson Lucius in Taymor's *Titus* (2000). The absence of any audience other than ghosts from the theatrical space depicted reminds us of a cinema audience's material absence from filmic performance space.

by the peculiar atmosphere of the show that follows). Accompanied on the soundtrack by a circus band of cymbals, accordion, saxophone, clarinet and um-pa-pa tuba, the clown's weirdly whimsical young female assistant hops out of the cart and as part of an extravagantly odd hoppity skippity dance sets out four camping stools in a row facing the cart. The Andronici have been formally designated the audience for the show and they temporarily collude in the game by taking their allotted seats.

With a grotesquely joyous abandon reminiscent of the *Grand Guignol*, the clown and his assistant then lay on their freakshow of horrors. Like theatrical impresarios, they raise the shutter on the side of the wagon and, as they do so, the soundtrack cuts suddenly from its crazy circus skittishness to silence. In the startling hush, their ghoulish exhibition is revealed both to their on-screen and off-screen audiences: the two sons' heads carefully preserved in glass specimen jars, the amputated hand mounted on a velvet cushion, and all three beautifully framed by a ruched silk background and a swish theatrical curtain. This is horror dressed up as a performative confection.

The scene is principally shot from behind Titus, Marcus, Lucius and Lavinia, looking over their shoulders with them at the wagon's grisly wares. The sight of the backs of the on-screen spectators therefore mimics and blends with the backs of the off-screen spectators sitting in the movie theatre. An identification is implied, and felt. We see the heads of the sons as if through the eyes of the father. 'When will this fearful slumber have an end?' (III.i.252) he asks, and the question resonates with us too. We, like him, are near the end of our endurance for the unremitting catalogue of sensational horrors by which we have been assailed. As Titus's shoulders, seen from behind, start to shudder, it is reasonable to wonder how much more suffering could he, could anyone – can we – bear? The shot then cuts to the front of Titus to reveal a man whose shaking shoulders are not those of a man sobbing, as we might have thought, but rather of a man laughing. Released by Titus's response, the scene's sick comedy has space to breathe. 'Why I have not another tear to shed' (III.i.266) says Titus by way of explanation, and his willingness to laugh marks a turning point in his responses to Tamora's elaborately choreographed taunts. Titus has allowed himself to be infected by the warped levity of the scene and will later make use of this new tone for his own projects. However, he can also channel the energy that comes with that levity into serious purpose. The instruction to Lavinia to carry the severed hand in her teeth – a piece of business which interrogates the extremes to which a performance can be taken and still resist farce – is here delivered and acted upon in all seriousness. It is aided by Elliot Goldenthal's weightily melancholic and brooding underscoring that replaces the silence of the unveiling. In a world of ludicrousness, other things may be bleakly funny, but the Taymor/Hopkins collaboration manages to sustain a gravity to the collecting and re(-)membering of Andronici body parts. Even Lavinia's portering role in the communal *exeunt* seems, in this rendering, reasonable as a means of including her in the clan's collaborative gathering-up of its own and regrouping in preparation for their own counter-strikes.

The *pièce de résistance* of the Andronici fight-back is the banquet scene. At its beginning, the quietly gruesome scene of the murder of Chiron and Demetrius cedes to a shot of two beautiful pies cooling by an open window where wholesomely white muslin curtains waft gently in the breeze. The comic incongruity of this cut from horror to a pastiche of a picture from a women's cookery magazine is greatly enhanced by the chirpy energy of the 1937 Carlo Buti/Cesare Andrea Bixio hit song *Vivere* (from the famous Italian film of that name) on the soundtrack. In among the film's humorous clashes of periods and styles reflecting Rome's successive waves of autocracy and institutionalised savagery, 1930s Italian fascism plays a prominent role in the film. The references implicit in, for example, the architecture of Mussolini's Government Building and Tamora's (Jessica Lange) shimmering 1930s evening dress are supported in the banquet scene by the seductively lilting rhythms of this

1930s song. *Vivere* (urging its audience to 'live') is ironically employed at the very moment in the film when the characters are unknowingly about to eat each other. More particularly, in the *Vivere* film it is the voice of a father which is heard urging his ailing daughter to live, ironically foreshadowing Titus's gently delivered instruction to *his* daughter to 'Die, die, Lavinia' (V.iii.46). The late 1930s moment evoked by this soundtrack is decadent, pleasure-seeking and unknowingly on the cusp of an outpouring of public violence. By 1945, Benito Mussolini's body, along with fifteen others (including that of his lover Claretta Petacci) would be hung upside down in a Milanese square, the Piazzale Loreto, where vast crowds would vent their fury by spitting at, kicking and even firing multiple further bullets into the bodies. It was to be a political piece of public theatre that would recall the uncompromising dynamics of the amphitheatre. The *Vivere* soundtrack for the banquet is not only therefore tonally witty in context, but it also purposefully evokes a moment of social and political anacrucis, the blissfully unaware anticipation of a thunderingly ugly conclusion. Titus's banquet is precisely such an anacrucis: mayhem, as Titus's mad dance in his white chef's outfit suggests, is imminent.

The ensuing bloody drama on the banqueting table replays the carnage on the boy's kitchen table at the film's opening, with a glancing suggestion that the one is, in effect, caused by the other, that bellicose instincts in children will have their effects on the adult world in due course. Once the scene is littered with bodies, Taymor uses 'time slice' to freeze all the action bar the child's transfixed, wide-eyed observation of his own father first spitting at and then shooting Saturninus. The body count now complete, the environment around the central scene of human attrition shifts for a tonally transformed coda. From within their freeze, the banqueters are magically transported from Titus's Roman villa back into the centre of the coliseum where the bodies of the dead, like those of Mussolini and associates, may, in effect, be offered as trophies to the waiting crowd.

And there *is* now a crowd in the previously empty amphitheatre. The film's use of the coliseum as its framing symmetry relates the two scenes that take place there. The audience's striking absence from the coliseum in the opening of the film throws into sharper relief its sudden presence in this final scene. However, unlike the hostile and violent crowds that greeted the exhibited bodies in the Pizzale Loreto, the amphitheatre crowds that look upon the bodies of Lavinia, Titus, Tamora and Saturninus in Taymor's film appear to register nothing but a numbed silence. As was announced in much of the film's publicity, in promotional interviews and in the published screenplay, the particular coliseum used for the shoot is in Pula, in Croatia's Istria County. As a known central European architectural landmark, it was a location of which the production crew were justly proud. Its presence in the film is, however, more than simply dramatically striking, though it is certainly that. Its specific geographical placement cannot help but trigger a range of historical and political associations for anyone who recognises, or who had seen the publicity about, the particular Balkan location on offer.

Since the amphitheatre is in Croatia, the silent extras watching the aftermath of the atrocities in this particular space are locally hired Croatians. The symbolism of these spectators watching a dramatic spectacle of clan on clan bloodshed in 1999 confirms the keenly contemporary spin to the drama's exploration of human barbarity, a spin that Taymor explicitly courted. Croatia's Istrian peninsula, not *directly* affected by the Balkan war (although necessarily partisan in it), was itself effectively part of the amphi-theatre stands for the ethnic atrocities perpetrated in Croatia's eastern counties and in Bosnia between 1991 and 1995. The presence of hundreds of Croatians in an auditorium just a few years later watching two clans – now the Andronici and the Goths – brutalising each other for historical reasons therefore carries real-life resonances that add a disturbing topicality to the catalogue of tribal horrors the film depicts. As the shot cuts between the silent faces of the spectating extras observing the staged theatrical carnage before them, it is difficult for anyone aware of the location of the shoot not to wonder whether these same faces might not already have had to look on worse in real life. The audience's absence from the opening scene may serve as a nod to the medium of cinema in which the drama is currently being played, from which an audience is necessarily absent. The particular identity of its 'sad-fac'd' (V.iii.67) presence in the final scene, however, testifies powerfully to the acuteness of the story's ongoing engagements with contemporary narratives of human atrocity. For all its stylised and heightened aesthetics that might, superficially, seem to remove it from the mundanity of the world the rest of us inhabit, this is a film whose references and interests are crucially bound up in the fabric of that world. Its purposeful breachings of the seemingly cool and removed beauty of its own frame borders can even ambush the spectator – this spectator at least – with the terrible force of its psychological and emotional impact.

In the final moments of the film, the boy Lucius deliberately reverses his own fate by picking up Aaron's baby and carrying him slowly *out* of this arena into which he had himself been carried at the film's opening. Throughout the drama he has had to witness (and has increasingly himself participated in) acts of cruelty being rendered performative and it is the coliseum whose architecture and associations have formalised this relationship between violence and entertainment. In removing the baby from the brutalising codes of the amphitheatre, young Lucius breaks the bond and tries to ensure that no further entertainment can be derived from the baby's sufferings. As he carries him out of this arena, the sound of many babies crying on the soundtrack invites us to take the one baby being rescued as representative of many more born into a space where entertaining spectacle is made of others' suffering. The walk is long and slow, through an arch and out towards a vast landscape beyond which a dawn is breaking. The sugar that the boy had frantically shaken over his toy soldiers at the beginning of the film had seemed ironically inappropriate at the time since there is little that is saccharine in the rest of the film. In this sentimentally conceived exit, however, a little of that sugar seems finally to be candying over some of the play's less forgiving angularities.

Taymor wanted the play's end to be made amenable to redemption. The walk towards the dawn is, she has said, 'a teeny-weeny ray of hope. I felt we needed it at the end of the film, given that we're moving into the next millennium.'[26] Richard Burt finds the iconography of this concessionary moment reminiscent of *ET* and, as such, schlocky (which it self-consciously is).[27] In the well-advertised context of its Croatian shooting location, however, it is more than this too. The sight of a child being rescued from this setting takes the potential for smaltz that Burt identifies and gives it a weighty centre by merging it with real-world associations. The enduring mythic dimension of such a rescue, a dimension to which Taymor's film points, is in part dependent on the existence of specific real-world examples of such narratives that cumulatively give historical resonance to the myth.

It is worth citing one such. The point in doing so is not to suggest that this particular reference was deliberate. It was not. Rather, it is intended to suggest a reception context for the film that would have been potentially receptive to such images specifically because they chime evocatively with half-familiar stories from the real world.

In 1992, for example, Michael Nicholson, an ITN television correspondent covering the siege of Sarajevo, found himself employed to observe and report on human atrocities to the watching world. So affected was he by the horrors being perpetrated in the region that he broke with the usual rules of journalistic engagement. He arranged for a convoy of babies and small children to be evacuated and himself rescued a child from both the carnage and the passivity of the watching world's gaze by taking her back with him (illegally) to England. It was an act of rare professional folly and, arguably, of personal courage. In 1993, Nicholson published an account of these events (*Natasha's Story*) and in 1997 Michael Winterbottom made his story into a film entitled *Welcome to Sarajevo*, starring Stephen Dillane.

Young Lucius's loss of objective detachment, like Nicholson's in Sarajevo, is incremental. Moreover, his eleventh-hour decisive rejection of his role as observer and unexpected intervention in the fate of the baby has obvious parallels with the story of the news reporter who impulsively steps in to participate in the troubling action he had been viewing. And knowing of such real-world stories in which a child is rescued from clan-on-clan violence – and in this particular case specifically in a Balkan setting – cannot but add a gritty piquancy to the otherwise sentimental walk at the end of *Titus*.

That the walk out of the amphitheatre can evoke real-world analogues in this way should not, needless to say, be allowed to detract from the far more general resonances about communal responsibility, compassion and hope that the scene also carries. What it can do is enrich its topical engagements with the historically scarred location in which it is performed and, as a consequence, with a troubled world to which the film is subsequently exhibited.

When Taymor first wrote to Hopkins in the hope of wooing him to play Titus, she was already seeking ways of thinking about the story that fused cinematic myth and real life. She described the part to him as 'ranging between . . . a General Schwarzkopf and a Hannibal Lecter'.[28] This joyously eclectic mixing of known fictions and known fact – of Hannibal Lecter and General Schwarzkopf, of *ET* (and, more deliberately, of the 1950s American sitcom *Father Knows Best*) and war in the Balkans – joins the extensive catalogue of other incongruous encounters, stylistic, temporal, tonal, to which the movie promiscuously and brilliantly plays host. Style and period are frequently employed as an economical thumbnail sketch of character. At the opening, Saturninus (Alan Cummings) is a maniacal fascist prototype and in recognition of this for his progress through Rome is invested with all the pomp of a 1930s military cavalcade. Titus, by contrast, is a man of old Rome who clings to the traditional orders: as such, he arrives in a chariot. As Titus's psychological defences are subsequently pared away in the course of the film, however, so too are his layers of protective clothing. His armour is first compromised by the undignified presence of a dressing gown over the top and then abandoned as he retreats into his family home in a baggy old cardigan. Eventually he is seen apparently entirely defenceless, naked in a bath. This impression of powerlessness is, however, deceptive since it is from this position of such telegraphed vulnerability that he then emerges to wreak his stylishly warped revenge. Having been stripped of all the usual defences he now reconstructs himself in elaborately theatricalised form. In the last section of the film Titus's wardrobe will no longer catalogue what has been done to him but will now become expressive of what he can do to others. Thus it is that his macabrely skittish decision to dress in a white chef's outfit represents him at his most dangerous.

The play *Titus Andronicus* is invested with an acute self-consciousness about its own dramatic and linguistic mechanisms. In it, Shakespeare may be seen as narrativising his own duelling allegiances between theatrical spectacle and the more rarified delights of poetry written for private consumption, or, in the terms of his dedication to *Venus and Adonis*, between the base things laid on for the 'vulgus' and the poeticism inspired by the Castalia spring. In fact, in its various explorations of the nature of a public performance, of the processes of

Hopkins' wardrobe throughout *Titus* (2000) reflects his level of control of his own destiny. With deliberate theatricality he presents himself as a chef to outdo even Tamora's self-presentation as Revenge.

spectatorship and of the role of language and action within such a performance, the play seems as finely aware of its own processes as subsequently Taymor's *Titus* was to be of its. In *Titus*, Taymor explores and documents the particularities of her own transference of performance medium, theatre to film, and includes specifically theatricalised moments, such as the presentation of the bottled heads, to illustrate the play's own systems of theatrical self-reference. Through the shots of the coliseum she offers us two transmuted versions of theatrical space – one visually bereft of an audience and the other in which an audience is visually present but where there is no reciprocal responsiveness between actors and audience. Both versions are expressive about the definitive separation of actor from audience in a work of cinema. In this concern with the potency of performance even in evacuated, deadened theatres and also in her encouragement of a hybridity of performance styles, Taymor allows her interest in the dynamics of both media to percolate richly throughout the film. Like Olivier's *Henry V*, this film has emerged from a practitioner whose medium affiliations are divided and whose film eloquently allegorises those divergent allegiances.

Olivier's *Henry V* is an extraordinary film. However, for historical reasons, it has become organically bound up in the British national psyche in ways that have traditionally placed it beyond compare. It is time to break with tradition in this respect. For the depth and range of its cinematic discussion of the processes of theatre and of film separately and in contrapuntal engagement with each other, *Titus* has a level of ferociously watchable sophistication comfortably beyond the reach even of Olivier's film.

*

Prospero's Books narrates the demise of the book and the ascendancy of digital technology for the recycling of Shakespeare. *Romeo+Juliet* finds a brutally clear symbol to illustrate the wearied status of the theatre – and even perhaps of public cinemas – as the site in which Shakespearean performance can now come alive. Almereyda's *Hamlet* offers competing cinematic styles and showcases one of them in digitised form on a palm-top computer, demonstrating the manipulability of a performance that can be freeze-framed, viewed and reviewed in reverse or at different speeds, rendered portable. *Titus* both laments the separation of audience and actor in the cinema for the presentation of a Shakespearean performance and mesmerisingly celebrates the power of cinema to reach across the divide in defiance of the spatial and temporal separation. While telling a Shakespearean story these films all draw attention repeatedly both to the (cinematic) terms in which it is being told, and to the (literary and theatrical) terms in which it might have been told, has been told elsewhere, but is not currently being told.

All texts are understood in relation to other texts, made sense of both in terms of what they are and of what they are not. This instinctive process of comparison and analogy is how the defined identity of anything is arrived at, and it takes place on multiple levels simultaneously in ways personally determined by the particularity of each person's experience at the moment of apprehension. What is striking about the films discussed in this chapter, in keeping with many others of the period, is that they are themselves specifically inscribed with a series of intertextual references that suggest particular routes to follow in the interpretive process of comparison and analogy. That is, they themselves configure points of 'like' and 'not like', of similarity and difference, as part of their own textual substance, inviting interpretation by prescribed comparison. And it is not only in relation to other film texts that these films define themselves, but crucially also in relation and contradistinction to other textual systems (architecture, painting, literature, music videos, television news, theatre). Thus they often act as signposts to other forms of cultural expression, to the performance history of their source texts, and to the weight of other media images by which we navigate our way through life. Not only, therefore, what it means to be *this* film and no other (for example, from the same director, featuring the same star or from the same source text), but also what it means to be a film *at all*, as opposed to some other art form, is consciously part of the identity.

Since the 1990s it has, therefore, rarely been found sufficient to tell a Shakespearean story in film: that story has also had to be inlaid with the story of its own cinematic telling. Such reflexivity could be considered a sign of interpretive exhaustion. It might indicate that film-makers feel they have nowhere else to go but inwards to attempts at self-definition using a string of foils for purposes of clarification. It is possible to criticise them for being self-consciously clever, and for lacking the courage to depart from the prevailing spirit of their moment by rejecting ironic self-awareness. In theory, such a position might be persuasive. In practice, however, these films do not read as documents in exhaustion. In acknowledgement of the fact that their reception will not take place in a vacuum, they playfully wish to participate in determining the network of references that each is destined to provoke in its spectators. Such ludic attempts to identify themselves in playful competition with other cultural forms in which such stories are peddled suggests an excess of energy rather than a lack of it. Bottom-like, they wish to expand their roles, to play the interpreter as well as the interpreted. Thus they are eager not just to dramatise the inherited story but with it the critical terms in which they might themselves be interrogated.

By coincidence, the chronology of the four films discussed in this chapter happens to document Shakespeare's career in reverse – beginning with his final solo act of writing for the stage, *The Tempest*, and ending with one of his earliest tragedies *Titus Andronicus*. If his late play *The Tempest* in part dramatises an artist's elegiac exploration of a moment just before abandoning theatrical control of his environment, *Titus Andronicus* partly dramatises the challenges involved in *assuming* dramatic control, of exploring what theatre is and what it can do. Without needing to be read in exclusively or reductively autobiographical terms, these plays are clearly expressive of challenges that were true not only for the characters but in oblique and thematic ways also for their creator in relation to the processes of creation.

Like most Elizabethan and Jacobean dramatists, Shakespeare frequently referenced the terms of his trade in his writing. He scripted discussion of plots, performances, acting, audiences, illusionism, and the theatricalised gap between playing and being throughout his writing career. In drawing attention to the tools of their own medium, these films therefore to some extent enact a Shakespearean project. The wonder of it is that for all their introspection they do not drown in their self-reference. *Prospero's Books* – as intellectually stimulating and visually awing as it is eventually emotionally numbing – is perhaps the exception. The others manage still to tell a story of love and loss, of greed and dissatisfaction, of displacement and revenge, of ambition and hate, of hope and fear. Moreover, they do so in language that as voiced by players of such variety and distinction as Harold Perrineau (Mercutio), Julia Stiles (Ophelia) and Anthony Hopkins (Titus) can still resonate in ways that both move and surprise. Those tempted to herald self-referential films as a symptom of 'endism', as the death rattle of vibrant interpretive performance, may yet be pleasantly surprised.

FURTHER READING

Michael Almereyda, *William Shakespeare's Hamlet: A Screenplay Adaptation* (London: Faber, 2000).

Peter Greenaway, *Prospero's Books* (London: Chatto & Windus, 1991).

Douglas Lanier, 'Drowning the Book', in James C. Bulman (ed.), *Shakespeare, Theory and Performance* (London: Routledge, 1996), pp.187–209.

Courtney Lehmann, *Shakespeare Remains* (Ithaca, NY and London: Cornell University Press, 2002). (See note 11 below.)

Alfredo Michel Modenessi, '(Un)Doing the Book "without Verona Walls"': A View from the Receiving End of Baz Luhrmann's *William Shakespeare's Romeo+Juliet'*, in Courtney Lehmann and Lisa S. Starks (eds), *Spectacular Shakespeare: Critical Theory and Popular Cinema* (London: Associated University Presses, 2002), pp.62–85.

Craig Pearce and Baz Luhrmann, *William Shakespeare's Romeo+Juliet: The Contemporary Film, the Classic Play* (London: Hodder Children's Books, 1997).

Carol Chillington Rutter. 'Looking Like a Child – or – Titus: The Comedy', *Shakespeare Survey* 56(2003), pp. 1–26.

Julie Taymor, *Titus: The Illustrated Screenplay* (New York: Newmarket Press, 2000).

NOTES

1. From L. Digges' dedicatory poem, 'To the Memoire of the deceased Author Maister W. Shakespeare'. 1623 First Shakespeare Folio, fol 5r, ll.11–12.

2. There are also, however, some slightly less self-denying helicopter shots in *The King is Alive*.

3. Interview with Rob Blackwelder, San Francisco, 26 April 2001. Transcript published online at http://www.rottentomatoes.com/click/author-1232/reviews.php?critic=other&page=7&rid235295.

4. The broad-brimmed tasselled cardinal's hat and cardinal's robes worn by Prospero when Miranda and Ferdinand first encounter each other automatically signify 'Jerome' in the artistic traditions of the late medieval and Renaissance periods. Writing in Bologna between 1334 and 1346/47, Giovanni d'Andrea had even sought to enshrine the hat quasi-officially as part of the accepted iconography for Saint Jerome: 'I have also established the way he should be painted, namely, sitting in a chair, beside him the hat that cardinals wear nowadays . . .' Giovanni d'Andrea, *Hironymianus* (Basel edn, 1514), fols 16v–17r. Quoted in Eugene F. Rice, *Saint Jerome in the Renaissance* (Baltimore, MD and London: Johns Hopkins University Press, 1985), p.65. If evidence were needed that the

cardinal's hat is consciously intended to refer to Jerome in this film, it is to be found in Greenaway's reproduction in the published filmscript of de la Tour's painting *Saint Jerome* in which the cardinal's hat is clearly present: Peter Greenaway, *Prospero's Books* (London: Chatto & Windus, 1991), p.40. In *The Pillow Book* (Greenaway, 1996), the same de la Tour painting of Jerome appears on the publisher's screen as testimony to Greenaway's ongoing interest in Jerome's scholarly presence. The Hieronymite references in that film are rendered fully explicit in the naming of the writer-translator character Jerome (Ewan McGregor).

5. The child Ariel's appropriation of Prospero-Shakespeare's quill in order to write in his book mimics Van Dyck's painting of Saint Jerome (*c.* 1620), held in the Museum Boijmans-van Beuningen, Rotterdam. In that painting, a youthful, naked cherub takes up Jerome's quill in order not merely to inspire him indirectly but, like Greenaway's cherubic Ariel, actually to do the writing for him.

6. Greenaway (1991), p.9.

7. See the brief critical discussion of Tufte's paper in George P. Landow, 'We Are Already Beyond the Book', in Warren Chernaik, Marilyn Deegan and Andrew Gibson (eds), *Beyond the Book: Theory, Culture and the Politics of Cyberspace*, No. 7, Office for Humanities Communication Publications (Oxford: Office for Humanities Communication, 1996), pp.23–32. Tufte's gesture is discussed on pp.23–4.

8. The Shakespearean grove, in keeping with the plethora of other updatings and temporal sleights of hand the film performs, is here transmuted into the name of the now ruined theatre. (These beach scenes were shot in the Mexican coastal village of Veracruz.)

9. 'To the melancholic strains of Mozart's "Serenade for Winds", we discover the ornate arch of what is left of a once splendid cinema.' Craig Pearce and Baz Luhrmann, *William Shakespeare's Romeo+Juliet: The Contemporary Film, The Classic Play* (London: Hodder Children's Books, 1997), p.17.

10. The film cost $14.5 million to make and grossed over $11 million in its opening weekend alone. See Russell Jackson's introduction to *The Cambridge Companion to Shakespeare on Film* (Cambridge: Cambridge University Press, 2000), pp.4–5 for comparative budgets and grosses of this and other Shakespeare films.

11. Just before delivering the manuscript for this book, I have come across Courtney Lehmann's stimulating new book *Shakespeare Remains* (Ithaca, NY and London: Cornell University Press, 2002). Among other more divergent areas of enquiry, there are some points of coincidence between her areas of interest and mine. These particularly concern the significance of the ruined theatre in Luhrmann's *William Shakespeare's Romeo+Juliet* and the ghostly status of *all* characters in Almereyda's *Hamlet*. It is a matter of regret that there is not time to absorb detailed reference to her argument into this chapter, but for a far more densely theoretical take on some of the same issues considered here, I warmly recommend her book.

12. Miramax's production notes. Viewed on microfiche at the British Film Institute.

13. Hamlet's flyer for 'The Mousetrap' is of an orange swirling vortex, deliberately reminiscent of the advertising poster for Hithcock's *Vertigo* (1958). Through the allusion to a cinematic classic, Hamlet nimbly satirises his own hubris.

14. Ethan Hawkes' Introduction to Michael Almereyda, *William Shakespeare's Hamlet: A Screenplay Adaptation* (London: Faber, 2000), p.xiv.

15. I am indebted to Barbara Hodgdon for this point. In her plenary lecture to the Scaena Conference, St John's College, Cambridge (August 2001), she commented persuasively on the striking remoteness of Gielgud's presence as viewed from within Almereyda's film.
16. I am grateful to Mike Cordner for alerting me to this possible reading of Polonius's 'all'.
17. The gravedigger scene was shot but cut in post-production. As a result, the film remained more tonally of a piece.
18. It was Taymor's record of stylised stage violence in her productions of *Oedipus Rex*, *Transposed Heads*, *Juan Darien* and *Salome* that had first led her to *Titus Andronicus*.
19. See Julie Taymor, *Playing with Fire*, updated and expanded edition (New York: Harry N. Abrams, 1999), p.186.
20. The poster is reproduced in Taymor (1999), p.182. I am indebted to Jonathan Statham for alerting me to this point of continuity.
21. Although the parallels in the role of Osheen Jones between the two films are striking, Taymor herself did not know Noble's film and was entirely unaware of Jones's role in it. Taymor, in personal conversation with the author, 11 April 2003.
22. The slight parallels with Noble's film are, however, purely coincidental. See note 21 above.
23. Taymor, in personal conversation with the author, 11 April 2003.
24. See Anthony Davies' elegant discussion of the spatial strategy of Olivier's film in *Filming Shakespeare's Plays* (Cambridge: Cambridge University Press, 1988), pp.26–37.
25. Christian Metz, *The Imaginary Signifier: Psychoanalysis and the Cinema*, trans. Celia Britton *et al.* (Bloomington: Indiana University Press, 1982), p.95.
26. Julie Taymor, in interview with Alan Cummings. *Interview* (January 2000), p.35.
27. Richard Burt, *Shakespeare After Mass Media* (New York: Palgrave, 2002), p.311.
28. Richard Stayton, 'Portrait of Shakespeare as an Angry Young Man', *Written By*, 4, 2 (February 2000), pp.39–43. This quotation p.41.

SELECT FILMOGRAPHY

Films are arranged chronologically. Archive details are given only for those films not commercially available. Where multiple prints exist, archive listings here are not exhaustive. The Library of Congress film archival holdings are available to view, by appointment, through the Library of Congress Motion Picture Division Reading Room. The National Film and Television Archive (NFTVA) is part of the British Film Institute (BFI) in London: their archival holdings are available to view by appointment. I have only indicated the nature of commercial availability for those titles whose distribution is restricted by format or region. Where no details are given, the title is widely available at the time of writing. All films are given here in their English release titles. NTSC (American) format videos are playable on almost all up-to-date European VCRs from PAL-based countries. Region 1 DVDs are playable on multi-regional European DVD players.

1899 *King John* (GB: British Mutoscope and Biograph Company)	BFI 'Silent Shakespeare' Video & DVD
1905 *The Tempest* (GB: Charles Urban and Beerbohm Tree)	No print survives
1905 *Duel Scene from Macbeth* (US: AMBC)	Included on *Othello* (1922) DVD
1907 *Shakespeare Writing Julius Caesar* (France: Star Films, dir. Méliès)	No print survives
1908 *The Tempest* (GB: Clarendon Film Corporation, dir. Percy Stow)	BFI 'Silent Shakespeare' Video & DVD
1908 *Romeo and Juliet* (US: Vitagraph)	George Eastman House, Rochester & Folger Library, Washington DC
1908 *Julius Caesar* (US: Vitagraph)	NFTVA & Library of Congress
1908 *Hamlet* (Italy: Cines)	NFTVA
1909 *King Lear* (US: Vitagraph)	NFTVA
1909 *Othello* (Italy: Film d'Arte Italiana)	No print survives
1909 *A Midsummer Night's Dream* (US: Vitagraph)	BFI 'Silent Shakespeare' Video & DVD
1910 *A Winter's Tale* (US: Thanhouser)	Library of Congress
1910 *The Merchant of Venice* (Italy: Film d'Arte Italiana)	BFI 'Silent Shakespeare' Video & DVD
1911 *Henry VIII* (GB: William Barker)	No print survives
1911 *Richard III* (GB: Co-operative Cinematograph Company)	BFI 'Silent Shakespeare' Video & DVD

1911	*Romeo and Juliet* (Italy: Film d'Arte Italiana)	Library of Congress
1913	*A Midsummer Night's Dream* (Italy: Tommasi-Huebner, dir. Azzuri)	Folger Library, Washington DC
1913	*Hamlet* (GB: Gaumont-Hepworth, dir. Hay Plumb)	NFTVA & Folger Library, Washington DC
1913	*Cymbeline* (US: Thanhouser)	Library of Congress
1914	*Othello* (Italy: Ambrosio)	Cineteca, Bologna
1916	*The Real Thing At Last* (GB: British Actors, dir. James Barrie)	No print survives
1916	*King Lear* (US: Thanhouser, dir. Ernest Warde)	Folger Library, Washington DC
1917	*Hamlet* (Italy: Rodolfi-Film, dir. Eleuterio Rodolfi)	Cineteca, Bologna
1920	*Hamlet* (Germany: Art-Film, dirs. Svend Gade/Heinz Schall)	Commercially available (NTSC)
1922	*Othello* (Germany: Woerner-Film, dir. Dmitri Buchowetski)	Commercially available (NTSC & Reg. 1 DVD)
1932	*Island of Lost Souls* (US: Paramount, dir. Erle C. Kenton)	Commercially available (NTSC)
1935	*A Midsummer Night's Dream* (US: Warner Brothers, dir. Reinhardt/Dieterle)	Commercially available (NTSC)
1939	*The Lion Has Wings* (GB: London Film, dirs. Korda, Powell etc)	Commercially available
1941	*Lady Hamilton* (GB: Korda Films, dir. Alexander Korda)	Commercially available (PAL)
1943	*The Life and Death of Colonel Blimp* (GB: The Archers, Powell & Pressburger)	Commercially available
1944	*This Happy Breed* (GB: Two Cities Film, dir. David Lean)	Commercially available
1944	*Henry V* (GB: Two Cities Film, dir. Laurence Olivier)	Commercially available
1953	*Julius Caesar* (US: MGM, dir. Joseph Mankiewicz)	Commercially available
1954	*Broken Lance* (US: Twentieth Century Fox, dir. Edward Dmytryk)	Commercially available
1955	*Joe Macbeth* (GB: Columbia, dir. Ken Hughes)	Not currently available
1956	*Forbidden Planet* (US: MGM, dir. Fred McLeod Wilcox)	Commercially available
1957	*Throne of Blood* (Japan: Toho, dir. Akira Kurosawa)	Commercially available
1969	*Magic Island* (w/dir. Michael Powell)	Film never made
1969	*Julius Caesar* (GB: Commonwealth Utd. Entertainment, dir. Stuart Burge)	Commercially available
1979	*The Tempest* (GB: Boyd's Company, dir. Derek Jarman)	Commercially available
1982	*Tempest* (US: Columbia, dir. Paul Mazursky)	Commercially available (NTSC)
1984	*A Midsummer Night's Dream* (GB/Spain: Cabochon, Kemp/Coronado)	Commercially available

1985	*Ran* (Japan: Herald Ace/Greenwich Film, dir. Akira Kurosawa)	Commercially available
1988	*Iguana* (US: Film Production Enterprise, dir. Monte Hellman)	Commercially available (NTSC)
1989	*Henry V* (GB: Renaissance, dir. Kenneth Branagh)	Commercially available
1991	*Men of Respect* (US: Central City Film, dir. William Reilly)	Commercially available (NTSC)
1990	*Hamlet* (UK: CARolco International, dir. Franco Zeffirelli)	Commercially available
1991	*Prospero's Books* (GB/Netherlands/France/ Italy: dir. Peter Greenaway)	Commercially available
1993	*Much Ado About Nothing* (GB/Italy: Renaissance, dir. Kenneth Branagh)	Commercially available
1994	*Renaissance Man* (US: Touchstone, dir. Penny Marshall)	Commercially available
1995	*A Midsummer Night's Dream* (GB: Channel Four *et al.*, dir. Adrian Noble)	Commercially available
1995	*Othello* (GB: Castle Rock, dir. Oliver Parker)	Commercially available
1996	*Hamlet* (GB: Castle Rock, dir. Kenneth Branagh)	Commercially available
1996	*William Shakespeare's Romeo+Juliet* (US: Bazmark, dir. Luhrmann)	Commercially available
1996	*The Pillow Book* (pan-European: Channel Four/Canal +, dir. Greenaway)	Commercially available
1999	*A Midsummer Night's Dream* (US: Fox Searchlight, dir. Hoffman)	Commercially available
2000	*Love's Labour's Lost* (GB: Miramax *et al.*, dir. Kenneth Branagh)	Commercially available
2000	*Titus* (US: Clear Blue Sky, dir. Julie Taymor)	Commercially available
2000	*O* (US: Lion Gate, dir. Tim Blake Nelson)	Commercially available (Reg. 1 DVD)
2000	*The King is Alive* (Denmark/Namibia: Dogme, dir. Kristian Levring)	Commercially available
2000	*Hamlet* (US: Miramax International, dir. Michael Almereyda)	Commercially available
2001	*Scotland PA* (US: Abandon Pictures *et al.*, dir. Billy Morrissette)	Commercially available (NTSC/Reg.1 DVD)

BIBLIOGRAPHY

UNPUBLISHED MATERIAL

Michael Powell Special Collection

Held by Thelma Schoonmaker Powell, Michael Powell's widow, and now also by Special Materials, British Film Institute. All typescript.

'The Tempest': Technical shooting script. With foreword. (Undated.) 99 pages.
Synopsis and Production Notes. (Undated.) 5 pages.
'The Magic Island'. Notes on the visual presentation of the screenplay. (1 January, 1971). 28 pages.
Memorandum. Budget and shooting schedule. (December, 1972). 7 pages.
Production Scheme and Timetable March 1973–March 1974. 7 pages.
List of Song Titles. MS. 1 page.

Derek Jarman Special Collection

Held by Special Materials, BFI.

Item 11. Picture album of photographs of scenes and personnel.
Item 12. MS (June 1976). Notebook containing treatment notes.
Item 13. Production file.
Item 14. Typescript film treatment (December 1978).
Item 16. MS (Autumn 1974). Notebook containing treatment notes and sketches.
Item 17. First draft typescript treatment (1976).
Item 18. Typescript treatment (October 1978).
Item 19. Typescript treatment (1976).
Item 20. Annotated treatment (20 December 1978).
Item 22. Bound photocopy treatment with sketches.
Item 23. Visual continuity notebooks, with costume designs.
Item 24. Transcript of interview with Toyah Wilcox.

Kenneth Branagh Special Collection

Held by Special Materials, BFI.

Item 1. First draft Screenplay of *Henry V* (January 1988). Typescript with handwritten marginalia by Bruce Sharman.
Item 2. Second Draft Screenplay of *Henry V* (October 1988).

Kenneth Branagh file

Held at The Theatre Museum, Covent Garden, London.

A useful bank of materials including programmes, newspaper articles, reviews and interviews.

Documents relating to *Forbidden Planet* (Fred McLeod Wilcox, 1956)

Held at the Library of Congress, Motion Picture Division Reading Room.

Continuity script. Copyright Registration: LP 6177–26B.

Documents relating to *Tempest* (Paul Mazursky, 1982)

Held at the Library of Congress, Motion Picture Division Reading Room.

Continuity script (dated 2 July 1982). Copyright Registration: PA 147–821.
Columbia press package (1982).
The Cassavetes/Rowlands interview in the H.F.P.A. transcript.
Columbia Pictures' Preliminary Production Notes (1982).

The American Mutoscope and Biograph Company's production log.

Held at the Library of Congress, Motion Picture Division Reading Room.

Documents relating to *Hamlet* (Michael Almereyda, 2000)

Held on microfiche at the BFI.

Miramax's Production Notes.

Documents relating to *Men of Respect* (William Reilly, 1991)

Held on microfiche at the BFI.

Columbia Pictures Production Information (catalogued as 'Pressbook').

Personal conversations with Julie Taymor

Quotations taken from author's notes.

11 April 2003/21 July 2003.

THESES

Guiguet, Claude and Matalan, Pierrette, *L'œuvre de Michael Powell*. Unpublished PhD Thesis: Paris VII, Monsieur Oriano, 1983.

Jackson, Robert Darrell, *Romeo and Juliet on Film: A Comparative Analysis of Three Major Film Versions of Shakespeare's Play*. Unpublished PhD Dissertation: Wayne State University, Michigan, 1978.

Pilkington, Ace G., *Screening Shakespeare*. Unpublished DPhil Thesis: University of Oxford, 1988.

Skoller, Donald S., *Problems of Transformation in the Adaptation of Shakespeare's Tragedies from Play-Script to Cinema*. Unpublished PhD Dissertation: New York University, 1968.

BOOKS

Abel, Richard (ed.), *French Film Theory and Criticism: A History/Anthology*, 2 vols. Princeton, NJ: Princeton University Press, 1988.

Almereyda, Michael, *William Shakespeare's Hamlet: A Screenplay Adaptation*. London: Faber, 2000.

Altman, Rick (ed.), *Sound Theory, Sound Practice*. London: Routledge, 1992.

Amis, Kingsley, *New Maps of Hell: A Survey of Science Fiction*. London: Gollancz, 1961.

Amis, Kingsley, *The Golden Age of Science Fiction*. London: Hutchinson, 1981.

Anderson, Joseph L. and Richie, Donald, *The Japanese Film: Art and Industry*. Tokyo: Charles E. Tuttle Company, 1959.

Andrew, Dudley, *Concepts in Film Theory*. Oxford: Oxford University Press, 1984.

Anzi, Anna Cavallone, *Shakespeare Nei Teatri Milanesi Del Novocento (1904–1978)*. Bari: Adriatica Editrice, 1980.

Balázs, Béla, *Theory of the Film: Character and Growth of a New Art*, trans. Edith Bone. London: D. Dobson, 1952.

Ball, Robert Hamilton, *Shakespeare on Silent Film: A Strange Eventful History*. London: Allen and Unwin, 1968.

Barthes, Roland, *Image Music Text*, trans. Stephen Heath. New York: Noonday, 1977.

Barthes, Roland, *Camera Lucida*, trans. Richard Howard. London: Jonathan Cape, 1982.

Barthes, Roland, *Mythologies*, trans. Annette Lavers. London: Vintage, 1993.

Bartholomeusz, Dennis, *The Winter's Tale in Performance in England and America 1611–1976*. Cambridge: Cambridge University Press, 1982.

Bate, Jonathan and Jackson, Russell (eds), *Shakespeare: An Illustrated Stage History*. Oxford: Oxford University Press, 1996.

Baxter, John, *Science Fiction in the Cinema*. London: Zwemmer, 1970.

Bazin, André, *What is Cinema?*, trans. Hugh Gray, 2 vols. Berkeley: University of California Press, 1967.

Bergeron, David M., *Reading and Writing in Shakespeare*. Newark, NJ: University of Delaware Press, 1996.

Berkoff, Stephen, *I Am Hamlet*. London: Faber and Faber, 1989.

Bingham, Madeleine, *The Great Lover: The Life and Art of Herbert Beerbohm Tree*. London: Hamish Hamilton, 1978.

Bodkin, Maud, *Archetypal Patterns in Poetry: Psychological Studies of Imagination*. London: Humphrey Milford, 1934.

Bolter, Jay David, *Writing Space: The Computer, Hypertext, and the History of Writing*. Hillsdale, NJ: Erlbaum, 1991.

Boose, Lynda E. and Burt, Richard (eds), *Shakespeare the Movie: Popularizing the Plays on Film, TV, and Video.* London and New York: Routledge, 1997.

Booth, Michael R., *Victorian Spectacular Theatre 1850–1910.* London: Routledge, 1981.

Bordwell, David, *Making Meaning: Inference and Rhetoric in the Interpretation of Cinema.* Cambridge, MA: Harvard University Press, 1989.

Branagh, Kenneth, *Beginning.* New York and London: W.W. Norton, 1989.

Branagh, Kenneth, *Hamlet by William Shakespeare: Screenplay, Introduction and Film Diary.* New York and London: W.W. Norton, 1996.

Branagh, Kenneth, *Henry V by William Shakespeare: A Screen Adaptation by Kenneth Branagh.* London: Chatto and Windus, 1989.

Branagh, Kenneth, *Much Ado About Nothing: Screenplay, Introduction, and Notes on the Making of the Movie.* New York and London: W.W. Norton, 1993.

Bristol, Michael, *Shakespeare's America/America's Shakespeare.* New York: Routledge, 1990.

Brode, Douglas, *Films of the Fifties:* Sunset Boulevard *to* On the Beach. New York: Carol Publishing Group, 1976.

Brosnan, John, *The Primal Screen: A History of Science Fiction Film.* New York: Little, Brown and Co., 1991.

Brown, Richard and Anthony, Barry, *A Victorian Film Enterprise: The History of the British Biograph and Mutoscope Company, 1897–1915.* Trowbridge: Flicks Books, 1999.

Buchman, Lorne, *Still in Movement: Shakespeare on Screen.* Oxford: Oxford University Press, 1991.

Bulman, James C. (ed.), *Shakespeare, Theory and Performance.* London: Routledge, 1996.

Burnett, Mark Thornton and Wray, Ramona (eds), *Shakespeare, Film, Fin de Siècle.* London: Macmillan, 2000.

Burt, Richard, *Unspeakable ShaXXXspeares: Queer Theory and American Kiddie Culture.* London: Macmillan, 1998.

Burt, Richard, *Shakespeare After Mass Media.* New York: Palgrave, 2002.

Callow, Simon, *Being An Actor,* new edn. London: Penguin, 1995.

Carroll, Noël, *Philosophical Problems of Classical Film Theory.* Princeton, NJ: Princeton University Press, 1988.

Casebier, Allan, *Film and Phenomenology: Towards a Realist Theory of Cinematic Representation.* Cambridge: Cambridge University Press, 1991.

Césaire, Aimé, *Une Tempête.* Paris: Seuil, 1974.

Chang, Kevin K.W. (ed.), *Kurosawa: Perceptions on Life, An Anthology of Essays.* Honolulu: Honolulu Academy of Arts, 1991.

Chernaik, W., Deegan, M. and Gibson, A. (eds), *Beyond the Book: Theory, Culture, and the Politics of Cyberspace.* Oxford: Office for Humanities Communication Publications no. 7, 1996.

Cheyfitz, Eric, *The Poetics of Imperialism: Translation and Colonization from* The Tempest *to* Tarzan. Oxford: Oxford University Press, 1991.

Christie, Ian, *Powell, Pressburger and Others.* London: British Film Institute, 1978.

Christie, Ian, *The Last Machine: Early Cinema and the Birth of the Modern World.* London: BBC Education and British Film Institute, 1994.

Christie, Ian, *Arrows of Desire: The Films of Michael Powell and Emeric Pressburger,* 2nd edn. London: Faber and Faber, 1994.

Christie, Ian (ed.), *The Life and Death of Colonel Blimp*. London: Faber and Faber, 1994.

Cohn, Ruby, *Modern Shakespeare Offshoots*. Princeton, NJ: Princeton University Press, 1976.

Coleridge, S.T., *Shakespeare Criticism*, 2 vols (ed.) T.M. Raysor. London: J.M. Dent, 1960.

Collick, John, *Shakespeare, Cinema and Society*. Manchester: Manchester University Press, 1989.

Conrad, Peter, *To Be Continued: Four Stories and Their Survival*. Oxford: Oxford University Press, 1995.

Coultass, Clive, *Images for Battle: British Film and the Second World War 1939–1945*. London and Toronto: Associated University Presses, 1989.

Coursen, H.R., *The Compensatory Psyche*. New York: University Press of America, 1986.

Coursen, H.R., *Watching Shakespeare on Television*. Rutherford, NJ: Farleigh Dickinson Press, 1993.

Cox, C.B. and Palmer, D.J. (eds), *Shakespeare's Wide and Universal Stage*. Manchester: Manchester University Press, 1984.

Crowl, Samuel, *Shakespeare Observed: Studies in Performance on Stage and Screen*. Athens: Ohio University Press, 1992.

Davies, Anthony, *Filming Shakespeare's Plays*. Cambridge: Cambridge University Press, 1988.

Davies, Anthony and Wells, Stanley (eds), *Shakespeare and the Moving Image*. Cambridge: Cambridge University Press, 1994.

Davis, Darrell William, *Picturing Japaneseness: Monumental Style, National Identity, Japanese Film*. New York: Columbia University Press, 1996.

Desmet, Christy and Sawyer, Robert (eds), *Shakespeare and Appropriation*. London and New York: Routledge, 1999.

Desser, David D. and Friedman, Lester D., *American-Jewish Filmmakers: Traditions and Trends*. Champaign: University of Illinois Press, 1993.

Dobson, Michael, *The Making of the National Poet: Shakespeare, Adaptation and Authorship, 1660–1769*. Oxford: Oxford University Press, 1992.

Dollimore, Jonathan, *Radical Tragedy: Religion, Ideology and Power in the Drama of Shakespeare and His Contemporaries*. 2nd edn. Hemel Hempstead: Harvester Wheatsheaf, 1989.

Dollimore, Jonathan and Sinfield, Alan (eds), *Political Shakespeare: Essays in Cultural Materialism*. 2nd edn. Manchester: Manchester University Press, 1994.

Donaldson, Peter S., *Shakespearean Films/Shakespearean Directors*. Boston: Unwin Hyman, 1990.

Downer, Alan S., *The Eminent Tragedian: William Charles Macready*. Cambridge, MA: Harvard University Press, 1966.

Dryden, John and Davenant, William, *The Tempest, or the Enchanted Island*. London, 1670. Available in facsimile in Guffey (1969).

Dryden, John, *Works*, 18 vols (ed.) W. Scott. London, 1808.

Durgnat, Raymond, *A Mirror for England: British Movies from Austerity to Affluence*. London: Faber and Faber, 1970.

Eames, John Douglas and Bergan, Ronald, *The MGM Story: The Complete History of Sixty-Nine Roaring Years*. London: Hamlyn, 1993.

Eckert, Charles W. (ed.), *Focus on Shakespearean Film*. Englewood Cliffs, NJ: Prentice-Hall, 1972.

Eco, Umberto, *The Role of the Reader: Explorations in the Semiotics of Texts.* Bloomington: University of Indiana Press, 1979.

Edgerton, Gary (ed.), *Film and the Arts in Symbiosis: A Resource Guide.* Westport, CT: Greenwood Press, 1988.

Fitzgerald, Percy H., *Principles of Comedy and Dramatic Effect.* London, 1870.

Foulkes, Richard (ed.), *Shakespeare and the Victorian Stage.* Cambridge: Cambridge University Press, 1986.

Freeman, Mark, *Rewriting the Self: History, Memory, Narrative.* London: Routledge, 1993.

Freud, Sigmund, *Art and Literature,* trans. James Strachey (ed.) Albert Dickson. London: Penguin, 1990. (Penguin Freud Library, XIV.)

Freud, Sigmund, *New Introductory Lectures on Pyschoanalysis,* trans. James Strachey (ed.) James Strachey with Angela Richards. London: Penguin, 1991. (Penguin Freud Library, II.)

Freud, Sigmund, *Civilzation, Society and Religion,* trans. James Strachey (ed.) Albert Dickson. London: Penguin, 1991. (Penguin Freud Library, XII.)

Friedmann, Herbert, *A Bestiary for Saint Jerome: Animal Symbolism in European Religious Art.* Washington, DC: Smithsonian Institution Press, 1980.

Garrett, John (ed.), *Talking of Shakespeare.* New York: Hodder and Stoughton, 1954.

Gayley, Charles Mills, *Shakespeare and the Founders of Liberty in America.* New York: Semin-Centennial Publications, 1917.

Gillies, John, *Shakespeare and the Geography of Difference.* Cambridge: Cambridge University Press, 1994.

Glavin, John, *After Dickens: Reading, Adaptation and Performance.* Cambridge: Cambridge University Press, 1999.

Goodwin, James E. (ed.), *Perspectives on Akira Kurosawa.* New York: G.K. Hall, 1994.

Greenaway, Peter, *Prospero's Books.* London: Chatto and Windus, 1991.

Greenblatt, Stephen, *Marvelous Possessions: The Wonder of the New World.* Oxford: Oxford University Press, 1991.

Gross, John (ed.), *After Shakespeare.* Oxford: Oxford University Press, 2002.

Guffey, George Robert (ed.), *After The Tempest.* Los Angeles: University of California Press, 1969.

Gurr, Andrew, *The Shakespearean Stage, 1574–1642.* 2nd edn. Cambridge: Cambridge University Press, 1980.

Halio, Jay L., *A Midsummer Night's Dream: Shakespeare in Performance.* Manchester: Manchester University Press, 1994.

Hamilton, Donna B., *Vergil and The Tempest.* Columbia: Ohio State University Press, 1990.

Hammerton, J.A., *Barrie: The Story of a Genius.* New York: Sampson Law, 1929.

Hanke, Lewis, *Aristotle and the American Indians: A Study in Race Prejudice in the Modern World.* Bloomington, IN: Hollis and Carter, 1959.

Harbage, Alfred, *Shakespeare Without Words and Other Essays.* Cambridge, MA: Harvard University Press, 1972.

Hardy, P. (ed.), *Science Fiction.* London: Aurum, 1991.

Hauser, Arnold, *The Social History of Art,* 4 vols. New York: Routledge, 1962.

Hawkes, Terence, *That Shakeskesperian Rag: Essays on a Critical Process.* London: Methuen, 1986.

Hawkins, Harriet, *Classics and Trash*. Hemel Hempstead: Harvester Wheatsheaf, 1990.

Hazlitt, William, *Characters of Shakespeare's Plays*. Cambridge: Cambridge University Press, 1915.

Higson, Andrew (ed.), *Dissolving Views: Key Writings on British Cinema*. London: Cassell, 1996.

Hoffman, Michael, *A Midsummer Night's Dream*. London: HarperCollins, 1999.

Holden, Anthony, *Olivier*. London: Weidenfeld and Nicolson, 1988.

Holderness, Graham (ed.), *The Shakespeare Myth*. Manchester: Manchester University Press, 1988.

Holderness, Graham (ed.), *The Politics of Theatre and Drama*. London: Macmillan, 1992.

Iappolo, Grace, *Revising Shakespeare*. Cambridge, MA: Harvard University Press, 1991.

Jackson, Russell (ed.), *The Cambridge Companion to Shakespeare on Film*. Cambridge: Cambridge University Press, 2000.

Jacobs, Margaret and Warren, John (eds), *Max Reinhardt: The Oxford Symposium*. Oxford: Oxford Polytechnic, 1986.

James, D.G., *The Dream of Prospero*. Oxford: Oxford University Press, 1967.

Jarman, Derek, *Dancing Ledge*. London: Quartet, 1984.

Jenkins, Roy, *Churchill*. Basingstoke and Oxford: Macmillan, 2001.

Jenks, Chris (ed.), *Visual Culture*. London: Routledge, 1995.

de Jongh, Nicholas, *Not in Front of an Audience: Homosexuality on Stage*. London: Routledge, 1992.

Jorgens, Jack, *Shakespeare on Film*. Bloomington: Indiana University Press, 1977.

Jourdain, Sylvester, *A Discovery of the Bermudas, Otherwise called the Ile of Divels* (1610). Facsimile edn, (ed.) J.Q. Adams. New York: Scholars Facsimiles and Reprints, 1940.

Jung, C.G., *Symbols of Transformation*, 2nd edn. London: Routledge, 1967. (Routledge *Complete Works*, V.)

Jung, C.G., *The Archetypes and the Collective Unconscious*, 2nd edn. London: Routledge, 1968. (Routledge *Complete Works*, IX.)

Jung, C.G., *Civilization in Transition*, 2nd edn. London: Routledge, 1970. (Routledge *Complete Works*, X.)

Kelly, J.N.D., *Jerome: His Life, Writings, and Controversies*. London: Duckworth, 1975.

Kennedy, Dennis, *Looking at Shakespeare: A Visual History of Twentieth Century Performance*. Cambridge: Cambridge University Press, 1993.

Kermode, Frank, *The Classic: Literary Images of Permanence and Change*. Cambridge MA: Harvard University Press, 1983.

Kipling, Rudyard, *How Shakespeare Came to Write 'The Tempest'*. New York: Dramatic Museum of Columbia University, 1916.

Kitchen, Laurence, *Drama in the Sixties: Form and Interpretation*. London: Faber and Faber, 1966.

Kliman, Bernice W., *Hamlet: Film, Television and Audio Performance*. Rutherford, NJ: Farleigh Dickinson University Press, 1988.

Knapp, Jeffrey, *An Empire Nowhere: England, America, and Literature from Utopia to The Tempest*. Berkeley: University of California Press, 1992.

Kott, Jan, *Shakespeare Our Contemporary*. London: Methuen, 1964.

Kozintsev, Grigori, *Shakespeare, Time and Conscience*. London: D. Dobson, 1967.

Kupperman, Karen Ordahl, *Settling with the Indians: The Meeting of English and Indian Cultures in America, 1580–1640*. London: J.M. Dent, 1980.

Kurosawa, Akira, *Something Like an Autobiography*, trans. Audie E. Bock. New York: Knopf, 1982.

Kurosawa, Akira, *Ran: The Original Screenplay and Storyboards*. Boston and London: Shambhala, 1986.

Lanier, Douglas, *Shakespeare and Modern Popular Culture*. Oxford: Oxford University Press, 2002.

Lapsley, R. and Westlake, M., *Film Theory: An Introduction*. Manchester: Manchester University Press, 1988.

Levin, Harry, *The Myth of the Golden Age in the Renaissance*. Bloomington: Indiana University Press, 1969.

Lloyd, Ann (ed.), *Movies of the Fifties*. London: Orbis, 1982.

Loney, Glen, *Peter Brook's Production of William Shakespeare's 'A Midsummer Night's Dream' for the Royal Shakespeare Company: The Complete and Authorised Acting Edition*. Stratford-upon-Avon, 1974.

Lotman, Yuri, *The Structure of the Artistic Text*, trans. Gail Lenhoff and Ronald Vroon. Michigan: Ann Arbor, 1977. (Michigan Slavic Contributions, no. 7.)

MacArthur, Brian, *Twentieth Century Speeches*. London: Viking, 1992.

MacCary, W. Thomas, *Friends and Lovers: The Phenomenology of Desire in Shakespearean Comedy*. New York: Columbia University Press, 1985.

McFarlane, Brian, *Novel to Film: An Introduction to the Theory of Adaptation*. Oxford: Oxford University Press, 1996.

McKernan, Luke and Terris, Olwen (eds), *Walking Shadows: Shakespeare in the National Film and Television Archive*. London: British Film Institute, 1994.

MacKinnon, Kenneth, *Greek Tragedy into Film*. Beckenham: Croom Helm, 1986.

Macready, William Charles, *Reminiscences and Selections from his Diary and Letters*, 2 vols (ed.) F. Pollock. London, 1875.

Maltin, Leonard, *Behind the Camera: The Cinematographer's Art*. London: Signet, 1971.

Mannoni, Octave, *Prospero and Caliban: The Psychology of Colonization*, trans. Pamela Powesland. London: Methuen, 1956.

Manvell, Roger, *Shakespeare and the Film*. London: Dent, 1971.

Manvell, Roger, *Theater and Film: A Comparative Study of the Two Forms of Dramatic Art, and the Problems of Adaptation of Stage Plays into Film*. Rutherford, NJ: Farleigh Dickinson University Press, 1979.

Marcus, Leah S., *Puzzling Shakespeare: Local Readings and Its Discontents*. Los Angeles: University of California Press, 1988.

Marsden, Jean I., *The Appropriation of Shakespeare: Post-Renaissance Reconstructions of the Works and the Myth*. Hemel Hempstead: Harvester Wheatsheaf, 1991.

Martin, Mrs Charles, *Life of St. Jerome*. London: Keagan Paul, Trench & Co., 1888.

Martyr, Peter, *De novo orbe, or The Historie of the West Indies*, trans. Richard Eden and Michael Lok. London, 1612.

Martyr, Peter, *The Decades of the New Worlde*, trans. Richard Eden (1555). Facsimile edn. Michigan University Press, Ann Arbor: 1966.

Marx, Leo, *The Machine in the Garden: Technology and the Pastoral Ideal in America*. New York: Oxford University Press, 1964.

Mast, G., Cohen, M. and Braudy, L. (eds), *Film Theory and Criticism, Introductory Readings*, 4th edn. Oxford: Oxford University Press, 1992.

Mazer, Cary M., *Shakespeare Refashioned: Elizabethan Plays on Edwardian Stages*. Michigan: UMI Research Press, 1981.

Mazursky, Paul and Capetanos, Leon, *Tempest: A Screenplay*. New York: Performing Arts Journal Publications, 1982.

Metz, Christian, *Film Language: A Semiotics of the Cinema*, trans. Michael Taylor. Chicago: University of Chicago Press, 1974.

de Montaigne, Michel E., *The Essays of Montaigne*, 3 vols, trans. John Florio (ed.) George Saintsbury. London, 1892.

Morley, Henry, *The Journal of a London Playgoer*. London: George Routledge and Sons, 1866, reprinted 1891.

Münsterberg, Hugo, *The Film: A Psychological Study*. New York: Dover Publications, 1970.

Murray, Gilbert, *The Classical Tradition in Poetry*. London: Oxford University Press, 1927.

Nagler, A.M., *A Source Book in Theatrical History*. New York: Dover, 1952.

Nash, Jay Robert and Ross, Stanley Ralph, *The Motion Picture Guide*, 12 vols. Chicago: Cinebooks, 1985–87.

Nichol, Allardyce, *Film and Theatre*. London: George G. Harrap, 1936.

Nuttall, A.D., *Two Concepts of Allegory: A Study of Shakespeare's The Tempest and the Logic of Allegory*. London: Routledge, 1967.

Odell, George C.D., *Shakespeare from Betterton to Irving*, 2 vols. London: Constable 1921.

Orgel, Stephen, *The Illusion of Power: Political Theatre in the English Renaissance*. Berkeley: University of California Press, 1975.

Ovid, *Metamorphoses*, trans. Mary Innes. London: Penguin, 1955.

Parish, James Robert and Pitts, Michael R., *The Great Science Fiction Picture*. Metuchen, NJ: Scarecrow, 1977.

Pearce, Craig and Luhrmann, Baz, *William Shakespeare's Romeo+Juliet: The Contemporary Film, The Classic Play*. London: Hodder Children's Books, 1997.

Pilard, Philippe, *Shakespeare au Cinéma*. Paris: Editions Nathan, 2000.

Plummer, Ken (ed.), *Modern Homosexualities*. London: Routledge, 1992.

Potter, Lois, *Othello*. Shakespeare in Performance Series. Manchester: Manchester University Press, 2002.

Powell, Michael, *Million-Dollar Movie: The Second Volume of His Life in the Movies*. London: Heinemann, 1992.

Prince, Stephen, *The Warrior's Camera: The Cinema of Akira Kurosawa*, revised and expanded edn. Princeton, NJ: Princeton University Press, 1991.

Propp, Vladimir, *The Morphology of the Folktale*. Austin: University of Texas Press, 1968.

Reinhardt, Gottfried, *Der Liebhaber: Erinnerungen seines Sohnes Gottfried Reinhardt an Max Reinhardt*. Stuttgart: Deutscher Bücherbund, 1973.

Rice, Eugene F. Jr., *Saint Jerome in the Renaissance*. Baltimore, MD and London: Johns Hopkins University Press, 1988.

Richie, Donald, *The Films of Akira Kurosawa*. Berkeley and LA: University of California Press, 1965.

Rollins, H.E. (ed.), *The Letters of John Keats*, Vol. I. Cambridge: Cambridge University Press, 1958.

Rothwell, Kenneth S. and Melzer, Annabell Henkin, *Shakespeare on Screen*. New York: Mansell, 1990.

Ryuta, Minami, Carruthers, Ian and Gillies, John (eds), *Performing Shakespeare in Japan*. Cambridge: Cambridge University Press, 2001.

Schmidgall, Gary, *Literature as Opera*. New York: Oxford University Press, 1977.

Shakespeare, William, *As You Like It* (Arden II) (ed.) Agnes Latham. London: Methuen, 1975.

Shakespeare, William, *Hamlet* (Arden II) (ed.) Harold Jenkins. London: Methuen, 1982.

Shakespeare, William, *King Henry V* (Arden II) (ed.) J.H. Walter. London: Routledge, 1988.

Shakespeare, William, *King Lear* (Arden II) (ed.) Kenneth Muir. London: Methuen, 1972.

Shakespeare, William, *Love's Labour's Lost* (Arden II) (ed.) Richard David. London: Methuen, 1956.

Shakespeare, William, *Macbeth* (Arden II) (ed.) Kenneth Muir. London: Routledge, 1988.

Shakespeare, William, *A Midsummer Night's Dream* (Arden II) (ed.) Harold F. Brooks. London: Methuen, 1979.

Shakespeare, William, *Much Ado About Nothing* (Arden II) (ed.) A.R. Humphreys. London: Methuen, 1981.

Shakespeare, William, *Othello* (Arden II) (ed.) M.R. Ridley. London: Methuen, 1965.

Shakespeare, William, *Romeo and Juliet* (Arden II) (ed.) Brian Gibbons. London: Methuen, 1980.

Shakespeare, William, *Twelfth Night* (Arden II) (ed.) J.M. Lothian and T.W. Craik. London: Routledge, 1975.

Shakespeare, William, *The Tempest* (Arden II) (ed.) Frank Kermode. 6th edn. London: Routledge, 1989.

Shakespeare, William, *Titus Andronicus* (Arden III) (ed.) Jonathon Bate. London: Routledge, 1995.

Sharp, Cecil J., *A Midsummer Night's Dream: Songs and Incidental Music Arranged and Composed by Cecil J. Sharp for Granville Barker's Production at the Savoy Theatre, Jan: 1914*. London: Simpkin, Marshall, Hamilton, Kent & Co. Ltd, Novelloe & Co., Ltd, 1914.

Simonson, Harold P., *Beyond the Frontier: Writers, Western Regionalism and a Sense of Place*. Fort Worth: Texas Christian University Press, 1989.

Speaight, Robert, *Shakespeare on the Stage*. London: Collins, 1973.

Staiger, Janet, *Interpreting Films: Studies in the Historical Reception of American Cinema*. Princeton, NJ: Princeton University Press, 1992.

Steiner, George, *Antigones: The Antigone Myth in Western literature, Art and Thought*. Oxford: Oxford University Press, 1984.

Stern, Ernst, *My Life, My Stage*, trans. Edward Fitzgerald. London: Gollancz, 1951.

Storr, Anthony, *Freud*. Oxford: Oxford University Press, 1989.

Strachey, William, 'A true repertorie of the wracke and redemption of Sir Thomas Gates, Knight' (1610), in *Purchas his Pilgrimes*. London, 1625.

Styan, J.L., *Max Reinhardt*. Cambridge: Cambridge University Press, 1982.

Suleiman, S. and Crosman, I. (eds), *The Reader in the Text: Essays on Audience and Interpretation*. Princeton, NJ: Princeton University Press, 1980.

Summers, Montague, *Shakespeare Adaptations*. London: Jonathan Cape, 1922.

Taylor, Gary, *Reinventing Shakespeare: A Cultural History from the Restoration to the Present*. London: Vintage, 1991.

Taymor, Julie, *Playing with Fire*, updated and expanded edn. New York: Harry N. Abrams, 1999.

Taymor, Julie, *Titus: The Illustrated Screenplay*. New York: Newmarket Press, 2000.

Thomas, Sari (ed.), *Film/Culture: Explorations of Cinema in its Social Context*. Metuchen, NJ: Scarecrow, 1982.

Tree, Herbert Beerbohm, *The Tempest: As Arranged for the Stage by Herbert Beerbohm Tree*, Souvenir Edition of *The Tempest* for the 50th performance in the run. London, 1904.

Tree, Herbert Beerbohm, *The Tempest: A Descriptive Theatre Programme*, His Majesty's Theatre, London, 1904.

Tree, Herbert Beerbohm, *Some Notes on A Midsummer Night's Dream, produced at His Majesty's Theatre (for the second time) on Easter Monday, April 17th, 1911, by Sir Herbert Beerbohm Tree*. London, 1911.

Trewin, J.C., *Shakespeare on the English Stage: 1900–1964*. London: Barrie and Rokcliff, 1964.

Uricchio, W. and Pearson, R.E., *Reframing Culture: The Case of the Vitagraph Quality Films*. Princeton, NJ: Princeton University Press, 1993.

Usai, Paolo Cherchi, *Burning Passions: An Introduction to the Study of Silent Cinema*. London: BFI, 1994.

Vardac, Nicholas, *Stage to Screen*. Cambridge, MA: Harvard University Press, 1949.

Vaughan, A.T. and Vaughan, V.M., *Shakespeare's Caliban: A Cultural History*. Cambridge: Cambridge University Press, 1991.

Vergil, *Æneidos* (ed.) R.D. Williams. Oxford: Oxford University Press, 1962.

Vickers, Brian, *Returning to Shakespeare*. London: Routledge, 1989.

Vining, Edward P., *The Mystery of Hamlet*. Philadelphia, 1881.

Waller, Gregory, A., *The Stage/Screen Debate. A Study in Popular Aesthetics*. New York: Garland, 1983.

Warren, William McCallum, *Keep Watching the Skies!: American Science Fiction Movies of the Fifties*, 2 vols. Jefferson, NJ: McFarland, 1982.

Wells, H.G., *The Island of Dr. Moreau* (1896). Harmondsworth: Penguin, 1962.

Wheale, Nigel (ed.), *The Postmodern Arts*. London: Routledge, 1995.

Williams, Gary Jay, *Our Moonlight Revels: A Midsummer Night's Dream in the Theatre*. Iowa City: University of Iowa Press, 1997.

Williams, Heathcote, *AC/DC*, playscript. London: J. Calder, 1971.

Williams, Heathcote, *The Immortalist*, playscript. London: J. Calder, 1978.

Williamson, Jack, *H.G. Wells: Critic of Progress*. Baltimore, MD: Mirage Press, 1973.

Yates, Fances A., *Theatre of the World*. London: Routledge, 1969.

Yates, Fances A., *The Rosicrucian Enlightenment*. London: Routledge, 1972.

Yoshimoto, Mitsuhiro, *Kurosawa: Film Studies and Japanese Cinema*. Durham, NC: Duke University Press, 2000.

CHAPTERS FROM BOOKS, JOURNAL ARTICLES, TRADE PAPERS AND NEWSPAPERS

Andrews, John F., 'Interview: Cedric Messina discusses *The Shakespeare Plays*', *Shakespeare Quarterly* 30 (1979): 134–7.

Andrews, Nigel and Kennedy, Harlan, 'Peerless Powell', *Film Comment* 15, 3 (May/June 1979): 49–55.

Arnold, Gary, 'Tempest: Steady Drizzle', *Washington Post* (24 September 1982): C3.

Badder, David, 'Powell and Pressburger: The War Years', *Sight and Sound* 48, 1 (Winter 1978/1979): 8–12.

Barber, Lester E., 'This Rough Magic: Shakespeare on Film', *Lit/FilmQuarterly* 1 (1973): 372–6.

Barker, Adam, 'A Tale of Two Magicians', *Sight and Sound* 1, 1 (May 1991): 26–30.

Barra, Allen, 'Dialogue with Paul Mazursky', *American Film* 15, 4 (January 1990): 18–21, 54–5.

Berger Jr., Harry, 'Miraculous Harp: A Reading of Shakespeare's *Tempest*', *Shakespeare Studies* 5 (1969): 253–83.

Billings, Josh, *Forbidden Planet*: review, *Kinematograph Weekly*, 2543 (10 May 1956): 18.

Bioscope, Film listings (17 December 1908): 7.

Bioscope, Synopsis of Vitagraph's *Dream* (3 March 1910): 47.

Bioscope 19, 348 (12 June 1913): 773.

Bioscope, 'The Filming of "Hamlet": Interview with Mr. Cecil Hepworth', 20, 354 (24 July 1913): 275.

Blumenthal, J., '*Macbeth* into *Throne of Blood*', *Sight and Sound* 34, 4 (Autumn 1965): 190–5.

Boyum, Joy Gould, Review of Mazursky's *Tempest*, *The Wall Street Journal* (20 August 1982): 20.

Brog, Review of *Forbidden Planet*, *Variety* (14 March 1956): 6.

Buchanan, Judith, '"Like this insubstantial pageant faded": Michael Powell's *The Tempest*', *Film Studies*, 1, 2 (March 2000): 79–90.

Buchanan, Judith, 'Virgin and Ape, Venetian and Infidel: Configurations of Otherness in Oliver Parker's *Othello*', Chapter 11 in Mark Thornton Burnett and Ramona Wray (eds), *Shakespeare, Film, Fin de Siècle*. Basingstoke: Macmillan, 2000: 179–202.

Buchanan, Judith, '*Forbidden Planet* and the Retrospective Attribution of Intentions', Chapter 11 in Cartmell, D., Hunter, I., Kaye, H. and Whelehan, I. (eds), *Retrovisions: Reinventing the Past in Film and Fiction*. London and Chicago: Pluto, 2001: 148–62.

Bulman, James C., 'The BBC Shakespeare and "House Style"', *Shakespeare Quarterly* 35 (1984): 571–81.

Burnett, Mark Thornton, 'Impressions of Fantasy: Adrian Noble's *A Midsummer Night's Dream*', in Mark Thornton Burnett and Ramona Wray (eds), *Shakespeare, Film, Fin de Siècle*. Basingstoke: Macmillan, 2000: 89–101.

Canby, Vincent, 'A Prospero for Today', *New York Times* (13 September 1982).

Cartmell, Deborah, 'Franco Zeffirelli and Shakespeare', Chapter 12 in Russell Jackson (ed.), *The Cambridge Companion to Shakespeare on Film*. Cambridge: Cambridge University Press, 2000: 212–21.

Christie, Ian and Collins, Richard, 'Interview with Michael Powell: The Expense of Naturalism', *Monogram* 3 (1972): 32–8.

Clarke, Frederick C. and Rubin, Steve, 'Retrospect: *Forbidden Planet*', *Cinéfantastique* 8, 2/3 (Spring, 1979): 4–67.

Clayton, Thomas, 'Aristotle on the Shakespearean Film; or, Damn Thee, William, Thou Art Translated', *Lit/Film Quarterly* 2 (1974): 183–9.

Cobos, Juan and Rubio, Miguel, 'Welles and Falstaff: An Interview with Welles', *Sight and Sound* 35 (Autumn, 1966): 158–63.

Crowl, Samuel, 'Stormy Weather: A New *Tempest* on Film', *Shakespeare on Film Newsletter* 5, 1 (December 1980): 1, 5–6.

Crowl, Samuel, 'Fathers and Sons: Kenneth Branagh's *Henry V*', Chapter 10 in *Shakespeare Observed: Studies in Performance on Stage and Screen.* Athens: Ohio University Press, 1992: 165–74.

Crowl, Samuel, 'Flamboyant realist: Kenneth Branagh', Chapter 13 in Russell Jackson (ed.), *The Cambridge Companion to Shakespeare on Film.* Cambridge: Cambridge University Press, 2000: 222–38.

Crowther, Bosley, 'Review of *Forbidden Planet*', *New York Times* 2 (4 May 1956): 21.

Cummings, Alan, An Interview with Julie Taymor, *Interview* (January 2000): 35.

Donaldson, Peter S., 'Taking on Shakespeare: Kenneth Branagh's *Henry V*', *Shakespeare Quarterly* 42 (Spring 1991): 60–71.

Dunn, Allen, 'The Indian Boy's Dream Wherein Every Mother's Son Rehearses His Part: Shakespeare's *A Midsummer Night's Dream*', *Shakespeare Studies* 20 (1988): 15–32.

Dyer, T.F.T., 'Foresters at Home', *Art Journal* (October 1885): 301.

Edmonds, Jill, 'Princess Hamlet', Chapter 3 in Gardner, Viv and Rutherford, Susan (eds), *The New Woman and Her Sisters: Feminism and Theatre 1850–1914.* Ann Arbor: University of Michigan Press, 1992: 59–76.

Farber, Celia, 'Whistling in the Dark: You May Think O.J. Simpson Killed His Wife, But Does That Mean You Can't Be Friends?' (A 'Q and A' with O.J. Simpson), *Esquire* (February 1998): 54–64.

Felton, Felix, 'Max Reinhardt in England', *Theatre Research* 5, 3 (ed.) Hans Knudsen (London, 1963): 134–42.

Fiedler, Leonhard M., 'Reinhardt, Shakespeare, and the "Dreams"', in Margaret Jacobs and John Warren (eds), *Max Reinhardt: The Oxford Symposium.* Oxford: Oxford Polytechnic, 1986: 79–95.

Film Daily, Review of *Forbidden Planet*, 109, 51 (15 March 1956): 6.

Film Directions, Derek Jarman: Interview, 2, 8 (1979): 14–15.

Forsyth, Neil, 'Shakespeare the Illusionist: Filming the Supernatural', Chapter 16 in Russell Jackson (ed.), *The Cambridge Companion to Shakespeare on Film.* Cambridge: Cambridge University Press, 2000: 274–94.

Freedman, Barbara, 'Critical Junctures in Shakespeare Screen History: The Case of *Richard III*', Chapter 3 in Jackson, Russell (ed.), *The Cambridge Companion to Shakespeare on Film.* Cambridge: Cambridge University Press, 2000: 47–71.

French, Philip, Review of Jarman's *Tempest*, *The Observer* (4 May 1980): 15.

Gerard, Jeremy, Review of *Clueless*, *Variety* (23 September 1996): 51–2.

Gerlach, John, 'Shakespeare, Kurosawa, and *Macbeth*: A Response to J. Blumenthal,' *Literature/Film Quarterly* 1, 4 (1973): 352–9.

Gilbert, Gerard, television previews, *The Independent* (23 November 1996): 32.

Goldberg, Jonathan, 'Textual Properties', *Shakespeare Quarterly* 37 (Summer, 1986): 213–17.

Grundmann, Roy, 'History and the Gay Viewfinder: An Interview with Derek Jarman', *Cinéaste* 18, 4 (1991): 24–7.

Halio, Jay L., 'Three Filmed Hamlets', *Lit/Film Quarterly* 2 (1973): 316–20.

Hapgood, Robert, 'Kurosawa's Shakespeare Films: *Throne of Blood, The Bad Sleep Well, and Ran,*' in Anthony Davies and Stanley Wells (eds), *Shakespeare and the Moving Image: The Plays on Film and Television.* Cambridge: Cambridge University Press, 1994: 234–49.

Hattaway, Michael, 'The Comedies on Film', in Russell Jackson (ed.), *The Cambridge Companion to Shakespeare on Film.* Cambridge: Cambridge University Press, 2000: 85–98.

Henderson's North of England Film Bureau, Advertisement, *Kinematograph and Lantern Weekly* (22 February 1912): 13.

Hewitt, Anne-Maree, 'This Jarman Man', *Cinema Papers* 65 (September 1987): 12–14.

Hodgdon, Barbara, 'Race-ing *Othello*, Re-engendering White-out', in Linda Boose and Richard Burt (eds), *Shakespeare the Movie.* London and New York: Routledge, 1997: 23–44.

Holland, Peter, 'Two-dimensional Shakespeare: *King Lear* on Film', Chapter 3 in Anthony Davies and Stanley Wells (eds), *Shakespeare and the Moving Image: The Plays on Film and Television.* Cambridge: Cambridge University Press, 1994: 50–68.

Holman, Sidney R., 'Criticism for the Filmed Shakespeare', *Lit/Film Quarterly* 5 (1977): 282–90.

Howard, Tony, 'Shakespeare's Cinematic Offshoots', Chapter 17 in Russell Jackson (ed.), *The Cambridge Companion to Shakespeare on Film.* Cambridge: Cambridge University Press, 2000: 295–313.

Jackson, Russell, 'Shakespeare's Comedies on Film', in Anthony Davies and Stanley Wells (eds), *Shakespeare and the Moving Image.* Cambridge: Cambridge University Press, 1994: 99–120.

Jackson, Russell, 'The Film Diary', in Kenneth Branagh, *Hamlet, by William Shakespeare: Screenplay, Introduction and Film Diary.* New York and London: W.W. Norton, 1996: 175–208.

Jackson, Russell, 'Shakespeare's Fairies in Victorian Criticism and Performance', in Jane Martineau (ed.), *Victorian Fairy Painting.* London: Royal Academy of Arts, 1997: 38–45.

Jackson, Russell, 'Kenneth Branagh's Film of *Hamlet*: The Textual Choices', *Shakespeare Bulletin* 15, 2 (Spring 1997): 37–8.

Jenkins, Will F., 'Forbidden Planet', *Screen Stories* 55, 4 (April 1956): 40–1, 60–3.

Johnson-Haddad, Miranda, 'A Time for *Titus*: An Interview with Julie Taymor', *Shakespeare Bulletin* 18, 4 (Fall 2000): 35.

Johnston, Sheila, Review of *Men of Respect, Independent* (28 February 1992): 18.

Johnstone, Ian, *Sunday Times* Sec. 5 (1 September 1991): 8.

Kahn, Coppélia, 'The Absent Mother in *King Lear*', in Margaret W. Ferguson, Maureen Quilligan, Nancy J. Vickers (eds), *Rewriting the Renaissance.* Chicago: University of Chicago Press, 1986: 33–49.

Kehr, David, 'Samurai *Lear*', *American Film* 10, 10 (September 1985): 21–6.

Kempley, Rita, 'Tempest: Apologies to the Bard', Time Life (24 September 1982): W/E 15.

Kennedy, Dennis, 'Shakespeare without the Language', in James C. Bulman (ed.), Shakespeare, Theory and Performance. London and New York: Routledge, 1996: 133–48.

Kennedy, Harlan, 'Prospero's Flicks', Film Comment (January/February 1992): 45–8.

Kinematograph and Lantern Weekly (14 May 1908): 19

Kinematograph and Lantern Weekly Film listings (26 November 1908): 11.

Kinematograph and Lantern Weekly Tyler Film Company, Advertisement (28 November 1912).

Kinematograph and Lantern Weekly Film listings (4 June 1914): 6.

Kinder, Marsha, 'Throne of Blood: A Morality Dance', Lit/Film Quarterly 5, 4 (1977): 339–45.

Kitchin, Laurence, 'Shakespeare on the Screen', Shakespeare Survey 18 (Cambridge 1965): 70–4.

Klass, Perri, 'The Lion King: Bambi for the 90's, via Shakespeare', New York Times (19 June 1994), Arts and Leisure: 1.

Kuhl, E.P., 'Shakespeare and the Founders of America: The Tempest', Philological Quarterly 41, 1 (January 1962): 123–46.

Lacourbe, Roland, 'Introduction à l'œuvre de Michael Powell', Image et Son 251 (June/July 1971): 22–70.

Lacourbe, Roland, 'Redécouvrir Michael Powell I', Ecran 76 (15 January 1979): 37–48.

Lacourbe, Roland, 'Redécouvrir Michael Powell II', Ecran 77 (15 February 1979): 34–40.

Landow, George P., 'We Are Already Beyond the Book', in Warren Chernaik, Marilyn Deegan and Andrew Gibson (eds), Beyond the Book: Theory, Culture, and the Politics of Cyberspace, no. 7, Office for Humanities Communication Publications. Oxford: Office for Humanities Communication, 1996: 23–32.

Lane, Anthony, 'The Current Cinema', The New Yorker (27 November 1989): 105.

Lanier, Douglas, 'Drowning the Book', in James C. Bulman (ed.), Shakespeare, Theory and Performance. London: Routledge, 1996: 187–209.

Lanier, Douglas, '"Art thou base, common and popular?": The Cultural Politics of Kenneth Branagh's Hamlet', in Courtney Lehmann and Lisa S. Starks (eds), Spectacular Shakespeare: Critical Theory and Popular Cinema. London: Associated University Presses, 2002: 149–71.

Lillich, Meredith, Film Review 7 (June/July 1956): 247–60.

MacCabe, Colin, 'Edward II: Throne of Blood', Sight and Sound 1, 6 (October 1991): 12–14.

McDonald, Keiko, 'The Noh Convention in The Throne of Blood and Ran', in Kevin K.W. Chang (ed.), Kurosawa: Perceptions on Life, An Anthology of Essays. Honolulu: Honolulu Academy of Arts, 1991: 24–32.

McFarlane, Brian, 'A Literary Cinema? British Films and British Novels', in Charles Barr (ed.), All Our Yesterdays. London: BFI, in association with the Museum of Modern Art, New York, 1986: 120–42.

McKernan, Luke, 'Beerbohm Tree's King John Rediscovered', Shakespeare Bulletin 11, 1 (Winter 1993): 35–6.

McKernan, Luke, 'Further News on Beerbohm Tree's *King John*', *Shakespeare Bulletin* 11, 2 (Spring 1993): 49–50.

McKernan, Luke, 'A Scene – *King John* – Now Playing at Her Majesty's Theatre', in Linda Fitzsimmons and Sarah Street (eds), *Moving Performance: British Stage and Screen, 1890s–1920s*. Trowbridge: Flicks Books, 2000: 56–68.

Maxwell, Hal, 'Review of *Forbidden Planet*', *Films in Review* 4 (April 1956): 174–6.

Millard, Barbara C., 'Shakespeare on Film: Towards an Audience Perceived and Perceiving', *Lit/Film Quarterly* 5 (1977): 352–7.

Modenessi, Alfredo Michel, '(Un)Doing the Book "without Verona walls": A View from the Receiving End of Baz Luhrmann's *William Shakespeare's Romeo+Juliet*', in Courtney Lehmann and Lisa S. Starks (eds), *Spectacular Shakespeare: Critical Theory and Popular Cinema*. London: Associated University Presses, 2002: 62–85.

Moffitt, Jack, '"Forbidden Planet": Class A Science Fiction Picture', *Hollywood Reporter* 138, 43 (12 March 1956): 3.

Monthly Film Bulletin, P.H., 'Review of *Forbidden Planet*', 23 (June 1956): 71–2.

Monthly Film Bulletin, T.B., 'Review of *Island of Lost Souls*', 26, 300 (January 1959): 3.

Morning Leader, Review of *King John*, Tree's stage production (21 September 1899): 4.

Motion Picture Herald, *Forbidden Planet*: Review (reviewer, J.D.I.), 202, 11 (17 March 1956): 818.

Moving Picture World 2, 24 (13 June 1908): 511.

Moving Picture World, *Twelfth Night*: review (19 February 1910): 257.

Moving Picture World, Advertisement for Thanhouser *Tempest*, 10, 8 (25 November 1911): 598.

Moving Picture World 21, 1 (4 July 1914): 21.

Myers, Caren, Review of *The Lion King*, *Sight and Sound* 4, 10 (October, 1994): 47–8.

New York Times, F.R. Review of *Forbidden Planet* 2 (6 March 1956): 1.

Newton, H. Chance, 'About Town', *The Sketch* (20 September 1899): 388.

Nilan, Mary M., '*The Tempest* at the Turn of the Century: Cross-currents in Production', *Shakespeare Survey* 25 (1972): 113–28.

O'Pray, Michael, 'If You Want To Make Films . . . : Art and Film', *Sight and Sound* Supplement (July 1994): 20–2.

Orgel, Stephen, 'The Authentic Shakespeare', *Representations* 21 (1988): 1–25.

Orgel, Stephen, 'What is a Text?', *Research Opportunities in Renaissance Drama* 24 (1981): 476–95.

Pally, Marcia, 'Order vs. Chaos: The Films of Peter Greenaway', *Cinéaste* 18, 3 (1991): 3–45.

Pearson, Roberta E. and Uricchio, William, '"Shrieking From Below the Gratings": Sir Herbert Beerbohm-Tree's *Macbeth* and His Critics', in A.J. Hoenselaars (ed.), *Reclamations of Shakespeare*. Amsterdsam and Atlanta: Rodopi, 1994: 249–71.

Pictures and the Picturegoer, 'Sir Herbert Tree Pleased', 9, 105 (19 February 1916): 483–4.

Pitcher, John, 'A Theatre of the Future: *The Aeneid* and *The Tempest*', *Essays in Criticism* 34 (1984): 193–215.

Poel, William, 'The Theatre and its Needs', *TLS* (6 April 1922).

Premiere (US) (November 1999): 122.

Raynor, Henry, 'Shakespeare Filmed', *Sight and Sound* 22 (1952): 117–21.

Reeves, Geoffrey, 'Shakespeare on Three Screens: An Interview with Peter Brook', *Sight and Sound* 34, 2 (1965): 66–70.

Rubin, Steve, 'Retrospect: *Forbidden Planet*', *Cinéfantastique* 4, 1 (Spring 1975): 4–13.

Rutter, Carol Chillington, 'Looking Like a Child – or – Titus: The Comedy', *Shakespeare Survey* 56 (2003): 1–26.

Sarris, Andrew, 'Tempest in a Teapot', *Voice* (17 August 1982): 45.

Sedgwick, John, 'Richard B. Jewell's RKO Film Grosses, 1929–1951: the C.J. Trevlin Ledger: A Comment', *Historical Journal of Film, Television and Radio* 14, 1 (1994): 54–60.

Sewell, John B., 'Shakespeare on the Screen II: An Updating of Our Lillich Article of Twelve Years Ago', *Films in Review* 20 (August/September 1969): 419–26.

The Sketch, King John: Review and Stills (27 September 1899): 413.

Skura, Meredith Anne, 'Discourse and the Individual: The Case of Colonialism in *The Tempest*', *Shakespeare Quarterly* 40 (1989): 42–69.

Slide, Anthony, 'Elisabeth Welch', *Films in Review* (October 1987): 480–3.

Smedley, W.T., *King John*: A Review, *Westminster Gazette* (21 September 1899): 4.

Smith, Emma, ' "Either for Tragedy, Comedy": Attitudes to *Hamlet* in Kenneth Branagh's *In the Bleak Midwinter* and *Hamlet*', Chapter 9 in Mark Thornton Burnett and Ramona Wray (eds), *Shakespeare, Film, Fin de Siècle*. Basingstoke: Macmillan, 2000: 137–46.

Smith, Emma, ' "Sir J. and Lady Forbes-Robertson Left for America on Saturday": Marketing the 1913 *Hamlet* for Stage and Screen', in Linda Fitzsimmons and Sarah Street (eds), *Moving Performance: British Stage and Screen, 1890s–1920s*. Trowbridge: Flicks Books, 2000: 44–55.

Southern, Richard, 'The Picture-Frame Proscenium of 1880', *Theatre Notebook* 5, 3 (1951): 59–61.

The Stage, King John: A Review (21 September 1899): 13.

Starks, Lisa S., 'The Displaced Body of Desire: Sexuality in Kenneth Branagh's *Hamlet*', Chapter 9 in Christy Desmet and Robert Sawyer (eds), *Shakespeare and Appropriation*. London and New York: Routledge, 1999: 160–78.

Stayton, Richard, 'Portrait of Shakespeare as an Angry Young Man', *Written By* 4, 2 (February 2000): 39–43.

Stenberg, Doug, 'The Circle of Life and the Chain of Being: Shakespearean Motifs in *The Lion King*', *Shakespeare Bulletin* 14, 2 (Spring 1996): 36–7.

Sterritt, David, 'Tempest in a Critical Teapot', *The Christian Science Monitor* (26 August 1982): 19.

Stoll, E.E., 'Certain Fallacies and Irrelevancies in the Literary Scholarship of the Day', *Studies in Philology* 24 (1927): 485–508.

Strick, Philip, 'Review of *Island of Dr. Moreau*', *Monthly Film Bulletin* 44, 525 (October 1977): 213.

Sunday Telegraph, 'Beatrice and Benedick in close-up' (25 July 1993): Review Section 9.

Tatler, The, Review of Granville Barker's *A Midsummer Night's Dream* 660 (18 February 1914): 197.

Tavernier, Bertrand and Prayer, Jacques, 'Michael Powell', *Midi-Minuit Fantastique* 20, (1968): 13.

Taylor, Noreen, An Interview with Kenneth Branagh, *The Times* (15 March 2000): 6–7.

Le Théâtre, 'Le Théâtre à Londres: *King John* de Shakespeare au Her Majesty's Theatre' (20 September 1899): 19.

Thorp, Margaret, 'Shakespeare and the Movies', *Shakespeare Quarterly* (Summer 1958): 357–66.

Today's Cinema, Forbidden Planet: Review, 86, 7518 (9 May 1956).

Traister, Rebecca, 'The Story of O, Weinstein Style: High-School *Othello* Is Held Up', *New York Observer* (13 November 2000): 1.

Views and Film Index (2 November, 1907).

Vogue, 'Hallowed Ground' (September 1989): 330.

Waxman, Sharon, 'Studio Keeps a Lid on 'O' After School Shootings', *Washington Post* (Saturday 10 March 2001): C01.

Welles, Orson, 'The Third Audience', *Sight and Sound* 23 (1954): 120–3.

Williams, Linda Ruth, 'Movie Nightmares', *Sight and Sound* (May 1993): 30–3.

Willson, Robert F., Jr., 'The Selling of *Joe Macbeth*', *Shakespeare on Film Newsletter* 7, 1 (December 1982): 1, 4.

Willson, Robert F., 'Recontextualising Shakespeare on Film: *My Own Private Idaho, Men of Respect, Prospero's Books*', *Shakespeare Bulletin* 10, 5 (Summer 1992): 34–7.

ONLINE RESOURCES

All online resources were checked for continuing availability in January 2003.

Steve Sohmer, 'Certain Speculations on Hamlet, the Calendar and Martin Luther', *Early Modern Literary Studies* (online), 2, 1 (April 1996). Available at: www.humanities.ualberta.ca/emls/02-1/sohmshak.html

Rita Kempley, *Washington Post*, 29 December 1995. Available on line at: www.washingtonpost.com/wp-srv/style/longterm/movies/videos/othellorkempley_c03fe2htm

Interview with Kristian Levring by Rob Blackwelder, San Francisco, 26 April 2001. Transcript published online at: http://www.rottentomatoes.com/click/author-1232/reviews.php?critic=other&page=7&rid235295

Joe Baltake, 'Pared-down 'Othello': is it really O.J.'s tale?', *The Sacramento Bee's MovieClub*, 29 December 1995. Available online at: http://www.movieclub.com/reviews/archives/95othello/othello.html

Roger Ebert, *Chicago Sun-Times*, 29 December 1995. Available at: http://www.suntimes.com/ebert/ebert_reviews/1995/12/1013460.html

Official website for Michael Hoffman's *A Midsummer Night's Dream* (1999): www.foxsearchlight.com/midfinal/html/piazza.html

AUDIO-VISUAL RESOURCES

Classic Mel Gibson: The Making of Hamlet (1991). HBO documentary, narrated by Mel Gibson.

Q. David Bowers, *CD Rom of History of the Thanhouser Film Company* (1995).

BBC1's *Omnibus* 'Peter Greenaway' (September 1991).

Kenneth Branagh, interviewed by Jenni Murray, *Woman's Hour*, BBC Radio 4, February 1997.

Richard Briers, interviewed by Sue Lawley, *Desert Island Discs*, BBC Radio 4, Sunday 22 December 2000.

Simon Russell Beale, interviewed by Ned Sherin, *Loose Ends*, BBC Radio 4, 6 January 2001.

INDEX